Lecture Notes in Computer Scien

T0237807

Commenced Publication in 1973
Founding and Former Series Editors:
Gerhard Goos, Juris Hartmanis, and Jan van Leeuwen

Fabrice Kordon   Tullio Vardanega (Eds.)

Reliable
Software Technologies –
Ada-Europe 2008

13th Ada-Europe International Conference
on Reliable Software Technologies
Venice, Italy, June 16-20, 2008
Proceedings

 Springer

Volume Editors

Fabrice Kordon
Université Pierre et Marie Curie
Laboratoire d'Informatique de Paris 6
Modeling and Verification
CNRS UMR 7606, 4 place Jussieu, 75252 Paris Cedex 05, France
E-mail: Fabrice.Kordon@lip6.fr

Tullio Vardanega
University of Padua
Department of Pure and Applied Mathematics
via Trieste 63, 35121 Padua, Italy
E-mail: tullio.vardanega@math.unipd.it

Library of Congress Control Number: 2008927854

CR Subject Classification (1998): D.2, D.1, D.3, C.2.4, K.6

LNCS Sublibrary: SL 2 – Programming and Software Engineering

ISSN   0302-9743
ISBN-10   3-540-68621-5 Springer Berlin Heidelberg New York
ISBN-13   978-3-540-68621-7 Springer Berlin Heidelberg New York

Typesetting: Camera-ready by author, data conversion by Scientific Publishing Services, Chennai, India
Printed on acid-free paper   SPIN: 12275687   06/3180   5 4 3 2 1 0

Preface

The 13th edition of the International Conference on Reliable Software Technologies (Ada-Europe 2008) marked its arrival in Italy by selecting the splendid venue of Venice. It did so after having been hosted twice in Switzerland, Spain and the UK (Montreux for its inauguration in 1996 and Geneva in 2007; Santander in 1999 and Palma de Mallorca in 2004; London in 1997 and York in 2005), and having visited Sweden (Uppsala, 1998), Germany (Potsdam, 2000), Belgium (Leuven, 2001), Austria (Vienna, 2002), France (Toulouse, 2003) and Portugal (Porto, 2006). It was certainly high time that the conference came to Italy!

The conference series, which is run and sponsored by Ada-Europe, chooses its yearly venue following two driving criteria: to celebrate the activity of one of its national member societies in a particular country, and/or to facilitate the formation, or the growth, of a national community around all aspects of reliable software technologies. The success of this year's conference, beside the richness of its technical and social program, will thus be measured by its lasting effects. We can only hope that the latter will be as good and vast as the former!

Owing to the absence of a national society associated with Ada-Europe in Italy, the organization of the conference was technically sustained by selected members of the Board of Ada-Europe, its governing body, with some invaluable local support. The Board thus faced the very serious challenge of having to keep up with the high standard of previous Ada-Europe conferences. With all aspects of the organization behind us, we can be satisfied that the success of the conference was confirmed, continued and increased.

The conference took place on June 16–20, 2008 and featured a rich, dense and attractive program. Following its usual style the conference spanned a full week, with 10 tutorials offered on Monday and Friday, and a technical program from Tuesday to Thursday, which included 3 keynote talks, 20 peer-reviewed papers, 12 industrial presentations, a special session on software engineering education, the traditional vendor session and the accompanying industrial exhibition. Let us now look at the highlights of the conference program in some more detail.

The keynote talks were given by eminent and inspired speakers:

- Alberto Sangiovanni-Vincentelli (University of California at Berkeley, USA), a most authoritative member of the embedded systems community worldwide, delivered a talk entitled: *Embedded Software Design: Art or Science?*
- Robert Dewar (New York University, USA), a renowned expert in programming technologies and a talented public speaker, discussed where programming languages are expected to go next in a talk evocatively entitled: *Lost in Translation.*
- Christian Queinnec (Université Pierre et Marie Curie, Paris, France), a leading researcher in programming language semantics and the programming of the Web, explored the inner heart of Service-Oriented Architecture in a talk entitled: *Three Ways to Improve SOA Reliability.*

Submissions to the peer-reviewed track of the conference came from 15 countries worldwide, which caused a fairly competitive selection process that resulted in the making of 7 technical sessions on topics ranging from formal verification to real-time systems via concurrency, embedded systems, language technologies, model-driven engineering and applications of Petri Nets. The conference proceedings published in this volume fully cover this track of the conference.

The tutorial program featured a rich variety of topics, all presented by recognized domain experts, in close match with the core scope of the conference, as follows:

- *AADL: Architecture Analysis and Design Language*, Jean-Pierre Rosen (Adalog, France)
- *The Best of Ada 2005*, John Barnes (John Barnes Informatics, UK)
- *Object-Oriented Programming in Ada 2005*, Matthew Heaney (On2 Technologies, USA)
- *Preserving Model-Asserted Properties at Run Time for High-Integrity Systems*, Tullio Vardanega (University of Padua, Italy) and Juan Antonio de la Puente (Technical University of Madrid, Spain)
- *Technical Basis of Model Driven Engineering*, and
- *Verification Techniques for Dependable Systems*, both by William Bail (The MITRE Corporation, USA)
- *A Practical Introduction to Model-Driven Software Development Using Eclipse*, Cristina Vicente-Chicote and Diego Alonso-Cáceres (Universidad Politécnica de Cartagena, Spain)
- *Languages for Safety-Critical Software: Issues and Assessment*, Benjamin Brosgol (AdaCore, USA)
- *Service-Oriented Architecture Concepts and Implementations*, Ricky Sward (The MITRE Corporation, USA)
- *Real-Time Scheduling Analysis of Ada Applications*, Frank Singhoff (University of Brest, France).

The industrial track received the largest number of submissions since its inception in 2005. We read this as a twofold token of the thriving activity of the high-integrity industry worldwide and of the need of its representatives to meet with researchers and practitioners in reliable software technologies. The conference program included the following industrial talks:

- *A Discussion on the U.S. Federal Aviation Administration's Use of and Experiences with Ada, Including the Current Modernization Efforts*, Jeffrey O'Leary (FAA, USA) and Alok Srivastava (Northrop Grumman Corporation, USA)
- *Experiences Developing the Flight Services Component of the ERAM System*, Howard Ausden (Lockheed Martin, USA)
- *Challenges in Implementing a Ravenscar Runtime in an ARINC 653 Partition*, Jean-Pierre Fauche and Tom Grossman (Aonix, France)
- *Binary Data Comparison Automation,* Matt Mark (Lockheed Martin, USA)
- *Industrial Feedback on the Separation of Functional and Real-Time Constraints, and Object Orientation for Embedded Application*, Mathieu Le Coroller, Gérald Garcia (ThalesAlenia Space, France)

- *Advanced Real-Time Analysis in ASSERT – Application on Satellite Central Flight Software*, Dave Thomas, Jean-Paul Blanquart (EADS/Astrium Satellites, France), Marco Panunzio (Università di Padova, Italy)
- *Porting Naval Command and Control Systems to Ada 2005*, Jeff Cousins (BAE Systems, UK)
- *Distributed Status Monitoring and Control Using Remote Buffers and Ada 2005*, Brad Moore (General Dynamics, Canada)
- *A Comparison of Industrial Coding Rules*, Jean-Pierre Rosen (Adalog, France)
- *Growing a Tree that Lives Forever: Automatic Storage Management and Persistence of Complex Data Structures*, S. Tucker Taft (SoftCheck, USA)
- *Exceptionally Safe*, Arnaud Charlet, Cyrille Comar, Franco Gasperoni (AdaCore, France)
- *Genesis. Automation, via Generation, via ASIS, of Tests of Ada Software*, Mário A. Alves, Nuno Almeida (Critical Software, Portugal).

The special session on software engineering education hosted four talks and a lively panel discussion. The following presentations were given:

- *A Rational Approach to Software Engineering Education or: Java Considered Harmful*, Ed Schonberg, Robert Dewar (New York University, USA)
- *Ada and Software Engineering Education: One Professor's Experiences*, John W. McCormick (University of Northern Iowa, USA)
- *Is Ada Education Important?*, Jean-Pierre Rosen (Adalog, France)
- *Use of Ada in a Student CubeSat Project*, Carl Brandon (Vermont Technical College, USA).

Reports on the tutorial program, the industrial track and the special session on software engineering education will all be published in issues of the Ada User Journal produced by Ada-Europe.

Before closing this preface, we would like to acknowledge the work of those who contributed to the success of the conference, in various roles, moments and levels of visibility. First and foremost we want to express our gratitude to the authors of all presentations included in the program: the success of the conference was also largely theirs. We would also like to thank the members of the program committee at large: while they operated mostly in the background, their effort was crucial to keeping the level of the program quality as high as expected by soliciting worthwhile submissions as well as by carrying out the critical task of peer-reviewing. A smaller group of people accomplished the year-long task of following the preparation, construction and execution of the conference program as a whole. They deserve to be thanked for their effort and dedication: the Local Chair, Sabrina De Poli; the Publicity Chair, Dirk Craeynest; the Exhibition Chair, Ahlan Marriott; and the Tutorial Chair, Jorge Real.

We, who had the privilege of running the organization team, do hope that the attendees enjoyed the conference, in both its technical and social program, as much as we enjoyed coordinating it. We close this volume with the confidence of a job well done and the satisfaction of a thoroughly enjoyable experience.

June 2008

Fabrice Kordon
Tullio Vardanega

Organization

Conference Chair

Tullio Vardanega, Università di Padova, Italy

Program Co-chairs

Tullio Vardanega, Università di Padova, Italy
Fabrice Kordon, Université P. & M. Curie, France

Tutorial Chair

Jorge Real, Universidad Politécnica de Valencia, Spain

Exhibition Chair

Ahlan Marriott, White Elephant GmbH, Switzerland

Publicity Chair

Dirk Craeynest, Aubay Belgium & K.U. Leuven, Belgium

Local Chair

Sabrina De Poli, Sistema Congressi srl, Italy

Ada-Europe Conference Liaison

Fabrice Kordon, Université P. & M. Curie, France

Sponsoring Institutions

AdaCore
Aonix
Ellidiss Software

Praxis High-Integrity Systems
Rapita Systems Ltd
Telelogic

Dipartimento di Matematica Pura ed Applicata, Università di Padova, Italy

Program Committee

Nabil Abdennadher, University of Applied Sciences, Switzerland
Alejandro Alonso, Universidad Politécnica de Madrid, Spain
Johann Blieberger, Technische Universität Wien, Austria
Maartin Boasson, University of Amsterdam, The Netherlands
Bernd Burgstaller, Yonsei University, Korea
Dirk Craeynest, Aubay Belgium & K.U. Leuven, Belgium
Alfons Crespo, Universidad Politécnica de Valencia, Spain
Juan A. de la Puente, Universidad Politécnica de Madrid, Spain
Raymond Devillers, Université Libre de Bruxelles, Belgium
Michael González Harbour, Universidad de Cantabria, Spain
José Javier Gutiérrez, Universidad de Cantabria, Spain
Serge Haddad, Université Paris-Dauphine, France
Andrew Hately, Eurocontrol CRDS, Hungary
Jerôme Hugues, Télécom Paris, France
Günter Hommel, Technische Universität Berlin, Germany
Hubert Keller, Institut für Angewandte Informatik, Germany
Yvon Kermarrec, ENST Bretagne, France
Fabrice Kordon, Université Pierre & Marie Curie, France
Albert Llemosí, Universitat de les Illes Balears, Spain
Kristina Lundqvist, MIT, USA
Franco Mazzanti, ISTI-CNR Pisa, Italy
John McCormick, University of Northern Iowa, USA
Stephen Michell, Maurya Software, Canada
Javier Miranda, Universidad Las Palmas de Gran Canaria, Spain
Daniel Moldt, Universität Hamburg, Germany
Laurent Pautet, Télécom Paris, France
Laure Petrucci, LIPN, Université Paris 13, France
Luís Miguel Pinho, Polytechnic Institute of Porto, Portugal
Erhard Plödereder, Universität Stuttgart, Germany
Jorge Real, Universidad Politécnica de Valencia, Spain
Alexander Romanovsky, University of Newcastle upon Tyne, UK
Jean-Pierre Rosen, Adalog, France
José Ruiz, AdaCore, France
Lionel Seinturier, Université de Lille, France
Man-Tak Shing, Naval Postgraduate School, USA
Alok Srivastava, Northrop Grumman, USA
Tullio Vardanega, Università di Padova, Italy
Andy Wellings, University of York, UK
Jürgen Winkler, Friedrich-Schiller-Universität, Germany
Luigi Zaffalon, University of Applied Sciences, Switzerland

Industrial Committee

Guillem Bernat, Rapita Systems, UK
Olivier Devuns, Aonix, France
Franco Gasperoni, AdaCore, France
Rei Stråhle, Saab Systems, Sweden
Dirk Craeynest, Ada-Europe (Vice-President), Belgium
Tullio Vardanega, Ada-Europe (President), Italy

Table of Contents

A New Approach to Memory Partitioning in On-Board Spacecraft Software*

Santiago Urueña, José A. Pulido, Jorge López,
Juan Zamorano, and Juan A. de la Puente

Universidad Politénica de Madrid (UPM), E28040 Madrid, Spain
{suruena,pulido,jorgel,jzamorano,jpuente}@dit.upm.es
http://www.dit.upm.es/rts/

Abstract. The current trend to use partitioned architectures in on-board spacecraft software requires applications running on the same computer platform to be isolated from each other both in the temporal and memory domains. Memory isolation techniques currently used in Integrated Modular Avionics for Aeronautics usually require a Memory Management Unit (MMU), which is not commonly available in the kind of processors currently used in the Space domain. Two alternative approaches are discussed in the paper, based on some features of Ada and state-of-the art compilation tool-chains. Both approaches provide safe memory partitioning with less overhead than current IMA techniques. Some footprint and performance metrics taken on a prototype implementation of the most flexible approach are included.

Keywords: Ravenscar Ada, high-integrity, hard real-time, embedded systems, integrated modular avionics.

1 Introduction

On-board embedded computers play a crucial role in spacecraft, where they perform both platform control functions, such as guidance and navigation control or telemetry and tele-command management, and payload specific functions, such as instrument control and data acquisition. One distinctive characteristic of on-board computer systems is that computational resources are scarce, due to the need to use radiation-hardened hardware chips and also to weight and power consumption constraints. In this kind of systems, the more computational resources on-board the higher energy consumption, which in turn results in more power cells and thus more weight, increasing the total weight and the costs required to launch the spacecraft. Another key aspect of these systems is the presence of high-integrity and hard real-time requirements, which raises the need for a strict verification and validation (V&V) process both at the system and software levels [1].

---

* This work has been funded in part by the Spanish Ministry of Education, project no. TIC2005-08665-C03-01 (THREAD), and by the IST Programme of the European Commission under project IST-004033 (ASSERT).

F. Kordon and T. Vardanega (Eds.): Ada-Europe 2008, LNCS 5026, pp. 1–14, 2008.

Current trends envisage systems with increased functionality and complexity. Such systems are often composed of several applications that may have different levels of criticality. In such a scenario, the most critical applications must be isolated from the less critical ones, so that the integrity of the former is not compromised by failures occurring in the latter. Isolation has often been achieved by using a *federated* approach, i.e. by allocating different applications to different computers. However, the growth in the number of applications and the increasing processing power of embedded computers foster an *integrated* approach, in which several applications may be executed on a single computer platform. In this case, alternate mechanisms must be put in place in order to isolate applications from each other. The common approach is to provide a number of *logical partitions*[1] on each computer platform, in such a way that each partition is allocated a share of processor time, memory space, and other resources. Partitions are thus isolated from each other both in the temporal and spatial domains. Temporal isolation implies that a partition does not use more processor time than allocated, and spatial isolation means that software running in a partition does not read or write into memory space allocated to another partition.

This approach has been successfully implemented in the aeronautics domain by so-called Integrated Modular Avionics (IMA) [2]. While IMA is industrially supported and effectively provides temporal and spatial isolation, its use in spacecraft systems raises some problems due to the need of complex computer boards that call for alternative, more flexible solutions. In this context, Ada 2005 [3] provides a new set of real-time mechanisms that open the way to new approaches to inter-partition isolation. Some strategies for providing temporal isolation using the new Ada execution-time monitoring mechanisms have already been developed by the authors [4], and prototype implementations have been built in the framework of the ASSERT project[2] [5].

This paper presents new research directed at providing spatial isolation based on alternative approaches to current IMA architectures, including features of the Ada language and operating system-level mechanisms. The basic idea behind the proposed strategies is to modify the compilation toolchain to make a better use of the scarce computational resources at run-time. The available hardware memory protection is still used at run-time, but predictability losses due to address translation in MMUs are avoided. The rest of the paper is organized as follows. Section 2 describes the main aspects of the current IMA architectures. Section 3 introduces some alternative approaches to spatial isolation. Section 4 discusses the architecture of real-time kernels with respect to memory protection, while section 5 details a set of changes needed in the compilation tool-chain needed to implement the two new strategies. Finally, section 6 references some related work, and section 7 summarizes the main conclusions of this paper.

---

[1] Notice that the term *partition* is not used here in the sense defined in the ALRM (10.2/2), but as an implementation of *protection* as specified in the DO-178B (2.3.1).

[2] http://www.assert-project.net/

2 Integrated Modular Avionics

Integrated Modular Avionics (IMA) is a generic term to describe an architecture where different avionics applications are executed independently on a single CPU. Applications may have different criticality levels [6], and be logically distributed on different partitions of the same processor or over a network of computers connected by a communication link.

In order to support different criticality levels, applications have to be isolated from each other. Otherwise all the code would have to be certified to the highest criticality, an extremely expensive (and probably impossible) burden. To this purpose, each computer node is divided into one or more partitions, each of which is a virtual container for one or more applications with the same level of criticality, which are isolated in the time and memory domain from applications running in other partitions. An important consequence of partitioning is that applications can be updated individually without requiring re-certification of the whole system. Figure 1 shows an example of an IMA system.

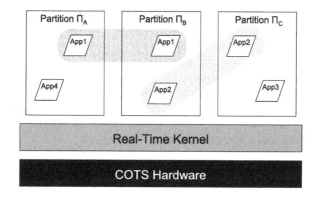

Fig. 1. Four applications with different criticality levels executing inside three partitions over the same computing node

Implementing an IMA architecture requires a specialized operating system layer that provides temporal and spatial isolation between partitions. The ARINC 653 standard [7] defines an architecture for such an operating system. There are diverse ARINC 653 implementations available from multiple vendors, and the standard has been successfully used in a number of commercial and military avionics systems. However, in spite of its success in the aeronautics field, its application to spacecraft systems raises some problems. First of all, the partition scheduling method is too rigid, and does not allow spare processor time to be re-allocated to other partitions. This may reduce the schedulability of applications on the comparatively slow processors that are currently used in spacecraft computers. The other main problem is that current ARINC 653 implementations require a MMU, which is seldom available on space computers. Indeed, current processors used by ESA[3], such as LEON2 [8], do not have an MMU. Therefore, other methods not relying on the presence of MMU devices should be explored in order to implement spatial isolation in spacecraft systems.

3   Approaches to Spatial Isolation

3.1   Static Analysis

SPARK is an Ada-based language designed for high-integrity systems. The language is restricted to a safe subset of Ada, augmented with formal annotations enabling efficient static analysis. A particular kind of annotation refers to the integrity—or criticality—level of program elements, enabling static analysis of violations in the criticality segregation [9]. In this way, static information-flow analysis of source code can be used to guarantee that an application will not write into the memory space of another application.

In principle this method can provide spatial isolation for a node with applications with high criticality levels, and it can also be used to ensure fault containment inside a specific application. However, this approach requires all the software in a computer node to be programmed in SPARK, a language intended only for high-criticality applications. Therefore, it is not suitable for the general case where low-criticality applications, possibly written in other languages, are present. On the other hand, it is an interesting approach to spatial isolation in computers which only host highly critical code, and can also be combined with other methods in a more general situation.

3.2   Run-Time Checks

A second approach is to use the extensive set of compile-time and run-time checks provided by the Ada language to detect possible violations of memory isolation. For example, forbidding using a memory pool in more than one partition seems a reasonable restriction. Following a similar reasoning, the run-time system can be designed so that there is a separate secondary stack for each partition, and an exception is raised in case of overflow. Additional run-time controls for checking that no task can write outside its partition memory area can also be implemented, e.g. when using general access objects a check can be made that the address is inside the partition space, and the same can be done for all access types if 'Unchecked_Access or Unchecked_Conversion is allowed.

Wahbe et al [10] proposed a different software technique to avoid writing outside the memory region of the application called *address sandboxing*. Some code is added before dereferencing a pointer which applies a mask to the high bits of the pointer so that the destination address always falls into the memory range of the application. Therefore, even if the pointer is incorrect, the mask ensures

---

[3] European Space Agency.

that it will not write outside its memory region. Address sandboxing does not detect failures, but can be more efficient than run-time checks.

The main problem of these approaches is that they add complexity to the compiler and run time support, which may make it difficult to certify high-criticality applications. They can be retained, however, to implement fault containment regions within a partition.

3.3 Hardware Protection

Some kind of hardware memory protection is available on virtually all processors, usually allowing read and write access, read-only access, or completely hiding a memory region. In addition, a memory area can be made non-executable, which is useful if the area contains only data. The memory protection setting cannot be modified when the processor is in user mode, but only in supervisor mode, and thus it can only be changed by the operating system. These mechanisms can thus be used to ensure that applications of mixed criticality can safely run on the same node. Furthermore, only the operating system must be certified to the highest criticality level, as it is the only subsystem that deals with memory protection.

An MMU is not always available in spacecraft computers because it is a complex hardware component with a comparatively high power consumption [11], as its internal cache for translating addresses, the TLB, is usually fully-associative and frequently accessed. Moreover, the possibility of TLB misses hinders the predictability of the system and introduces some overhead due to address translation and TLB flushes [12]. The complexity of MMU chips also makes them prone to single event upsets (bit flips due to high-energy particles) [2].

There is another main kind of hardware memory protection mechanism, *fence registers*. Fence registers provide a limited functionality, protecting a fixed number of memory segments of any size. In contrast, an MMU can provide sophisticated memory management schemes, including pagination, segmentation, and virtual memory. While such schemes are usually required in general-purpose operating systems, they are of less use in embedded computing, even with reprogrammability in mind, due to the fact that embedded hard real-time applications are usually statically loaded at system initialization time, at least in spacecrafts. For example, the LEON2 processor has a pair of fence registers that can be used to avoid writings outside the two specified segments of the SRAM.

In this case, there is no hardware relocation, and therefore all applications share a single address space. Memory reads are always allowed by the fence registers. This limits their usefulness as a spatial isolation mechanism, as attempts to read or execute outside the allowed memory area are not detected. In spite of this limitation, fence registers are a simple and robust mechanism without the complexity and comparatively high power consumption of MMUs. Two schemes for implementing spatial isolation based on generic fence registers are described in the following sections.

4   Kernel Architecture

4.1   Architecture of Current Real-Time Kernels

The current practice in the space domain is to execute all the embedded software in supervisor mode, i.e. any application and not only the kernel can execute privileged instructions. Furthermore, all the code executes inside a single (flat) memory space, and all the applications are linked statically into a single binary image, also including the real-time kernel, regardless of their criticality. As shown in figure 2, all the executable code is linked into a single .text section, the global variables are located in the .data and .bss sections, and the stack for each thread is created in the .bss section during initialization.

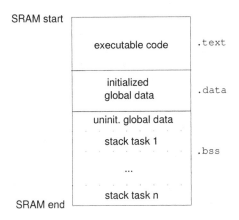

Fig. 2. Current memory map

   This model has several advantages, like increased CPU performance and memory footprint reduction. There is no code duplication because all the applications share the same code, including static libraries. The operating system can be simpler, e.g. there is no application loader. However, hardware memory protection cannot be used to provide complete memory isolation because all the global variables are located in the same section (.data or .bss), regardless of their criticality level. Only the task stacks can have some memory protection because they are clearly separated in memory. ORK, RTEMS, and ThreadX are examples of real-time kernels currently used in the European space industry that follow this memory allocation model.

4.2   Needed Architectural Changes

Some changes to the above scheme are required in order to implement spatial isolation using fence registers. Specifically, the global data and stacks (and heap, if available) of each partition must be allocated to separate memory areas, so that the kernel can provide write permission only to the data area of the partition of the thread that is currently executing.

An example of a memory map implementing this principle is shown in figure 3. In this figure, the code and data of each partition (including the kernel) are grouped into dedicated memory zones. Other schemes are possible, for example one with all the executable code in an adjacent area, which can be more efficient as only one segment has to be used for protecting non-executable memory.

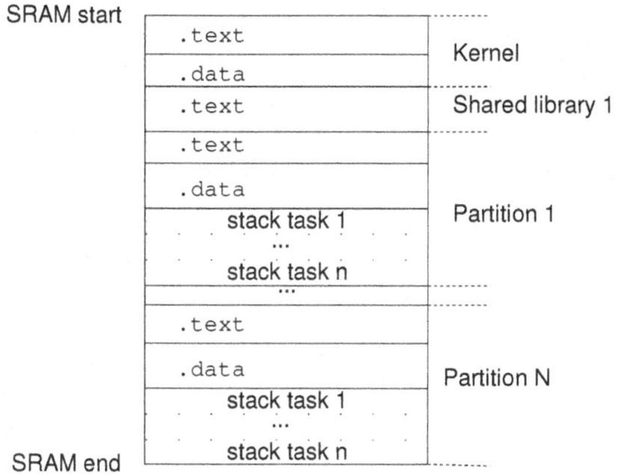

Fig. 3. Memory map for spatial isolation

It should be noticed that the code shared among partitions is compiled as shared libraries, i.e. each partition using a specific shared library reserves in its private data section the space required for the global variables of the shared library. Otherwise, the code would be duplicated in each partition thus increasing the memory footprint. In addition, it is worth noting that some free memory space should be reserved for on-line reprogrammability.

The above schemes show that implementing spatial isolation with fence register requires changes not only in the real-time kernel, but in the compilation and linking process as well. These changes are discussed in the next section.

5   Modifying the Compilation Toolchain

5.1   Basic Considerations

In order to implement a partitioned system, the tasks and global data that are included in each partition must be identified in the first place. Possible communication between co-operating applications running on different partitions must also be analysed. This in turn requires some kind of inter-partition communication mechanism to be defined.

In the following paragraphs two alternative strategies for developing partitioned systems are explored. The first one is based on building a custom *linking script* for the partitioned system, and the second one uses a new tool called *meta-linker*. In both cases the compilation model and the linking method that are used to produce the executable code are modified with respect to the basic model described in section 4.

5.2   Custom Linking Script

Compilation model. The current practice when using common compilation toolchains is to have all applications in the same computer node compiled as a single Ada program. Spatial isolation can be achieved if all applications are programmed according to a set of rules that clearly mark the tasks and data belonging to each application, e.g. using new pragmas or formal annotations. An ASIS [13] tool can then be used to check the source code and detect possible problems at a system-wide level and to generate a custom script that is used by the linker to produce an appropriate memory map (figure 4).

This approach requires a precise set of Ada rules for partitioning to be defined. Some rules are straightforward, e.g. "tasks belonging to different applications may not be declared in the same package", but some others are more complex, e.g. those on data types transmitted to other applications in order to avoid cross-partition pointers. Overall, a set of rules similar to the Ada Distributed Systems Annex (DSA) [3, App. E] can be defined, with the difference that the run-time system can be shared among all the partitions in the same computer node.

Protected objects (marked with a specific pragma) can be used for inter-partition communication (note again footnote 1). Such objects are located in a specific shared memory region, independent of those allocated to partitions. However, when the *proxy-model* implementation of protected objects is used (as in e.g. GNAT), a task can execute some entry code on behalf of some other task [14]. This means that the proxy task may need to write some results in a stack belonging to another partition. One possible solution is to forbid out parameters in protected entries that are used for inter-partition communication. In this case, the entry is used only for signalling the arrival of an inter-partition message, and a protected procedure is then called to read the data.

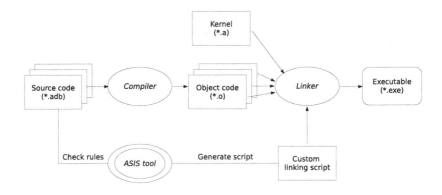

Fig. 4. Approach 1: Custom linking-script

Linking method. The linker binds each symbol (subprogram or global data) to a specific memory address [15]. This first approach relies on using an appropriate linking method for partitioning code and data into disjoint memory areas, in order to be able to take advantage of hardware memory protection. This approach also requires the kernel to be slightly modified so that it creates the stack of each thread in the global data area allocated to its partition.

The simplest way to implement this approach is to make an ASIS tool that checks the programming rules and generates a custom *linking script* for the system. The script specifies the location of each piece of data and each memory stack according to the partition it belongs to. The linker uses this custom script to generate an executable image with code and data allocated to the specified areas and symbol resolution (see figure 4).

An important advantage of this strategy is that existing response time analysis techniques can still be used. However, a new set of complex programming rules needs to be defined in order to provide partitioning among applications, and some of them may not be amenable to efficient static checking. In addition, the tool must support all the programming languages used in the system, which may be infeasible in some cases.

5.3   Meta-Linker

Compilation model. The second strategy for memory isolation is based on compiling each partition as a separate Ada program, with all its tasks and global data belonging to that partition. Task priorities are global, i.e. the scheduler does not have any notion of partitions. On the other hand, no global variables can be shared among partitions. Hence, a new kernel service for inter-partition communication, similar to a message queue, has to be implemented. This service can be specially crafted to be very efficient in CPU time and memory space. Only one-way communication is needed, so blocking time can be minimized with respect to intra-partition synchronization primitives. The main requirement is that inter-partition communications must be predictable so that response time analysis can still be performed.

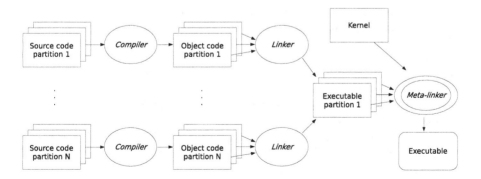

Fig. 5. Approach 2: Meta-linker

The problem with this approach is how to perform application-wide analysis with applications running in multiple partitions. Since there are no global shared data, the Ada Distributed Systems Annex can be used as a basis. Notice that the DSA also supports partition-wide strong typing enforcing by the compiler. The DSA is designed so that each partition has a separate run-time system. However, in this case the run-time can be shared among all partitions in order to reduce memory footprint. Distribution transparency is achieved as any partition can be moved to another node without source code modification. Therefore Ada provides all the needed support, and there is no need for language extensions like new pragmas as in the previous approach.

Linking method. Under this approach each partition is first linked separately, but relocation information is retained in a linkable output format (e.g. ELF offers this possibility). Then a new tool called *meta-linker* finally sets the memory area of each partition, the kernel, and all shared libraries (including the Standard Ada Libraries) into a single executable. The data of each partition are bound to a separate location by the meta-linker so hardware memory protection can be used, taking into account the size and alignment requirements. The meta-linker also creates some data structures describing the layout of the partition. This information is needed by the kernel to adjust the fence registers in each context switch.

The meta-linker can be seen as an alternative to the address translation performed by an MMU, although in this case the address translation is performed statically within the compilation chain. It can be simple enough to be a qualified tool [6, §12.2], and therefore there is no need to certify again all the partitions if a change in the size of one of them results in modifying their base addresses.

It is often required that a partition can be independently modified without a need for re-linking and re-certifying other partitions. This can be done in two ways. The first one is that the linker resolves all symbols with an arbitrary base address, retaining all the relocation information for each symbol in the object code. The meta-linker adjusts the base address of all symbols for each partition at the time of building the final executable. The alternative is to generate Position Independent Code (PIC), so that the meta-linker only needs to adjust some symbols and specific pointers to global data. The problem with the first solution is that it makes the meta-linker more complex, and it also may require some changes in the compiler and linker, this making qualification more difficult. On the other hand, compiling as PIC often leads to larger and slower code, which may be a problem when computing resources are scarce.

5.4   Prototyping

In order to evaluate performance penalties, a meta-linker prototype and a new version of GNAT/ORK for LEON (a variant of GNAT[4] which uses an evolved version of the ORK kernel [16]), which can generate PIC, have been built.

The first problem that has been investigated is a potential increase in footprint. Preliminary measurements have been taken in order to evaluate the

---

[4] http://www.adacore.com/

differences between PIC and non-PIC executables. Compiling both synthetic benchmarks and real code used in space projects, the increase in the number of instructions can be considered tolerable for this type of embedded systems. The size increase of the executable code (.text section) has been found to be about 7–15%, and the penalty in the total memory usage is only 1–4%, including also the data and stack segments, as shown in table 1.

Table 1. Footprint increase of Position Independent Code (PIC)

	Executable code		Global data		Stacks	Total	
	non-PIC	PIC	non-PIC	PIC		non-PIC	PIC
Benchmark 1	59 KB	67 KB	383 KB	384 KB	220 KB	661 KB	670 KB
Benchmark 2	104 KB	118 KB	385 KB	387 KB	420 KB	908 KB	925 KB
Application 1	439 KB	478 KB	422 KB	429 KB	320 KB	1181 KB	1227 KB
Application 2	1060 KB	1134 KB	599 KB	610 KB	320 KB	1979 KB	2064 KB

Position Independent Code (PIC) also has an execution time penalty when calling to a function in a shared library or referring to a global variable. As the linker cannot know where the code will be loaded, non-static routines must be called via a Procedure Linkage Table (PLT) and two actual jumps are performed instead of just one as usual. In order to measure the negative impact on performance, a set of composite benchmarks and high-level algorithms from the Performance Issue Working Group (PIWG) test suite were used. Table 2 shows the results which for the Dhrystone and Whetstone benchmarks, as well as three complex algorithms. The significant differences are just in the Dhrystone and Whetstone benchmarks, as the differences in the high level algorithm tests and other PIWG tests are negligible or even favour PIC.

The most significant difference is in the Dhrystone benchmarks with full optimization where the performance penalty of PIC is about 38%. The penalty is about 21% for this test with no optimization. However, the Dhrystone benchmark consists of composite calls to integer routines with a very short execution time. Conversely, the Whetstone benchmark routines perform floating point calculations with considerably longer execution times. In this cases, the penalty ranges from 0.5% to 4.5%. Of course, a program calling mostly short routines will pay a comparatively higher penalty due to extra jumps.

The real situation is likely to be closer to the high level algorithms, where the maximum penalty is about 12%, and the minimum one is negligible. Therefore, it can be said that the penalty of using PIC is acceptable both in footprint and performance for typical real situations. It must be noticed that using an MMU approach for spatial isolation also pays a significant performance penalty due to heavier context switches.

In summary, it can be said the best way to provide spatial isolation based on fence registers as the only hardware support is the second proposed strategy, i.e. writing separate source code for each application and compiling and linking each partition separately, keeping the relocation information. A qualified meta-linker is then used to examine the sizes of the kernel, the shared libraries, and

Table 2. Comparison in execution time

Description	No optimization		Full optimization	
	non-PIC	PIC	non-PIC	PIC
Dhrystone	91.50 μs	111.52 μs	30.56 μs	41.66 μs
Whetstone manufacturers math routines	228.00 ms	233.50 ms	128.62 ms	131.88 ms
Whetstone with built-in math routines	207.76 ms	208.76 ms	66.68 ms	69.56 ms
NASA Orbit determination	586.00 ms	635.50 ms	281.50 ms	316.50 ms
JIAWG Kalman benchmark	185.76 ms	186.00 ms	20.28 ms	20.18 ms
Tracker centroid algorithm	5.64 ms	5.58 ms	2.08 ms	2.08 ms

the partitions, adjust the base address of the whole application, and generate a single binary image. Finally, the real-time kernel adjusts the fence registers and processor mode at run time in order to provide the required strong hardware memory protection between partitions.

This is an elegant and powerful solution as it enables distributed applications (e.g. using a specialized DSA implementation) to be written in any programming language, including Ravenscar Ada and SPARK for high-criticality applications, or full Ada and C for low-criticality ones. It enables the performance and predictability problems of an MMU to be avoided, and allows individual partitions to be modified without having to certify again the whole system.

No modifications are required to current compilers, assemblers, or linkers, and the meta-linker is designed to be simple enough to be qualified for the development of high-integrity software. Furthermore, no extensions are required to the Ravenscar profile for enabling spatial isolation using the meta-linker approach. The few and localized additions to the kernel are not expected to hinder certification, being less complex or at least comparable to the software implementation support required by an MMU.

6 Related Work

The implications of the MMU in Integrated Memory Avionics have also been studied by Audsley and Bennet [12]. Using SPARK for mixed criticality high-integrity systems was proposed by Amey and others [9].

The performance penalties with respect to Position Independent Code have been analysed by several authors. However, measurements comparing PIC and non-PIC executables for embedded systems are not easy to find. One example of measurements for general purpose C++ applications is presented by Hamilton [17].

Other industrial domains could take advantage of the proposed techniques for achieving spatial isolation. For example, Autosar [18] is an automotive standard with a similar objective as Integrated Modular Avionics. The target CPUs used in those systems do not usually have an MMU, and therefore the standard does not consider spatial isolation. However, some of the techniques proposed in this paper can be a solution to provide memory protection on such systems.

7   Conclusions

Spatial isolation is needed to comply with the requirements of the the next-generation systems in the aerospace domain. A Memory Management Unit is commonly used for this purpose in general purpose operating systems, but performance and predictability problems appear when using MMUs in hard real-time embedded systems. Indeed, processors currently used in the European space industry an other embedded application domains, only include basic memory protection mechanisms, such as fence registers.

Several techniques have been explored in order to find a memory isolation scheme that can be used in this type of systems, most of them taking advantage of the unique characteristics of the Ada language. The recommended approach for systems composed only of high-integrity code is to use a safe subset of the language, such as SPARK, which also enables the absence of errors to be statically proved under appropriate conditions.

For systems composed of high- and low-criticality applications, a novel and powerful solution, involving a separate compilation of each partition, and a qualified meta-linker to generate the final executable, has been proposed. This flexible approach provides the same features as traditional techniques like strong memory partitioning, independent certification of partitions and maintenance, but it requires less hardware functionality and adds less overhead as specific processing is done statically at build time. Finally, additional Ada run-time checks can be used to detect programming errors inside each partition. A special-purpose implementation of the Ada Distributed Systems Annex can be used to enable static program-wide analysis of applications spanning multiple partitions, a characteristic which is often required for the certification of high-integrity systems.

A meta-linker prototype has been implemented as a proof of concept of the whole approach. The tool is simple enough to be qualified to a high-integrity level, and experimental performance and footprint metrics show that there is not a substantial penalty if the partitions are compiled as Position Independent Code. No modifications are required to the compiler, assembler or linker.

Future work includes specific compiler modifications to improve the generation of position independent code for embedded platforms, and research about how to reduce the impact of processor mode changes in space processors.

References

1. ECSS: ECSS-Q-80B Space Product Assurance — Software Product Assurance. Available from ESA (2003)
2. Rushby, J.: Partitioning for safety and security: Requirements, mechanisms, and assurance. NASA Contractor Report CR-1999-209347, NASA Langley Research Center (June 1999) Also to be issued by the FAA
3. Tucker Taft, S., Duff, R.A., Brukardt, R.L., Plödereder, E., Leroy, P.: Ada 2005 Reference Manual. LNCS, vol. 4348. Springer, Heidelberg (2006)

4. Pulido, J.A., Urueña, S., Zamorano, J., de la Puente, J.A.: Handling Temporal Faults in Ada 2005. In: Abdennahder, N., Kordon, F. (eds.) Ada-Europe 2007. LNCS, vol. 4498, pp. 15–28. Springer, Heidelberg (2007)
5. Zamorano, J., de la Puente, J.A., Hugues, J., Vardanega, T.: Run-time mechanisms for property preservation in high-integrity real-time systems. In: OSPERT 2007 — Workshop on Operating System Platforms for Embedded Real-Time Applications, Pisa. Italy (July 2007)
6. RTC: RTCA SC167/DO-178B — Software Considerations in Airborne Systems and Equipment Certification (1992); Also available as EUROCAE document ED-12B
7. ARINC: Avionics Application Software Standard Interface — ARINC Specification 653-1 (October 2003)
8. Gaisler Research: LEON2 Processor User's Manual (2005)
9. Amey, P., Chapman, R., White, N.: Smart Certification of Mixed Criticality Systems. In: Vardanega, T., Wellings, A.J. (eds.) Ada-Europe 2005. LNCS, vol. 3555, pp. 144–155. Springer, Heidelberg (2005)
10. Wahbe, R., Lucco, S., Anderson, T.E., Graham, S.L.: Efficient software-based fault isolation. ACM SIGOPS Operating Systems Review 27(5), 203–216 (1993)
11. Chang, Y.J., Lan, M.F.: Two new techniques integrated for energy-efficient TLB design. IEEE Transactions on Very Large Scale Integration (VLSI) Systems 15(1), 13–23 (2007)
12. Bennett, M.D., Audsley, N.C.: Predictable and efficient virtual addressing for safety-critical real-time systems. In: Proceedings of the 13th Euromicro Conference on Real-Time Systems (ECRTS 2001), pp. 183–190. IEEE Computer Society Press, Los Alamitos (2001)
13. ISO: Ada Semantic Interface Specification (ASIS). ISO/IEC- 15291:1999 (1999)
14. Giering, E.W., Baker, T.P.: Implementing Ada protected objects—interface issues and optimization. In: TRI-Ada 1995: Proceedings of the conference on TRI-Ada 1995, pp. 134–143. ACM Press, New York (1995)
15. Levine, J.R.: Linkers and Loaders. Morgan Kaufmann, San Francisco (2000)
16. Urueña, S., Pulido, J.A., Redondo, J., Zamorano, J.: Implementing the new Ada 2005 real-time features on a bare board kernel. Ada Letters XXVII(2), 61–66 (2007); Proceedings of the 13th International Real-Time Ada Workshop (IRTAW 2007)
17. Hamilton, G., Nelson, M.N.: High performance dynamic linking through caching. Technical report, Sun Microsystems, Inc., Mountain View, CA, USA (1993)
18. Heinecke, H., Schnelle, K.P., Fennel, H., Bortolazzi, J., Lundh, L., Leflour, J., Maté, J.L., Nishikawa, K., Scharnhorst, T.: AUTomotive Open System Architecture — an industry-wide initiative to manage the complexity of emerging Automotive E/E-Architectures. In: Convergence 2004 (2004)

Design and Development of Component-Based Embedded Systems for Automotive Applications

Marco Di Natale

Scuola Superiore S. Anna, Pisa, Italy
marco@sssup.it

Abstract. Automotive software systems are characterized by increasing complexity, tight safety and performance requirements, and need to be developed subject to substantial time-to-market pressure. Model- and component-based design methodologies can be used to improve the overall quality of software systems and foster reuse. In this work, we discuss challenges in the adoption of model-based development flows, and we review recent advances in component-based methodologies, including existing or upcoming standards, such as the MARTE UML profile, ADL languages and AUTOSAR. Finally, the paper provides a quick glance at results on a methodology based on virtual platforms and timing analysis to perform the exploration and selection of architecture solutions.

1 Introduction

The automotive domain is experiencing evolutionary changes because of the demand for new advanced functions, technological opportunities and challenges, and organizational issues. The increased importance and value of electronics systems and the introduction of new functions with unprecedented complexity, timing and safety issues are changing the way systems are designed and developed and are bringing a revolution in the automotive supply chain. New standards and methodologies are being developed that will likely impact not only automotive electronics systems, but also other application domains, which share similar problems.

The automotive supply chain is currently structured in tiers

- *Car manufacturers (or Original Equipment Manufacturers OEMs)*.
- *Tier 1 suppliers* who provide electronics subsystems to OEMs.
- *Tier 2 suppliers* e.g., chip manufacturers, IP providers, RTOS, middleware and tool suppliers, who serve OEMs and more likely Tier 1 suppliers.
- *Manufacturing suppliers* providing manufacturing services.

Currently, automotive systems are an assembly of *components* that are designed and developed in house or, more often, by Tier 1 suppliers. These subsystems have traditionally been loosely interconnected, but the advent of active-safety and future safety-critical functions, including by-wire systems, and the interdependency of these functions is rapidly changing the scenario. Furthermore,

F. Kordon and T. Vardanega (Eds.): Ada-Europe 2008, LNCS 5026, pp. 15–29, 2008.
© Springer-Verlag Berlin Heidelberg 2008

subsystems are developed using different design methods, software architectures, hardware platforms, real-time operating systems and middleware layers. To give an idea of architecture complexity, the number of Electronic Control Units (ECUs) in a vehicle is presently in the high tens, and further increasing. In the face of this scenario, OEMs need to understand and control the emerging behavior of the complex distributed functions, resulting from the integration of subsystems. This includes both functional and para-functional properties, such as timing and reliability. The supply process, traditionally targeted at simple, black-box integrated subsystems, will evolve from the current situation, where the specifications issued to the OEMs consist of the message interface and general performance requirements, to more complex component specifications that allow plug-and-play of portable software sub-systems.

The essential technical problem to solve for this vision is the establishment of standards for interoperability among IPs, both software and hardware, and tools. AUTOSAR [1], a world-wide consortium of almost all players in the supply chain of automotive electronics, has this goal very clear in mind. However, several issues need to be solved for function partitioning and subsystem integration, in the presence of real-time and reliability requirements, including:

- **Composability and refinement of subsystems.** The automotive industry together with the avionic industry was the first to embrace model-based design, as a tool to remove coding errors and to speed up the software development process. This approach was made possible by the introduction of powerful simulation tools where the functionality of the system is captured with a mathematically-oriented formalism, such as Simulink [12]. However, the definition of a process that goes from system-level to component models, in which behaviors are formally and unambiguously defined, such that they can verified at design time, and that allows for automatic code generation, is a quite challenging task. Such a process would indeed require that all relevant functional and non-functional constraints and properties are captured by the models used at all levels and that model semantics is preserved at each refinement/transformation steps. In Section 2 we discuss the issues related to model-based development and we review the impact of AUTOSAR on the design methodology.
- **Time predictability.** This issue is related to the capability of predicting the system-level timing behavior (latencies and jitter), resulting from the synchronization between tasks and messages, but also from the interplay that different tasks can have at the RTOS level and the synchronization and queuing policies of the middleware. The timing of end-to-end computations depends, in general, on the deployment of the tasks and messages on the target architecture and on the resource management policies. In Section 3, we review issues in this domain.
- **Dependability.** The deployment of the functions onto the ECUs and the communication and synchronization policies must be selected to meet dependability targets. A system-level design tool should integrate support for design patterns suited to the development of highly-reliable systems with

fault containment both at the functional level and at the timing level. Such tools should also support the automatic construction of fault-trees to compute the probability of a hazard occurrence.

Complex automotive functions, including active-safety and safety-critical systems, are characterized by non-functional requirements, including timing and performance, requirements for safety, and cost, together with reusability and extensibility of the architecture artifacts. System-level analysis and new modeling and analysis methods and tools are not only needed for predictability and composability when partitioning end-to-end functions, but also for providing guidance and support in the evaluation and selection of the electronics and software architectures. In Section 4, we provide the description of a design methodology based on virtual platforms in which models of the functions and of the possible solutions for the physical architecture are defined and matched to select the best possible hardware platform with respect to performance. Opportunities for the automatic synthesis of the software architecture are also discussed.

2   Model-Based Design, Composability and AUTOSAR

Model-based design methodologies are increasingly adopted for improving the quality and the reusability of software. A model-based environment allows the development of control and dataflow applications in a graphical language that is familiar to control engineers and domain experts. The possibility of defining components (subsystems) at higher levels of abstraction and with well defined interfaces allows separation of concerns and improves modularity and reusability. Furthermore, the availability of verification tools (often by simulation) gives the possibility of a design-time verification of the system properties. However, when considered in the context of a design flow that starts from the early stages of architecture exploration and analysis and supports complex interacting functions with real-time requirements, deployed on a distributed architecture, most modern tools for model-based design have a number of shortcomings

Lack of separation between the functional model and the architecture model: such a separation is fundamental for exploring different architecture options with respect to a set of functionality and for reusing an architecture platform with different functions.

Lack of support for the definition of the task and resource model: Most model-based flows support the transition from the functional model directly to the code implementation. The designer has limited control on the generation of the task set and the task and resource model is scantly addressed. Placement of tasks in a distributed environment is typically performed at the code level. The specification of the task and message design and of the resource allocation is necessary to evaluate the timing and dependability properties of the system.

Insufficient support for the specification of timing constraints and attributes: The definition of end-to-end deadlines, as well as jitter constraints is often not considered by modeling languages.

Lack of modeling support for the analysis and the back-annotation of scheduling-related delays: Most tools support simulation and verification of the functional model, which is typically based on an assumption of zero communication and computation delays. The definition of the deployment on a given architecture allows the analysis of the delays caused by resource sharing. In a sound design flow, tools should support this type of analysis, and the communication and scheduling delays should be back-annotated into the model to verify the performance of the function on a given architecture solution.

Issue of semantics preservation: The generation of the code starting from a model description is not always performed in such a way that the original semantics is preserved. It is important that designers and developers understand under what conditions the code generation stage can preserve the model semantics and what are the implications of an incorrect implementation.

Some of these issues can be reviewed in more detail, with reference to an abstract design flow, which encompasses all the refinement steps, from the system-level view, down to the code implementation (Figure 1).

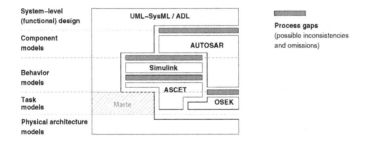

Fig. 1. An abstract development flow: standards and process gaps

The highest level in the description of the system corresponds to the early decomposition of high-level end-to-end functions (typically derived from user requirements). The system description is characterized by a behavior specification, but also by reliability and time requirements. Candidate languages and standards for system-level modeling, which may include a first-level decomposition into major functional blocks or subsystems, are the Unified Modeling Language (UML) and its specialized profile SysML, and Architecture Description Languages (ADL), like the EAST/ADL [22].

In order to allow for the specification and modeling of time and reliability requirements, UML has recently been extended by two profiles (specialized restrictions of the language semantics), the MARTE profile for the specification of timing requirements and properties [20] and the UML Profile for Modeling QoS and Fault Tolerance Characteristics and Mechanisms [21]. Both standards are expected to provide support for expressing time and reliability properties and requirements. However, because of the need of dealing with the generality of the UML language, they are typically cumbersome (the MARTE profile specification is currently 658 pages long) and must rely on faithful and efficient implementation by tool vendors, which presently cannot be guaranteed.

Subsystem specifications are then passed from OEMs to Tier-1 suppliers, who are responsible for their development. Although UML can still be used at this stage, the AUTOSAR development partnership [1], including several OEM manufacturers, Tier-1 suppliers, tool and software vendors, has been created with the purpose of developing an open industry standard for component specification and later integration.

To achieve the technical goals of modularity, scalability, transferability and re-usability of functions, AUTOSAR provides a common software infrastructure based on standardized interfaces for the different layers. The current version of the AUTOSAR model includes a reference architecture and interface specifications. AUTOSAR has been focused on the concepts of location independence, standardization of interfaces and portability of code. While these goals are undoubtedly of extreme importance, their achievement is not a sufficient condition for improving the quality of software.

The current specification has at least two major shortcomings. The AUTOSAR metamodel, as of now, is affected by the *lack of a clear and unambiguous communication and synchronization semantics* and the *lack of a timing model*. The AUTOSAR consortium recently acknowledged that the specification was lacking a formal model of components for design time verification of their properties. As a result, the definition of the AUTOSAR metamodel was started. Similarly to UML, the AUTOSAR metamodel is sufficiently mature in its static or structural part, but offers an often incomplete behavioral description, which is planned for significant updates in its upcoming revision. Furthermore, the standard does not address adequately issues related to timing and performance, therefore underestimating the complexity of current and future applications, in which component interactions generate a variety of timing dependencies due to scheduling, communication, synchronization, arbitration, blocking, buffering. The reuse of a component requires that the behavior of the reused components and the result of the composition with respect to time can be predicted in the new configuration. If this problem is not addressed, the composition will eventually lead to (possibly transient) timing problems. The definition of a timing model for AUTOSAR and the development of a standardized infrastructure for the handling of time specifications is the objective of the ITEA project TIMMO, which started in April 2007 and includes car manufacturers like Audi, PSA, Volvo Technology and Volkswagen, as well as electronics and tool suppliers, including Bosch, Continental, ETAS, Siemens VDO, Symtavision and TTTech.

On a separate context, a discussion of the issues that need to be considered when mapping UML into AUTOSAR (and vice-versa) and the possible gaps and inconsistencies in this transformation can be found in [22].

Components must be characterized by (a set of) behavior requirements and a corresponding internal behavior model. In AUTOSAR, the behavior of Atomic-SoftwareComponents is represented by a set of RunnableEntities (Runnables for short) communicating with each other over the ports of the container structural entities (components). Like in UML, structural and behavioral entities are linked to each other but are kept separated. AUTOSAR provides several mechanisms for Runnables to access the data items for sender/receiver communication and the services of client/server communication, *but the synchronization and timing semantics in the execution of Runnables is only partly specified.* In AUTOSAR, the runtime environments (RTEs) of each ECU are responsible for establishing the communication between the Runnables (local or remote) and triggering their execution using the following events:

- *Timing Event* triggering periodical execution of Runnables.
- *DataReceivedEvent* upon reception on a Sender/Receiver communication.
- *OperationInvokedEvent* for invocation of Client/Server service.
- *DataSendCompleteEvent* upon sending a Sender/Receiver communication.
- *WaitPoint* allows blocking a runnable while waiting for an Event.

Behavioral models are not supported in AUTOSAR, but the standard relies on external behavioral modeling tools like Simulink and ASCET, which brings the issue of the composition of (possibly heterogeneous) models. Therefore, any integration environment (EAST-ADL2 [22] is an example), must define the triggering and execution semantics of functions. This semantic should be deterministic to allow execution verification.

An example of the possible issues in the definition of the execution semantics (and also an example of model translation issues) can be found in Figure 2 (adapted from [22]), in which three models of a control algorithm, respectively in Simulink, UML (activity diagram) and AUTOSAR are represented.

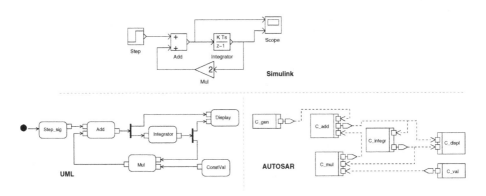

Fig. 2. Model-to-model transformation issues

Despite a similarity in their structure, the three models differ in the execution order of the actions. Contrary to UML activity diagrams, in Simulink, blocks are not executed in lexicographic order. In Simulink, blocks for which the output does not depend on the input at any given time, such as the *Integrator* in the Figure, can be executed before the others. Indeed, the simulation behavior of the depicted Simulink model will start with the output of the *Integrator*, and then continue with the *Mul* and *Add* blocks. In the UML activity diagram, the *Add* action will run before the *Integrator* block. The difference in the execution order may lead to different model behaviors and different simulation results.

In UML, in fact, the triggering order is defined when operations are called, but the execution order is undefined in the case of communication by data (streams) received on ports. SysML tries to define the semantics of data reception on ports, but the bindings between behavior parameters, and either the flow properties or the containing block properties are a semantic variation point [22]. In conclusion, for triggering semantics that differ from the loose UML standard definition, designers are required to explicitly define their own semantics by introducing stereotypes (specializing generic UML concepts by additional constraints and tagged values) in a dedicated profile .

However, execution order is not the only problem with our example. In Simulink, all blocks react at the same time and produce outputs in zero time (according to the Synchronous Reactive semantics), which leads to possible problems when the model has algebraic loops (instantaneous cyclic dependencies of signals from themselves). In this case, the system may have a fixed point solution or the model may be simply not correct. The definition of a Synchronous Reactive semantics in UML is probably possible by leveraging the Marte profile, but it would require the adoption of a stereotyped (discrete) time model. Additional diagrams are probably required to synchronize triggers and/or enforcing the correct execution order (possibly state diagrams). Finally, in case other types of timing constraints on end-to-end computations exist, an additional sequence diagram (and a stereotyped notation for timed events) would be required as well.

Finally, the AUTOSAR specification is based on the OSEK specification for Operating Systems. In an OSEK system, tasks are executing concurrently with priorities and subject to preemption. Hence, special care must be taken in the code generation stage, when the structural and behavioral part of the specification are mapped into concurrent tasks using automatic code generation techniques. Runnables and functional blocks must be executed by tasks in such a way to ensure data consistency of the variables implementing the communication links, and also time determinism in the execution of blocks. Furthermore, the implementation must guarantee the enforcement of the set of partial orders in the execution of blocks, as determined by the model semantics.

3   Timing Predictability, Timing Isolation and Standards

The automotive domain has been traditionally receptive to methods and techniques for timing predictability and time determinism. The standard Controller Area Network (CAN) bus [6] for communication is based on the concept of a deterministic resolution of the contention and on the assignment of priorities to messages. The OSEK standard for real-time operating systems [14] not only supports predictable priority-based scheduling [10], but also bounded worst-case blocking time through an implementation of the immediate priority ceiling protocol [17] and the definition of non-preemptive groups [18] for a possible further improvement of some response times and to allow for stack space reuse. In the absence of faults, and assuming that the worst-case execution time of a task can be safely estimated, these standards allow the designer to predict the worst-case timing behavior of computations and communications.

Priority-based scheduling of tasks and messages fits well within the traditional design cycle, in which timing properties are largely verified a-posteriori and applications require conformance with respect to worst-case latency constraints rather than tight time determinism. Furthermore, control algorithms are designed to be tolerant with respect to small changes in the timing behavior and to the nondeterminism in time that possibly arises because of preemption and scheduling delays [7], or even possibly to overwritten data or skipped task and message instances because of temporary timing faults. Finally, although formally incorrect, there is a common perception that small changes in the timing parameters (decreased periods and/or wrong estimates of the computation times) typically only result in a graceful degradation of the response times of tasks and messages and that such degradation will in any case preserve the high priority computations.

These assumptions can be misleading and faulty. The worst-case response times of tasks and messages, scheduled on priority-based systems, such as those defined by the OSEK and CAN standards can be computed using a fixed point formula. For a periodic task τ_i, activated with period T_i and worst-case computation time C_i, the worst-case response time r_i is given by (in case $r_i \leq T_i$, the general case is discussed in [11])

$$r_i = B_i + C_i + \sum_{j \in hp(i)} \left\lceil \frac{r_i}{T_j} \right\rceil C_j \tag{1}$$

Where $j \in hp(i)$ means all the indexes of the generic tasks τ_j with a priority higher than τ_i and B_i is the worst-case blocking time in which the task cannot execute because of an activity (typically a critical section or an interrupt handler) executed on behalf of a lower priority task. The worst-case latency of a CAN message can be upper bound as shown in [9], where the factor B_i is the largest transmission time of any message frame.

$$w_i = B_i + \sum_{j \in hp(i)} \left\lceil \frac{w_i}{T_j} \right\rceil C_j \ (w_i > 0)$$
$$r_i = w_i + C_i \tag{2}$$

In the face of the development of larger and more complex applications, which are deployed with a significant amount of parallelism on each ECU and consist of a densely connected graph of distributed computations, and of new safety-critical functions, which require tight deadlines and guaranteed absence of timing faults, a new rigorous science needs to be established. A number of issues need to be considered with respect to the current standards and the use of priority based scheduling of tasks and messages.

- Priority-based scheduling can lead to discontinuous behavior in time and timing anomalies. The dependency of the response time of a lower priority task or message with respect to the computation time (or period) of a higher priority task is not linear and not even continuous. Furthermore, especially in distributed systems, it may even be possible that shorter computation times result in larger latencies [16]. A recently developed branch of worst-case timing analysis is focusing on sensitivity analysis [5][16] as a means for understanding which computation and communication loads are critical for the preservation of deadlines.
- Variability of the response times between the worst-case and the best case scenario, together with the possible preemptions, can lead to the violation of time-deterministic model semantics in the implementation of software models by priority scheduled tasks and messages [4].
- Extensibility and (to some degree) tolerance with respect to unexpectedly large resource requirements from tasks and messages that is allowed by priority-based scheduling comes at the price of additional jitter and latency and lack of timing isolation.
- Future applications, including safety critical (x-by-wire) and active safety need shorter latencies and time determinism (reduced jitter) because of increased performance. The current model for the propagation of information, based on *communication by periodic sampling*, among non-synchronized nodes has very high latency in the worst-case and a large amount of jitter between the best case and the worst-case delays. Even if communication-by-sampling can be formally studied and platform implementations can be defined to guarantee at least some fundamental properties of the communication flow (such as data preservation), time determinism is typically disrupted and the application must be able to tolerate the large latencies caused by random sampling delays.
- The deployment of reliable systems requires timing isolation in the execution of the software components, and protection from timing faults. One of the major downsides of priority-based scheduling of resources is that faulty high priority computation or communication flows can easily obtain the control of the ECU or the bus, subtracting time from lower priority tasks or messages. For example, an excessive request of computation time from any high priority task impacts the response time of lower priority tasks on the same ECU. Timing protection is even more important in the light of AUTOSAR, when components from Tier1 suppliers are integrated into the same ECU, leveraging the standardization of interfaces, and faulty behaviors (functional and temporal) need to be contained and isolated.
- The development of future applications will also require the enforcement of composability and compositionality not only in the functional domain but also for para-functional properties of the system, including the timing behavior of the components and their reliability. (see next section)

Time-based schedulers, including those supported by the FlexRay and OSEK-Time [13] standards force context switches on the ECUs and the assignment of the communication bus at predefined points in time, regardless of the outstanding requests from the tasks for computation and communication bandwidth. Therefore, they are better suited to provide temporal protection, except that the enforcement of a strict time window for the execution and communication requires a much better capability of the designer in predicting the worst case execution times of tasks so that the execution window can be appropriately sized, and guardians are needed to ensure that an out-of-time transmission will not disrupt the communication flow on the bus.

4   Platform-Based Design for Architecture Selection

Platform-based design requires/entices the identification of clear abstraction layers and a design interface that allows for the separation of concerns between the refinement of the functional architecture specification and the abstractions of possible implementations. The application-layer software components are thus decoupled from changes in microcontroller hardware, ECU hardware, I/O devices, sensors, actuators, and communication links. The basic idea is captured on the left side of Figure 3. The vertex of the two cones represents the combination of the functional model and the architecture platform. Decoupling the application-layer logic from dependencies on infrastructure-layer hardware or software enables the application-layer components to be reused without changes across multiple vehicle programs. A prerequisite for the adoption of the platform-based

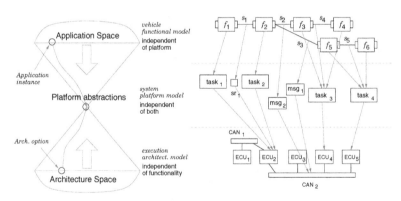

Fig. 3. Platform-based design and models

design and of the meet-in-the-middle approach is the definition of the right models and abstractions for the description of the functional platform specification and for the architecture solutions at the top and the bottom of the hourglass of Figure 3. The platform interface must be isolated from lower-level details but, at the same time, must provide enough information to allow design space exploration with a fairly accurate prediction of the properties of the implementation. This model may include size, reliability, power consumption and timing; variables that are associated to the lower level abstraction.

Design space exploration consists of seeking the optimal mapping of the system platform model into the candidate execution platform instances. The mapping must be driven by a set of methods and tools providing a measure of the fitness of the architecture solutions with respect to a set of feasibility constraints and optimization metric functions. This work focuses on timing constraints and metrics. In Section 4.2, we discuss the possibility for the automatic selection of part of the platform configuration by software tools. The technology, however, is not mature yet for a full synthesis of the task and message design and the definition of the architecture mapping. The approach that is currently viable is a what-if analysis where different options are selected as representatives of the principal platform options and evaluated according to measurable metrics.

Functional Model
The starting point for the definition of ECS based vehicle architecture is the specification of the set of features that the system is expected to provide. A feature is a very high level description of a system capability, such as an active-safety function. The software component of each feature is further developed by control engineers who devise algorithms fulfilling the design goals. Typically, these algorithms are captured by a hierarchical set of block diagrams produced with commercial tools for control design. The functional model(s) are created from the decomposition of the feature in a hierarchical network of components encapsulating a behavior, within a provided and required interface, expressed by a set of ports or by a set of methods with the corresponding signature. This view abstracts from the details of the functional behavior and models only the interface and the communication semantics, including the specification of the activation signal for each functional block, be it periodic, sporadic, or arriving, together with the incoming data, from one of its input ports. The functional description is further endowed with the required constraints. For example, timing constraints are expressed in the context of the functional architecture by adding end-to-end deadlines to the computation paths, maximum jitter requirements to any signal and time correlation constraints between any signal pair.

Architecture Model
The model of the architecture is hierarchical and captures the logical topology of the vehicle network, including the communication buses, such as CAN [6] and time triggered links, the number of processors for each ECU and the resource management policies that control the allocation of each ECU and BUS. At this stage, the hardware and software resources that are available for the execution of the application tasks and the resource allocation and scheduling policies must also be specified.

Platform Model
The system platform model is where physical concurrency and resource requirements are expressed. The system platform model(s) are a representation of the mapping process. Tasks are defined as units of computation processed concurrently in response to environment stimuli or prompted by an internal

clock. Tasks cooperate by exchanging messages and synchronization or activation signals and contend for use of the processing and communication resource(s) (e.g., processors and buses) as well as for the other resources in the system. The system platform model entities are, on one hand, the implementation of the functional model and, on the other hand, are mapped onto the target hardware. The mapping phase consists of allocating each functional block to a software task and each communication signal variable to a virtual communication object (right side of Figure 3). The task activation rates are derived from the functional blocks activation rates. As a result of the mapping of the platform model into the execution architecture, the entities in the functional models are put in relation with timing execution information derived by worst-case execution time analysis or back-annotations extracted from physical or virtual implementation. Given a mapping, it is possible to determine which signals are local (because the source and destination functions are deployed onto the same ECU) and which are remote and, hence, need to go over the network. Each communication signal is therefore mapped to a message, or to a task private variable or to a protected shared variable. Each message, in turn, is mapped to a serial data link. The mapping of the threads and message model into the corresponding architecture model and the selection of resource management policies allows the subsequent validation against timing constraints.

4.1   What-If Analysis

The procedure for architecture selection and evaluation is a what-if iterative process. First, the set of metrics and constraints that apply to the design is defined. Then, based on the designer's experience, a set of initial candidate architecture configurations is produced. These architectures are evaluated and, based on the results of the quantitative analysis, a solution can be extracted from the set as the best fit. If the designer is not satisfied with the result, a new set of candidate architectures can be selected. The iterative process continues, until a solution is obtained. The intervention of the designer is required in two tightly related stages of the exploration cycle. The designer must provide the initial set of architecture options. After the options have been scored and annotated by the analysis and simulation tools, the designer must understand the results of the analysis and select the architecture options that are the best fit to the exploration goals and (more importantly) understand the results of the analysis to add other options to the next set of configurations that needs to be evaluated. The set of analysis methods that are available for architecture evaluation are:

- Evaluation of end-to-end latency and schedulability against deadlines for chains of computations spanning tasks and messages scheduled with fixed priority [19].
- Sensitivity analysis for tasks and messages scheduled with fixed priorities and sensitivity analysis for resources scheduled with fixed priorities [5].

- Evaluation of message latencies in CAN bus networks [8].
- System level simulation of time properties and functional behaviors (based on the Metropolis engine [3]).
- Analysis of fault probability and cutsets (conditions leading to critical faults) based on fault trees.

4.2   Automatic Configuration of the SW Architecture

The mapping of the functional model into the execution platform is part of the platform-based design referred in the previous sections and of the Y-chart design flow [2] shown in Figure 4, where the application description and architectural description are joined in an explicit mapping step. The mapping definition and the creation of the task and resource models can be performed in several ways. In single processor systems, the problem is usually very simple, and often subsumed by the code generation phase. In distributed architectures, the design of the software architecture is a more complex task and it is very often delegated to the experience of the designer. When a software implementation is not feasible because of resource constraints, design iterations may be triggered and the functional model itself or the architecture configuration may be modified.

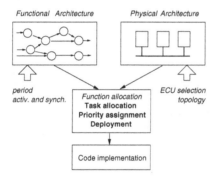

Fig. 4. Design flow stages and period synthesis

Once the function and the architecture are defined, there are several possible options for the intermediate layer, and automated tools can provide guidance in the selection of the optimal configuration with respect to the timing constraints and a performance-related metric function.

The mapping consist of the following stages: function to task mapping; task to ECU deployment and signal to message mapping, and, finally, of the assignment of priorities to tasks and messages. When iterations are required on the functional model, a different selection of the execution periods of the functions, or different synchronization and communication solutions may be explored.

We defined solutions based on mixed integer linear programming (MILP) and geometric programming (GP), respectively, for the problem of optimizing the activation mode of tasks and messages [19] and the selection of task periods [8].

The effectiveness of these approaches has been demonstrated by application to on an experimental vehicle system case. We are currently exploring approximated solutions for the selection of a feasible mapping of tasks to ECUs and signals to messages and the assignment of priorities to tasks and messages.

5 Conclusions

The structure of the automotive electronic industry and the state-of-the-art of automotive electronics design methodology was summarized. Issues on model-based design, composability and timing protection and a quick look at the opportunities and the limitations of the existing standards were also discussed. We concluded with a proposed methodology for architecture exploration, based on virtual platforms and the separation of functional and physical architecture models. We envision the availability of an intermediate platform layer in which the functions are mapped into the architecture option and the result is evaluated with respect to para-functional metrics and constraints related to timing, dependability and cost. It will be of highest importance to support the evolution of the automotive standards to ensure the feasibility of a correct and robust design flow based on virtual platform.

References

1. AUTOSAR. Consortium web page, www.autosar.org
2. Balarin, F., et al.: Hardware-Software Co-Design of Embedded Systems – The Polis Approach. Kluwer Academic Publishers, Dordrecht (1997)
3. Balarin, F., Lavagno, L., Passerone, C., Watanabe, Y.: Processes, interfaces and platforms. Embedded software modeling in Metropolis. In: Proc. of the 2nd ACM EMSOFT, Grenoble, France (October 2002)
4. Baleani, M., Ferrari, A., Mangeruca, L., Sangiovanni-Vincentelli, A.: Efficient embedded software design with synchronous models. In: Proc. of the 5th ACM EMSOFT. ACM Press, New York (2005)
5. Bini, E., Natale, M.D., Buttazzo, G.: Sensitivity analysis for fixed-priority real-time systems. In: Euromicro ECRTS, Dresden, Germany (June 2006)
6. Bosch, R.: Controller area network specification, version 2.0. Stuttgart (1991)
7. Caspi, P., Benveniste, A.: Toward an approximation theory for computerised control. In: Sangiovanni-Vincentelli, A.L., Sifakis, J. (eds.) EMSOFT 2002. LNCS, vol. 2491, pp. 294–304. Springer, Heidelberg (2002)
8. Davare, A., Zhu, Q., Natale, M.D., Pinello, C., Kanajan, S., Sangiovanni-Vincentelli, A.: Period optimization for hard real-time distributed automotive systems. In: Design Automation Conference, San Diego, CA (June 2007)
9. Davis, R.I., Burns, A., Bril, R.J., Lukkien, J.J.: Controller area network (can) schedulability analysis: refuted, revisited and revised. Real-Time Systems 35, 239–272 (2007)
10. Harbour, M.G., Klein, M., Lehoczky, J.: Timing analysis for fixed-priority scheduling of hard real-time systems. IEEE Transactions on Software Engineering 20(1) (January 1994)

11. Lehoczky, J.P., Sha, L., Ding, Y.: The rate-monotonic scheduling algorithm: Exact characterization and average case behavior. In: Proc. of the 10th RTSS, Santa Monica, CA (December 1989)
12. Mathworks. The Mathworks Simulink and StateFlow User's Manuals, http://www.mathworks.com
13. OSEK. OSEK/VDX Steering Committee: Time-Triggered Operating System, http://www.osek-vdx.org
14. OSEK. OS vers. 2.2.3 specification (2006), http://www.osek-vdx.org
15. DSpace TargetLink product page, http://www.dspaceinc.com
16. Racu, R., Ernst, R.: Scheduling anomaly detection and optimization for distributed systems with preemptive task-sets. In: 12th RTAS, San Jose (April 2006)
17. Sha, L., Rajkumar, R., Lehoczky, J.P.: Priority inheritance protocols: An approach to real-time synchronization. IEEE Transactions on computers 39(9), 1175–1185 (1990)
18. Wang, Y., Saksena, M.: Scheduling fixed priority tasks with preemption threshold. In: Proc. of the RTCSA Conference (December 1999)
19. Zheng, W., Natale, M.D., Pinello, C., Giusto, P., Sangiovanni-Vincentelli, A.: Synthesis of task and message activation models in real-time distributed automotive systems. In: Proc. of the DATE conference, Nice, April 15-18 (2007)
20. Object Management Group MARTE profile: Modeling and Analysis of Real-time and Embedded systems, http://www.omgmarte.org/
21. Object Management Group UML Profile for Modeling QoS and Fault Tolerance Characteristics and Mechanisms, http://www.omg.org/cgi-bin/doc?ptc/2006-12-02
22. ATESST Advanced Traffic Efficiency and Safety through Software Technology Deliverable 3.2 Report on behavior modeling with the EAST-ADL 2.0 (July 12, 2007)

On the Timed Automata-Based Verification of Ravenscar Systems

Iulian Ober[1] and Nicolas Halbwachs[2]

[1] Université de Toulouse - IRIT
118 Route de Narbonne, 31062 Toulouse, France
iulian.ober@irit.fr
[2] CNRS - VERIMAG
2, av. de Vignate, 38610 Gières, France
Nicolas.Halbwachs@imag.fr

Abstract. The Ravenscar profile for Ada enforces several restrictions on the usage of general-purpose tasking constructs, thereby facilitating most analysis tasks and in particular functional and timing verification using model checking. This paper presents an experiment in translating the Ravenscar fragment of Ada into the input language of a timed model checker (IF [7, 8]), discusses the difficulties and proposes solutions for most constructs supported by the profile. The technique is evaluated in a small case study issued from a space application, on which we present verification results and conclusions.

1 Introduction

This paper discusses an experiment in applying model checking techniques to the verification of functional and non-functional (timing) aspects of Ada systems complying with the Ravenscar profile [1, 10].

We targeted the IF model checker [7, 8] for several reasons including its ability to handle complex structured data, dynamic object allocation (necessary to simulate the procedural control flow of Ada), both timed and non-timed execution aspects, and last but not least for the automatic abstraction features of the IF tool which help to cope efficiently with large specifications.

Ravenscar is a standardized set of restrictions for the Ada language and runtimes, set forward in order to facilitate the verification of concurrent real-time programs and to make their implementation more reliable and efficient. The incentive to apply model checking to Ravenscar systems was the fact that the profile is used as the runtime and semantic baseline by several work tracks [5, 22] within the IST ASSERT European project[1], and it has recently been formalized in [17]. ASSERT aims at developing novel systems engineering methods for distributed and embedded real time systems in the aerospace domain, based on formal model-centric techniques.

---

[1] This work was partially supported by ASSERT, an Integrated Project of the 6th Framework Programme IST of the EU, see http://www.assert-project.net

The paper is structured as follows. Section 2 is a brief overview of the Ravenscar Ada profile. Section 3 presents the IF language and tools. Section 4 is the main part of the paper, describing the mapping of the main Ada concepts to IF, and discussing how the Ravenscar profile restrictions may help. Then, in Section 5 we present experimental results on a small case study, before concluding.

2   The Ravenscar Ada Profile

The Ada language exhibits a rich set of constructs for programming concurrent and time-aware systems. However, as analyzed in [10, 1], the total freedom granted by the tasking and inter-task communication model of the language comes at a high cost. Firstly, this freedom exposes the systems to various runtime problems related to schedulability (like unbounded blocking times or priority inversion) and concurrency control (like deadlocks). Secondly, it makes it impossible to apply most currently available analysis techniques to verify the resulting system: known schedulability analyses [12] like rate monotonic analysis [20] or response time analysis [19] do not work on such general models, and the application of more general purpose techniques like model checking [13] is hindered.

Several factors cause the aforementioned problems, among which: tasks may be created dynamically (either explicitly or implicitly), their activation patterns are arbitrary (a task may be suspended and activated by arbitrary **delay** statements, by rendez-vous, etc.), they may communicate in various ways (through rendez-vous, through shared protected objects, etc.).

The Ravenscar profile makes a number of restrictions on the tasking and synchronisation constructs that may be used, and additionally it imposes a scheduling policy – namely *fixed priority* preemptive scheduling with *priority ceiling protocol* (for a description, see for example [12]) – thus aiming to render the resulting systems analysable and to guarantee by construction certain properties such as absence of deadlocks and mutual exclusive access to shared resources. The restrictions, defined in [1] and motivated in [10], are the following:

- The task set is static and flat, i.e. there is no dynamic task creation, and all tasks are created at package level and depend directly on the environment task. Tasks are also not permitted to terminate or abort.
- Interrupt handlers are only attached statically to interrupts.
- Task rendez-vous is forbidden, only protected objects can be used for inter-task communication and synchronization. Moreover, the set of protected objects is static as they are only allowed to be created at package level. Protected objects are also subject to further restrictions: they may have *at most one protected entry* (along with any number of procedures and functions), the maximum queue length at the entry is *one* (otherwise, an exception is raised), the entry *barrier* must be a simple Boolean variable, and *requeue* is not allowed.
- All delays must be absolute (that is, only **delay until** statements are legal).

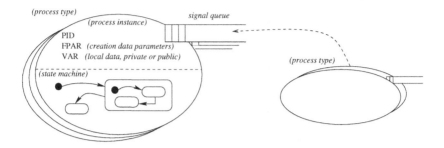

Fig. 1. Constituents of an IF model

To achieve analysability of the resulting systems, all tasks must be structured such that they are either periodic or sporadic (i.e., event driven with a minimum inter-arrival time enforced). This restriction is not formally imposed by the Ravenscar profile since it can be verified neither statically nor at run-time. However, [10] contains coding patterns for these two types of tasks.

To end this section, we note that there are currently two runtimes which comply with the Ravenscar profile requirements: the commercial ObjectAda Real-Time RAVEN from Aonix [4] and the open source Open Ravenscar Real-Time Kernel ORK [14].

3   The IF Model Checker

The validation approach proposed in this work is based on the formal model of communicating extended timed automata, as it is embodied in the IF language and the execution and validation environment built around this language [7, 8]. This section provides a brief overview of IF, necessary for understanding the rest of the paper.

The IF language is dedicated to modeling *distributed systems* that can manipulate *complex data*, may involve *dynamic process creation* and *real time constraints*. The language constructs allow to represent the behavior of a system at an arbitrary level of abstraction, ranging from very abstract descriptions involving lots of non-determinism and un-interpreted actions, to very concrete descriptions involving concrete data manipulation, algorithmic structures, etc. In particular, the richness of the language allows to describe the semantics of higher level formalisms, like UML [16] or SDL [18], and has been used as a format for inter-connecting modelling and validation tools.

The main purpose of IF models is validation by formal techniques (simulation, property verification), which explains why some features of the language presented below, such as default transition atomicity, could be considered "unrealistic" from an implementation perspective.

Communicating extended timed automata. An IF system is composed of a set of communicating *processes* that run in parallel (see figure 1). Processes are instances of *process types*, they have an identity (PID), may own data variables and their behavior is defined by a *state machine*. The state machine may be hierarchical (i.e., making use of composite states) and the effect of transitions is described by usual structured imperative statements.

Data variables are statically typed, and may contain either simple scalars (boolean, integer, real) or structured data (arrays, records, objects).

Processes inter-communicate by sending *asynchronous signals*, which are stored in per-process signal *queues* until the destination process is ready to handle them. Additionally, processes may communicate via *shared variables*, which are public variables exported by some process and that every other process can read/write. Parallel processes are composed asynchronously (i.e., they progress independently from each other). The model also allows *dynamic creation* of processes, which is an essential feature for modeling object-based systems or procedural control flow, as will be shown later in this paper.

The link between system execution and time progress may be described in a precise manner, and thus offers support for modeling real time constraints. For this, IF uses the constructs of *timed automata with urgency* [6]: there are special variables called *clocks* which measure time progress. All clocks progress at the same rate during a system run, and they differ only by the moments when they are started; a dedicated statement, *set $x:= 0$*, is used to (re)start a clock x. Comparisons between a clock and an integer value may be used in transition guards. A special attribute of each transition, called *urgency*, specifies if time may progress when the transition is enabled.

Dynamic priorities. On top of the above model, *priority rules* allow for specifying dynamic priorities as partial orders between processes. The theoretical foundation of this framework is given in [3].

A priority rule has the following form:

`p1 < p2 if state_condition(p1,p2)`

where `state_condition(p1,p2)` is a boolean expression with free PID variables `p1` and `p2`, which can be interpreted in the context of a given system state. The semantics of the rule is the following: given a system state, for any pair of processes `P1` and `P2` which have enabled transitions in that state, if the (closed) formula `state_condition(P1,P2)` evaluates to true then the transitions of `P1` are not allowed to execute (i.e., `P2` has priority over `P1`).

It is shown in [3] how this kind of rules may be used to model different scheduling policies, including fixed priority scheduling, Earliest Deadline First (EDF) and others.

Property specification with observers. Behavioral properties of IF models may be expressed using *observer automata*. These are special processes that monitor the changes in a system's *state* (variable values, contents of queues, etc.) and the *events* occurring during the execution of transitions (inputs, outputs, creation and destruction of processes, etc.). To express desired *safety* properties of a system, some of the observer states are labeled as *error* states: if a system execution leads to such a state then the property represented by the observer was violated. This allows to express arbitrary *safety properties*.

Analysis techniques: the IF toolbox. The IF toolbox [7, 8] is the validation environment built around the formalism presented before. It is composed of three categories of tools. **Behavioral tools** are used for simulation, verification of properties, automatic test generation, state space minimization and comparison. The tools implement techniques such as *partial order reductions* and *symbolic simulation* of time, and thus present a good level of scalability. **Static analysis tools** provide source-level optimizations (*data flow analysis* such as dead variable reduction, *slicing*, etc.) that help reducing further the state space of the models. **Front-ends and exporting tools** which provide coupling to higher level languages (UML, SDL) and to other verification tools.

4   The Mapping of Ravenscar Ada to IF

In this section we describe the principles of the mapping of Ada programming constructs to IF model elements. In IF the only first class language citizen is the process: it is used for encapsulating data and behavior, it is the only one that can be referenced (by PID), can be dynamically created and killed. Therefore, most of the constructs of Ada like packages, tasks, procedures, protected objects and referenced data will be encoded using processes.

Note that although this encoding significantly increases the number of processes employed to "simulate" a Ravenscar system, it does not add to the combinatorial complexity of system behavior, as most of the processes are just passively encapsulating data or waiting for some event (see §4.2). In general, the number of "active" processes in a given state is equal to the number of active threads in the corresponding configuration of the Ada system.

4.1   Packages, Data and Statements

Ada packages are static containers for various types of content: data variables, tasks, protected objects, procedures, types and other packages. Some of the content has an actual runtime existence (variables, tasks, objects) while in the case of procedures, types and nested packages, the encapsulating package acts only as a static namespace.

In IF, a package is mapped to a process which only contains variables corresponding to the Ada data, task or object variables. The static namespace function of a package cannot be fulfilled directly by an IF process since nesting is not allowed, therefore we use a naming scheme for mapping qualified Ada entity names to flat IF process names. This kind of manipulation is common in all compilers which generate low-level object code from a high level language with complex scoping rules. Similarly, generic packages and instantiation are also handled using naming rules and code replication (code size optimization is not important for verification).

Scalar data is restricted to the types supported by IF: `boolean`, `integer` and `real`. This limitation is not very strong when the goal is formal verification of high-integrity systems, since the control flow of such systems is rarely affected by other types of data. Complex data types are constructed using the IF `array` and `record` constructors, or by encapsulation within dedicated processes (e.g., for constructing records with *variants*). Processes are also used to represent any entity which is handled *by reference*, like tasks and protected objects (the reference is then the PID).

The mapping of computation statements is defined as follows:

- The points of control before and after a statement are represented by IF *states*, and the statements are represented by *transitions* between states.
- Assignments and elementary operations have a direct counterpart in IF.
- Procedure and function calls and evaluation of expressions containing calls is done according to the simple principles described in §4.2.
- Control flow statements like alternatives and loops are encoded in the structure of the state / transition graph.

We note that several statements, like those involved in (bounded) rendez-vous, etc., are forbidden by the Ravenscar profile. Other statements, which are not forbidden (e.g., `delay until`), are explained below.

4.2 Procedural Control Flow and Tasks

Procedures, functions and protected object entries (collectively referred to as subroutines in this section) are represented by processes which are dynamically created upon call and killed upon return of control. Thus, the runtime call stack of a task has a direct representation in IF as a linked list of processes. The processes hold the subroutine local variables and parameters, and realize the subroutine behavior by their automaton.

IF allows passing data parameters (`fpars`) at process creation which allows us to represent very directly the passing of `in` parameters. Along with these, a caller also passes as parameter its identity and the identity of the *task* on behalf of which the call is made. These references are used for returning the control, which is represented by the sending of a `return_<procedure name>` signal from the callee to the caller, just before the callee kills itself. The signal also carries the `out` parameters of the procedure, if any.

Figure 2 shows the mapping of a complete procedure, illustrating the mechanisms of call and return (as well as the implementation of actions by automata, the access to variables, etc.). For clarity, we have presented the IF process in a graphical form which is isomophic to the textual form actually used by the tool.

Finally, *tasks* are mapped to processes which encapsulate local task variables and realize the task behavior (body) by their automaton.

4.3 Protected Objects

Protected objects are the synchronization mechanism used in Ravenscar Ada. They provide functions (which may only read but not modify object attributes) that can be executed concurrently, together with procedures and entries that are

```
procedure Compute
 (Value : in out Natural) is
begin
  OPCS.Compute (Value);
end Compute;
```

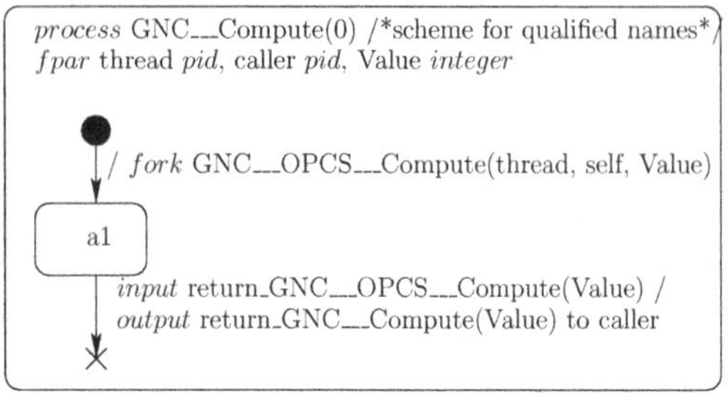

Fig. 2. Mapping of procedural control flow

```
protected body OBCS is
  ...
 function Count_Requests
   return Integer is
begin
   ...
   return x;
 end Get_Request;
end OBCS;
```

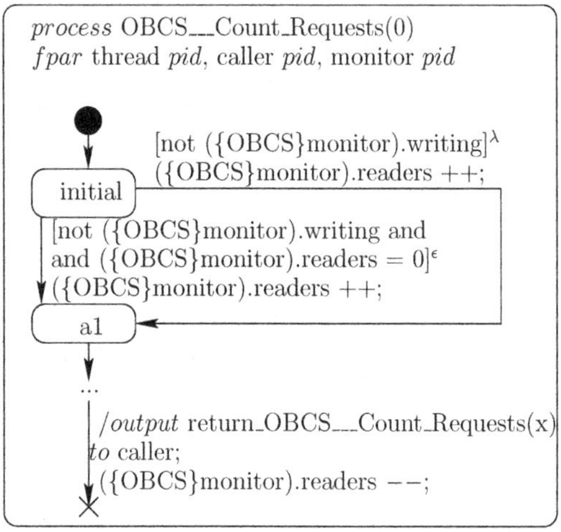

Fig. 3. Mapping of protected objects: functions

executed in mutual exclusion from each other and from functions. This corresponds to the classical *readers-writers* problem and Ada runtimes solve it using lower level mutual exclusion mechanisms. In IF however, the solution is much facilitated by the fact that the language offers mutually exclusive and atomic *transitions* by default, and transitions are provided with *guard conditions* that may be readily used for conditional waiting.

A protected object is mapped to a process that encapsulated its data, together with two additional variables used for implementing the readers-writers protocol: a boolean **writing** and an integer **readers**. Functions, procedures and entries are, as mentioned before, mapped to processes that are created upon calling and they receive an additional parameter – **monitor** – pointing to owning the protected object. The readers-writers protocol implemented in our mapping is a variant of the classical solution that may be found in many textbooks (see for ex. [11]):

– Procedures and entries begin by waiting in an **initial** state until **readers=0** and **not writing**. For entries, this condition is augmented with the barrier.

When this condition is true, it is followed atomically by `writing := true`. At the end of procedures/entries, `writing` is reset to false.
- Functions begin by waiting in an `initial` state until `not writing`. When this condition is true, they atomically increment `readers`. At the end of the function, `readers` is decremented.

To preserve the generality of the solution, we also allow functions to stay in the `initial` state if at least one other function is executing in the object. Thus, the model includes both the behavior where functions eagerly begin execution regardless of waiting procedures/entries (possibly leading to the starvation of the latter), and the behavior where functions lazily wait giving the possibility to procedures/entries to start (possibly leading to the starvation of tasks executing the functions).

At the level of IF (see Figure 3), this is achieved by declaring the transition from `initial` as having *lazy* urgency (see [6]). However, a reader function is not allowed to wait when the protected object is free of any access, i.e. when `readers = 0 and not writing`. To enforce this, a second (*eager*) transition is added.

The mapping of functions is illustrated in Figure 3 (for space reasons we do not include an illustration for procedures, described above). Note that the transition *guards* are represented inside square brackets, with the urgency specified as an exponent (λ for *lazy*, ϵ for *eager*). They are followed by a slash and the actions executed (atomically) by the transition. Also, note that the expression (`{A}p`).`B` in IF (used for accessing variables from the `monitor` process) denotes the casting of an untyped PID `p` to the type of process `A` followed by access to variable `B` exported by `p`.

Since Ravenscar disallows more than one task waiting on an entry, we need not represent the waiting queues in the IF model. The waiting tasks are simply those whose calls are in the `initial` state. Note that one interesting use of IF may be to verify the satisfaction of the queue length restriction.

4.4   Time and Delays

As mentioned before, in Ravenscar tasks may suspend themselves only using absolute delays. In practice, the coding patterns presented in §5 of [10] show that the absolute dates are always computed relatively to a "timestamp" (e.g., obtained with `Ada.Real_Time.Clock`). This kind of waiting falls within the expressive power of timed automata. In Figure 4 we show how the *Cyclic* task from [10] is mapped to IF using clocks (see the description of clocks in §3).

4.5   Scheduling Policy and Timing Model

The Ravenscar profile fixes the scheduling policy to FIFO within priorities with priority ceiling locking. One can suppose that every task and protected object contains a `pragma Priority` directive, and that the assigned priority levels observe the ceiling rule.

```
task body Cyclic is
 Next_Period : Ada.Real_Time.Time;
 Period : constant
   Ada.Real_Time.Time_Span := ...;
begin
  Next_Period :=
    Ada.Real_Time.Clock + Period;
  loop
    delay until Next_Period;
    Next_Period := Next_Period
      + Period;
    ...
  end loop;
end Cyclic;
```

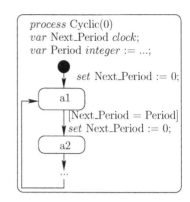

Fig. 4. Mapping of a cyclic task

The dynamic priority framework of IF is more expressive than this policy, and therefore it allows a quite straightforward mapping for it. The mapping idea is that every process corresponding to a task has a `priority` attribute, which is dynamically updated to reflect the ceiling priority when entering/exiting subroutines of a protected object. Then, the policy is simply modeled by an IF dynamic priority rule equivalent to this:

$$x < y \text{ if } x.priority < y.priority$$

(The actual IF rule, equivalent to this one, is slightly more complex because attribute access like `x.priority` cannot be directly made for non-typed PIDs like x and y. Such implementation details are out of scope here.)

The only aspect which is not captured by the mapping above is the FIFO rule for equal priority tasks. In such cases, there will be a non-deterministic choice between tasks x and y. This induces an overapproximation of the system behavior (in the sense that the set of behaviors modeled in IF is a superset of those of the real system), which is a *conservative* abstraction for any *safety* properties verified on the IF model [13].

Timed automata are in principle not expressive enough to model *execution times* in preemptive systems (for which a *stopwatch* concept strictly stronger than the timed automata clocks is in general necessary). There are particular cases in which an encoding is possible, like the one in [15] which only works for systems of tasks with fixed execution time (i.e., best case and worst case execution times are equal), but they are rarely applicable in real systems. Another possibility is to use discrete (integer) counters instead of clocks to model execution times (or, equivalently, to use discrete representations for clocks in analysis), but this yields complex models and worsens the perspectives for combinatorial explosion during verification. For Ravenscar systems, the use of such techniques for schedulability analysis is *not justified*, since the constraints imposed by the profile render them analyzable for example by response time analysis (RTA) techniques rooted in [19].

Consequently, we base the timing of the IF model not on the worst case execution times of tasks, but on the response times previously computed by RTA. Concretely, every task has an associated `response` clock which is not allowed to grow past a `max_response_time` issued from RTA, a condition that is clearly expressible with classical timed automata clocks. This timing model also yields a conservative overapproximation of the real system's timing (the proof of this statement is considered out of scope here).

4.6   Interrupts and the Environment

In order to verify properties on the IF model resulting from an Ada system, one has to close it with a model of the environment, which embodies the hypotheses that are made about what it is reasonable to expect from it. Typically, the environment can interact with a system either by triggering interrupts or by calling sub-programs of the system, and the hypotheses concern the order in which such events arrive, the inter-arrival times, etc. Currently the environment's behavior is modeled directly in IF and we do not pose any restrictions on how this is done. An interrupt can be modeled as a call to the *attached* procedure.

We note that the behavioral and temporal non-determinism allowed in IF is key to a simple and expressive modelling of the environment hypotheses, which generally contain some degree of uncertainty.

5   Experimental Results

5.1   The Case Study

We validated the mapping defined in §4 on a typical task synchronization example issued from a spaceborne application provided by Astrium Space Transportation within the ASSERT project. Although the functionality of the example is quite simple, the number of Ada objects involved and the size of the code is significant owing to the fact that the code is automatically generated from a high-level architecture description (conforming to the approach described in [5]) and contains different mechanisms for separating functional and architectural aspects, for implementing "archetypical" architectural elements like cyclic and sporadic tasks, etc. The code features two tasks, three protected objects and some 20 procedures, functions and object entries, all spread across 8 packages (including generic ones).

A simplified view of the architecture of the example is depicted in Figure 5. (The notation is inspired from AADL [21]. Rounded rectangles stand for packages, rectangles stand for protected objects, dotted parallelograms stand for tasks, double line connectors signify access to operations. For simplicity, we have renamed some of the system entities to more meaningful names.) In short, the functionality of the example is as follows:

 - A task TMTC receives sporadic requests (in reality, telecommands from a ground system) upon which it attempts to update an attribute of a protected object (POS). For receiving the requests, TMTC uses a protected object

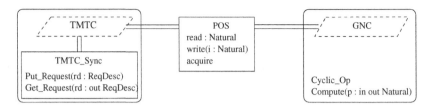

Fig. 5. Architecture of the example

(`TMTC_Sync`) which exhibits a `Put_Request` procedure and a `Get_Request`
entry. The sporadic task implements a protection mechanism against requests made more often than a minimum inter-arrival time ($MIAT$).
- Another task, `GNC` (for *Guidance-Navigation-Control*), periodically reads the
  attribute of `POS`, performs some computation based on its value, and finally
  updates it.
- It is required that, when a `TMTC` request comes, the value written to `POS`
  shall not be overwritten by a value written by the `GNC`, (so that the next
  cyclic read by the `GNC` reads the value sent by the ground). In the example,
  this is achieved by encapsulating the entire `GNC` read-compute-write cycle in
  a protected operation (called `acquire`) of `POS`, thus rendering it mutually
  exclusive with the writes from `TMTC`.

The property that one wants to verify on this model corresponds to the requirement stated informally above. The requirement is however not sufficiently
precise, and one has to express it in terms of strictly defined events like the
reception of a `Put_Request` by the `TMTC_Sync`, the effective execution of `Write`
by `POS` after acquiring the monitor lock, etc. While doing so, we realized that
the requirement is actually a conjunction of two simpler safety properties:

P1. After the effective execution of `POS.write` with value `p` on behalf of the
   `TMTC` task, the next execution of `POS.read` on behalf of `GNC` returns `p`.

   By itself this property is not sufficient since it does not exclude unfair
   executions in which an effective `TMTC` write is delayed for several `GNC` cycles
   after the request arrives. Consequently, we added the following property
   which expresses the fact that a telecommand is effectively handled at latest
   at the end of the current GNC cycle.

P2. The `POS.write` executed by the `TMTC` after receiving `TMTC_Sync.Put_Request`
   must start before the next cycle of GNC starts execution.

The two properties can be expressed as IF observers, the automata structures
are shown in Figure 6 (the event observation details are omitted).

In order to verify the model, we had to close it with a model of the environment. The chosen environment is a time-non-deterministic ground component
which calls `TMTC_Sync.Put_Request` from time to time (though no more often
than 1 time unit). In order to reduce the verification state space, we discard traces
where a second TC is sent while the previous TC is still pending in `TMTC_Sync`.

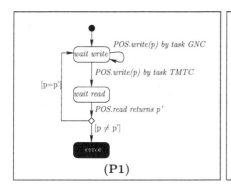 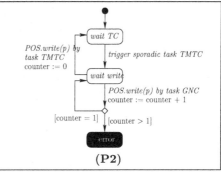

Fig. 6. Desired properties of the example

5.2 Verification Results

Two temporal parameters come into play when verifying the satisfaction of properties by the model: the minimum inter-arrival time ($MIAT$) enforced for TMTC requests, and the cycle time of the GNC. The values specified initially in the Ada code were respectively 10ms and 8ms. However, it should be noted that the $MIAT$ is seen as a protection mechanism of the sporadic TMTC task, and may not be actually observed by the environment, which may try to send requests more often.

We have experimented with the following combinations of values (state space size, verification times and results are summarized in Table 1):

- GNC *Cycle=8ms,* TMTC *MIAT=10ms, actual MIAT observed by the environment < 10ms (1ms).* In this case **P1** is verified, but **P2** may be violated. The result is not surprising, since when a second TMTC request comes sooner than expected, it may be delayed for a certain time, and more than one Read request from the GNC may overtake it.
- GNC *Cycle=8ms,* TMTC *MIAT=10ms, actual MIAT observed by the environment=10ms.* Both P1 and P2 are verified.

Table 1. Verification results

Parameters	Results	State space metrics	User time
GNC Cycle=8ms, TMTC MIAT=10ms, actual env. MIAT=1ms	P1:true P2:false	(stopped after 30 error scenarios)	$< 1s$
GNC Cycle=8ms, TMTC MIAT=10ms, actual env. MIAT=10ms	P1:true P2:true	45332 states / 122953 transitions	$< 5s$
GNC Cycle=8ms, TMTC MIAT=6ms, actual env. MIAT=1s	P1:true P2:true	336487 states / 902696 transitions	$< 46s$

- GNC *Cycle=8ms*, TMTC *MIAT < 8ms (e.g., 6ms), actual MIAT observed by the environment=1ms*. Both **P1** and **P2** are verified. Note that when the TMTC MIAT is less than the length of the GNC cycle, **P2** is verified regardless of the frequency with which the environment sends the requests.

Note that **P1**, which is the essential property of the system (no value written by the TMTC is ever overwritten by the GNC) is satisfied in all configurations.

6   Conclusions

We have proved the feasibility of formal verification of Ada Ravenscar systems by translation to a sufficiently powerful formal language based on timed automata, which is supported by the model-checker IF [7, 8]. Due to particular features of the IF language, like dynamic process creation, we have been able to produce a mapping which is structure-preserving, meaning that every construct of the initial Ada specification can be identified as an entity in the resulting code (in general an IF *process*). This potentially allows traceability between the two representations, with the obvious benefits. Previous applications of model checking to Ada systems, such as the one presented in [9], do not offer this kind of structure preservation (and consequently, they also lend themselves less easily to automation), in general because of the lack of expressivity in the target language (UPPAAL in [9]).

The translation overhead (in terms of verification state space) also proves to be moderate in our case: for example, the case study presented in §5 yields a large set of 34 IF processes, but thanks to the efficient sub-state sharing algorithms used in IF this does not contribute significantly to the size of the state space, only the combinatorial complexity generated by the two tasks does.

The first part of this work was concerned with defining the translation method and with validating it on a prototypical example. In order for these results to be applicable in practice, an implementation in the form of a compiler is needed. For that, we could rely on the GNAT-based open-source implementation of Ravenscar. Resources allowing, these are our plans for the future.

Acknowledgements. We wish to thank the ASSERT team from the University of Padua for providing the Ada code of the example as well as the initial motivation for this work. We also thank all other partners of the ASSERT project for fruitful discussions around the topics presented here.

References

[1] Tucker Taft, S., Duff, R.A., Brukardt, R.L., Plödereder, E., Leroy, P. (eds.): Ada 2005 Reference Manual. LNCS, vol. 4348. Springer, Heidelberg (2006)
[2] Abdennahder, N., Kordon, F. (eds.): Ada-Europe 2007. LNCS, vol. 4498. Springer, Heidelberg (2007)

[3] Altisen, K., Gößler, G., Sifakis, J.: A Methodology for the Construction of Scheduled Systems. In: Joseph, M. (ed.) FTRTFT 2000. LNCS, vol. 1926, pp. 106–120. Springer, Heidelberg (2000)

[4] Aonix. ObjectAda Real-Time RAVEN,
http://www.aonix.com/objectada_raven.html

[5] Bordin, M., Vardanega, T.: Correctness by construction for high-integrity real-time systems: A metamodel-driven approach. In: [2], pp. 114–127

[6] Bornot, S., Sifakis, J.: An algebraic framework for urgency. Inf. Comput. 163(1), 172–202 (2000)

[7] Bozga, M., Graf, S., Mounier, L.: IF-2.0: A Validation Environment for Component-Based Real-Time Systems. In: Brinksma, E., Larsen, K.G. (eds.) CAV 2002. LNCS, vol. 2404, pp. 343–348. Springer, Heidelberg (2002)

[8] Bozga, M., Graf, S., Ober, I., Ober, I., Sifakis, J.: The IF Toolset. In: Bernardo, M., Corradini, F. (eds.) SFM-RT 2004. LNCS, vol. 3185, pp. 237–267. Springer, Heidelberg (2004)

[9] Burns, A., Wellings, A.J.: How to verify concurrent Ada programs: the application of model checking. ACM SIGADA Ada Letters 19(2), 78–83 (1999)

[10] Burns, A., Dobbing, B., Vardanega, T.: Guide for the use of the Ada Ravenscar profile in high integrity systems. Ada Lett. XXIV(2), 1–74 (2004)

[11] Burns, A., Wellings, A.: Real-Time Systems and Programming Languages, 3rd edn. Addison-Wesley, Reading (2001)

[12] Buttazzo, G.: Hard Real-Time Computing Systems: Predictable Scheduling Algorithms and Applications, 2nd edn. Real-Time Systems Series, vol. 23. Springer, Heidelberg (2005)

[13] Clarke, E.M., Grumberg, O., Peled, D.A.: Model Checking. MIT Press, Cambridge (1999)

[14] de la Puente, J.A., Ruiz, J.F., Zamorano, J.: An open Ravenscar real-time kernel for GNAT. In: Keller, H.B., Plödereder, E. (eds.) Ada-Europe 2000. LNCS, vol. 1845, pp. 5–15. Springer, Heidelberg (2000)

[15] Fersman, E., Mokrushin, L., Pettersson, P., Yi, W.: Schedulability Analysis Using Two Clocks. In: Garavel, H., Hatcliff, J. (eds.) TACAS 2003. LNCS, vol. 2619, pp. 224–239. Springer, Heidelberg (2003)

[16] Object Management Group. Unified modeling language,
http://www.omg.org/spec/UML/

[17] Hamid, I., Najm, E.: Operational semantics of Ada Ravenscar. In: 13th International Conference on Reliable Software Technologies - AdaEurope, Proceedings. LNCS, vol. 5026. Springer, Heidelberg (2008)

[18] ITU-T. Languages for telecommunications applications – Specification and Description Language (SDL). ITU-T Revised Recommendation Z.100 (1999)

[19] Joseph, M., Pandya, P.: Finding response times in a real-time system. The Computer Journal 29(5), 390–395 (1986)

[20] Liu, C.L., Layland, J.W.: Scheduling algorithms for multiprogramming in a hard-real-time environment. Journal of the ACM 20(1), 46–61 (1973)

[21] SAE Aerospace. Architecture Analysis & Design Language (AADL). SAE Technical Standard (November 2004)

[22] Zalila, B., Hamid, I., Hugues, J., Pautet, L.: Generating distributed high integrity applications from their architectural description. In: [2], pp. 155–167

Operational Semantics of Ada Ravenscar

Irfan Hamid and Elie Najm

Telecom ParisTech – LTCI-UMR 5141 CNRS
46, rue Barrault, 75013 – Paris, France
Irfan.Hamid@enst.fr, Elie.Najm@enst.fr

Abstract. The Ada programming language has been designed from the ground up for safety-critical real-time systems. This trend has continued with the Ada 2005 language definition which has incorporated the Ravenscar Profile for high-integrity systems into the language standard. Here we describe the operational semantics for Ada Ravenscar code generated automatically from an architecture description of the system given in the Architecture Analysis and Design Language.

1 Introduction

The Ada Ravenscar Profile [2] is a restriction of the rich tasking subset of the Ada language and associated runtime that aims to make the language more amenable to the development of safety-critical real-time systems. The Architecture Analysis and Design Language (AADL) [13] is an architecture description language targeted specifically to the real-time and avionics domain. The code generation rules given with the AADL standard are incomplete and rely on the existance of an "AADL executive", in effect, an operating system that provides all the services needed by an AADL application.

Since such an operating system does not exist, we used ORK [6], a Ravenscar-compliant executive. We developed code generation rules for AADL to Ada that faithfully preserve semantics when run on the ORK platform. We also developed a code generator as an Eclipse plugin (ARC http://aadl.enst.fr/arc/) that transforms AADL models to Ada source. The code generation rules and toolset were introduced in [9]. In this paper, we present a static semantics for the Ravenscar code that we generate, which is a subset of Ada Ravenscar. We also present a structured operational semantics that represents the dynamic evolution of the generated system. The Ravenscar Profile restrictions on Ada eliminate certain features from the language and associated runtime:

- All tasks must be either periodic or sporadic (for schedulability analysis)
- Tasks may only communicate among themselves through protected objects
- No dynamic creation or destruction of tasks or protected objects
- Rendezvous are prohibited (no entries on Ada tasks)
- Protected objects may have at most one entry
- A protected object entry's queue is of size 1
- All delays must be absolute (no `delay  <time_expression>` allowed)

F. Kordon and T. Vardanega (Eds.): Ada-Europe 2008, LNCS 5026, pp. 44–58, 2008.

- Scheduling is priority based, priority assignment is RMA [15] or RTA [3]
- The priority ceiling protocol [16] is used for access to protected objects

ARC relies upon the OSATE AADL toolkit [14] to parse AADL models. The OSATE toolkit uses the Eclipse Modeling Framework [1] to represent the abstract syntax of the parsed model. Instead of directly generating Ada code from the AADL model, we chose to implement an intermediate meta-model to represent the Ravenscar system. The front-end transforms the AADL model to an instance of this meta-model. The code generator traverses this intermediate model—which we call the Ravenscar Meta-model (RMM)—to generate Ada code. Two advantages of this approach are a reduction in complexity (RMM is simpler than the AADL meta-model), and ease of writing code generators for other languages. Because all AADL models cannot be transformed to Ravenscar-compliant code, we verify the AADL model against a set of Object Constraint Language rules before a model transformation from AADL to an instance of the RMM is carried out. The paper is structured as follows. Sec. 2 presents the static semantics. Sec. 3 presents the dynamic semantics of the generated Ravenscar code using a structured operational semantic approach [12]. Sec. 4 relates our contribution to past and ongoing research and concludes.

2   Static Semantics

The static semantics provided in this section are a formalization of the structure of the RMM using set theory, and mirrors the static structure of code generated by ARC. This static semantics will be used in the ensuing section on dynamic semantics, specifically to manipulate the entities in the operational semantic transitions.

2.1   Ravenscar Computational Units

A Ravenscar system is given by five *finite* and *pairwise disjoint* sets, endowed with five functions and related by four relations. The five sets are:

$$\textbf{Periodic tasks } \mathcal{T}_p = \{P_1 \ldots P_n\}$$
$$\textbf{Sporadic tasks } \mathcal{T}_s = \{S_1 \ldots S_m\}$$
$$\textbf{Interrupts } \mathcal{U} = \{U_1 \ldots U_k\}$$
$$\textbf{Synchronisers } \mathcal{D} = \{D_1 \ldots D_l\}$$
$$\textbf{Exchangers } \mathcal{E} = \{E_1 \ldots E_r\}$$

- *Sporadic tasks* are dispatched upon the reception of an event. A minimum time—characteristic to each task—between successive dispatches is enforced
- *Periodic tasks* are dispatched at regular time intervals called their *period*
- *Interrupts* can be raised at any time except if a previous occurence is already being executed. Thus, at any time, there can be at most $k = |\mathcal{U}|$ interrupts present in the system

- *Exchangers* are protected objects with an internal data buffer and Get and Set procedures. They are used for simple data exchange among tasks
- *Synchronisers* are protected objects with an internal queue of events that expose a Send_Event procedure for depositing events. A Get_Event *entry* is exposed upon which the associated sporadic task waits for dispatch

We define four derived sets, namely, **Tasks** ($\mathcal{T}$), **Activities** ($\mathcal{A}$), **Protected objects** ($\mathcal{PO}$), and **Computational units** ($\mathcal{C}$); as follows:

$$\mathcal{T} = \mathcal{T}_p \cup \mathcal{T}_s$$
$$\mathcal{A} = \mathcal{T}_p \cup \mathcal{T}_s \cup \mathcal{U}$$
$$\mathcal{PO} = \mathcal{E} \cup \mathcal{D}$$
$$\mathcal{C} = \mathcal{A} \cup \mathcal{PO}$$

2.2   Functions on Computational Units

Five functions on computation units are defined with the following signatures:

$$\text{PRIORITY} : \mathcal{C} \rightarrow \quad \text{ANYPRIORITY} \tag{1}$$
$$\text{HOLDINGTIME} : \mathcal{T} \rightarrow \quad \text{TIME} \tag{2}$$
$$\text{PROG} : \mathcal{C} \rightarrow \quad \text{PROGS} \tag{3}$$

TIME is a discrete time domain. HOLDINGTIME is defined as the period for a periodic and minimum inter-dispatch time for a sporadic task. ANYPRIORITY is a bounded subset of the set $\mathbb{N}$ of natural numbers and gives valid priorities. PROGS is the subset of Ada 95 that the code of computational units conforms to. The code of a computational unit γ is given by PROG(γ).

2.3   Conformant PROGS Programs

We focus on an abstraction of programs that represents execution steps relevant to our semantics, which gives legal instructions and their sequencing:

- comp: A sequential execution step
- Set(E): A Set call to exchanger E
- Get(E): A Get call to exchanger E
- Send_Event(D): A Send_Event call to synchroniser D
- Get_Event(D): A Get_Event call to synchroniser D
- delay until: request to be suspended until a future instant
- ret: return statement

The legal execution sequences of these steps depend on the type of the computational unit. They are defined using BNF grammars. The code of each computational unit must respect its prescribed grammar (BP is for periodic tasks, BS for sporadic, BU for interrupts, BE for exchangers, BD for synchronizers):

$BP := \texttt{comp}; BP \mid \texttt{Set}(E); BP \mid \texttt{Get}(E); BP \mid \texttt{Send\_Event}(D); BP \mid \texttt{delay until}$
$BS := \texttt{Get\_Event}(D); BP$
$BU := \texttt{Send\_Event}(D) \mid \texttt{Set}(E)$
$BE := [\texttt{Set} -> CC \,, \texttt{Get} -> CC \,]$
$BD := [\texttt{Send\_Event} -> CC, \texttt{Get\_Event} -> CC \,]$
$CC := \texttt{comp} ; CC \mid \texttt{ret}$

2.4   Topological Relations on Computational Units

By an analysis of the set of programs PROG, we can construct the communication topology between the various computational units. Four topological relations, *sets*, *gets*, *sends_event*, and *gets_event* are induced by PROG:

$$sets : \dfrac{}{\texttt{Set}} \subset \mathcal{A} \times \mathcal{E} \tag{4}$$

$$gets : \dfrac{}{\texttt{Get}} \subset \mathcal{T} \times \mathcal{E} \tag{5}$$

$$sends\_event : \dfrac{}{\texttt{Send\_Event}} \subset \mathcal{A} \times \mathcal{D} \tag{6}$$

$$gets\_event : \dfrac{}{\texttt{Get\_Event}} \subset \mathcal{T}_s \times \mathcal{D} \tag{7}$$

they are defined according to the following conditions:

$$\texttt{Set}(E) \text{ occurs-in PROG}(\alpha) \quad \Leftrightarrow \quad \alpha \dfrac{}{\texttt{Set}} E \tag{8}$$

$$\texttt{Get}(E) \text{ occurs-in PROG}(T) \quad \Leftrightarrow \quad T \dfrac{}{\texttt{Get}} E \tag{9}$$

$$\texttt{Send\_Event}(D) \text{ occurs-in PROG}(\alpha) \quad \Leftrightarrow \quad \alpha \dfrac{}{\texttt{Send\_Event}} D \tag{10}$$

$$\texttt{Get\_Event}(D) \text{ occurs-in PROG}(S) \quad \Leftrightarrow \quad S \dfrac{}{\texttt{Get\_Event}} D \tag{11}$$

We also need three derived relations, namely: *dispatches* ($\overline{DIS}$), *writes_to* ($\overline{WTO}$) and *accesses* ($\overline{ACC}$). *dispatches* is the inverse of *gets_event*, *writes_to* is the union of *gets* and *sends_event*, and *accesses* is the union of the four primitive relations. Formally:

$$D \overline{DIS} S \triangleq S \dfrac{}{\texttt{Get\_Event}} D \tag{12}$$

$$\alpha \overline{WTO} \pi \triangleq (\pi \in \mathcal{E} \ \wedge \ \alpha \dfrac{}{\texttt{Set}} \pi) \vee (\pi \in \mathcal{D} \ \wedge \ \alpha \dfrac{}{\texttt{Send\_Event}} \pi) \tag{13}$$

$$\begin{aligned}
\alpha \overline{ACC} \pi \triangleq {}& (\pi \in \mathcal{E} \ \wedge \ \alpha \dfrac{}{\texttt{Set}} \pi) \vee (\pi \in \mathcal{E} \ \wedge \ \alpha \dfrac{}{\texttt{Get}} \pi) \\
& \vee (\alpha \in \mathcal{A} \ \wedge \ \pi \in \mathcal{D} \ \wedge \ \alpha \dfrac{}{\texttt{Send\_Event}} \pi) \\
& \vee (\alpha \in \mathcal{T}_s \ \wedge \ \pi \in \mathcal{D} \ \wedge \ \alpha \dfrac{}{\texttt{Get\_Event}} \pi)
\end{aligned} \tag{14}$$

The topological relations must satisfy the following constraints:

$$\forall \ D, \ \exists \ S \text{ unique satisfying: } D \xrightarrow[DIS]{} S \tag{15}$$

$$\forall \ S, \ \exists \ D \text{ unique satisfying: } S \xrightarrow[\text{Get\_Event}]{} D \tag{16}$$

$$\forall \ U, \ \exists \ \pi \text{ unique satisfying: } U \xrightarrow[WTO]{} \pi \tag{17}$$

$$U \xrightarrow[WTO]{} \pi \text{ and } U' \xrightarrow[WTO]{} \pi \ \Rightarrow \ U = U' \tag{18}$$

At most one task is dispatched by a synchronizer (15). For every sporadic task, there exists one and only one synchronizer that dispatches it (16). Each interrupt writes on one and only one protected object (17). At most one interrupt may write to a protected object (18). Constraints (15) and (16) imply that relations $\overleftarrow{DIS}$ and $\overleftarrow{\text{Get\_Event}}$ are bijective and mutually inverse functions. From (17) and (18) it follows that relation $\overleftarrow{WTO}$, when restricted to $\mathcal{U}$, is an injective function with co-domain in $\mathcal{PO}$.

Priority Ceiling Protocol. All priorities must comply with PCP. Function PRIORITY must satisfy the following property ($\overleftarrow{ACC}$ from equation 14):

For any activity α and any protected object π :

$$(\alpha \xrightarrow[ACC]{} \pi) \ \Rightarrow \ \text{PRIORITY}(\pi) \geq \text{PRIORITY}(\alpha) \tag{19}$$

3   Dynamic Semantics

The dynamic semantics of the system will be described using a form of *structured operational semantics* [12] which describes the evolution of the system over time.

3.1   Execution Context

$$\text{Execution context } c = \begin{cases} \sigma, \sigma_s & \text{Scheduler} \\ \iota & \text{Idle task} \\ a & \text{An active execution context} \end{cases}$$

The above equation states that three entities may possess processing resources, the scheduler (σ and σ_s), the system idle task (ι), or an activity (a). The scheduler can be in one of two states: σ when the scheduler has seized control, σ_s when the scheduler is ready to grant control. Thus, σ and σ_s represent two steps in the excution of the scheduler functions, allowing the assignment of different execution times to both in order to accurately model context switches. An active context, a, may have one of the following forms:

Sporadic tasks: $S, \ S\xrightarrow[\text{Set}]{}E, \ S\xrightarrow[\text{Send\_Event}]{}D, \ S\xrightarrow[\text{Get}]{}E, \ S\xrightarrow[\text{Get\_Event}]{}D$

Periodic tasks: $P, \ P\xrightarrow[\text{Set}]{}E, \ P\xrightarrow[\text{Send\_Event}]{}D, \ P\xrightarrow[\text{Get}]{}E$

Interrupts: $U, \ U\xrightarrow[\text{Set}]{}E, \ U\xrightarrow[\text{Send\_Event}]{}D$

The PRIORITY function is extended to active contexts and in conformance with the priority ceiling protocol, as follows (where the form $\alpha \underset{x}{\text{---}} \pi$ corresponds to the context of a protected object π executing a call x issued by activity α):

$$\text{PRIORITY}(\alpha \underset{x}{\text{---}} \pi) = \text{PRIORITY}(\pi) \qquad (20)$$

We use a record notation—as defined in [4]—to maintain the state information of computational units. The fields corresponding to each computational unit are given in Table 1. We will use the dot notation to extract fields from records. $T\cdot\mathsf{Beh}$ is the value of field Beh in the record T. The update of a field in a record is performed as in the following example where D' is the record obtained by updating in record D the field Bar with true and field Queue with ϵ:

$$D' = \langle D \leftarrow \mathsf{Bar} = \mathsf{true} \leftarrow \mathsf{Queue} = \epsilon \rangle$$

Table 1. Fields present in state records of Ravenscar Computational Units

Description of field	Name	Type	D	$\mathcal{E}$	T_s	T_p	$\mathcal{U}$
Current program state	Beh	PROGS	✓	✓	✓	✓	✓
Next dispatching time	Nd	TIME			✓	✓	
Elapsed time	Et	TIME			✓	✓	✓
Processing time	Pt	TIME			✓	✓	✓
Queue on entry	Queue	$T_s \cup \{\epsilon\}$	✓				
Barrier state	Bar	BOOL	✓				
Event count	Ec	$\mathbb{N}$	✓				

3.2 Ready Queue

A ready queue, R, is made of a (possibly empty) sequence of active execution contexts. We use $\circ$ as a sequence operator, hence, if a is an execution context and R a ready queue then $(a \circ R)$ is a ready queue whose head is a and whose tail is R. The empty ready queue will be denoted by ϵ. Ready queues satisfy the *priority-ordered* property, which is inductively defined as follows:

(i) ϵ is *priority-ordered*

(ii) $a \circ R$ is *priority-ordered* iff: — R is *priority-ordered* and
                                    — $\forall a' \in R : \text{PRIORITY}(a') \leq \text{PRIORITY}(a)$

The satisfaction by a queue R of the *priority-ordered* property implies that R is an ordered list of queues having the form: $R = r_{p_1} \circ \ldots \circ r_{p_n}$ where for each r_{p_n}:

$$\forall i, j : i < j \Rightarrow p_i > p_j \qquad \text{and} \qquad (21)$$

$$\forall i, \forall a \in r_{p_i} : \text{PRIORITY}(a) = p_i \qquad (22)$$

All active contexts in the same subqueue have the same priority (22), and subqueues are ordered according to their priorities (21). We define priority head insertion and priority tail insertion for ready queues as both methods are used:

Let $p_k = \text{PRIORITY}(a)$
Priority Head Insertion $a \odot R =$

$$r_{p_1} \circ \ldots \circ a \circ r_{p_k} \circ \ldots \circ r_{p_n} \quad \text{when } R = r_{p_1} \circ \ldots \circ r_{p_k} \circ \ldots \circ r_{p_n}$$
$$r_{p_1} \circ \ldots \circ r_{p_i} \circ a \circ r_{p_j} \ldots r_{p_n} \quad \text{when } R = r_{p_1} \circ \ldots \circ r_{p_i} \circ r_{p_j} \circ \ldots \circ r_{p_n} \wedge p_i < p_k < p_j$$
$$(23)$$

Priority Tail Insertion $R \odot a =$

$$r_{p_1} \circ \ldots \circ r_{p_k} \circ a \circ \ldots \circ r_{p_n} \quad \text{when } R = r_{p_1} \circ \ldots \circ r_{p_k} \circ \ldots \circ r_{p_n}$$
$$r_{p_1} \circ \ldots \circ r_{p_i} \circ a \circ r_{p_j} \ldots r_{p_n} \quad \text{when } R = r_{p_1} \circ \ldots \circ r_{p_i} \circ r_{p_j} \circ \ldots \circ r_{p_n} \wedge p_i < p_k < p_j$$
$$(24)$$

A task taken from the blocked set to the ready queue is inserted at the tail of the ready queue for its priority, whereas one that is preempted during execution by the scheduler is inserted at the head of the ready queue for its priority.

3.3   Structure of the State of a Ravenscar System

The state of a Ravenscar system has a static part made up of the set of records of all computational units, and a dynamic part which is given by the vector:

$$IL \rightsquigarrow [c, R, B, \mathsf{ns}, \mathsf{t}] \qquad (25)$$

- *IL*: list of interrupts present in the system, waiting to be handled. When the list of interrupts is empty, the leading "$IL \rightsquigarrow$" may be ommitted
- *c*: current execution context
- *R*: ready queue
- *B*: set of blocked tasks
- ns: time of the next system clock tick when control is passed to the scheduler
- t: current time, i.e.: the current age of the system

Each of the execution context types (scheduler, idle, or active) may perform specific execution steps. These steps cause the state of the system to evolve over time. The steps performed by the active context depend on the current state of the code of its activity, given by the Beh field of the state record of the activity. The steps performable by the scheduler are: (i) *suspending activity a and taking control* $(a \xrightarrow{\text{as}} \sigma)$; (ii) *suspending idle task and taking control* $(\iota \xrightarrow{\text{is}} \sigma)$; (iii) *self suspension to handle interrupts* $(\sigma_s \xrightarrow{\text{ss}} \sigma)$; (iv) *handling an interrupt* $(\sigma \xrightarrow{\text{ih}} \sigma)$; (v) *updating the ready queue* $(\sigma \xrightarrow{\text{ud}} \sigma_s)$; (vi) *granting control to activity a* $(\sigma_s \xrightarrow{\text{sa}} a)$; (vii) *granting control to idle task* $(\sigma_s \xrightarrow{\text{si}} \iota)$. The idle task performs one type of steps which is *idling*: $(\sigma_s \xrightarrow{\text{idling}} \iota)$.

3.4   Initial State of a Ravenscar System

The initial state of a Ravenscar system is given by:

$$[\sigma, R_0, B_0, 0, 0] \qquad (26)$$

where the initial ready queue, R_0, is a *priority-ordered* list of all tasks: $R_0 = T_1 \circ \ldots \circ T_n$, and B_0 the initial set of blocked tasks is an empty set: $B_0 = \{\}$. Moreover, the initial state of each of the periodic tasks, the sporadic tasks, the synchronisers and the exchangers, is given by their associated records:

$$P = \langle\ \mathsf{Beh} = \mathrm{PROG}(P), \mathsf{Nd} = 0, \mathsf{Et} = 0, \mathsf{Pt} = 0\ \rangle$$
$$S = \langle\ \mathsf{Beh} = \mathrm{PROG}(S), \mathsf{Nd} = 0, \mathsf{Et} = 0, \mathsf{Pt} = 0\ \rangle$$
$$E = \langle\ \mathsf{Beh} = \mathrm{PROG}(E)\ \rangle$$
$$D = \langle\ \mathsf{Beh} = \mathrm{PROG}(D), \mathsf{Queue} = \epsilon, \mathsf{Ec} = 0, \mathsf{Bar} = \mathsf{false}\ \rangle$$

3.5   State Transitions of a Ravenscar System

The execution of a Ravenscar system is given by the set of structured operational semantics rules, having the structure of a fraction:

$$\frac{Antecedents}{IL \rightsquigarrow [c, R, B, \mathsf{ns}, \mathsf{t}] \xrightarrow{act} IL' \rightsquigarrow [c', R,' B', \mathsf{ns}', \mathsf{t}]\ \hat{+}\ \delta(act)} \quad SHORT\ NAME$$

Antecedents (numerator) are conditions which need to hold for the *Consequent* (denominator) part to be applied. *Antecedents* depend on the current state of the system. *Consequent* part denotes the transition taken and the action—*act*—performed. *act* represents the smallest possible uninterruptible instruction. It is an indivisible unit; interrupts will either be fired before or after such an instruction. Complex instructions like `delay until` are considered a sequence of simpler instructions with the final indivisible one actually having the intended impact. *IL* and *IL'* are optional, they represent the list of interrupts present before and after the transition. $\delta(act)$ is the time consumed by the transition, and $\hat{+}\ \delta(act)$ is the *ageing* operator. It is formally defined as follows:

$$[c, R, B, \mathsf{ns}, \mathsf{t}]\ \hat{+}\ \delta = [c\ \hat{+}\ \delta,\ R\ \hat{+}\ \delta,\ B,\ \mathsf{ns},\ \mathsf{t} + \delta]$$

where:

$$c\ \hat{+}\ \delta = \begin{cases} \sigma & \text{if} \quad c = \sigma \\ \iota & \text{if} \quad c = \iota \\ \langle \alpha \leftarrow \mathsf{Et} = \alpha \cdot \mathsf{Et} + \delta \leftarrow \mathsf{Pt} = \alpha \cdot \mathsf{Pt} + \delta \rangle & \text{if} \quad c = \alpha \vee c = \alpha\frac{}{x}\pi \end{cases}$$

$$R\ \hat{+}\ \delta = \langle a_1 \leftarrow \mathsf{Et} = a_1.\mathsf{Et} + \delta \rangle \circ \ldots \circ \langle a_n \leftarrow \mathsf{Et} = a_n.\mathsf{Et} + \delta \rangle \text{ for } R = a_1 \circ \ldots \circ a_n$$

The above equations state that if the currently executing task is either the scheduler or the idle task then the ageing operator has no effect on it. However, if the excution context is an active one then the ageing operator adds the $\delta(action)$ amount of time to both the elapsed time (Et) and processing time (Pt) fields of the record of the activity. On the other hand, for all tasks in the ready queue R, the ageing operator only adds the $\delta(action)$ amount of time to the elapsed time field (they are not budgeted for this time). We now provide the transition rules, starting with the system idle task and ending with rules for interrupt handling.

Idling: Rule *IDLE* shows the idle task executing. The antecedent shows that the system can only idle if it hasn't reached the next scheduling instant ns. The *age* of the system advances by an amount δ(idling).

$$\frac{t < \mathsf{ns}}{[\iota, R, B, \mathsf{ns}, \mathsf{t}] \xrightarrow{\text{idling}} [\iota, R, B, \mathsf{ns}, \mathsf{t}] \,\widehat{+}\, \delta(\text{idling})} \quad IDLE$$

Pure Computation Steps: The *CMPT* and *CMPO* transitions represent sequential computations that have no side-effects on tasking or inter-task communication. *CMPT* denotes a task carrying out a sequential computation, *CMPO* denotes a protected object carrying out a sequential computation. The behavior (Beh) must in both cases have comp instruction at the head, the current time must be less than the next dispatching time for the scheduler.

$$\frac{T \cdot \mathsf{Beh} = \mathsf{comp}; \mathsf{C} \;\wedge\; \mathsf{t} < \mathsf{ns}}{[T, R, B, \mathsf{ns}, \mathsf{t}] \xrightarrow{\text{comp}} [T', R, B, \mathsf{ns}, \mathsf{t}] \,\widehat{+}\, \delta(\text{comp})} \quad CMPT$$

$$T' = \langle T \leftarrow \mathsf{Beh} = \mathsf{C}\rangle$$

$$\frac{\pi \cdot \mathsf{Beh} = \mathsf{comp}; \mathsf{C} \;\wedge\; \mathsf{t} < \mathsf{ns}}{[\alpha \mathrel{\overline{\tau}} \pi, R, B, \mathsf{ns}, \mathsf{t}] \xrightarrow{\text{comp}} [\alpha \mathrel{\overline{\tau}} \pi', R, B, \mathsf{ns}, \mathsf{t}] \,\widehat{+}\, \delta(\text{comp})} \quad CMPO$$

$$\pi' = \langle \pi \leftarrow \mathsf{Beh} = \mathsf{C}\rangle$$

Protected Objects: The rule *NBCL* represents an activity (task or interrupt) calling a procedure of a protected object. The antecedent states that the current behaviour of the activity is a call to a procedure, and that the current time is less than the next scheduler launching time. The consequent is that the code of the protected object is being executed in the context of the activity α ($\alpha' \mathrel{\overline{x}} \pi$).

$$\frac{\begin{array}{c}\alpha \cdot \mathsf{Beh} = x(\pi); C \;\wedge \\ x \in \{\text{Get, Set, Send\_Event}\} \;\wedge\; \mathsf{t} < \mathsf{ns}\end{array}}{[\alpha, R, B, \mathsf{ns}, \mathsf{t}] \xrightarrow{x} [\alpha' \mathrel{\overline{x}} \pi, R, B, \mathsf{ns}, \mathsf{t}] \,\widehat{+}\, \delta(x)} \quad NBCL$$

$$\alpha' = \langle \alpha \leftarrow \mathsf{Beh} = C\rangle$$
$$\pi' = \langle \pi \leftarrow \mathsf{Beh} = \text{PROG}(\pi).x\rangle$$

The transitions *RET1* through *RET4* depict how calls from protected objects return. *RET1* represents the **return** from a protected object procedure. The consequent shows that the execution time is budgeted to the task's processing time Pt. The calling activity is placed at the head of the ready queue and the scheduler takes control to evaluate barriers. *RET2* shows a synchronizer returning from a **Send_Event** procedure when the entry queue is empty. Transition *RET3* shows a synchronizer returning from a **Send_Event** procedure when the entry queue is *not* empty. The blocked `Get_Event` entry is immediately executed in the context of the task waiting on it. *RET4* gives the situation where a synchronizer returns from `Get_Event` entry call. The task in whose context the execution was taking place is preempted and is placed at the head of its ready queue, and the scheduler takes over.

$$\frac{E \cdot \mathsf{Beh} = \mathsf{ret} \quad \wedge \quad x \in \{\mathrm{Get, Set}\} \quad \wedge \quad \mathsf{t} < \mathsf{ns}}{[\alpha \underset{x}{\frown} E, R, B, \mathsf{ns}, \mathsf{t}] \xrightarrow{\mathsf{ret}} [\sigma, \alpha' \circ R, B, \mathsf{ns}, \mathsf{t}] \,\widehat{\mp}\, \delta(\mathsf{ret})} \; RET1$$

$$\alpha' = \langle \alpha \leftarrow \mathsf{Pt} = \alpha \cdot \mathsf{Pt} + \delta(\mathsf{ret}) \rangle$$

$$\frac{D \cdot \mathsf{Beh} = \mathsf{ret} \quad \wedge \quad D \cdot \mathsf{Queue} = \epsilon \quad \wedge \quad \mathsf{t} < \mathsf{ns}}{[\alpha \underset{\mathrm{Send\_Event}}{\frown} D, R, B, \mathsf{ns}, \mathsf{t}] \xrightarrow{\mathsf{ret}} [\sigma, \alpha' \circ R, B, \mathsf{ns}, \mathsf{t}] \,\widehat{\mp}\, \delta(\mathsf{ret})} \; RET2$$

$$D' = \langle D \leftarrow \mathsf{Bar} = \mathsf{true} \leftarrow \mathsf{Ec} = D \cdot \mathsf{Ec} + 1 \rangle$$
$$\alpha' = \langle \alpha \leftarrow \mathsf{Pt} = \alpha' \cdot \mathsf{Pt} + \delta(\mathsf{ret}) \rangle$$

$$\frac{D \cdot \mathsf{Beh} = \mathsf{ret} \wedge D \cdot \mathsf{Queue} = S \wedge \mathsf{t} < \mathsf{ns}}{[\alpha \underset{\mathrm{Send\_Event}}{\frown} D, R, B, \mathsf{ns}, \mathsf{t}] \xrightarrow{\mathsf{ret}} [S' \underset{\mathrm{Get\_Event}}{\frown} D', \alpha' \circ R, B', \mathsf{ns}, \mathsf{t}] \,\widehat{\mp}\, \delta(\mathsf{ret})} \; RET3$$

$$B' = B \setminus \{S\}$$
$$S' = \langle S \leftarrow \mathsf{Nd} = \mathsf{t} + \textsc{holdingtime}(S) \rangle$$
$$D' = \langle D \leftarrow \mathsf{Bar} = \mathsf{true} \leftarrow \mathsf{Ec} = D \cdot \mathsf{Ec} + 1 \rangle$$
$$\alpha' = \langle \alpha \leftarrow \mathsf{Pt} = \alpha \cdot \mathsf{Pt} + \delta(\mathsf{ret}) \rangle$$

$$\frac{D \cdot \mathsf{Beh} = \mathsf{ret}; \; \mathsf{C} \quad \wedge \quad \mathsf{t} < \mathsf{ns}}{[S \underset{\mathrm{Get\_Event}}{\frown} D, R, B, \mathsf{ns}, \mathsf{t}] \xrightarrow{\mathsf{ret}} [\sigma, S' \circ R, B, \mathsf{ns}, \mathsf{t}] \,\widehat{\mp}\, \delta(\mathsf{ret})} \; RET4$$

$$D' = \langle D \leftarrow \mathsf{Bar} = (D \cdot \mathsf{Ec} > 1) \leftarrow \mathsf{Ec} = D \cdot \mathsf{Ec} - 1 \leftarrow \mathsf{Queue} = \epsilon \rangle$$
$$S' = \langle S \leftarrow \mathsf{Pt} = S \cdot \mathsf{Pt} + \delta(\mathsf{ret}) \rangle$$

Rules *OBCL* and *CBCL* represent a sporadic task issuing a `Get_Event` call. Rule *OBCL* represents when the barrier is open and the call is immediately executed. Rule *CBCL* represents when the barrier is closed, the call remains blocked on the entry until a `Set_Event` is issued by another task or interrupt.

$$\frac{S \cdot \mathsf{Beh} = \mathtt{Get\_Event}(D); \; \mathsf{C} \wedge D \cdot \mathsf{Bar} = \mathsf{True} \wedge \mathsf{t} < \mathsf{ns}}{[S, R, B, \mathsf{ns}, \mathsf{t}] \xrightarrow{\mathrm{Get\_Event}} [S' \underset{\mathrm{Get\_Event}}{\frown} D', R, B, \mathsf{ns}, \mathsf{t}] \,\widehat{\mp}\, \delta(\mathrm{Get\_Event})} \; OBCL$$

$$S' = \langle S \leftarrow \mathsf{Beh} = \mathsf{C} \leftarrow \mathsf{Nd} = \mathsf{t} + \textsc{holdingtime}(S) \rangle$$
$$D' = \langle D \leftarrow \mathsf{Beh} = \textsc{prog}(D) \cdot \mathsf{Get\_Event} \rangle$$

$$\frac{S \cdot \mathsf{Beh} = \mathtt{Get\_Event}(D); \ \mathsf{C} \ \wedge \ D \cdot \mathsf{Bar} = \mathrm{False} \ \wedge \ \mathsf{t} < \mathsf{ns}}{\left[S, R, B, \mathsf{ns}, \mathsf{t}\right] \ \xrightarrow{\ \mathtt{Get\_Event}\ } \ \left[S', R, B, \mathsf{ns}, \mathsf{t}\right] \mathbin{\hat{+}} \delta(\mathrm{Get\_Event})} \quad CBCL$$

$$S' = \langle S \leftarrow \mathsf{Beh} = C \leftarrow \mathsf{Bar} = \mathrm{true}\rangle$$
$$D' = \langle D \leftarrow \mathsf{Queue} = S\rangle$$

Scheduler. The scheduler also takes control at certain points called *scheduling points*. Some of these have already been explained (the RET_i transitions). Others occur when the active context executes a `delay until` instruction, and when the scheduler is *scheduled* to execute, represented by the `ns` variable in the system configuration and calculated just before the scheduler cedes control. *NS-IDLE* and *NS-ACT* represent the scheduler preempting the idle task and an activity (respectively) as its launch time arrives. *SDELAY* and *PDELAY* show a sporadic task and a periodic task (respectively) execute a `delay until`. `ns` is the minimum of `Nd` fields of all tasks in the blocked set where `Nd` represents the next dispatching time for the task: $\mathsf{ns} = \min_{T_i \in B}(T_i \cdot \mathsf{Nd})$. *SCUD* is the evolution of the scheduler as it evaluates and updates the ready queue and blocked tasks. *SCAC* shows the scheduler calculating its next dispatching time and then granting control to the highest priority ready task. *SCID* is the action carried out by the scheduler when the ready queue is empty.

$$\frac{\mathsf{ns} \leq \mathsf{t}}{\left[\iota, R, B, \mathsf{ns}, \mathsf{t}\right] \ \xrightarrow{\ \mathrm{is}\ } \ \left[\sigma, R, B, \mathsf{ns}, \mathsf{t}\right] \mathbin{\hat{+}} \delta(\mathrm{is})} \quad NS\text{-}IDLE$$

$$\frac{\mathsf{ns} \leq \mathsf{t}}{\left[a, R, B, \mathsf{ns}, \mathsf{t}\right] \ \xrightarrow{\ \mathrm{as}\ } \ \left[\sigma, a \circ R, B, \mathsf{ns}, \mathsf{t}\right] \mathbin{\hat{+}} \delta(\mathrm{as})} \quad NS\text{-}ACT$$

$$\frac{T \cdot \mathsf{Beh} = \mathtt{delay}; \mathsf{C} \ \wedge \ \mathsf{t} < \mathsf{ns}}{\left[T, R, B, \mathsf{ns}, \mathsf{t}\right] \ \xrightarrow{\ \mathrm{delay}\ } \ \left[\sigma, R, B', \mathsf{ns}, \mathsf{t}\right] \mathbin{\hat{+}} \delta(\mathrm{delay})} \quad SDELAY$$

$$T' = \langle T \leftarrow \mathsf{Beh} = \mathrm{PROG}(T) \leftarrow \mathsf{Pt} = T \cdot \mathsf{Pt} + \delta(\mathrm{delay})\rangle$$
$$B' = B \cup \{T'\}$$

$$\frac{T \cdot \mathsf{Beh} = \mathtt{delay} \ ; \ \mathsf{C}, \quad \mathsf{t} < \mathsf{ns}}{\left[T, R, B, \mathsf{ns}, \mathsf{t}\right] \ \xrightarrow{\ \mathrm{delay}\ } \ \left[\sigma, R, B', \mathsf{ns}, \mathsf{t}\right] \mathbin{\hat{+}} \delta(\mathrm{delay})} \quad PDELAY$$

$$T' = \langle T \leftarrow \mathsf{Beh} = \mathrm{PROG}(T) \leftarrow \mathsf{Pt} = T \cdot \mathsf{Pt} + \delta(\mathrm{delay})$$
$$\leftarrow \mathsf{Nd} = T \cdot \mathsf{Nd} + \mathrm{HOLDINGTIME}(T)\rangle$$
$$B' = B \cup \{T'\}$$

$$\frac{-}{\big[\sigma, R, B, \mathsf{ns}, \mathsf{t}\big] \xrightarrow{\mathsf{ud}} \big[\sigma_s, R', B', \mathsf{ns}, \mathsf{t}\big] \widehat{+}\, \delta(\mathsf{ud})} \; SCUD$$

$$B' = B \setminus \mathrm{ready}(B, \mathsf{t})$$
$$R' = R \odot \mathrm{ready}(B, \mathsf{t})$$
$$\mathrm{ready}(B, \mathsf{t}) = \{T \in B \mid T\cdot\mathsf{Nd} \geq \mathsf{t}\}$$

$$\frac{-}{\big[\sigma_s, a\circ R, B, \mathsf{ns}, \mathsf{t}\big] \xrightarrow{\mathsf{sa}} \big[a, R, B, \mathsf{ns}', \mathsf{t}\big] \widehat{+}\, \delta(\mathsf{sa})} \; SCAC$$

$$\mathsf{ns}' = \mathrm{Min}_{T \in B}(T\cdot\mathsf{Nd})$$

$$\frac{-}{\big[\sigma_s, \epsilon, B, \mathsf{ns}, \mathsf{t}\big] \xrightarrow{\mathsf{si}} \big[\iota, \epsilon, B, \mathsf{ns}', \mathsf{t}\big] \widehat{+}\, \delta(\mathsf{si})} \; SCID$$

$$\mathsf{ns}' = \mathrm{Min}_{T \in B}(T\cdot\mathsf{Nd})$$

Interrupt Handling. Rule *NEWI* models the arrival of a new interrupt. *I-AS* and *I-US* depict the scheduler preempting an activity and an idle task (respectively) in presence of interrupts in order to handle them. In case of arrival of interrupt during interrupt handling by the scheduler, the scheduler is restarted (transition *I-SS*). *I-IH* depicts the scheduler selecting the highest priority interrupt and inserting it at the tail of its priority list in the ready queue (all interrupt priorities are greater than all task priorities so an interrupt *will* preempt a task).

$$\frac{U \notin (\{c\} \cup R \cup IL)}{IL \rightsquigarrow \big[c, R, B, \mathsf{ns}, \mathsf{t}\big] \longrightarrow IL \circ U \rightsquigarrow \big[c, R, B, \mathsf{ns}, \mathsf{t}\big]} \; NEWI$$

$$\frac{IL \neq \phi}{IL \rightsquigarrow \big[a, R, B, \mathsf{ns}, \mathsf{t}\big] \xrightarrow{\mathsf{as}} IL \rightsquigarrow \big[\sigma, a\odot R, B, \mathsf{ns}, \mathsf{t}\big] \widehat{+}\, \delta(\mathsf{as})} \; I\text{-}AS$$

$$\frac{IL \neq \phi}{IL \rightsquigarrow \big[\iota, R, B, \mathsf{ns}, \mathsf{t}\big] \xrightarrow{\mathsf{is}} IL \rightsquigarrow \big[\sigma, R, B, \mathsf{ns}, \mathsf{t}\big] \widehat{+}\, \delta(\mathsf{is})} \; I\text{-}IS$$

$$\frac{IL \neq \phi}{IL \rightsquigarrow \big[\sigma_s, R, B, \mathsf{ns}, \mathsf{t}\big] \xrightarrow{\mathsf{ss}} IL \rightsquigarrow \big[\sigma, R, B, \mathsf{ns}, \mathsf{t}\big] \widehat{+}\, \delta(\mathsf{ss})} \; I\text{-}SS$$

$$\frac{-}{U \circ IL \rightsquigarrow \big[\sigma, R, B, \mathsf{ns}, \mathsf{t}\big] \xrightarrow{\mathsf{ih}} IL \rightsquigarrow \big[\sigma, R\odot U, B, \mathsf{ns}, \mathsf{t}\big] \widehat{+}\, \delta(\mathsf{ih})} \; I\text{-}IH$$

3.6 Discussion

One of the outcomes of providing a formal semantics (of a model, language or algorithm) is that it allows to disambiguate the informal description in the natural language. One can thus formally reason about properties of the system thus described. As an example, in our semantics, we made a choice in the way the inter-dispatch time is computed. If we had strictly obeyed the Ravenscar code patterns, we would have used a modified syntax for sporadic tasks in ℙℝ𝕆𝔾𝕊 whereby we would have made explicit the capture of the current clock from the system. We would have also had to decompose rules *RET3* and *CBCL*, introducing an additional step reflecting the capture of the current clock. A small discrepancy would then arise due to the non-atomic nature of the sporadic task release and computation of the next dispatch time, i.e., a higher priority task may preempt the sporadic task between these two actions. In case of a preemption by a higher priority task between the release of the task and the computation of the next release, a longer than stipulated inter-dispatch time may be enforced. This does not impact schedulability but can result in the sporadic tasks responding more sluggishly. This problem can be solved by assigning synchronizers the maximum priority in the system (`Max_Interrupt_Priority`), and returning the instance of time when the entry is executed. The maximum priority ensures that a task *cannot* be preempted while it is in the entry, thus ensuring the atomicity of the two actions. In our semantics, we chose a solution whereby the computation of the next release of sporadic tasks is performed as a side effect of the sporadic task entering the synchroniser. One may think of the scheduler performing this computation. Indeed, although the scheduler is not explicitly stated in rules rules *RET3* and *CBCL*, nevertheless, it is the scheduler which is responsible for granting control of the sporadic task when it enters the synchroniser. Thus, the scheduler performs the computation in an atomic fashion.

4   Conclusions

Previously, work has been undertaken ([8], [10], [17] and [7]) to formalize the semantics of real-time kernels and Ravenscar-like executives. In [7], the author defines an extension of CCS aimed at studying muti-tasking systems. Similarly to our approach, the general behaviour of systems made of concurrent tasks can be modeled. However, in our work, we represent the kernel functions explicitly, allowing us to account for system overhead. The work that is the closest to ours is perhaps [8] where the authors use the RTL and PVS formalisms to develop a Ravenscar-like kernel. A major difference with our contribution is that [8] aims at prescribing the development of the kernel functions whereas our contribution does provide an operational semantics which captures the global behaviour of Ravenscar systems (composed from the kernel and the running application). Another main difference with existing work is that our paper is the first direct approach at providing semantics using the structured operational semantics and not requiring any other notational support. In [11], the authors present a timed automata-based approach to the verification of Ravenscar systems.

The structured operational semantic formalization of RMM is pivotal to our tool chain as it provides to developers a direct and unambiguous description of the running behaviour of their hard real-time applications. Our semantics helped also to explicitly define the kernel functions and scheduler overheads due to context switches and interrupt handling. While the AADL is an architecture description language with open and loose semantics, our AADL to RMM transformation tool determines a rigourous semantic definition for a subset of AADL (the subset that is translatable into RMM). It must be kept in mind that the semantics given here are for executable systems generated from AADL models that are to run on a Ravenscar executive.

As stated in the introduction, with the RMM semantics we have a complete and unambiguous description of the interaction of functional code with the generated framework. This is possible due to the abstraction of functional code into the set of PROGS legal programs for all units. The work achieved can be usefully extended according to the approach of "semantic anchoring", whereby our operational semantics could be transposed using Abstract State Machines as a supporting anchoring language [5].

Acknowledgements. Work funded via the ASSERT project (IST-FP6-2004 004033) funded in part by the European Commission. We would like to thank Tullio Vardanega and Juan Antonio de la Puente for their insightful remarks.

References

1. Budinsky, F., Steinberg, D., Merks, E., Ellersick, R., Grose, T.: Eclipse Modeling Framework. Addison-Wesley, Reading (2004)
2. Burns, A., Dobbing, B., Vardanega, T.: Guide for the use of the Ada Ravenscar Profile in High Integrity Systems. Ada Lett. XXIV(2), 1–74 (2004)
3. Burns, A., Wellings, A.: Real-Time Systems and Programming Languages, 3rd edn. Addison-Wesley, Reading (2001)
4. Cardelli, L., Mitchell, J.C.: Operations on Records. In: Proceedings of the fifth international conference on Mathematical Foundations of Programming Semantics, pp. 22–52. Springer, New York (1990)
5. Chen, K., Sztipanovits, J., Neema, S.: Toward a Semantic Anchoring Infrastructure for Domain-specific Modeling Languages. In: EMSOFT 2005: Proceedings of the 5th ACM international conference on Embedded software, pp. 35–43. ACM Press, New York (2005)
6. de la Puente, J.A., Ruiz, J.F., Zamorano, J.: An Open Ravenscar Real-Time Kernel for GNAT. In: Keller, H.B., Plödereder, E. (eds.) Ada-Europe 2000. LNCS, vol. 1845, pp. 5–15. Springer, Heidelberg (2000)
7. Fidge, C.J.: The Algebra of Multi-tasking. In: Rus, T. (ed.) AMAST 2000. LNCS, vol. 1816, pp. 213–227. Springer, Heidelberg (2000)
8. Fowler, S., Wellings, A.: Formal Development of a Real-Time Kernel. In: RTSS 1997: Proceedings of the 18th IEEE Real-Time Systems Symposium (RTSS 1997), p. 220. IEEE Computer Society, Washington, DC (1997)
9. Hamid, I., Zalila, B., Najm, E., Hugues, J.: A Generative Approach to Building a Framework for Hard Real-Time Applications. In: 31st Annual NASA Goddard Software Engineering Workshop (SEW 2007) (March 2007)

10. Lundqvist, K., Asplund, L.: A Formal Model of a Run-Time Kernel for Ravenscar. In: RTCSA 1999: Proceedings of the Sixth International Conference on Real-Time Computing Systems and Applications, p. 504. IEEE Computer Society, Washington, DC (1999)
11. Ober, I., Halbwachs, N.: On the Timed Automata-based Verification of Ravenscar Systems. In: Ada-Europe 2008. LNCS, vol. 5026, pp. 30–43. Springer, Heidelberg (to appear, 2008)
12. Plotkin, G.D.: A Structural Approach to Operational Semantics. Technical Report DAIMI FN-19, University of Aarhus (1981)
13. SAE. Architecture Analysis & Design Language (AS5506) (September 2004), http://www.sae.org
14. SEI. Open Source AADL Tool Environment (2006), http://la.sei.cmu.edu/aadl/currentsite/tool/osate.html
15. Sha, L., Klein, M.H., Goodenough, J.B.: Rate Monotonic Analysis for Real-Time Systems. Computer 26(3), 73–74 (1993)
16. Sha, L., Rajkumar, R., Lehoczky, J.P.: Priority Inheritance Protocols: An Approach to Real-Time Synchronization. IEEE Transactions on Computers 39(9), 1175–1185 (1990)
17. Vardanega, T., Zamorano, J., de la Puente, J.A.: On the Dynamic Semantics and the Timing Behavior of Ravenscar Kernels. Real-Time Syst. 29(1) (2005)

Practical, Fast and Simple Concurrent FIFO Queues Using Single Word Synchronization Primitives*

Claude Evéquoz

University of Applied Sciences Western Switzerland
CH-1400 Yverdon-les-Bains, Switzerland
`Claude.Evequoz@heig-vd.ch`

Abstract. We present an efficient and practical non-blocking implementation of a concurrent array-based FIFO queue that is suitable for preemptive multi-threaded systems. It is well known that concurrent FIFO queues relying on mutual exclusion cause blocking, which have several drawbacks and degrade overall system performance. Link-based non-blocking queue algorithms have a memory management problem whereby a removed node from the queue can neither be freed nor reused because other threads may still be accessing the node. Existing solutions to this problem introduce a fair amount of overhead and are shown to be less efficient compared to array-based algorithms, which inherently do not suffer from this problem. In addition to being independent in advance knowledge of the number of threads that can access the queue, our new algorithm improves on previously proposed algorithms in that it does not require any special instruction other than a load-linked/store-conditional atomic instruction operating on pointer-wide number of bits.

Keywords: Concurrent queue, lock-free, non-blocking, compare-and-swap (CAS), load-linked/store-conditional (LL/SC).

1 Introduction

Lock-free data structures have received a large amount of interest as a mechanism that ensures that the shared data is always accessible to all threads and a temporarily or permanently inactive thread cannot render the data structure inaccessible. A concurrent data structure implementation is *non-blocking* (or *lock-free*) if it guarantees that at least one thread is guaranteed to finish its operation on the shared objects in a finite number of steps, even if there are other halted or delayed threads currently accessing the shared data structure. By definition, non-blocking implementations have no critical sections in which preemption can occur. These data structures also do not require any communication with the kernel and have been repeatedly reported to perform better than their counterparts implemented with critical sections [11]. There are two other classes of progress guarantee other than non-blocking synchronization. *Wait-free synchronization* [4] is a stronger progress guarantee since it advocates designing

---

* This work was partially funded by the University of Applied Science of Western Switzerland (HES-SO) research project no. 15516 RASMAS.

F. Kordon and T. Vardanega (Eds.): Ada-Europe 2008, LNCS 5026, pp. 59–72, 2008.

implementations that guarantee that any thread can complete any operation in a finite number of steps, irrespective of the execution speed of other threads. Unfortunately, eliminating starvation has proved in general to be difficult to implement efficiently, thereby motivating weaker progress guarantees such as non-blocking and *obstruction-free* synchronizations where starvation can theoretically occur. *Obstruction-free synchronization* [6] guarantees progress only in the absence of contention, thus allowing both starvation and livelock. This is the weakest progress guarantee but it is usually sufficient on uniprocessors where threads are scheduled by priority levels or by round-robin. On these schedulers, a thread is allotted more than enough time to complete alone an operation on the shared data structure before being preempted.

First-in-first-out (FIFO) queues are an important abstract data structure lying at the heart of most operating systems and application software. They are needed for resource management, message buffering and event handling. As a result, the design of efficient implementations of FIFO queues has been widely researched. A FIFO queue supports 2 operations: an *enqueue* operation inserts a new item at the *tail* of the queue, and a *dequeue* operation removes an item from the *head* of the queue if the queue is not empty.

This paper addresses the problem of designing a practical non-blocking FIFO queue based on a bounded circular array using only widely available pointer-wide atomic instructions. We begin by reviewing previous work done on FIFO queues and the memory reclamation problem inherent in link-based algorithms. Of particular interest in that section are algorithms that can adapt to a varying number of threads; these algorithms are called *population-oblivious* [7]. Section 3 presents the problems that must to be dealt with when designing non-blocking circular array FIFO queues. Section 4 introduces our algorithm, which is population-oblivious and has a space consumption depending only on the number of items in the queue. Its correctness is presented in Section 5. Performance evaluations of our algorithm are conducted in Section 6. The paper concludes in Section 7.

2   Related Work

Most non-blocking algorithms are based on the popular compare-and-swap (CAS) instruction, which takes 3 parameters: the address of a memory location, an expected value, and a new value. The new value is written into the memory location if and only if the location holds the expected value and the returned value is a Boolean indicating whether the write occurred.

Practical algorithms of non-blocking FIFO queues fall into two categories. The first category consists of algorithms based on finite or infinite arrays. Herlihy and Wing [3] gave a non-blocking FIFO queue algorithm requiring an infinite array. Wing and Gong [17] later removed the requirement of an infinite array. In their implementation, the running time of the dequeue operation is proportional to the number of completed enqueue operations since the creation of the queue. Treiber [14] also proposed a similar algorithm that does not use an infinite array. Although the enqueue operation requires only a single step, the running time needed for the dequeue operation is proportional to the number of items in the queue. These last two algorithms are thus inefficient for large queue lengths and many dequeue attempts. Valois [16] also presented an algorithm based on a bounded circular array. However, both enqueue and dequeue operations require that two array locations which may not be adjacent be simultaneously updated with a CAS primitive. Unfortunately this primitive is not available on modern processors. Shann et al. [13] present an efficient FIFO queue based on a circular array where each array element stores 2 fields: a data field and a reference counter field that prevents the so-called ABA problem (see section 3). Their algorithm is useful for processors that offer atomic instructions that can manipulate an array element as a whole. Because certain 32-bit architectures (e.g., Pentium) support 32- and 64-bit atomic instructions, the data field may also represent a pointer to a record when there is a need to expand the data field size. Current and emerging 64-bit architectures do not provide atomic access to more than 64-bit quantities, thus it is no longer possible to pack a large reference counter along with pointer-wide values in 64-bit applications. When application software exploiting these 64-bit capabilities becomes widespread [2], their algorithm will be of limited use. Tsigas and Zhang [15] proposed the first practical non-blocking FIFO queue based on a circular array using single word synchronization primitives found on all modern architectures and suitable for 64-bit applications. Their algorithm applies only to queued items that are pointers to data and they show that it outperforms link-based FIFO queues. However, for queueing operations to appear as FIFO (*linearizability* property [3]), the algorithm assumes that an enqueue or a dequeue operation cannot be preempted by more than s similar operations, where s is the array size. Their algorithm is therefore not population-oblivious.

The second category of FIFO queues is implemented by a linked list of queued nodes. Michael and Scott [10] proposed an implementation based on a single-linked list consisting of a *Head* pointer, which points to a dummy node, and a *Tail* pointer that points to the dummy node when the queue is empty or to the most recently inserted node. An enqueue operation adds a new node by making the last inserted node point to the new node and adjusting the *Tail* pointer to the new node. A dequeue operation advances the *Head* pointer, frees the dummy node and returns the data found in the now new dummy node. An enqueue operation requires 2 successful CAS operations and a dequeue operation completes after a single successful CAS. More recently, Ladan-Mozes and Shavit [8] presented an algorithm based on a doubly-linked list requiring one successful atomic synchronization instruction per queue operation. Although there are more pointers to update, all but *Head* and *Tail* are updated by simple reads and writes. They show that their algorithm consistently performs better than the single-linked list suggested in [10].

Although the advantage of linked-based FIFO queues over array-based implementations is that the size of the queue and the number of nodes it holds may vary dynamically, these queues are subject to a memory management problem. A dequeued node can be freed and made available for reuse only when the dequeuer is the only thread accessing the node. It would seem that array-based FIFO queues face the same problem, as an array slot cannot be overwritten if a dequeuer is still accessing the slot. However this problem can easily be avoided if array items are pointers to the data. In this case, a dequeuer can atomically exchange the pointer with a null marker to free the slot and be the only thread referencing the data. For linked-based FIFO queues, the easiest approach to deal with this problem is to ignore it and assume the presence of a garbage collector. However not all systems and languages provide garbage collector support. Another approach is to never free the node and to store it in a free pool for subsequent reuse once it is dequeued. When a new node is required, the node is obtained from the free pool. An important drawback of this approach is that the actual size of FIFO is equal to the maximum queue size since its initialization and is not really dynamically sized. Valois [16] presented an approach that actually frees a dequeued node. The mechanism associates a reference counter field with each node. Each time a thread accesses a node, it increments the node's reference counter; when it no longer accesses the node, it decrements the counter. The reference counter reflects the number of pointers that point to the node. A node can be freed only if the value of its reference counter drops to zero. Although the scheme is simple, a basic problem arises making this scheme impractical. Suppose a thread accesses a node and is then delayed before it can increment the reference counter associated with the node it is pointing to; while the thread is not running, it is possible that another thread dequeues and removes the last reference to the node. The solution proposed by Valois [16] and later corrected by Michael and Scott [9] involves 3 steps: (1) a pointer is set to the node that is to be accessed, (2) the reference counter of the possibly reclaimed node is then incremented, and (3) the pointer is verified that it still points to the correct node. Should the verification step (3) fail, the reference counter is decremented and all three steps repeated. Note that the reference counter of a node can be accessed and modified even after it has been freed. None of the reclaimed node can thus be definitely released to the memory allocator and reused for arbitrary purposes without possibly corrupting memory locations; all must again be stored in some free pool. Detlefs et al. [1] alleviate the above problem by performing steps (1) and (2) atomically. But because the reference to a node and its associated reference counter are not contiguous in memory, the needed primitive requires the atomic update of two arbitrary memory locations that is not supported in hardware by any modern processor.

Michael [12] presented a lock-free memory management technique that allows safe memory reclamation. Whenever a thread is about to reference a node, it publishes the address of the node in a global memory location. When the dequeuer removes a node from the queue, it scans the published accesses of the other threads. If a match is not found, the node may safely be freed. Otherwise the node is stored until a subsequent scan. A similar scheme, but not using pointer-wide instructions, was also independently proposed by Herlihy et al. [5].

Doherty et al. [2] present the first link-based FIFO queue that is population-oblivious and has a space consumption depending only on the number of queued items and the number of threads currently accessing the queue. However, their algorithm introduces significant overheads and trades memory space for computational time.

3 ABA Problem

The ABA problem is a well-known problem in the context of data structures implemented by CAS statements. The desired effect of a CAS operation is that it should succeed only if the value of a location does not change since the previous reading of the contents of the location. A thread may read value A from a shared location and then attempt to modify the contents of the location from A to some other value.

However it is possible that between the read and the CAS other threads change the contents of the location from A to B and then back to A again. The CAS therefore succeeds when it should fail. The semantics of read and CAS prevent them from detecting that a shared variable has not been written after the initial read. This problem is a common source of bugs in algorithms based on CAS operations.

In a circular list based on a finite array, there are 3 different ABA problem sources. First, the Head and Tail indices are each prone to the ABA problem, which we call the *index*-ABA problem. Next, each slot in the array holds 2 different value types: a queued data item and a null item that indicates that the slot is empty and available for reuse. Each of these 2 data values gives rise to an ABA problem that may be solved differently. In order to distinguish them, we respectively refer to them as the *data*-ABA and the *null*-ABA problem. In the following we illustrate an instance of how each identified ABA problem manifests itself and the means to elude the problem.

The enqueue and dequeue operations increment their respective indices once they have inserted or removed an item in or from the array. If these operations are delayed immediately prior to the increment but after modifying the contents of the array, other threads may successfully complete $s - 1$ identical operations and leave the index concerned by the delayed operation in the same state, where s is the size of the circular array. When the delayed operation resumes, it wrongly adjusts its index. Fig. 1 illustrates such a scenario.

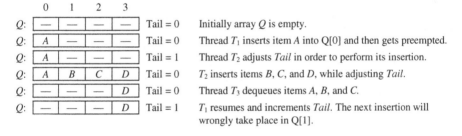

Fig. 1. Scenario with 3 threads illustrating the index-ABA problem

The index-ABA problem can easily be dealt with if we let each counter occupy a word and only increment these counters. The enqueue and dequeue functions can then map the counter into a valid index before accessing an array slot with a modulo operator. Although this solution does not guarantee that the ABA problem will not occur, its likelihood is extremely remote. On a 32-bit word with a million of increment operations per second, a wraparound occurs roughly after 1 hour. For the ABA problem to occur with a probability of $2 \cdot 10^{-10}$ (or 2^{-32}), there should also be a thread that is suspended in the midst of one of the queueing functions for a period longer than an hour while other threads monopolize the processor.

A simple example of the data-ABA problem can be given for an array having 2 slots. Assume that the array initially contains a single item A. Since a dequeue operation must first read the contents of the slot before removing it, a dequeuer may read item A and then be preempted before it gets a chance to remove A from the array. During its preemption, another thread may dequeue item A and then successively enqueue items B and A. The array is now full and when the preempted dequeue operation resumes, it wrongly removes item *A* instead of *B*. The implementation proposed in [15] circumvents this difficulty by assuming that the duration of preemption cannot be greater than the time for the indices to rewind themselves. This assumption may result into an exceedingly oversized array or be impossible to meet when the upper bound on the number of threads is unknown.

If we assume for the ease of explanation that the array is infinite, the array can be divided into 3 consecutive intervals: a possibly empty succession of empty slots that held removed items, a possibly empty series of enqueued items, and finally a series of empty slots that never held any item. A null-ABA problem occurs when an enqueuer mistakenly inserts an item into a free slot that belongs to the first interval. An enqueuer reads the contents of the first slot in the 3rd interval, notices that it is empty but gets preempted before inserting its item in the slot. Another thread may then insert an item and dequeue all the items in the array. When the enqueuer resumes, it incorrectly inserts its item in the first interval of the array. This flaw is corrected in [15] by cleverly having 2 empty indicators. Initially the array slots are set to $null_0$ (3rd interval) and once items are removed from the array the slots are marked with $null_1$ to become part of the 1st interval. When the head index rewinds to 0, the interpretations of the null values are switched from their corresponding intervals. The most common solution to this and other ABA problems is to split each shared memory location into 2 parts that are accessed simultaneously: a part for a version number or counter and a part for the shared data item; when a thread updates the memory location it also increments the counter in the same atomic operation. Because the version number is not unbounded, this technique does not guarantee the ABA scenario will not occur but it makes it extremely unlikely. Shann et al. [13] rely on this technique to solve the data-ABA and null-ABA problem for their FIFO queue implemented by a circular array. Algorithm designers using this technique usually assume that the version number and the data item each occupy a single word and that the architecture supports double-word atomic operations. In practice, this assumption is valid for some 32-bit architectures, but it is invalid for the emerging 64-bit architectures.

4 A New FIFO Algorithm

Modern instruction-set architectures, such as ARMv6 and above, DEC Alpha, MIPS II and PowerPC processors, do not provide atomic primitives that read and update a memory location in a single step because it is much more complex than a typical RISC operation and difficult to pipeline. Instead these processors provide an alternative mechanism based on two atomic instructions, *load-linked* (LL, also called load-lock or load reserve) and *store-conditional* (SC). The usual semantics of LL and SC assumed by most algorithm designers are given in Fig. 2. A shared variable X accessed by these instructions can be regarded as a variable that has an associated shared set of thread identifiers $valid_X$, which is initially empty. Instruction LL returns the value stored in the shared location X and marks it as reserved by including the calling thread identifier in set $valid_X$. This read operation always succeeds. Instruction SC takes the address of a shared location X and a value Y as parameters. It checks if the calling thread's identifier is in $valid_X$, and if so, completely clears $valid_X$ and updates the location before returning success; otherwise the instruction returns failure without modifying location X.

LL(X) $\equiv$ $valid_X \cup \{threadID\}$; **return** X
SC(X,Y) $\equiv$ **if** $threadID \in valid_X$ **then** $valid_X \leftarrow \varnothing$; $X \leftarrow Y$; **return** *true*
            else return *false*
            end if

Fig. 2. Equivalent atomic statements specifying the theoretical semantics of LL/SC

Based on the semantics of the LL and SC instructions, we can design a FIFO queue that is immune to ABA problems. Fig. 3 shows our algorithm in a self-explanatory pidgin C notation. For clarity, various type casts are missing but pointer dereferencing follows strict C notation. Following standard practice, all global variables have identifiers beginning with an uppercase letter and variables completely in lowercase are local to an operation.

Our FIFO queue is implemented as a circular list by an array of Q_LENGTH slots named Q, along with two indices named Head and Tail. An array slot contains either a pointer to a data item or the value *null* to indicate that it is currently free. Prior to calling an enqueue operation, enqueued items are allocated by a memory allocator. These items are later returned to the memory allocator for arbitrary future reuse once removed from the queue and no longer used by the dequeuer. Head refers to the first slot of the queue that may hold an item. Tail designates the next free slot where a new item can be inserted. To avoid the index-ABA problem, Head and Tail are incremental counters that are mapped into valid array indices by means of a modulo Q_LENGTH operation. The queue is empty when Head is equal to Tail, and it is full when Head + Q_LENGTH equals Tail. We assume that Q_LENGTH is a power of 2 so that Head and Tail can wraparound without skipping array slots. Finally, the array slots are initialized to *null* and the indices are set to 0 prior to calling an enqueue or a dequeue operation.

To add a data item, the enqueuer first reads the current Tail value (line E5) and proceeds only if there is an available free slot in the queue. The free slot the enqueuer intends to insert the item into and mapped by Tail is then marked (line E9). The test on line E10 verifies that the reserved slot still corresponds to the one mapped by Tail, and its purpose is to avoid the null-ABA problem. After successfully marking an array slot, the enqueuer checks the contents of the slot. If the slot is not empty, another concurrent thread has successfully inserted an item but was preempted before it had the chance to update Tail and the Tail value read on line E5 is lagging behind. In this case, the enqueuer helps the delayed thread and advances the Tail index (line E13) on its behalf before restarting its loop. If the marked slot is empty, the enqueuer tries to insert its item into it with a SC instruction (line E15) that can only succeed if no other enqueuer has changed the contents of the slot since the LL instruction on line E9. On success, the enqueuer updates Tail for the next enqueue operation (E17). If the SC instruction on line E15 fails, the enqueuer is notified that a concurrent operation took place and that the value of Tail read on line E5 was modified or needs to be updated. In this case the enqueuer starts over again from the beginning.

```
       Q: array[0..Q_LENGTH-1] of *DATA;          // Circular list
       unsigned int Head, Tail;                   // Extraction and insertion indices
E1:    BOOL Enqueue(DATA *node) {
E2:       unsigned int t, tailSlot;
E3:       DATA *slot;
E4:       while (true) {
E5:          t = Tail;                            // Get current Tail index
E6:          if (t == Head + Q_LENGTH)            // Check for full queue
E7:             return FULL_QUEUE;                // Return failure
E8:          tailSlot = t % Q_LENGTH;            // Get starting slot
E9:          slot = LL(&Q[tailSlot]);            // Reserve the slot
E10:         if (t == Tail) {                     // Check consistency
E11:            if (slot != null) {               // Got an empty slot?
E12:               if (LL(&Tail) == t)            // Tail is lagging behind
E13:                  SC(&Tail,t+1);              // Adjust for this insertion
E14:            }
E15:            else if (SC(&Q[tailSlot],node)) { // Try to insert node
E16:               if (LL(&Tail) == t)            // Adjust for next insertion
E17:                  SC(&Tail,t+1);
E18:               return OK;                     // Return success
E19:            }
E20:         }
E21:      }
E22: } /* end of Enqueue */

D1:    DATA *Dequeue(void) {
D2:       unsigned int h, headSlot;
D3:       DATA *slot;
D4:       while (true) {
D5:          h = Head;                            // Get current Head index
D6:          if (h == Tail)                       // Is queue empty?
D7:             return null;                      // Return failure
D8:          headSlot = h % Q_LENGTH;            // Get starting slot
D9:          slot = LL(&Q[headSlot]);            // Read and reserve slot
D10:         if (h == Head) {                     // Check consistency
D11:            if (slot == null) {               // Is Head lagging behind?
D12:               if (LL(&Head) == h)            // Adjust for current dequeue
D13:                  SC(&Head,h+1);
D14:            }
D15:            else if (SC(&Q[headSlot],null)) { // Remove new node
D16:               if (LL(&Head) == h)            // Adjust for next dequeue
D17:                  SC(&Head,h+1);
D18:               return slot;                   // Return node
D19:            }
D20:         }
D21:      }
D22: } /* end of Dequeue */
```

Fig. 3. ABA problem-free implementation of a FIFO queue

The dequeue operation removes the oldest item in the queue and returns it to its caller. The first 10 lines of the dequeue operation are similar to those of the enqueue operation. A dequeuer reads the current Head index, checks that the queue is not empty before carrying on by marking the array slot mapped by the read Head index. The test on line D10 confirms that the marked slot is indeed the oldest item that can be removed. Without this check, a dequeuer can read the current Head index, say h, and be preempted anywhere between lines D5 and D10. During this preemption, other threads can enqueue and dequeue items wrapping the array as they do so. When the preempted dequeuer resumes its execution and carries out the LL operation on line D9, Q[h] may hold an item that is not the oldest. Fig. 4 illustrates such a scenario for a queue with 5 slots.

	0	1	2	3	4	
Q:	—	A	B	—	—	Snapshot of Q when a dequeue operation begins. `Head` $= h = 1$, `Tail` $= 3$
Q:	E	F	—	C	D	Snapshot of Q when the dequeuer executes line D10. $h = 1$, `Head` $= 3$, and `Tail` $= 2$

Fig. 4. Possible snapshots experienced by a dequeuer immediately prior to and following its preemption.

After the test on line D10, the slot may be in one of two states. If it is empty, the dequeuer can infer that the `Head` index is falling behind since the dequeuer checked that the queue was not empty (line D6) before attempting to remove an item. In this case, the dequeuer tries to update `Head` before restarting from the beginning. On the other hand, if the slot is not empty, the dequeuer attempts to substitute the slot for a *null* with a SC instruction (line D15) and then, if it succeeds, tries to update `Head` before returning the dequeued item. The SC instruction fails when other concurrent operations have invalidated the LL instruction on line D9 and the dequeuer must start anew from the beginning.

5 Correctness

In this section, we prove that our algorithm satisfies liveness and certain safety properties.

5.1 Lock Freedom and Liveness

By definition of lock freedom applied to a FIFO queue, an implementation is lock-free if it guarantees that for an active thread trying to execute an enqueue or dequeue operation, the operation performed by the same or some other thread completes within a finite number steps. Lock freedom guarantees progress to at least one thread, theoretically allowing starvation but not livelock.[1]

Lemma 1. *One enqueue operation always completes regardless of the operations performed by other concurrent operations.*

Proof. We say that an operation is delayed at line i if the operation on line $i - 1$ is completed but the one on line i is not yet completely done. The enqueue operation contains a single unbounded loop that can delay the termination of the operation. The loop can reiterate for 3 different reasons.

Case 1: The SC operation on line E15 fails.
An enqueuer fails its store if it loses its reservation for the slot *tailSlot* it acquired on line E9. Since a dequeue operation can remove an item from slot *tailSlot* on line D15 only if the slot is not empty and since slot *tailSlot* was empty prior to the store on line

[1] On uniprocessor systems, the quantum allotted to a thread is greater than the time needed to perform several enqueue or dequeue operations. For our algorithm to perform efficiently on multiprocessor systems, we require that the contention for the FIFO queue to be such that a thread can execute at least an iteration of an enqueue or dequeue operation without any interference by other threads.

E15, a concurrent enqueue operation modified slot *tailSlot*. This store only occurs on line E15. Therefore some other enqueue operation succeeded E15 and terminated through line E18.

Case 2: The condition on line E11 is true.

When the enqueuer executed the condition on line E10, either slot *tailSlot* it reserved on line E9 was empty or it was not. Assume that it was: another concurrent enqueue operation succeeded its store into slot *tailSlot*. Assume that it wasn't: since the enqueue operation failed the condition on line E6, the queue is not full and Tail is lagging behind. Therefore another concurrent enqueue operation was delayed at line E16 or E17 at the time Tail was read on line E5. In both cases an enqueue operation terminates.

Case 3: The condition on line E10 fails.

Tail changed value from the time it was read on line E5. Tail can change only by means of successful SC instructions on lines E13 and/or E17. For the SC to succeed on line E13, another concurrent enqueue operation verified that its reserved slot is no longer empty on line E11. By Case 2 of this lemma, that enqueue operation reiterates its loop because of a 3rd concurrent enqueue operation, which terminates.

The SC operation on line E17 succeeds when another concurrent enqueue operation successfully inserted its item into the array (line E15). Therefore that enqueue operation terminates.

In all 3 cases, one enqueue operation always completes.   □

Lemma 2. *One dequeue operation always completes regardless of the operations performed by other concurrent operations.*

Proof. The proof follows exactly the same reasoning as Lemma 1 and is omitted.   □

5.2   Safety

Each operation is defined by 2 events: an event that modifies the state of the array, and an event that modifies the counter associated with the operation. For the enqueue operation, we denote these events by $ENQ(x)$ (line E15) and $INC\_TAIL(x)$ (lines E13 and E17), where x is the element to insert. For the dequeue operation, the corresponding events are $DEQ(x)$ (lines D15) and $INC\_HEAD(x)$ (lines D13 and D17). A *history* is an ordered sequence of events on a linear time axis, and each concurrent operation occupies a time interval on the axis. The precedence relation $\rightarrow$ is a strict partial order that relates operations or events in a history; $OP_1 \rightarrow OP_2$ means that OP_2 starts only when OP_1 ends. Operations unrelated by $\rightarrow$ are said to be *concurrent* or to *overlap*.

Lemma 3. *Enqueue operations cannot overlap.*

Proof. The statement is equivalent to stating that an enqueue operation can begin if and only if the previous enqueue operation is complete.

Assume that there are 2 items, x and y, that are concurrently being inserted into the FIFO array.

We first show that events $ENQ(x)$ and $ENQ(y)$ cannot occur at the same time. An $ENQ(x)$ event can occur only when a thread executes the SC instruction on line E15.

For the SC to succeed, the contents of Q[tailSlot] must not change since it was last read on line E9 and its contents must be equal to null, otherwise the SC instruction is not reached. Once a SC instruction succeeds, the value stored into the slot is non-null. Therefore, for ENQ(x) and ENQ(y) to occur at the same time, these events must operate on different slots, i.e., on different tail values. We now show that this is impossible. To simultaneously execute their respective SC instruction, both enqueue operations execute lines E5 through E15. As these lines only read Tail, both SC operations operate on the same slot, a contradiction.

Since events ENQ(x) and ENQ(y) cannot occur at the same time, they must occur one after the other. Assume that ENQ(x) → ENQ(y). We need to show that if INC_TAIL(x) is done, then ENQ(y) can occur. Assume INC_TAIL(x) is done. Event INC_TAIL(x) can occur if (1) Tail is not modified since it was last read on line E5, and (2) Q[Tail **mod** Q_LENGTH] ≠ null. Since INC_TAIL(x) is done, it was done by an enqueue operation executing line E13 or E17. In either case, statement (2) is true. After INC_TAIL(x), Tail indicates the next available slot, the slot on which ENQ(y) can occur. For ENQ(y) to occur, the SC instruction on line E15 must succeed. To succeed, the following 4 statements must be true: (1) Tail < Head + Q_LENGTH, i.e., the queue is not full, (2) Tail does not change value since it was last read on line E5, (3) Q[Tail **mod** Q_LENGTH] = null, and (4) Q[Tail **mod** Q_LENGTH] has not changed since it was last read on line E9. Provided the queue is not full, statements (2) and (4) are eventually true by Lemma 1. Because of INC_TAIL(x), statement (3) is also true, and ENQ(y) can occur. So, if INC_TAIL(x) is done, then ENQ(y) can be done.

We need to prove the converse to complete the proof. Assume that ENQ(y) can occur, i.e., the SC on line E15 can succeed. Let t_y = Tail **mod** Q_LENGTH. To succeed, Q[t_y] = null, otherwise line E15 is unreachable. But because ENQ(x) occurred before, it modified Q[t_x], where t_x = Tail **mod** Q_LENGTH. Hence, Q[t_x] ≠ null. For ENQ(y) to succeed, $t_y ≠ t_x$. The only instructions that modify Tail are E13 and E17, and either one generated INC_TAIL(x). So, if ENQ(y) can occur, then INC_TAIL(x) is done.

Therefore ENQ(y) can occur if and only if the previous enqueue operation is completely done.   □

As a consequence of Lemma 3, we can infer that regardless of the number of concurrent enqueue operations performed, the events associated with the operations do not overlap in the history. In other words, the enqueue events appear to be sequential. This is also the case for dequeue operations.

Lemma 4. *Dequeue operations cannot overlap.*

Proof. The proof follows the same line of reasoning as Lemma 3 and is omitted.   □

Lemma 5. *An item can be dequeued if and only if the enqueue operation that inserted the item is complete.*

Proof. We need to prove that DEQ(x) can occur if and only if INC_TAIL(x) is done. Assume DEQ(x) can occur. In order to do so, it must succeed the SC instruction on line D15. Thus, condition on line D10 is true, and Head cannot change since it was last read on line D5. But Head indicates which slot to remove on line D15, and the condition on line D6 must fail. Hence Head $\neq$ Tail. Since the enqueue operation inserts x into the slot indicated by Tail, if DEQ(x) can occur, then INC_TAIL(x) is done.

We need to prove the converse to complete the proof. Assume INC_TAIL(x) is done. Since INC_TAIL(x) is generated after ENQ(x), x is in the queue. Assume x occupies slot s. If s is equal to Q[t **mod** Q_LENGTH], then Tail is equal to $t + 1$ at the time INC_TAIL(x) occurs. To dequeue an item, the following 2 statements must be true: (1) slot s is not empty, and (2) Head = $t \neq$ Tail. Therefore, DEQ(x) can occur. So, if INC_TAIL(x) is done, then DEQ(x) can occur.

Therefore, DEQ(x) can occur if and only if INC_TAIL(x) is done.   □

We are now in position to prove our main result.

Lemma 6. *If* ENQ(x) $\rightarrow$ ENQ(y) *then* DEQ(x) $\rightarrow$ DEQ(y).

Proof. Assume ENQ(x) $\rightarrow$ ENQ(y). By Lemmas 3 and 5, we also have ENQ(x) $\rightarrow$ INC_TAIL(x) $\rightarrow$ ENQ(y) $\rightarrow$ INC_TAIL(y) $\rightarrow$ ENQ(y). Because elements are dequeued in increasing values of Head and provided that Head = Tail when the queue is empty, DEQ(x) occurs before DEQ(y), and by Lemma 5, after INC_TAIL(x).   □

6 Experimental Results

We evaluated the performance of our FIFO queue algorithm relative to other known algorithms by running a set of synthetic benchmarks written in C using *pthreads* for multithreading. In all our experiments, each thread performs 10000 iterations consisting of a series of 5 enqueue operations followed by 5 dequeue operations. Each enqueue operation is immediately preceded by allocating a new node and each dequeued node is freed. We synchronized the threads so that none can begin its iterations before all others finished their initialization phase. We report the average of 50 runs where each run is the mean time needed to complete the thread's iterations.

We conducted experiments on a PowerPC G4 1.5 GHz running on Darwin 8.8.0, which has only pointer-wide LL/SC instructions that can be accessed in C by implementing them as functions written in assembler. 32-bit CAS operations are provided by *libkern*, which are implemented by LL/SC instructions. On the PowerPC, we were able to compare our algorithm with 2 different implementations of Michael and Scott's link-based FIFO algorithm [10] that allow safe memory reclamation. The first implementation uses hazard pointers [12] (MS-Hazard Pointers) and the second is the algorithm proposed in [2] (MS-Doherty et al.). Both implementations require only pointer-wide CAS instructions.

Fig. 5 shows the normalized running times of the selected algorithms as a function to the number of threads. The basis of normalization was chosen to be our implementation.

As can be seen from the graph, the normalized running time of the MS-hazard implementation steadily increases as a function of the number of threads. This is because the accessed nodes by a thread are stored in a list that needs to be traversed before freeing a node. When memory reclamation is an issue, an array-based implementation is approximately 70 to 110% faster.

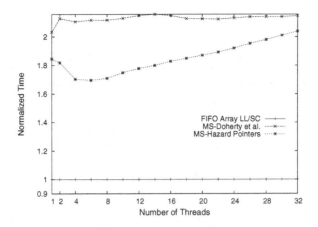

Fig. 5. Normalized running time as a function of the number of threads

7 Conclusions

We have presented a non-blocking implementation of a concurrent FIFO queue based on a bounded circular array, which uses load-linked/store conditional atomic instructions. Compared to concurrent non-blocking link-based FIFO queues, we showed that array-based implementations are approximately twice as fast when considering memory management problems. Compared to other non-blocking FIFO queue implementations, our new algorithm improves on previous ones by using only pointer-wide atomic instructions, as well as reducing space requirements and the need for advance knowledge of the number of threads that will access the queue.

We believe that our new algorithm is of highly practical interest for multithreaded applications because it is based on atomic primitives that are available in today's processors and microcontrollers.

Acknowledgments. The author would like to express his gratitude to the anonymous reviewers for their invaluable remarks and comments, which helped to improve the quality of this paper.

References

1. Detlefs, D.L., Martin, P.A., Moir, M., Steele Jr., G.L.: Lock-Free Reference Counting. In: Proc. of the 20th Annual ACM Symposium on Principles of Distributed Computing (PODC 2001), August 2001, pp. 190–199 (2001)
2. Doherty, S., Herlihy, M., Luchangco, V., Moir, M.: Bringing Practical Lock-Free Synchronization to 64-bit Applications. In: Proc. of the 23rd Annual ACM Symposium on Principles of Distributed Computing (PODC 2004), July 2004, pp. 31–39 (2004)
3. Herlihy, M.P., Wing, J.M.: Linearizability: A Correctness Condition for Concurrent Objects. ACM Trans. Progrmg. Lang. Syst (TOPLAS) 12(3), 463–492 (1990)

4. Herlihy, M.P.: Wait-Free Synchronization. ACM Trans. Progrmg. Lang. Syst (TOPLAS) 13(1), 124–149 (1991)
5. Herlihy, M., Luchangco, V., Moir, M.: The Repeat Offender Problem: A Mechanism for Supporting Dynamic-Sized, Lock-free Data Structures. In: Malkhi, D. (ed.) DISC 2002. LNCS, vol. 2508, pp. 339–353. Springer, Heidelberg (2002)
6. Herlihy, M.P., Luchangco, V., Moir, M.: Obstruction-Free Synchronization: Double-Ended Queues as an Example. In: Proc. 23rd IEEE Int. Conf. on Dist. Comp. Sys. (ICDCS 2003), Providence, RI, May 2003, pp. 522–529 (2003)
7. Herlihy, M., Luchangco, V., Moir, M.: Space- and Time-adaptive Nonblocking Algorithms. In: CATS 2003 Proc. of Computing: The Australasian Theory Symposium, April 2003, pp. 260–280 (2003)
8. Ladan-Mozes, E., Shavit, N.: An Optimistic Approach to Lock-Free FIFO Queues. In: Guerraoui, R. (ed.) DISC 2004. LNCS, vol. 3274, pp. 117–131. Springer, Heidelberg (2004)
9. Michael, M.M., Scott, M.L.: Correction of a Memory Management Method for Lock-Free Data Structures. Technical Report, Computer Science Department, University of Rochester (1995)
10. Michael, M.M., Scott, M.L.: Nonblocking Algorithms and Preemption-Safe Locking on Multiprogrammed Shared Memory Multiprocessors. J. Parallel Distrib. Comput. 51(1), 1–26 (1998)
11. Michael, M.M.: High Performance Dynamic Lock-Free Hash Tables and List-Sets. In: Proc. of the 14th Annual ACM Symposium on Parallel Algorithms and Architectures (SPAA 2001), August 2002, pp. 73–82 (2002)
12. Michael, M.M.: Hazard Pointers: Safe Memory Reclamation for Lock-Free Objects. IEEE Trans. on Parallel and Distributed Systems 15(6), 491–504 (2004)
13. Shann, C.-H., Huang, T.-L., Chen, C.: A Practical Nonblocking Queue Algorithm Using Compare-And-Swap. In: Proc. of the 7th International Conf. on Parallel and Distributed Systems (ICPADS 2000), July 2000, pp. 470–475 (2000)
14. Treiber, R.: Systems Programming: Coping With Parallelism. Technical Report RJ5118, IBM Almaden Research Center (April 1986)
15. Tsigas, P., Zhang, Y.: A Simple, Fast and Scalable Non-Blocking Concurrent FIFO Queue for Shared Memory Multiprocessor Systems. In: Proc. of the 13th Annual ACM Symposium on Parallel Algorithms and Architectures (SPAA 2001), July 2001, pp. 134–143 (2001)
16. Valois, J.D.: Lock-Free Linked Lists Using Compare-And-Awap. In: Proc. of the 14th ACM Symposium on Principles of Distributed Computing (PODC 1995), August 1995, pp. 214–222 (1995)
17. Wing, J.M., Gong, C.: Testing and Verifying Concurrent Objects. J. Parallel Distrib. Comput. 17(1-2), 164–182 (1993)

A Modelling Approach with Coloured Petri Nets

Christine Choppy[1], Laure Petrucci[1], and Gianna Reggio[2]

[1] LIPN, Institut Galilée - Université Paris XIII, France
[2] DISI, Università di Genova, Italy

Abstract. When designing a complex system with critical requirements (e.g. for safety issues), formal models are often used for analysis prior to costly hardware/software implementation. However, writing the formal specification starting from the textual description is not easy. An approach to this problem has been developed in the context of algebraic specifications [CR06], and was later adapted to Petri nets [CP04, CPR07]. Here, we show how such a method, with precise and detailed guidelines, can be applied for writing modular coloured Petri nets. This is illustrated on a model railway case study, where modules are a key aspect.

Keywords: specification method, modelling method, coloured Petri nets, modular design.

1 Introduction

While formal specifications are well advocated when a good basis for further development is required, they remain difficult to write in general. Among the problems are the complexity of the system to be developed, and the use of a formal language. Hence, some help is required to start designing the specification, and then some guidelines are needed to remind essential features to be described.

Petri nets have been successfully used for concurrent systems specification. Among their attractive features, is the combination of a graphical language and an effective formal model that may be used for formal verification. Expressiveness of Petri nets is dramatically increased by the use of high-level Petri nets [JKW07], and also by the addition of modularity allowing for quite large case studies.

While the use of Petri nets becomes much easier with the availability of high quality environments and tools, to our knowledge, little work had been devoted to a specification method for writing Petri nets.

Inspired by the work on algebraic specifications in [CR06], we proposed a method, providing detailed and precise guidelines. An initial approach was presented in [CP04], and further developed in [CPR07] where the different steps for building a coloured Petri net from a textual description of a system are shown.

In this paper, we push our work a step further and start introducing the use of modularity. Section 2 gives an overview of our design method. The role of the different steps is explained. In the following sections, these steps are detailed individually before being applied to a model railway case study. First, section 3

F. Kordon and T. Vardanega (Eds.): Ada-Europe 2008, LNCS 5026, pp. 73–86, 2008.

describes the running example and its expected behaviour in an informal way, as could be given to a designer. The *constituent features* and *modular structure* of our system are derived from the description. Section 4 expresses the expected properties of the system in terms of the previously identified elements. Then, sections 5 and 6 show how this is all transformed into a modular coloured Petri net and the properties validated. In these different steps, the basic operations from [CPR07] are summarised while focusing on the new modular aspects. In particular, we shall see that sometimes it is sufficient to consider modules independently of one another, whereas for other issues it is necessary to consider the system as a whole. Finally, section 7 discusses re-engineering (because some properties were not valid). This re-engineering phase modifies part of the train routing policy in some modules identified during the properties verification phase. The conclusion (section 8) summarises the design method and draws lessons from this experience w.r.t. modularity, refinement and re-engineering.

2   Overview of the Design Method

The goal of the proposed method is to obtain a modular coloured Petri net modelling a given system. The general approach is described in Fig. 2. While a modular structure is being built, the method is based on two key ingredients, the *constituent features*, that are *events* and *state observers*. *Events* are, as usual, e.g. an action of some component, or a change in some part of the system. A *state observer* instead defines something that may be observed on the states of the system, defined by the values of some type. These constituent features are grouped into the relevant *modules*, that represent the different components (or subsystems) of the system. Both events and state observers can *appear in different modules* when they are part of their interface (e.g. synchronised events and shared resources).

Starting from an informal (textual) description, the first step consists in identifying the state observers and the events characterising the system, as well as the components in which they take part. This leads to a set of modules, each with two lists of events and state observers: those that are proper (local) to the module, and those that are part of its interface. The identified data types may also be local or global,

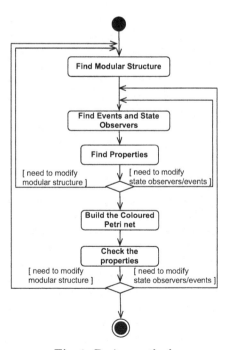

Fig. 1. Design method

depending on whether they are used
by a single module or several. Note that in Figure 2, the identification of modules and constituent features are separated. This is due to the re-engineering phase, which may lead to modifications at a more or less large extent.

Associated properties are then determined and expressed, leading to possible modifications of state observers and events. New ones can be introduced and conversely others may be removed if they are duplicates. The lists of identified elements are updated accordingly.

When reaching a stable set of events, state observers, datatypes and properties, the modular coloured Petri net can be built and the properties checked. Several modular constructs for Petri nets exist, which basically correspond to place and transition fusion. We chose to adopt the presentation of [Kin07] since it has a clear presentation of both modules and their interface, and is considered as a good candidate within the Petri nets extensions standardisation process (ISO/IEC 15909-3 [Pet07]).

The analysis may lead to modifications of the model, in which case the process should be repeated. The nature of the modifications may be within the modules, or involve large parts of the system and therefore require reconsidering the modular structure.

In the following sections, we describe shortly the different steps and apply them to a model railway case study. For more details about the individual steps in a non-modular framework, the reader is referred to [CPR07].

3   Analysing the System Description

3.1   Guidelines for Identifying Modules and Constituent Features

The first task of the proposed method is to find the events and the state observers that are relevant. A grammar-based analysis of an informal description is proposed, as advocated by classical object-oriented methods (see e.g. [CY91]). Some figures may be part of this description, and be refered to and/or (partly) commented in the text.

The text describing the system is examined, and the verbs, the nouns (or better the verbal and the noun phrases), and the adjectives outlined. Unless the same words are used for different meanings, phrases are outlined only once. Note that verb phrases and noun phrases can be nested. There may also be sentences that do not carry any information, and are therefore discarded.

In general, the outlined verbs (or verbal phrases) lead to find out the events, while the outlined nouns and adjectives lead to find out the modules, the state observers and the datatypes.

Thus all outlined verbs are listed, grouping together the synonyms or different phrases refering to the same concept, and each one is examined in order to decide whether it should yield an event. Each event is then given a name (an identifier), accompanied by a short sentence describing it. Similarly, the outlined nouns and adjectives are listed, grouping synonyms, and examined in order to decide whether they yield modules, datatypes or state observers. Each outlined state observer is then given a name (an identifier) and a type, accompanied by a short sentence describing what it observes in the system.

All the datatypes needed to type the state observers should be listed apart, together with a (chosen) name and if possible a definition or some operations.

The picture and the textual description can lead to identify *modules*, either because a particular complex entity is mentioned (e.g. a sender and a receiver in a network protocol) or because it becomes obvious that some of the other elements are strongly related to each other. In this latter case, these elements should be grouped together within a same module. It might also be the case that this module structure does not appear at this stage, but later on.

When modules are identified, they contain state observers and/or events. They are also linked to other modules in the global system, through an *interface*. The elements of the interface can be state observers or events participating in several modules whereas the other ones are local to the sole module they are involved in. As concerns datatypes, they can either be particular to a single module (e.g. a characteristic of a sender process) and can be declared locally, or shared by several modules (e.g. a message type) in which case we shall consider them as global.

For the system and each module, three lists are resulting from this step: (i) events, (ii) state observers, (iii) datatypes.

3.2   Case Study: Identifying Events and State Observers

The running example is a model railway issued from [BP01], where it was used as a case study for a students' project. It is complex enough to show how our method could help to specify it and obtain a coloured net model.

The informal description of this case study is given below with emphasis on **verbal phrases**, *noun phrases*, or ***both*** (when nested).

Informal description. The model railway is depicted in Figure 2. It consists of *about 15 meters of tracks, divided into 12 sections (blocks B1 to B12) connected by four switches.* The way **the trains can pass the switches** is indicated by the arrows in Figure 2. **The traffic on all tracks can go both ways.** *The railway is connected to a computer via a serial port which allows to read information from sensors and send orders to trains through the tracks or directly to switches. Each section is equipped with one sensor at each end,* **to detect the entrance or**

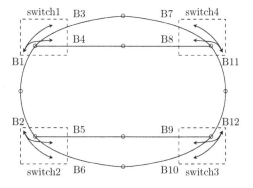

Fig. 2. The tracks of the model railway

exit of a train. **The orders sent to trains can be either stop or go forward/backwards at a given speed**.

This railway is used by a toy shop to attract people in the store. Hence the company wants to **run several trains at the same time**, but these should *not be subject to accidents (i.e. there should be no collision)* and should **run forever without human intervention**. Thus, an adaptive routing strategy will be adopted: **the behaviour of trains adapts to local conditions instead of following a pre-determined route**. Namely, at each switch, **the train route can be chosen among several tracks and a train may even go back when it cannot continue forward**.

Informal description analysis. The first task to achieve is to analyse the textual description (as described in Sect. 3.1) so as to find out relevant elements about *subsystems* (or modules), the *events*, the state of the system (expressed in terms of *state observers*), and the *data* involved (either directly mentioned in the text, or returned by the state observers).

Here we also have to deal with a picture, and parts of it are commented in the text, but not necessarily all. For instance, the picture clearly suggests the switches as subparts, which may yield some `Switch` *modules* in a hierarchy. Note that, in the picture, all switches are alike, i.e. there is one track on one side and two on the other. The arrows also indicate that a train goes from one side of the switch to the other side (e.g. from B1 to B3, and not from B3 to B4).

In this analysis of the text, we discard sentences that do not bring any elements for our concern, e.g. :
"The model railway is depicted in Figure 2."
"This railway is used by a toy shop to attract people in the store."

The text is not fully a "processing narrative", different levels of discourse are mixed, such as the "physical (or hardware) level" (e.g. describing how the railway is connected to a computer) which is not relevant for us, and the "logical level" which provides us with the needed information. There are also some slightly ambiguous parts, e.g. the "speed" of trains is mentioned but from the context we can assume it is expected to be constant except when the train stops. It is also mentioned that a train can stop, however, again from the context of the shop we understand that the trains are not supposed to remain stopped.

We also choose the category (verbal or nominal phrase) depending on the kind of information we expect to extract, for instance in the sentence:
"It consists of *about 15 meters of tracks, divided into 12 sections (blocks B1 to B12), connected by four switches.* ", "it consists" is not a verb potentially related to any event. We rather have a description of the (here permanent) state of the tracks display. Sentences about "sensors" are usually related with state observers, while sentences about "orders" may be related with some events.

We first list the verb phrases and the noun phrases and discuss for each whether it leads to relevant information. Redundant texts (that describe the same thing) are grouped together. Then, the modules, events, state observers and datatypes lists are extracted.

Verbs (verbal phrases)

– Several sentences refer to the moves and the positions of the trains:
  - **the trains can pass the switches**
  - **The traffic on all tracks can go both ways**
  - **a train may even go back when it cannot continue forward.**
  - **The orders sent to trains can be either stop or go forward/backwards at a given speed.**

  ⇒ the changeTrackSec event expresses that a train is moving from one track section to another, and the changeTrackSwitch event expresses that a train is moving from one track section to another through a switch. As mentioned above, an order is often associated with some events that are induced by the order "completion". Some event(s) may be associated with a train passing a switch (specified, e.g. by its number). It is also mentioned that trains can go "both ways", this information can be expressed either by a state parameter of a train (forward/backward/stopped), and/or by stating the tracks from and to which a train is travelling. The "speed" does not need to be a state parameter of a train.

– **run several trains at the same time** ⇒ here is an example of a verbal phrase that may refer to a state of the system where several trains are travelling at the same time, and this may be observed

– **run forever without human intervention** ⇒ rather a property of the system that does not reach a final state

– ⇒ The two sentences below express a non-determinism property
  - **the behaviour of trains adapts to local conditions instead of following a pre-determined route.**
  - **the train route can be chosen among several tracks and ...**

List of events
There are several events of two kinds:

changeTrackSec. A train is moving from one track section to another (not via a switch), for instance from B1 to B2, and from B2 to B1, ...

changeTrackSwitch. A train is moving from one track section to another through a switch, e.g. for Switch1, from B1 to B3, from B1 to B4, from B4 to B1, and from B3 to B1.

Nouns (noun phrases)
– *about 15 meters of tracks, divided into 12 sections (blocks B1 to B12), connected by four switches.* ⇒ as mentioned above, this refers to the permanent state of the tracks display, and this sentence does not describe in detail which track is connected to which others, and whether it is a simple connection or via a switch, since all this information is shown in Figure 2; often, state observers relate to some chosen information (rather than to the whole state), and further work (on the properties) will point out which are needed. However, it should be appropriate to have the TrackSection datatype. As mentioned earlier, we have Switch modules. Similarly, we can have modules associated with the (non-switch) connections between sections.

- *The railway is connected to a computer via a serial port which allows to read information from sensors and send orders to trains through the tracks or directly to switches.* ⇒ this describes the electronic part of the system which is not considered in the specification.
- *Each section is equipped with one sensor at each end,* **to detect the entrance or exit of a train.** ⇒ a sensor typically is an observer, trainPresent observes whether a train is present on a given track section (or not), thus the Train datatype provides either a train identifier or "none" that denotes that there is no train.
- *not be subject to accidents (i.e. there should be no collision)* ⇒ this is a property that should be ensured by the system.

List of datatypes

TrainId   ::= $\{t_1, \ldots, t_n\}$ where n is the number of trains.
TrackSection   ::= B1 | B2 | ...B12   **Train** ::= TrainId | none

List of state observers

trainPresent : TrackSection → Train
  observes whether a train is present on a given track section (or not)

List of modules

System is the (toplevel) module of the whole system.
Switch1, Switch2, Switch3, Switch4 are the four modules associated with the four switches, where the details of the train moves within a switch are expressed. As noted before, they are all alike and can be instantiations of a same module **Switch**. Each switch is connected to one track section on one side (that we shall name 0 afterwards) and two on the other (T1 and T2). The corresponding event names are constructed with the name of the initial track and the name of the destination track, e.g. OT1 means a move from 0 to T1.
MoveSec1, ... MoveSec6 similarly, we can introduce details of the train moves from one section to another one simply connected (no switch) in both ways, as instantiations of a module **MoveSec** (with sections S1 and S2).

In table 1, we summarise the elements identified for each module. Those in the **System** are global for the system and thus inherited by the other modules. The other modules have a local part and an interface.

Table 1. Events, state observers and datatypes per module

System	Switch	MoveSec
TrackSection	local: changeTrackSwitch	local: changeTrackSec
Train, TrainId	OT1, OT2, T1O, T2O	S1S2, S2S1
trainPresent	interface: 0, T1, T2: Train	interface: S1, S2: Train

4   Expected Properties

Let us assume that we have the three lists (events, state observers and datatypes) produced in the previous step. Now we consider the task of finding the most relevant/characteristic properties of the system and of its behaviour, and to express them in terms of the identified events and state observers (using also the identified datatypes). Our method helps to find out these properties by providing precise guidelines for the net designer to examine all relevant relationships among events and state observers, and all aspects of events and state observers.

4.1   Finding Properties

For each state observer SO returning a value of type DT (declared as SO: DT), we look for:

- properties on the values returned by SO (e.g. assuming DT = INT, SO should always return positive values);
- properties relating the values observed by SO with those returned by other state observers (e.g. the value returned by SO is greater than the value returned by state observer SO_1).

The state observers also allow for expressing the following properties:

- *initial condition*: a property about state observers that must hold in any initial state;
- *final condition*: a property about state observers that must hold in all final states, if any.

For each event EV we look for its:

- *precondition* which must hold before EV happens;
- *postcondition* which must hold after EV happened;
- other properties:
  - *on the past* : properties on the possible pasts of EV;
  - *on the future* : properties on the possible futures of EV;
  - *vitality* when it should be possible for EV to happen;
  - *incompatibility*: the events EV_i such that there cannot exist a state in which both EV and EV_i may happen.

While writing the properties, we may have to revise the lists obtained at the previous step, either to add new elements or to remove duplicates.

4.2   Properties of the Model Railway Case Study

Event properties

changeTrackSec   a train tr is moving from one track section ts1 to another ts2
  precondition the two tracks should be connected (we introduce a new state observer connected), there should be no train on ts2, and the train is on ts1 and is moving in the direction of ts2 (in the given layout of Figure 2 a simple and generic way to denote the train direction td is clockwise and

anticlockwise that are the two values of a TrainDirection type, and the TrainId should now include this information together with an operation direction to retrieve it ; moreover, the connected observer should include this parameter)

connected (ts1, ts2, td) ∧ direction (tr)=td ∧ trainPresent (ts1)= tr ∧ trainPresent (ts2)=none

postcondition the train is on ts2, and there is no train on ts1 anymore

trainPresent (ts2)=tr ∧ trainPresent (ts1)=none

more incompatibility properties (it is not possible that several events occur concurrently towards the same track).

changeTrackSwitch a train tr is moving from one track section ts1 to another ts2 through a switch

precondition the two tracks should be connected via a switch (we introduce a new state observer switched), there should be no train on ts2, and the train should be moving in the direction of ts2

switched (ts1, ts2, td) ∧ direction (tr)=td ∧ trainPresent (ts1)= tr ∧ trainPresent (ts2)=none

postcondition the train is on ts2, and there is no train on ts1 anymore

trainPresent (ts2)=tr ∧ trainPresent (ts1)=none

more incompatibility properties (it is not possible that several events occur concurrently towards the same track).

While expressing the properties of the events, we identified the following new state observers, datatypes and operations:

(New) List of state observers

connected : TrackSection × TrackSection × TrainDirection → BOOL
switched : TrackSection × TrackSection × TrainDirection → BOOL

(New) datatypes and operations over the TrainId datatype

TrainNumber ::= $\{t_1, \ldots, t_n\}$ where n is the number of trains.
TrainDirection ::= clockwise | anticlockwise
TrainId ::= pair (TrainNumber,TrainDirection)
    direction: TrainId → TrainDirection
    direction (pair (tn,td))=td
Train ::= TrainId | none   (unchanged)

State observers properties

trainPresent : TrackSection → Train
    observes whether a train is present on a given track section (or not), and this depends on the state of the system

connected : TrackSection × TrackSection × TrainDirection → BOOL
    these are axioms about the layout, e.g.
    connected (B2, B1, clockwise)=true; connected (B2, B4, anticlockwise)=false;
switched : TrackSection × TrackSection × TrainDirection → BOOL
    these are axioms about the layout, e.g.
    switched (B3,B1,anticlockwise)=true; switched (B3,B5,clockwise)=false;

initial state. Initially, n trains are on different tracks, each heading one direction or the other.

$\forall$tr $\in$ TrainNumber : $\exists$!ts $\in$ TrackSection : $\exists$d $\in$ TrainDirection :
trainPresent(ts) $=$ (tr, d)

final state. There should not be any final state, since the system should never terminate.

Note that switches 1 and 3 behave identically since a train present on 0 heading clockwise can go on either T1 or T2, while it is the case in switches 2 and 4 if the train is running anticlockwise. Therefore, the Switch module can be parameterised with the direction (as in section 5.2). This entails that for a module Switch(dir), we have: switched (0,T1,dir)=true; switched (0,T2,dir)=true; switched (T1,0,!dir)=true; switched (T2,0,!dir)=true, where !dir is the direction opposite to dir, and all the other possibilities are false. A similar approach can be applied to connected in the Move Sec modules.

5   Construction of the Modular Coloured Petri Net

At this point, we can assume that we have the list of modules with their interfaces, as well as the state observers and events (plus the list of used datatypes with their operations) resulting from the previous steps, and that for each event the pre/postconditions have been expressed. Other properties about the state observers and the events have also been found, that will be checked in the last step of the method, once the net is built.

5.1   Deriving the Net

Starting from the above elements, a coloured Petri net modelling the system can be built from the different modules and their interfaces. For each module, we first express the conditions in a canonical way. The *canonical form* requires that:

1. each state observer has type MSet(T) for some type T;
2. the pre/postconditions have the following form [1]

   pre $(\wedge_{i=1,...,n} exp_i \leq SO_i) \wedge (\wedge_{j=n+1,...,m} exp_j \leq SO_j) \wedge cond,$
   post $(\wedge_{i=1,...,n} SO_i' = SO_i - exp_i + exp_i') \wedge (\wedge_{j=n+1,...,m} SO_j' = SO_j - exp_j) \wedge$
   $(\wedge_{h=m+1,...,r} SO_h' = SO_h + exp_h') \wedge cond',$

   where
   - SO_l $(l = 1,...,r)$ are all distinct,
   - the free variables occurring in exp_l and exp_l' $(l = 1,...,r)$ may occur in $cond$ and in $cond'$,
   - no state observer occurs in $cond$, $cond'$, exp_l and exp_l' $(l = 1,...,r)$,
   - and $cond$ and $cond'$ are first order formulae.

---

[1] $\leq$, $+$ and $-$ denote respectively the inclusion, union and the difference between multisets.

In [CPR07], some often encountered schemes have been identified so as to obtain a canonical form.

Assume that all elements are in the canonical form. The coloured Petri net is defined as follows. The state observers and the events determine the places and the transitions, while the pre/postconditions determine the arcs. Each state observer SO : MSet(T) becomes a place named SO coloured by T, and each event EV becomes a transition, named EV. Pre/postconditions of an event EV lead to the set of arcs as pictured in Fig. 3.

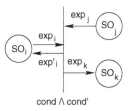

Fig. 3. Deriving arcs

5.2   Coloured Petri Net Modelling the Railway

We deduce from the previous analysis that the net modelling the railway is composed of 4 Switch (figure 5(b)) and 6 MoveSec modules (figure 5(a)). Moreover, a *toplevel* structure (figure 4) indicates how these different modules are linked together via their interfaces. The notations adopted here are those of [Kin07]. For the sake of figures readability, anticlockwise and clockwise are shortened to acl and cl respectively. Note that the track sections are modelled by places containing a token with the contents of the section itself.

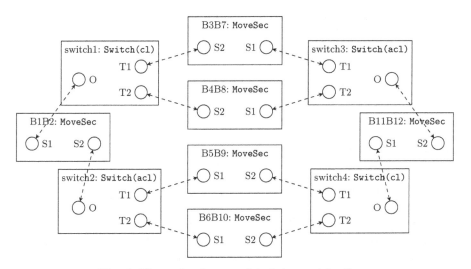

Fig. 4. The toplevel net model of the model railway

6   Checking the Properties

6.1   Checking the Expected and Required Properties

The previous steps of our design method did exhibit several properties which must be satisfied by the system. These properties should be expressed according to the language accepted by the coloured Petri nets tool to be used. Then the

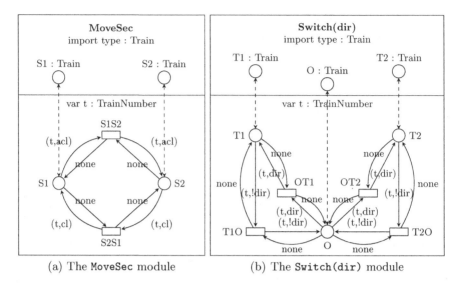

(a) The `MoveSec` module   (b) The `Switch(dir)` module

Fig. 5. The modules

properties should be checked using the tool, e.g. generate the occurrence graph
and check that all states satisfy the properties.

6.2   The Railway Properties

After generating the occurrence graph for an initial marking with 4 trains, we
check the expected properties. We find that there are deadlocks, e.g. with a
train going clockwise in B11 and a train going in the other direction in B12.
The other deadlocks are similar with either adjacent track sections or sections
connected by a switch. Hence the policies for moving between adjacent tracks
must be improved in both kinds of modules.

7   Re-engineering

7.1   Modifying the Model

In case some properties do not hold, the designer should investigate the causes
of the problem by e.g. closely examining the states not satisfying the property
and the paths leading to these states. This gives insight to locate the source of
the problem. The model then has to be modified accordingly, and the process
repeated until all properties hold. It might also be the case that some properties
derived from the informal specification are not correctly expressed. Then the
properties should be changed and the new ones checked.

7.2   New Version of the Railway Model

The policy in module `MoveSec` is changed by having a new event `retboth` where
both trains return when each of them wants to go on the other train track, as

depicted in figure 6(a). Similarly, the policy in module Switch is improved by
adding an event retO where in case of deadlock, the train on the side of the switch
with a single section returns to go in the opposite direction as in figure 6(b).

The new model is analysed again and the properties are satisfied.

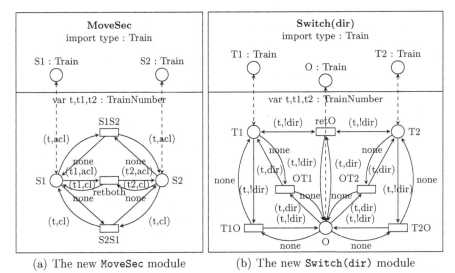

(a) The new MoveSec module   (b) The new Switch(dir) module

Fig. 6. The new modules

8   Conclusion and Future Work

Designing a formal specification has proved to be important to check properties
of a system prior to hardware and software costly implementation. However,
even if such an approach reduces both the costs and the experimenting time,
designing a formal model is difficult in general for an engineer.

This paper gives guidelines to help with the design process. The main idea is
to derive key features from the textual description of the problem to model, in a
rather guided manner so as to deduce the important entities handled, and then
to transform all this into Petri net elements. At the same time, some properties
inherent to the system appear, that are also formalised and should be proven
valid on the model at an early stage. When a coloured net is obtained, with
these properties satisfied, further analysis can be carried out, leading to possible
changes in the specification.

Our method, inspired by [CR06], was developed in [CPR07] for writing flat
coloured Petri nets. Here, we have started exploring the addition of a modular
structure, which is most helpful when designing large systems. The process is
applied to a simple model railway case study, which nevertheless raises issues for
future work.

The process for obtaining modules should be investigated further and formalised. In the case study, the Switch module emerged early in the specification
process. On the contrary, it seemed relevant and consistent to introduce MoveSec.

The notations used for the description of modules are those of [Kin07]. However, it does not completely take into account the main (toplevel) system description. Therefore, a clean expression of the hierarchy and the connection between components interfaces is required.

When listing the constituent features of the modules, some were obviously part of a single module, hence local, while others were shared by several modules. This is particularly the case for datatypes. We chose here to make these latter global by declaring them at the system level. However, for efficiency purposes, in particular during the analysis phase, we should rather consider which modules use them and which ones do not.

Our case study did exhibit several instances of a same module, and then a parameterised one. Here, finding these elements was rather simple, but we should investigate different cases where the use of such concepts is worthwhile.

The last phase of our method aims at checking that the system model satisfies the expected properties. However, we could imagine adding some refinement procedure there, in order to describe part of the system with additional detail.

Finally, the verification was performed using CPNTOOLS [JKW07]. For the moment, no tool suite handles these modular mechanisms, having an interface to modules with possibly both places and transitions. The development of modular nets in the framework of ISO/IEC 15909-3 standardisation will not only enhance the theoretical constructs and notations, but also be an incentive for adequate tool implementation.

References

[BP01]   Berthelot, G., Petrucci, L.: Specification and validation of a concurrent system: An educational project. Journal of Software Tools for Technology Transfer 3(4), 372–381 (2001)

[CP04]   Choppy, C., Petrucci, L.: Towards a methodology for modelling with Petri nets. In: Proc. Workshop on Practical Use of Coloured Petri Nets, Aarhus, Denmark, October 2004, pp. 39–56 (2004) Report DAIMI-PB 570, Aarhus, DK

[CPR07]   Choppy, C., Petrucci, L., Reggio, G.: Designing coloured Petri net models: a method. In: Proc. Workshop on Practical Use of Coloured Petri Nets, Aarhus, Denmark (October 2007)

[CR06]   Choppy, C., Reggio, G.: A formally grounded software specification method. Journal of Logic and Algebraic Programming 67(1-2), 52–86 (2006)

[CY91]   Coad, P., Yourdon, E.: Object-Oriented Analysis. Prentice-Hall, Englewood Cliffs (1991)

[JKW07]   Jensen, K., Kristensen, L., Wells, L.: Coloured Petri Nets and CPN Tools for modelling and validation of concurrent systems. Journal of Software Tools for Technology Transfer 9(3-4), 213–254 (2007)

[Kin07]   Kindler, E.: Modular PNML revisited: Some ideas for strict typing. In: Proc. AWPN 2007, Koblenz, Germany (September 2007)

[Pet07]   Petrucci, L.: ISO/IEC 15909 — Part 3: Extensions (November 2007) Working document of ISO/IEC JTC1-SC7-WG19, ref. PA2-018

A Tailored V-Model Exploiting the Theory of Preemptive Time Petri Nets

Laura Carnevali, Leonardo Grassi, and Enrico Vicario

Dipartimento di Sistemi e Informatica - Università di Firenze
{carnevali,grassi,vicario}@dsi.unifi.it
http://www.dsi.unifi.it

Abstract. We describe a methodology that embeds the theory of pre-emptive Time Petri Nets (pTPN) along development and verification activities of a V-Model lifecycle to support the construction of concurrent real time SW components. Design activities leverage on a pTPN specification of the set of concurrent timed tasks. This supports design validation through simulation and state space analysis, and drives disciplined coding based on conventional primitives of a real-time operating system. In verification activities, the pTPN model comprises an Oracle for unit and integration testing and its symbolic state space supports test case selection, test sensitization and coverage evaluation.

Keywords: concurrent real-time systems, V-Model, preemptive Time Petri Nets, formal methods, state space analysis.

1 Introduction

Intertwined effects of concurrency and timing comprise one of the most challenging factors of complexity in the development of safety critical SW components. Formal methods may provide a crucial help in facing this complexity, supporting both design and verification activities, reducing the effort of development, and providing a higher degree of confidence in the correctness of products.

Integration of formal methods in the industrial practice is explicitly encouraged in certification standards such as RTCA/DO-178B [1], with specific reference to software with complex behavior deriving from concurrency, synchronization, and distributed processing, under the recommendation that proposed methods are smoothly integrated with design and testing activities prescribed by a defined and documented SW lifecycle. This recommendation can be effectively referred to the framework of the V-Model [22], which is often adopted by process oriented standards ruling the development of safety critical software subject to explicit certification requirements, such as airborne systems [1], railway and transport applications [17], medical control devices [21].

In this paper, we describe a tailoring of the V-Model life cycle that leverages on the theory of preemptive Time Petri Nets (pTPN) [5] to support design, coding and testing of complex concurrent and real time task sets. The proposed tailoring spans over the activities of Preliminary and Detailed SW Design, SW

F. Kordon and T. Vardanega (Eds.): Ada-Europe 2008, LNCS 5026, pp. 87–100, 2008.

Implementation, and SW Integration. During SW design, the architecture of the task set is specified using the intuitive formalism of timelines, which can be automatically translated into a pTPN model. In turn, this supports validation of design with respect to sequencing and timeliness requirements through timed simulation and/or timed state space analysis. During SW implementation, the pTPN specification of the task set is implemented through a disciplined coding approach relying on conventional primitives of a real time operating system. The implementation produces a so-called operational architecture which supports incremental integration and testing of low-level SW components. During SW Integration, the pTPN specification comprises an Oracle for integration testing, while symbolic state space analysis supports test-case-selection, test-sensitization and coverage-evaluation.

The rest of the paper is organized in six sections. The specification of the real-time task set architecture and its validation are discussed in Sect.2, while Sect.3 describes how to implement the specification model on top of LinuX RTAI APIs. Sect.4 illustrates how pTPNs support testing activities, both in test case selection/sensitization and in the evaluation of executed tests. Sect.5 organizes all the activities to outline a tailoring of the V-Model SW life cycle. Conclusions are drawn in Sect.6.

2   Preemptive Time Petri Nets in the Specification and Architectural Validation of Real-Time Task Sets Using the Oris Tool

In this section, we introduce preemptive Time Petri Nets (pTPN) [5][8], showing how they support the modeling of real-time task sets and how simulation and analysis of the specification model are employed in the architectural validation of the task set itself, supporting tight schedulability analysis and verification of the correctness of logical sequencing.

2.1   Specification of Real-Time Task Sets through Timelines

We assume a general setting that includes the patterns of process concurrency and interaction which are commonly encountered in the context of real-time systems [9].

The task set is comprised by tasks. Tasks release jobs in recurrent manner with three different possible release policies: i) *periodic*, in which tasks have a deterministic release time; ii) *sporadic*, in which tasks have a minimum but not a maximum release time; and iii) *jittering*, in which tasks have a release time constrained between a minimum and a maximum. Task deadline is usually coincident with its minimum release period.

Jobs can be internally structured as a sequence of chunks, each characterized by a nondeterministic execution time constrained within a minimum and a maximum value. Chunks may require preemptable resources, notably one or more processors. In this case, they are associated with a priority level and run under static priority preemptive scheduling. Chunks may be synchronized through binary semaphores, to guarantee mutual exclusion in the use of shared resources: a chunk acquires a semaphore before starting its execution and releases it at the end of its execution.

Task sets can be conveniently specified through timelines, which represent a temporal scheme annotated with parameters of tasks and chunks (release period, deadline, resource request, priority). Fig.4 reports an example with 4 tasks. T_1 is a periodic task synchronized by semaphore m_1 to the sporadic task T_4; tasks T_2 and T_3 are periodic and synchronized through semaphore m_2.

2.2 Preemptive Time Petri Nets

A timeline schema can be easily translated into an equivalent pTPN. Preemptive Time Petri Nets [8][5] extend Time Petri Nets (TPN) [10][11] with an additional mechanism of resource assignment, making the progress of timed transitions be dependent on the availability of a set of preemptable resources. Syntax and semantics are formally expounded in [5], and we report here only an informal description. As in TPN, each transition is associated with a static firing interval made up of an earliest and a latest static firing time, and each enabled transition is associated with a clock evaluating the time elapsed since it was newly enabled: a transition cannot fire before its clock has reached the static earliest firing time, neither it can let time pass without firing when its clock has reached the static latest firing time. In addition, each transition may request a set of preemptable resources, each request being associated with a priority level: an enabled transition is progressing and advances its clock if no other enabled transition requires any of its resources with a higher priority level; otherwise, it is suspended and maintains the value of its clock. This supports representation of the suspension mechanism and thus of preemptive behavior, attaining an expressivity that compares to that of stopwatch automata [7][6][5].

Translating a timeline schema into a pTPN model: The Oris Tool supports both the editing of a timeline schema and its automatic translation into an equivalent preemptive Time Petri Net. Repetitive job releases performed by a task are modeled as an always-enabled transition with static firing interval equal to the task release range; chunks are modeled as transitions with static firing intervals corresponding to their min-max range of execution time and with the same resource requests and priority. A binary semaphore is modeled by a place containing one token, which represents the permission to acquire the semaphore itself.

Priority inversion frequently occurs in practical systems and limiting its adverse effects is extremely important in a system where any kind of predictable response is required. For instance, priority inversion can occur when a high priority chunk requires exclusive access on a resource that is being currently accessed by a low priority chunk: if one or more medium priority chunk then run while the resource is locked by the low priority chunk, the high priority chunk can be delayed indefinitely. To avoid priority inversion, we extend pTPN formalism to assume priority ceiling emulation protocol, which raises the priority of any locking chunk to the highest priority of any chunk that ever uses that lock (i.e., its priority ceiling).

Fig.5 reports the pTPN modeling the timeline schema of Fig.4.

Timeliness expressivity: In principle, the specification model could be expressed directly using pTPNs. However the usage of timelines, that represent an intuitive formalism, augments modeling convenience and facilitates industrial acceptance and interoperability. In addition, timelines provide a structural restriction on the expressivity of pTPNs which gives meaning to some relevant concepts in the theory of real-time systems such as task, job, chunk, hyperperiod and idle state. As a drawback, this restriction prevents an explicit representation of priority ceiling emulation protocol within timeline formalism.

2.3   Architectural Validation through Simulation or State Space Enumeration of the pTPN Model

The pTPN specification model can be simulated or analyzed to perform architectural validation of the real-time task set.

The state of a pTPN can be represented as a pair $s = \langle M, \tau \rangle$, where M is a marking and τ is a vector of times to fire for enabled transitions. Since τ takes values in a dense domain, the state space of a pTPN is covered using *state classes*, each comprised of a pair $S = \langle M, D \rangle$, where M is a marking and D is a firing domain encoded as the space of solutions for the set of constraints limiting the times to fire of enabled transitions. A reachability relation is established among classes: a state class S' is reachable from class S through transition t_0 , and we write $S \overset{t_0}{\rightarrow} S'$, if and only if S' contains all and only the states that are reachable from some state collected in S through some feasible firing of t_0. This reachability relation, sometimes called AE relation [12], defines a graph of reachability among classes that we call *state class graph* (SCG).

The AE reachability relation turns out to collect together the states that are reached through the same firing sequence but with different times [11][13][14]. A path in the SCG thus assumes the meaning of *symbolic run*, representing the dense variety of runs that fire a given set of transitions in a given qualitative order with a dense variety of timings between subsequent firings. A symbolic run is then identified by a sequence of transitions starting from a state class in the SCG, and it is associated to a completion interval, calculated over the set of completion times of the dense variety of runs it represents. Note that the same sequence of firings may be firable from different starting classes. According to this, we call *symbolic execution sequence* the finite set of symbolic runs with the same sequence of firing but with different starting classes.

If the model does not include preemptive behavior, i.e. if it can be represented as a TPN, firing domains can be encoded as Difference Bound Matrixes (DBM), which enable efficient derivation and encoding of successor classes in time $O(N^2)$ with respect to the number of enabled transitions N. Moreover, the set of timings for the transitions fired along a symbolic run can also be encoded as a DBM, thus providing an effective and compact profile for the range of timings that let the model run along a given firing sequence [14].

When the model includes preemptive behavior, then derivation of the successor class breaks the structure of DBM, and takes the form of a linear convex polyhedron. This results in exponential complexity for the derivation of classes and, more importantly, for their encoding [8][5][6][15]. To avoid the complexity, [5] replaces classes with their tightest enclosing DBM, thus yielding to an over-approximation of the SCG. For any selected path in the over-approximated SCG, the exact set of constraints limiting the set of feasible timings can be recovered, thus supporting clean-up of false behaviors and derivation of exact tightening durational bounds along selected critical runs. In particular, the algorithm provides a tight bound on the maximum time that can be spent along the symbolic run and provides an encoding of the linear convex polyhedron enclosing all and only the timings that let the model execute along a symbolic run.

The Oris tool [16] supports enumeration of the SCG, selection of symbolic runs attaining specific sequencing and timing conditions and tightening of their range of timings. The example of Fig.5 has a symbolic state space comprised by 29141 state classes, having 134 different markings. For each task, the analysis of the SCG allows the identification of the paths starting with the release of a job and ending with its completion, which we call *task symbolic runs*, and of the corresponding execution sequences, which we call *task execution sequences*. Specifically, tasks T_1, T_2, T_3 and T_4 have 6915, 10816, 22093 and 13837 symbolic runs and 244, 951, 2823 and 1935 symbolic execution sequences, respectively. The analysis provides the worst case completion time for each task (70, 100, 170 and 140 time units for T_1, T_2, T_3 and T_4, respectively), thus verifying that deadlines are met and with which minimum laxity (80, 80, 70 and 220 time units for T_1, T_2, T_3 and T_4, respectively).

3   Coding Process

The pTPN specification model enables a disciplined coding of the task set architecture on top of conventional primitives of a real-time operating system. The procedure is described with reference to the APIs of Linux RTAI, a patch for the Linux kernel which introduces a hardware abstraction layer and an application interface supporting the development of real-time applications for several processor architectures.

The task set is implemented as a kernel module, with functions *init_module()* and *cleanup_module()* as entry points for loading and unloading. Tasks are created in *init_module()* through *rt_task_init()* and they are started by calling *rt_task_make_periodic()* or *rt_task_resume()* depending on they are recurrent or one-shot tasks, respectively; they are destroyed in *cleanup_module()* by invoking *rt_task_delete()*. Chunks are implemented as C functions, invoked by their respective tasks. Semaphore operations must be appropriately combined with priority handling, to guarantee proper implementation of the specification model. RTAI provides resource semaphores, which implement priority inheritance, and binary semaphores, which instead leave the programmer control over priority handling. We use binary semaphores to obtain an implementation conforming to the semantics of pTPN models with static priorities, though dynamic priorities could also be encompassed in pTPN expressivity and analysis [8]. More specifically, when a low priority task acquires a semaphore, priority boost requested for priority ceiling emulation must precede semaphore wait operation; viceversa, at release, priority must be restored to the previous level after semaphore signal operation. Data structures of the application, such as semaphores and real-time FIFO queues, are created and destroyed in *init_module*() and *cleanup_module*(), respectively.

In our approach, a disciplined manual translation has been preferred to non-supervised, model-based code generation. By leaving the programmer the responsibility of the coding process, we ensure human control over the implementation and we preserve the readability and maintainability of the output source code. Disciplined coding enables to fully exploit the flexibility of programming languages in the realization of real time design patterns; besides, the axiomatic semantics of programming languages and IPC primitives ensure construction (i.e. types) and procedural consistency and are still to be retained as better specified than the semantics and notation of formal modeling languages.

However, we believe that automatic code generation is achievable without considerable efforts on the part of the developers and without critically impacting the proposed approach. As a proof, let's consider the structural decomposition of a pTPN specification into its semantic components, i.e. tasks, jobs chunks and synchronization structures. In our approach, each model component has a context-free translation into a corresponding code element, i.e. a C function or a OS IPC primitive; according to this partitioning, the entire specification model can be modularly implemented by composing code structures inductively derived from individual pTPN elements.

This seems to greatly reduces the complexities related to the generation of code and to the verification of its correctness thus allowing to seamlessly integrate automated model-to-code translation within the development process.

4 Supporting the Testing Process through Preemptive Time Petri Nets and the Oris Tool

We address the testing phase and, in order to detect failures in the implementation, we show how the pTPN specification model can be employed in the evaluation of logs produced during testing and in test case selection and execution.

Fault model and failure detection: We consider failures deriving from types of fault that do not guarantee a proper implementation of the specification model with respect to the sequencing and the timing of individual actions (i.e. job releases, chunk completions, signal and wait operations): *i) time frame violation fault*, i.e. a fault in the chunk implementation leading a an action to assume values out of its nominal interval; *ii) cycle stealing fault*, i.e. the presence of additional tasks which steal computational resources (these can be unexpected tasks, services provided by the operating system, or tasks intentionally not represented in the specification because considered not critical for the real-time application to be realized); *iii) faults in concurrency control and task interactions*, i.e. a wrong priority assignment, a semaphore operation which is not appropriately combined with priority handling, or in general, a wrong implementation of any IPC mechanism.

We assume that the implementation is instrumented so as to provide a time-stamped log of actions represented in the specification model [20]. Therefore, each run provides a finite sequence of timed actions $tr = \{\langle a_n, \tau_n \rangle\}_{n=1}^{N}$, where a_n is an action corresponding to a unique transition t_n in the pTPN model and τ_n represents the time at which a_n has occurred. According to this, the operational semantics of the pTPN model can be exploited as a *time-sensitive Oracle* in order to evaluate an execution run. The Oracle off-line simulates the execution of the sequence of timed actions and emits a failure verdict as soon as any timed action is not accepted by the simulator; a pass verdict is emitted when the run is finished.

It can be easily verified that any time frame violation fault, as well as any fault in concurrency control and task interaction, is detected as a failure by the time-sensitive Oracle, either because a transition is not firable or because it is firable but not with the observed timing. Viceversa, a cycle stealing fault is recognized provided that its duration exceeds the laxity between an actual computation and its expected upper bound.

The time-sensitive Oracle somehow performs the function of the observers proposed in [2] [15]. In [2], an observer is an automaton employed online during the testing process to collect auxiliary information that is used for coverage evaluation. In [15], an observer is used to evaluate quantitative properties through state space enumeration of the specification model augmented with additional places and transitions. Differently from both the concepts of observer, our Oracle evaluates off-line the execution logs produced by an implementation. This is done by verifying if the sequence of timed actions is a subset of the dynamic behavior that the semantics of the specification model may accept.

Test case selection and execution: While the analysis of the specification model supports early validation of the process architecture, confidence in the conformance of the implementation to the specification can be achieved through testing. In this step, which is in any case requested for certification purposes [1][17], the state space of the specification model can be exploited to select test cases and to identify timed inputs that let the system run along selected cases [2][3][4][18]. Both steps face the existence of behaviors that are legal in the specification model but cannot be observed in a real implementation. In fact, when the specification of a software component is developed, various temporal parameters are necessarily associated with a nondeterministic range of variation, not only to accommodate changes in the embedding context and allow a margin of laxity for the implementation, but also to support a re-engineering process or reuse of a component within a modular architecture. Also, specification models usually neglect dependencies among temporal parameters, both to keep the specification model relatively simple and to avoid the difficulty in quantifying these dependencies. Besides, when software requires high Integrity Levels, the implementation must be deterministic.

According to this, coverage criteria cannot rely on the selection of deterministic test cases, as many of these could be not feasible. We thus propose that test cases be specified as symbolic runs, as they represent the dense variety of runs that follow the same sequence of actions with a dense variety of timings. A test case is considered covered when any of its runs has been executed. As proposed in [2], a symbolic run can be selected as the witness of a specific test purpose determined trough a model checking technique, or it can be part of a test suite identified through a coverage criterion defined on the state class graph (i.e. all nodes, all edges, all paths). Regardless of the number of identified failures, a metric of coverage is needed to provide a measure of confidence in the absence of residual faults and it can be derived by mapping on the state class graph the sequence of actions reproduced by the time-sensitive Oracle.

A procedure to sensitize a selected test case has been proposed in [19]. It is based on the observation that not all temporal parameters are controllable: in fact, periodic and asynchronous release times can be effectively controlled through conventional primitives of a real-time operating system, whereas controlling computation times is often impractical. This gives a major relevance to state classes of the specification where no computational chunk is pending and all jobs are waiting for their next release, that we call *idle classes*. Given a test case ρ with initial class S_{target}, the procedure identifies the temporal constraints representing the necessary condition to first reach S_{target} starting from an idle class S_{idle} and then execute ρ. Therefore, the IUT is started from any state within S_{idle} and controllable actions are forced to occur within the identified constraints.

5   Using Preemptive Time Petri Nets within the Software Life Cycle V-Model

In this section we show how the theory of preemptive Time Petri Nets can be smoothly integrated as a formal method in the V-Model of the software life cycle, also with reference to the RTCA/DO-178B standard, which provides guidelines for the production of software for avionic systems. In particular, we illustrate how the effort at modeling a real-time task set through pTPNs provides relevant advantages in the subsequent stages of software development: in fact, as also evidenced in the previous sections, analysis and simulation of pTPN models support both design and verification activities.

The V-Model of the German Federal Administration regulates the processes of system development, maintenance and modification in the software life cycle. The standard describes the development process from a functional point of view, defining a set of activities and products (results) that have to be produced. Since it has general validity and it is publicly available, it has been adopted by many companies and *tailored* to a variety of specific application contexts. Fig.1 reports

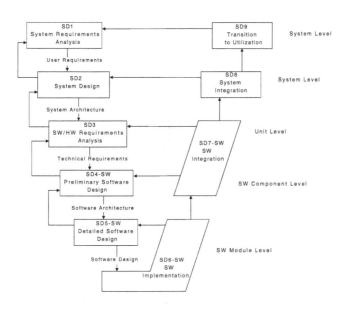

Fig. 1. Overview of Activities of Submodel System Development of the V-Model

a graphical representation of the activities pertaining the System Development (SD) submodel, emphasizing the integration between design and verification activities (left/right) and the hierarchical decomposition from System to Module Levels (top/down). Even if the order of activities appears sequential, iterations are very common during the development process.

With reference to a case example, we illustrate how pTPNs can be casted in the development life cycle of real-time software, focusing on those activities of the V-Model which the adoption of pTPNs as a formal method mainly supports.

5.1   Casting pTPNs within the V-Model of the Software Life Cycle

As a case example, we consider the activities pertaining the development of an avionic radar system. Fig.2 evidences the first three design activities. *System Requirements Analysis* (SD1) defines User Requirements, specifying both functional requirements and non-functional requirements, such as transmission radius, power and frequencies. *System Design* (SD2) identifies main system units (a receiving/transmission antenna unit, a receiver unit, a converter unit, a signal/data processing unit) and allocates User Requirements to each of them. *Software/Hardware Requirements Analysis* (SD3) examines both software and hardware resources of each unit, decomposing them into software and hardware components which, according to the notation of Software Configuration Management, are referred to as Computer Software Configuration Items (CSCIs) and Hardware Configuration Items (HCIs). Referring to the example, requirements pertaining the signal/data processing unit are allocated to three separate CSCIs: a raw-image elaborator, a tracker and a central processor. It is worth noting that

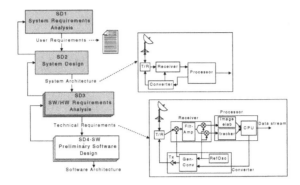

Fig. 2. The first three design activities in the development of an avionic radar system

SD1 and SD2 pertain the entire system under development, while subsequent design activities are repeated for each unit.

Preliminary Software Design (SD4-SW, see Fig.3) defines the *Software Architecture* of each CSCI, allocating it to a task set defined in terms of communicating tasks with assigned functional modules and prescribed release times and deadlines. *Detailed Software Design* (SD5-SW, see Fig.3) allocates resources and time requirements to software modules and produces the *Software Design* of each CSCI; in particular, the sub-activity of *Analysis of Resources and Time Requirements* (SD5.2-SW, not shown in Fig.1) addresses the evaluation of architecture feasibility. pTPNs allow the description of a shared resource environment

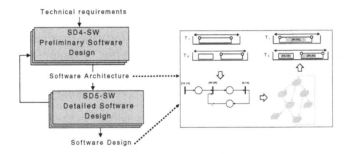

Fig. 3. Preliminary and Detailed Design activities in the development of an avionic radar system

with concurrent tasks subject to temporal constraints and running under priority preemptive scheduling, thus supporting both design activities. More specifically, Software Architecture of a CSCI can be modeled through a pTPN where timing requirements on computational chunks are left unspecified. This pTPN model can then be refined through the definition of low-level requirements, by associating each computational chunk with a minimum and a maximum execution time. It is worth noting that constraints on computation times can be assigned conservatively through estimations based on emulators or by attained experience with reused components and prototypes. However, they can also be assigned without any measurement on code but only according to a resource allocation policy. Hence, pTPNs as a formal method can be smoothly integrated within design activities; in addition, modeling convenience can be enhanced by considering the equivalent timeline schema.

Referring to the example, Fig.4 and Fig.5 show the timeline and the pTPN model, respectively, pertaining the Software Design of the tracker CSCI. Simulation and analysis of the pTPN specification model is employed in the architectural validation of the task set (*Analysis of Resources and Time Requirements*, SD5.2-SW, not shown in Fig.1), supporting tight schedulability analysis and verification of the correctness of logical sequencing.

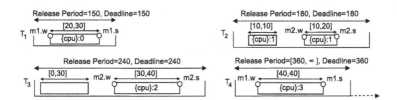

Fig. 4. The timeline schema of the Tracker CSCI, composed of four tasks synchronized by two semaphores. T_1 is a periodic task (period 150 ms) for the retrieval of radar data from Raw Image Processor CSCI. T_2 is a periodic task (period 180 ms) for the transmission of track data to the CPU CSCI. T_3 is a periodic task (period 240) representing plot extraction, fusion and Track-while-Scan (TWS) tracking. T_4 is a sporadic task (minimum interarrival time 360 ms) for the management of console commands (i.e. the request of radar pulse change). T_1 releases jobs made of a unique chunk, having an execution time constrained between 20 and 30 ms and requiring resource *cpu* with priority level 0 (low priority numbers correspond to high priority levels). This chunk is synchronized through semaphore m_1 with the unique chunk of T_4. The acquisition (*wait*) and the release (*signal*) of a semaphore performed by a chunk are represented through two circles embracing the rectangle which represents that chunk.

The refined and validated pTPN model enables a disciplined coding of the CSCI (*Software Implementation*, SD6-SW, see Fig.6) which relies on conventional primitives of a real-time operating system, as reported in Sect.3.

Verification processes proceed from Module to System Levels through subsequent integrations, which may provide a feedback to the corresponding design activity. Software Implementation (SD6-SW) includes an activity of testing on single modules (*Self Assessment of the Software Module*, SD6.3-SW, not shown in Fig.1), which is aimed at testing single modules within an emulated environment. *Software Integration* (SD7-SW) achieves the integration of CSCIs and their modules into a software unit, performing self-assessment of both CSCIs and units, whereas *System Integration* (SD8) composes units and performs self-assessment of the system. *Transition To Utilization* (SD9) comprises tasks that are required to install a completed system at the intended application site and to put it into operation. Note that the integration process (SD7-SW and SD8)

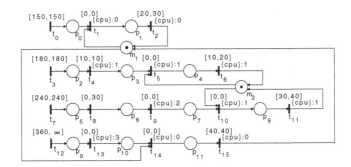

Fig. 5. The pTPN model for the timeline schema of Fig.4. Transitions t_0, t_3, t_7 and t_{12} account for repetitive job releases for tasks T_1, T_2, T_3 and T_4, respectively. They all have an output place, enabling the transition modeling the first chunk of the corresponding task. Subsequent chunks are modeled by chaining the transition representing the chunk and its input place. Places m_1 and m_2 model the two semaphores synchronizing the tasks. Transition t_1 models the acquisition of semaphore m_1 performed by the first chunk of T_1 with null execution time. Its firing enables transition t_2, which represents the nondeterministic execution time of the chunk and also performs release of the semaphore, having place m_1 as an output place. Since priority ceiling emulation protocol is assumed, in the translation from the timeline schema to the pTPN model, priority of tasks T_3 and T_4 is modified at the acquisition of semaphores m_2 and m_1, respectively. In particular, immediate transitions t_9 and t_{13} are added to T_3 and T_4, respectively, to model priority boost operations. The corresponding de-boost operations are represented by transitions t_{11} and t_{15}, which also model signal operations on semaphores m_2 and m_1, respectively.

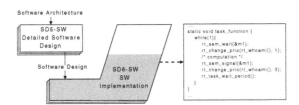

Fig. 6. Implementation activity in the development of an avionic radar system

is carried out iteratively, due to the replacement of dummies (such as simulators, prototypes and emulators) with operative software and due to the exchange of modules/components/units with improved versions or off-the-shelf products: therefore, during integration, software components and units can be tested in isolation or within an emulated environment, and integration may be run until all dummies in the system have been replaced. As described in Sect.4, pTPNs can be effectively integrated within verification activities, to enable test case selection and to support test case execution and subsequent evaluation.

6 Conclusions

In this paper, we described how preemptive Time Petri Nets can be smoothly integrated into the life cycle of real-time software, supporting both design and verification stages. Preemptive Time Petri Nets permit modeling of a task set subject to temporal constraints, enabling architectural validation of the specification through its analysis and simulation. The pTPN specification model drives the implementation stage, supporting a disciplined coding of the task set architecture, and enables the definition of oracles which can be employed in the evaluation of time-stamped logs produced during the execution. We pointed out how coverage criteria can be defined on the symbolic state space of the pTPN model and motivated the adoption of paths in the state space as test cases, illustrating a procedure to sensitize them.

For large models, validation of process architecture through state space enumeration may become unfeasible due to state space explosion. However, partial verification limited to a portion of the state space can provide a relevant support in testing activities. In fact, the pTPN model of the specification can still be employed as an oracle in failures detection, also providing a level of coverage with respect to the portion of the state space which has been enumerated. In addition, the state space, even if uncomplete, can be employed to select critical behaviors to be tested and sensitized.

Acknowledgments. This research was supported as a part of *Iniziativa Software* FINMECCANICA. We are grateful to R. Loiacono, S. Orsi and P. Viliani of GA - Firenze, for their precious contribution in filling the gap between theory and practice.

References

1. RTCA (Radio Technical Commission for Aeronautics). Do-178b, software considerations in airborne systems and equipment certification, http://www.rtca.org/
2. Hessel, A., Larsen, K., Nielsen, B., Pettersson, P., Skou, A.: Time-Optimal Real-Time Test Case Generation Using Uppaal. In: Petrenko, A., Ulrich, A. (eds.) FATES 2003. LNCS, vol. 2931, pp. 114–130. Springer, Heidelberg (2004)
3. Larsen, K., Mikucionis, M., Nielsen, B.: Online Testing of Real-Time Systems Using UPPAAL: Status and Future Work. Perspectives of Model-Based Testing (2005)
4. Krichen, M., Tripakis, S.: Black-Box Conformance Testing for Real-Time Systems. In: Graf, S., Mounier, L. (eds.) SPIN 2004. LNCS, vol. 2989, pp. 109–126. Springer, Heidelberg (2004)
5. Bucci, G., Fedeli, A., Sassoli, L., Vicario, E.: Timed state space analysis of real time preemptive systems. IEEE Trans.on Soft.Eng. 30(2), 97–111 (2004)
6. Roux, O.H., Lime, D.: Time Petri Nets with Inhibitor Hyperarcs. Formal Semantics and State Space Computation. In: Cortadella, J., Reisig, W. (eds.) ICATPN 2004. LNCS, vol. 3099, pp. 371–390. Springer, Heidelberg (2004)
7. Larsen, K.G., Cassez, F.: The Impressive Power of Stopwatches. In: Palamidessi, C. (ed.) CONCUR 2000. LNCS, vol. 1877. Springer, Heidelberg (2000)

8. Bucci, G., Fedeli, A., Sassoli, L., Vicario, E.: Modeling flexible real time systems with preemptive time petri nets. In: Proceedings of the 15th Euromicro Conference on Real-Time Systems (ECRTS 2003) (2003)
9. Buttazzo, G.: Hard Real-Time Computing Systems. Springer, Heidelberg (2005)
10. Merlin, P., Farber, D.J.: Recoverability of communication protocols. IEEE Trans.on Communications 24(9) (1976)
11. Berthomieu, B., Diaz, M.: Modeling and verification of time dependent systems using time petri nets. IEEE Trans. on Soft. Eng. 17(3) (1991)
12. Penczek, W., Półrola, A.: Specification and Model Checking of Temporal Properties in Time Petri Nets and Timed Automata. In: Cortadella, J., Reisig, W. (eds.) ICATPN 2004. LNCS, vol. 3099, pp. 37–76. Springer, Heidelberg (2004)
13. Berthomieu, B., Menasche, M.: An enumerative approach for analyzing time Petri nets. In: Information Processing: proc. of the IFIP congress, vol. 9, pp. 41–46 (1983)
14. Vicario, E.: Static analysis and dynamic steering of time dependent systems using time petri nets. IEEE Trans. on Soft. Eng. (2001)
15. Berthomieu, B., Lime, D., Roux, O.H., Vernadat, F.: Reachability problems and abstract state spaces for time petri nets with stopwatches. LAAS Report (2004)
16. Sassoli, L., Vicario, E.: Analysis of real time systems through the oris tool. In: Proc. of the 3rd Int. Conf. on the Quant. Evaluation of Sys. (QEST) (2006)
17. CENELEC-prEN50128: Railway applications: Sw for railway control and protection systems (1997)
18. Jard, C., Jéron, T.: Tgv: theory, principles and algorithms, a tool for the automatic synthesis of conformance test cases for non-deterministic reactive systems. Software Tools for Technology Transfer (STTT) 6 (2004)
19. Carnevali, L., Sassoli, L., Vicario, E.: Sensitization of symbolic runs in real-time testing using the oris tool. In: Proc. of the 12th IEEE Conference on Emerging Technologies and Factory Automation (ETFA) (2007)
20. Carnevali, L., Sassoli, L., Vicario, E.: Casting preemptive time petri nets in the development life cycle of real-time software. In: Proc. of the 19-th Euromicro Conference on Real-Time Systems (ECRTS) (2007)
21. IEC 62304 International Standard Edition 1.0 Medical device software - Software life cycle processes (2006)
22. Developing Standard for IT Systems of the Federal Republic of Germany. Lifecycle Process Model General Directive No. 250. (1997)

Concurrent Program Metrics Drawn by Quasar

Claude Kaiser[1], Christophe Pajault[1], and Jean-François Pradat-Peyre[2]

[1] CEDRIC - CNAM Paris
292, rue St Martin, F-75003 Paris
{kaiser,pajault}@cnam.fr
[2] LIP6 - Université Pierre et Marie Curie
104 avenue du Président Kennedy, F-75016 Paris
peyre@lip6.fr
http://quasar.cnam.fr/

Abstract. Aiming at developing reliable concurrent software, the engineering practice uses appropriate metrics. Our tool Quasar analyses automatically the concurrent part of programs and produces data reporting its analysis process. We attempt to use the data as metrics for concurrent programming. The first aim of Quasar is the validation of concurrent code; in addition, the reported data may be relevant to mark the quality of code, to evaluate different concurrency semantics, to compare the execution indeterminism of different implementations of a concurrency pattern and to estimate the scalability of a solution. As a case study we analyse with Quasar several implementations of a distributed symmetric non-deterministic rendezvous algorithm. We consider two possible uses of the collected data for indeterminism estimation and for concurrent software quality.

1 Concurrent Program Metrics

Metrics are used for program quality control. Following the seminal works of McCabe in 1976 [15] and Halstead in 1977 [10], several metrics are now available through specific software engineering tools (such as Telelogic Logiscope, IBM-Rational tools suite, IPL klockwork). Source code programming style guides (such as GSS [17], JavaRanch [19]) emphasize qualitative characteristics such as style, readability, concision, good structure, absence of design and coding errors.

Asynchronous execution of concurrent processes is highly non deterministic. Thus concurrency introduces temporal dimensions of correctness, i.e., safety (absence of deadlock or livelock, coherence of shared variables) and liveness (absence of starvation), which are central concerns in any concurrent design and implementation. Besides static or dynamic tools used for concurrency correctness, additional metrics may help to deal with concurrency complexity [5,18], effective parallelism usage, response time, indeterminism [4], execution behaviour observability, implementation comparison, scalability of concurrent solutions.

We have developed Quasar, a static analysis tool based on the use of slicing [20,21] and of model checking [6]. We believe that, besides its initial validation purpose, this tool can deliver some metrics for concurrency.

F. Kordon and T. Vardanega (Eds.): Ada-Europe 2008, LNCS 5026, pp. 101–114, 2008.
© Springer-Verlag Berlin Heidelberg 2008

We base our assumption on the following. A way of evaluating a program code (with available documentation) consists of giving it to an expert for appraisal. Of course this is crude, subjective, the expert is more or less competent, may get tired, makes errors; thus this method has been refined and has led to elaborate code review techniques. As Quasar also analyses the source code, it proceeds rather like the expert, systematically trying to get rid of unimportant parts and to reduce the analysis by means of structural properties or symmetries, finally focusing on the most crucial part of concurrent code. Quasar produces data, which reports on this analysis and reduction process and which we attempt to use as concurrency metrics.

2   Quasar

Quasar is an automatic concurrency analysis tool. It takes as input the application source code and uses it to generate and validate a semantic model.

Like any validation method, this one has to confront the explosion in the number of states which need to be analysed. Therefore the number of states that Quasar must consider is automatically reduced as soon as possible so far as the program structure allows it.

The analysis of the program concurrent behaviour is performed in four automatic steps.

1. First, the original text of the program is automatically sliced in order to remove parts of the program that are not relevant to the concurrency property the user wants to check. The sliced program is an executable and smaller program, equivalent to the original one for the checked property. This program will be easier to analyse in the next steps.
2. Second, the sliced program is translated into a concurrency model using a library of patterns. A pattern is a meta model of coloured Petri net corresponding to a declaration, a statement or an expression. Each pattern definition is recursive in such a way that its definition may contain one or several other patterns. The target model mapping the whole sliced program is obtained by replacing each meta-net by its corresponding concrete sub-nets and by merging all sub-nets. Performing structural reductions, also called static reductions, on the target model optimises this mapping.
3. In the third step Quasar checks the required property on the target model, generating a reachability graph. Quasar uses graph reductions such as delta marking which allow a symbolic storage of states, and a coloured stubborn sets technique which optimises state based enumeration (model-checking). These reductions are called dynamic reductions.
4. Finally, if the required property is not verified, Quasar displays the state in which the application is faulty and a reports a sequence leading to the faulty state.

A detailed description of this process can be found in [7,8].

The current Quasar version focuses on Ada concurrent programs.

Besides the property check, Quasar displays a) the sliced executable program, b) the number of places and transitions of the coloured Petri net model, c) reachability graph data, especially the number of graph states, the number of graph arcs and the number of arcs visited during the graph traversal, the graph compilation time and the graph searching time for model checking, the size of the memory used for storing the graph elements, d) the memory size and CPU time used.

3   Comparing Several Versions of a Concurrent Program

Several implementations of non-deterministic pairing provide static analysis data, which serve as a basis for their comparison and for an attempt to define metrics.

3.1   Non-deterministic Symmetric Pairing

Non-deterministic pairing occurs in a system when a concurrent process becomes a candidate to constitute a pair with any other candidate process. The pairing is said to be symmetrical since candidate partners all behave similarly, i.e. they all have the same capabilities for sending or receiving partner requests. The pair is the result of the non-deterministic interaction between two (or more) candidate partners. Once paired the processes are no longer candidates and become partners. One of them is chosen to lead the pair interactions: the leader calls while the other accepts a call (this dissymetry prevents deadlock). The partnership ends after a while allowing both processes of the pair to return to the state of possible candidate partners. The absence of candidate partners will not last forever.

The functionality required is very simple; once two candidates A and B have been selected for connection, the pairing specification is:

$$\{(A, Partner(A) = nil, Leader(A) = nil) and (B, Partner(B) = nil, Leader(B) = nil)\}$$
$$Pairing$$
$$\{(A, Partner(A) = B, Leader(A) = Leader(B)) and (B, Partner(B) = A, Leader(B) = Leader(A))\}$$

The challenge is to carry out a connexion as soon as possible once at least two processes are candidates. Pairing must concern two and only two processes. No third process should be allowed to disturb the creation of a single pair and the notification to each pair member of its partner name.

We consider a distributed system made of a set of at least two asynchronous non-failing concurrent processes and we propose to examine two algorithms. In the first one, a candidate process takes advantage of a shared pairing service; in the second one, it has to send requests to other processes until it finds one which is also candidate. A more detailed specification, which is outside the scope of this paper, can be found in [12,13].

3.2   The Different Implementations of Non-deterministic Pairing

We compare several reliable (i.e. deadlock free) solutions corresponding to various concurrency features. The main program declares and creates N concurrent processes and calls each of them to allocate unique Ids. Thus each process starts accepting a call to grasp its unique Id and then loops forever. Each cycle starts by a call to the pairing component to get a current partner and performing a peer-to-peer transaction with it. This partnership is delimited by two rendezvous: Start_Peering and Finish_Peering.

Shared agora. In this first solution a meeting place, called the Agora, is known to all seeking processes that use it as a pairing data container [13]. Implementations use shared data and shared procedures controlled by semaphores or by a monitor [11].

The semaphore implementation (*AgoraServerPosix*) programs explicitly a mutual exclusion and uses the synchronisation technique called "passing the baton" [2]. It corresponds to the style of concurrency expression allowed by POSIX. We simulate each semaphore by an Ada protected object.

Several possible monitor based concurrency semantics have been used in the past and a classification is presented in [3]. Every implementation provides mutual exclusion during the execution of a distinguished sequence (synchronised method in Java, lock in C#, protected object subprograms in Ada) using a lock for every object. The semantics differ in the chosen policies for blocking, signalling and awaking processes. Three kinds of monitor structure are used for experimentation in this paper.

Three implementations use explicit self-blocking and signalling instructions and are based on Java style using wait(), notify() and notifyAll() clauses with a unique waiting queue per encapsulated object (termed synchronized). We simulate the Java concurrency structure in Ada [9]. The first implementation (*AgoraServerJava*) emulates a native Java concurrency semantic with its weak fairness which moves awoken threads into a single system queue of ready threads. This weak semantic requires defensive programming in order to avoid deadlock. The other two implementations (*AgoraServerJavastrong* and *AgoraServerJavaStrongdc*) enforce a strong fairness semantic and give precedence to the awoken threads over other ready threads. In the first one the defensive code has not been coded although it has been kept in the second despite being useless.

The third monitor structure implemented (*AgoraServerAda*) uses implicit self-blocking and signalling [14] as provided by Ada protected objects [16] with entry barriers and automatic entry re-evaluation. The strong fairness semantic is the result of the so-called Ada eggshell model for protected objects which gives precedence to awaken calls over new calls. The requeue statement enables a request to be processed in several steps, each one associated with an entry call.

Shared remote server. In this second solution, all the seeking processes call up an additional process which acts as a shared pairing server. Two implementations (*RendezvousServerMonitor* and *RendezvousServerNested*) take advantage of the Ada rendezvous between tasks. The task of the first one acts as a monitor structure for its clients while the task of the second one realizes an anonymous rendezvous which hooks two calling client tasks [12].

Distributed cooperation. The third solution [12] is fully distributed and does not use a common agora or a common server. Each candidate process consults other processes until it discovers a candidate process and, since the pairing is symmetrical and non-deterministic, it must also answer requests of other candidate processes. This behaviour excludes a deadlock situation where all processes have called the others or where all processes wait for a call. Thus each process must be non-deterministically either requesting or listening. A requesting candidate sends only one request at a time (there is no calling concurrency to manage). A listening process picks and serves its received requests one at a time (there is no listening concurrency to manage). Each called process must answer indicating whether it is a candidate or not. The pairing implies that both partners are candidates and that one is requesting and the other is listening. Finally the pairing decision is taken by the listening partner (thus no distributed consensus is required).

The implementation (*CooperativeAdaTask*) associates each process with a local assistant task, which takes advantage of the Ada selective non-deterministic rendezvous between tasks and which cooperates with other assistant tasks.

Dummy component. This implementation (*Dummy*) provides a low bound model with just a shared procedure call which returns a predefined partner name, the same for all candidates (since this call is superfluous for concurrency, it is normally sliced. Quasar provides a means for signalling that a statement should not be sliced). All transactions performed with the fixed predefined partner are no longer peer-to-peer transactions. This choice maintains a reliable solution.

List of reliable implementations
Monitor like implementations:

AgoraServerAda:	Ada protected object
AgoraServerJava:	native Java semantic: plus defensive programming
AgoraServerJavaStrong:	Java modified for strong fairness
AgoraServerJavaStrongdc:	same as above plus defensive programming
AgoraServerPosix:	Semaphore solution

Remote server implementations:

RendezvousServerMonitor:	classical Ada style
RendezvousServerNested:	Ada rendezvous server task

Distributed cooperation:

CooperativeAdaTask:	fully distributed

Dummy component:

Dummy:	a fixed partnership

3.3   The Verdict Returned by Quasar

All these implementations have been ultimately written in Ada and use Ada tasks as process structure, declaration and activation. When POSIX semaphores and Java monitors are concerned, they have been emulated and their emulation is used instead of Ada concurrency features directly. All implementations have thus been analysed and proven deadlock free by Quasar. They are available on the Quasar Website [1]. Previously some, detected as faulty, had been corrected by adding defensive code (*AgoraServerJava* and *RendezvousServerMonitor*).

The first group of data drawn by Quasar concerns the coloured Petri net model. The sliced Ada program, which contains only concurrency relevant text, is automatically compiled into its coloured Petri net model. This model is simplified by structural reductions, which operate on superfluous places or transitions due to verbose programming or to the automatic generation in the compilation phase. $\mathcal{P}/\mathcal{P}_r$ (resp. $\mathcal{T}/\mathcal{T}_r$) records the number of places (resp. transitions) in the original and in the reduced Petri net model.

The second group of data concerns the reachability graph that is built during the model-checking step. It records the number of states and the number of arcs visited to check that the required property is not violated. The ratio compares the sizes of the graphs for two successive values of the number of concurrent processes.

The last group of data concerns CPU and memory used by Quasar for its analysis. Execution records the time (in seconds) needed to compile the Petri net and the time spent in the graph traversal while model checking (recorded as Comp/Trav).

3.4   Metrics and Insights Derived from the Collected Data

We have tried to obtain some insight from the data recorded from the different implementations of the pairing component. The results are recorded in Table 1.

Quality of code. The size of the Petri net gives an idea of the conciseness of code and of the style of programming. It can be used as a quality assessment metric for the concurrent part of a program, extending the cyclomatic complexity of functions. Note that the coloured Petri net of a given implementation is the same for all values N of the number of concurrent processes and that Quasar performs a static reduction of about 4.

As foreseeable the distributed cooperation is the most complex. Surprisingly the reduced Petri net of the distributed solution is only twice as large as the rendezvous server monitor which uses also rendezvous between tasks.

All shared paring service solutions are roughly equivalent. This reflects the fact that they use the same algorithm. The differences result from the additional code used for emulation.

The homogeneity of the metrics also reflects the fact that all the examples have been programmed with the same algorithm and by the same person(s).

Nondeterminism. The reachability graph records all the successive states that a program execution will visit. It does it for all possible executions of a program. The lower the number of elements in the graph, the less complex is the program execution; but also: the lower the number of elements, the less task interleaving. The graph size is thus related both to the execution efficiency and to the execution indeterminacy.

Again the distributed cooperation is the most complex. Let us compare the distributed cooperation and the rendezvous server monitor and examine the ratio

Table 1. Quasar data collected for pairing with peer to peer transaction

Program name	T	$\mathcal{P}/\mathcal{P}_r$	$\mathcal{T}/\mathcal{T}_r$	#States stored	#Arcs visited	Ratio N/N-1	Exec. (s) Comp/Trav	Space (Mb)
	4			4 182	4 369	-	146/0	10.6
AgoraServerAda	5	267/70	249/52	138 980	147 901	33.8	159/5	12.4
	6			5 256 768	5 652 471	38.2	421/368	89.6
	4			8 292	8 633	-	253/1	10.7
AgoraServerJava	5	392/93	372/73	312 619	330 480	38.3	549/18	15.1
	6			13 140 700	14 027 263	42.4	351/1142	207
	4			6 542	6 729	-	121/0	10.6
Ag.ServerJavaStrong	5	338/88	318/68	215 708	224 629	33.4	136/9	13.6
	6			8 104 338	8 500 041	37.8	138/389	128
	4			8 326	8 565	-	166/0	10.6
Ag.ServerJavaStrongdc	5	395/100	375/80	280 641	291 914	34.1	162/10	14.6
	6			9 920 178	10 323 753	35.4	148/686	160
	4			162 912	212 221	-	97/12	12.7
AgoraServerPosix	5	414/89	396/69	27 779 147	37 633 949	177	103/4 757	401
	5			4 739	4 926	-	139/0	10.6
RdvServerMonitor	6	329/78	308/57	152 218	160 839	32.7	223/5	12.6
	7			5 638 789	6 018 940	37.4	148/182	87.2
	5			2 824	3 011	-	98 /0	10.6
RdvServerNested	6	238/61	219/42	99 040	107 289	35.6	232/6	11.8
	7			3 822 728	4 169 915	38.8	262/177	60.3
	7			23 266	24 070	-	356/1	10.9
CooperativeAdaTasks	9	550/126	519/95	2 277 347	2 374 070	98.5	363/177	48.5
	4			108	109	-	99/1	10.5
Dummy	5	225/51	212/38	151	153	1.4	107/1	10.5
	6			194	197	1.8	107/0	10.5
	7			237	241	2.2	97/1	10.5

of the number of arcs visited in the reachability graph; this ratio is about 6 for 3 processes and about 14 for 4 processes.

The shared pairing service solutions show a difference between monitor like features (in Ada and Java) and low level semaphore programming. This latter is more complex because the analysis (and the execution) cannot consider that the critical sections of code embedded by programmed P and V operations of a mutual exclusion semaphore are really sequential, as it can be supposed when a monitor is used. Thus the analysis has to consider the interleaving of the instructions of the critical section instead of considering them as serializable.

The genuine Java like solution has more execution indeterminacy since the weak fairness semantic creates more process switching possibilities. When using strong fairness semantic as in *AgoraServerJavaStrong*, the indeterminacy is at least 25% less. If the defensive code is kept as in *AgoraServerJavaStrongdc*, the indeterminacy is still less than with the regular Java semantic.

Comparison of implementations. The shared pairing service solutions can be ordered in terms of Petri net or reachability graph sizes. The same order holds for the Petri net size as for the reachability graph size.

For high-level concurrency structures the best is the *RendezvousServerNested* implementation, since it has no shared variables and the information is thus passed from input parameter to output parameter. The second best is the

Ada protected object implementation, showing the quality of this feature. The increasing order is:

RendezvousServerNested > AgoraServerAda > RendezvousServerMonitor > AgoraServerJavaStrong > AgoraServerJava > CooperativeAdaTask.

Note that being able to compare the different implementations of a concurrency pattern can be a useful criterion of choice for automatic code generation.

Scalability. Analysing solutions with different process number provides some insight into the indeterminacy scalability.

For the shared pairing services, the scale factor is about 35 when they are implemented with high-level concurrency structures. It may be conjectured about 180 for the semaphore implementation. This results probably from the interleaving of the instructions within the critical section.

For the distributed cooperation, the scale factor seems to be near 100.

Comparing with a simpler utilization of the shared component. As Quasar analyses the global behaviour of programs, not the behaviour of a component per se, we wonder whether the comparison of the different implementations is modified when the component is used differently. Thus the pairing component has been used in a simpler program where the processes call the pairing component only and have no other interactions. The results are available on [1]. The preceding comparisons remain true. However some anomalies may be observed.

Some indeterminacy anomalies. Since the program with an empty sequence of process interaction is shorter than the program with a peer-to-peer transaction, which has two additional rendezvous, its Petri net and its reachability graph should be smaller. This is not the case for some component implementations (*AgoraServerJava, AgoraServerPosix, CooperativeAdaTasks*).

Let us examine some possible explanations.

In *AgoraServerJava* (genuine Java), the weak fairness semantic induces much process context switching due to the move of released processes into the system ready queue. When processes are in a peer to peer transaction, they cannot be in the ready queue and the combinatorics is smaller. Note that this anomaly is not present when using strong fairness with Java.

For *CooperativeAdaTasks*, the same effect occurs, there are fewer processes that are in effective possible competition since at least two of them are already in peer-to-peer interaction.

For *AgoraServerPosix* the mutual exclusion is not known by Quasar, thus the critical section of code is not considered as a unique serializable flow of program and all its instructions may be interleaved causing very large combinatorics.

4   About Indeterminacy Estimation

We consider now two other possible uses of this data. First we observe how they evolve when a component is combined with other concurrency features. Second we examine a possible estimation of software quality.

4.1   Program Code Incrementations

We have analysed two sets of programs with 3 processes calling a pairing component, one using the Ada protected object implementation (*AgoraServerAda*), the other using the dummy implementation (*Dummy*). Each set starts with a program in which the processes repeatedly get a partner and have no other interaction with it. Each subsequent program of the set is built by adding a new protected object or a new rendezvous used by the partner. This provides data for insights on program code implementation. The results are available on the Quasar website [1].

As the Petri net model is built gradually, adding a pattern for each feature, we may expect that the original and reduced Petri net sizes reflect this additive structure. We inspect the data to detect whether the indeterminacy variation may be somehow predictable, although model checking evolution is not linear, even in such a simple case.

The set of data collected by Quasar are displayed in [1] in Tables 3, 4 and 5. The latter table presents the results when Quasar is used without setting the usual static or dynamic reductions (also in this paper in Table 2).

Adding a protected object causes an almost fixed Petri net growth: it adds about 24 places and 22 transitions to the original net, about 7 places and 4 transitions to the reduced net. The non reduced reachability graph extension shows in both cases an extension due to an additional indeterminism: tasks are either before the call to the protected object or after the call. The size of the ultimately reduced reachability graph does not necessarily follow this augmentation, thanks to dynamic reductions performed during its construction.

Adding a rendezvous also causes some fixed Petri net extension with again two situations: the first rendezvous introduction adds 37 places and 36 transitions to the original net, 8 places and 7 transitions to the reduced net, while the other extensions add only 20 places and 19 transitions to the original net, 4 places and 3 transitions to the reduced net. This difference can be explained by the fact that in the last cases some places are shared between different rendezvous patterns while this is not possible in the first case (which contains a unique rendezvous).

This underlines the difficulty of evaluating the complexity of a program through the size of the corresponding Petri net or through the size of the reachability graph of the model.

Firstly, the Petri net size cannot be easily predicted since the Petri net is not generated by a simple juxtaposition of patterns; in fact, patterns are meta models of Petri nets from which concrete subnets are derived recursively and some of these subnet places are merged to provide the final net. Predicting a Petri net size is therefore as imprecise as predicting the size of the code generated by an optimizer compiler.

Secondly, model checking is highly combinatorial and is not a process decomposable into separate parts. Thus the number of states, and therefore the indeterminacy, grows exponentially and depends on the number of tasks, synchronisation points, statements, ...

Finally, estimating the metrics of a concurrent program from the metrics defined for its components, as can be done for sequential code, is still an open problem.

4.2   The Reduction Ability as a Quality Factor

Quasar can be used without setting the static or dynamic reductions. This allows another examination of a concurrent program, although limited because of the huge size of the graph without reductions. Let us do this analysis for the preceding programs. Results are displayed in Table 2 and summarized by Figure 1. They display high reduction factors, especially when the code contains few process interactions and is almost parallel. The reductions operating on the shared procedure component produce a ratio of at least 690 for static reduction, and of at least 118 108 for static followed by dynamic reduction. The respective ratios for the protected object component are 188 and 5 137. Let us explain how Quasar proceeds.

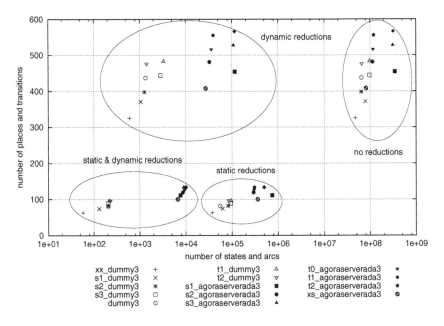

Fig. 1. Graph summarizing the different reductions performed by Quasar

When process code includes sequences of statements which are serializable (in this case their behaviour is easily understandable), Quasar reduces the size of the Petri net model since these serializable sequences of actions are detected and replaced by equivalent atomic actions. We can observe this on data provided: the simpler the sequences of actions performed by tasks, the higher the structural (static) reduction ratio.

Table 2. Quasar data with different kind of reductions

Different contincrementations	$\mathcal{P}$	ratio	$\mathcal{T}$	ratio	#States stored	ratio	#Arcs visited	ratio
Dummy component with a shared procedure								
xx_Dummy3 (0 RV, 0 PO)								
no reduction	168	-	157	-	9 608 380	-	37 388 544	-
static reduction only	37	4.5	26	6	8 548	1124	28 758	1 300
dynamic reduction only	168	-	157	-	303	31 711	303	123 395
static + dynamic reduction	37	4.5	26	6	29	331 323	29	1 289 260
s1_Dummy3 (0 RV, 1 PO)								
no reduction	192	-	179	-	16 062 612	-	62 491 204	-
static reduction only	44	4.4	30	6	14 185	1 132	48 147	1 298
dynamic reduction only	192	-	179	-	526	30 537	528	118 355
static + dynamic reduction	44	4.4	30	6	65	247 117	65	961 403
s2_Dummy3 (1 RV, 0 PO)								
no reduction	205	-	193	-	13 160 577	-	50 916 986	-
static reduction only	47	4.3	35	5.5	19 081	690	63 071	807
dynamic reduction only	205	-	193	-	632	20 824	633	80 437
static + dynamic reduction	47	4.3	35	5.5	102	129 025	103	494 340
s3_Dummy3 (1 RV, 1 PO)								
no reduction	229	-	215	-	19 989 509	-	77 383 894	-
static reduction only	52	4.4	37	5.8	21 861	914	72 483	1 067
dynamic reduction only	229	-	215	-	1 422	14 057	1 430	54 115
static + dynamic reduction	52	4.4	37	5.8	102	195 976	103	751 300
Dummy3 (2 RV, 0 PO)								
no reduction	225	-	212	-	13 312 421	-	51 459 540	-
static reduction only	47	4.8	34	6.2	13 053	1 020	42 511	1 210
dynamic reduction only	225	-	212	-	670	19 869	671	76 690
static + dynamic reduction	47	4.8	34	6.2	103	129 247	104	494 803
t1_Dummy3 (2 RV, 1 PO)								
no reduction	249	-	234	-	20 166 873	-	78 017 848	-
static reduction only	56	4.4	40	5.8	22 185	909	72 281	1 079
dynamic reduction only	249	-	234	-	1 662	12 134	1 672	46 661
static + dynamic reduction	56	4.4	40	5.8	108	186 730	109	715 760
t2_Dummy3 (3 RV,0 PO)								
no reduction	245	-	231	-	13 464 265	-	52 002 094	-
static reduction only	55	4.5	41	5.6	19 705	683	64 607	805
dynamic reduction only	245	-	231	-	708	19 017	709	73 346
static + dynamic reduction	55	4.5	41	5.6	114	118 108	115	452 192
AgoraServerAda Ada protected object implementation								
xs_AgoraServerAda3 (0 RV, 0 PO)								
no reduction	212	-	196	-	17 316 336	-	64 230 366	-
static reduction only	58	3.7	42	4.7	91 878	188	268 874	239
dynamic reduction only	212	-	196	-	13 534	1 279	13 669	4 699
static + dynamic reduction	58	3.7	42	4.7	3 279	5 281	3 414	18 814
s1_AgoraServerAda3 (0 RV, 1 PO)								
no reduction	236	-	218	-	72 406 616	-	273 741 102	-
static reduction only	65	3.6	46	4.7	182 484	397	561 181	488
dynamic reduction only	236	-	218	-	57 282	1 264	58 351	4 691
static + dynamic reduction	65	3.6	46	4.7	3 766	19 226	3 901	70 172
s2_AgoraServerAda3 (1 RV, 0 PO)								
no reduction	249	-	232	-	23 798 499	-	88 896 730	-
static reduction only	68	3.7	51	4.5	75 223	316	218 483	407
dynamic reduction only	249	-	232	-	16 342	1 456	16 503	5 387
static + dynamic reduction	68	3.7	51	4.5	4 208	5 656	4 369	20 347
s3_AgoraServerAda3 (1 RV, 1 PO)								
no reduction	273	-	254	-	65 691 467	-	247 715 698	-
static reduction only	73	3.7	53	4.8	123 451	532	369 703	670
dynamic reduction only	273	-	254	-	53 720	1 223	54 567	4 540
static + dynamic reduction	73	3.7	53	4.8	4 416	14 876	4 577	54 122
AgoraServerAda3 (2 RV, 0 PO)								
no reduction	267	-	249	-	24 563 347	-	91 637 360	-
static reduction only	72	3.7	54	4.6	77 077	319	222 947	411
dynamic reduction only	267	-	249	-	17 980	1 366	18 167	5 044
static + dynamic reduction	72	3.7	54	4.6	4 572	5 373	4 759	19 256
t1_AgoraServerAda3 (2 RV, 1 PO)								
no reduction	293	-	273	-	66 789 871	-	251 631 984	-
static reduction only	77	3.8	56	4.9	125 593	532	374 887	671
dynamic reduction only	293	-	273	-	56 494	1 182	57 391	4 385
static + dynamic reduction	77	3.8	56	4.9	4 780	13 973	4 967	50 661
t2_AgoraServerAda3 (3 RV,0 PO)								
no reduction	287	-	268	-	25 355 511	-	94 456 846	-
static reduction only	76	3.8	57	4.7	78 931	321	227 411	415
dynamic reduction only	287	-	268	-	19 722	1 286	19 935	4 738
static + dynamic reduction	76	3.8	57	4.7	4 936	5 137	5 149	18 345

When performing dynamic reductions (reductions performed during the building of the reachability graph), Quasar tries to detect independent behaviours and, depending on some conditions, reduces the number of states and arcs that have to be built and explored (without altering the true value of the analysed property); thus the more independent the processes are (and consequently the more understandable the program) the higher the dynamic reduction ratio is. This is the case for the *Dummy* component. Remember that its shared procedure has no effect on concurrency and was prevented from being sliced. Consequently the shared procedure is suppressed by any later reduction. In *xx_Dummy* (no additional rendezvous, no protected object) the remaining code is parallel and is analysed with 29 states only (with 9 million states without reduction, this corresponds to a reduction factor of over 300 000).

Many reductions performed by Quasar are favoured by the presence in the code of purely parallel structure and symmetries, by high-level synchronisation structures (for example the monitor concept), by code structuring (for example paradigm and pattern use), evidence and clarity of code. These code properties, which are required engineering practices when reliable code is needed, also have a positive side effect on concurrency analysis.

As all reductions performed by Quasar aim to concentrate the analysis to the genuine part of synchronisation which is involved in the property examined, the ability of a program to be strongly reduced by Quasar may be considered as a credible mark of its code readability and concurrency quality.

5   Conclusion

We have compared several implementations of a concurrent non-deterministic rendezvous algorithm. Data provided by their static analysis with Quasar have enabled us to:

- Verify whether a concurrency property, as absence of deadlock, holds,
- Give insights into the quality of the concurrent code,
- Provide a metrics for execution indeterminacy,
- Compare different implementations of a given concurrent pattern,
- Give an idea of the scalability evolution of a given implementation,
- Consider estimations for compound programs,
- Attempt to use the reductions performed as quality indicators.

All the programs and the data collected by their Quasar analysis are available on the Quasar website [1].

We envisage creating an extension to use programmers' assumptions of critical section of statements or of serialization of statements (similar to writer sequence and reader sequence). Quasar may benefit from these assumptions and verify them a posteriori. The slicing phase may also be extended to automatically generate causality time stamps and to use them at run-time to perform dynamic testing as in [22] as a complement to the static code analysis performed by Quasar.

From this analysis we can feedback some guidelines for reliable concurrent program design. (1) A high level language derives benefit from its large grain of mutual exclusion access. (2) A monitor based structure controlled by assertions is a good way of improving determinism. (3) Strong fairness semantic facilitates reliability. Moreover weak fairness requires defensive programming to counterbalance this weakness and to provide reliability. (4) Using concurrency paradigms rather than ad hoc concurrency code helps to provide code that is easier to understand and to observe.

Acknowledgments

Olivier Alzeari, Sami Evangelista, Claude Kaiser, Christophe Pajault, Jean-François Pradat-Peyre and Pierre Rousseau contributed to the present version of Quasar. We thank the 5 anonymous reviewers for their precious advice.

References

1. Quasar website, http://quasar.cnam.fr/files/concurrency_papers.html
2. Andrews, G.R.: Concurrent programming: principles and practice. Benjamin-Cummings Publishing Co. Inc., USA (1991)
3. Buhr, P.A., Fortier, M., Coffin, M.H.: Monitor classification. ACM Comput. Surv. 27(1), 63–107 (1995)
4. Cha, S., Chung, I.S., Kwon, Y.R.: Complexity measures for concurrent programs based on information-theoretic metrics. Inf. Proc. Lett. 46(1), 43–50 (1993)
5. Chung, C.-M., Shih, T.K., Wang, Y.-H., Lin, W.-C., Kou, Y.-F.: Task decomposition testing and metrics for concurrent programs. In: Proc. of the 7th Int. Symposium on Software Reliability Engineering (1996)
6. Peled, D., Clarke, E., Grumberg, O.: Model Checking. MIT Press, Cambridge (1999)
7. Evangelista, S., Kaiser, C., Pradat-Peyre, J.-F., Rousseau, P.: Quasar: A New Tool for Concurrent Ada Programs Analysis. In: Rosen, J.-P., Strohmeier, A. (eds.) Ada-Europe 2003. LNCS, vol. 2655, pp. 168–181. Springer, Heidelberg (2003)
8. Evangelista, S., Kaiser, C., Pradat-Peyre, J.F., Rousseau, P.: Verifying linear time temporal logic properties of concurrent ada programs with quasar. In: Proc. of the 2003 Annual ACM Int. Conf. on Ada (SIGAda 2003), pp. 17–24 (2003)
9. Evangelista, S., Kaiser, C., Pradat-Peyre, J.-F., Rousseau, P.: Comparing Java, C# and Ada monitors queuing policies: a case study and its Ada refinement. Ada Letters XXVI(2), 23–37 (2006)
10. Halstead, M.H.: Elements of Software Science. Operating and programming systems series. Elsevier Science Inc., New York (1977)
11. Hoare, C.A.R.: Monitors: an operating system structuring concept. Commun. ACM 17(10), 549–557 (1974)
12. Kaiser, C., Pajault, C., Pradat-Peyre, J.-F.: Modelling remote concurrency with Ada. Case study of symmetric non-deterministic rendez-vous. In: Abdennahder, N., Kordon, F. (eds.) Ada-Europe 2007. LNCS, vol. 4498, pp. 192–207. Springer, Heidelberg (2007)
13. Kaiser, C., Pradat-Peyre, J.F.: Chameneos, a concurrency game for Java, Ada and others. In: Int. Conf. ACS/IEEE AICCSA 2003 (2003)

14. Kessels, J.L.W.: An alternative to event queues for synchronization in monitors. Commun. ACM 20(7), 500–503 (1977)
15. McCabe, T.J.: A complexity measure. IEEE Transactions on Software Engineering 2, 308–320 (1976)
16. Brukardt, R., Tucker Taft, S., Duff, R.A., Plödereder, E.: Consolidated Ada Reference Manual. Language and Standard Libraries. LNCS, vol. 2219. Springer, Heidelberg (2001)
17. Geotechnical Software Services. Java programming style guidelines (2007)
18. Shatz, S.M.: Towards complexity metrics for Ada tasking. IEEE Trans. on Softw. Eng. 14(8), 1122–1127 (1988)
19. JavaRanch Project standards. Java programming style guide (2007)
20. Tip, F.: A survey of program slicing techniques. Journal of programming languages 3, 121–189 (1995)
21. Xu, B., Qian, J., Zhang, X., Wu, Z., Chen, L.: A brief survey of program slicing. SIGSOFT Softw. Eng. Notes 30(2), 1–36 (2005)
22. Yu, Y., Rodeheffer, T., Chen, W.: Racetrack: efficient detection of data race conditions via adaptive tracking. ACM SIGOPS OSR 39(5), 221–234 (2005)

A Comparison of the Object-Oriented Features of Ada 2005 and Java™

Benjamin M. Brosgol

AdaCore; 104 Fifth Ave., New York NY 10011 USA
brosgol@adacore.com

Abstract. Ada 2005 and Java offer comparable Object-Oriented Programming ("OOP") support, but exhibit significant differences in both their general philosophies and their specific features. Each language allows the programmer to define class inheritance hierarchies (including a limited form of multiple inheritance through "interfaces") and to employ encapsulation, polymorphism, and dynamic binding. Whereas OOP forms the foundation of Java's semantic model, OOP in Ada is largely orthogonal to the rest of the language. In Java it is difficult to avoid using OOP; in Ada OOP is brought in only when explicitly indicated in the program. Java is a "pure" OO language in the style of Smalltalk, with implicit pointers and implementation-provided garbage collection. Ada is a methodology-neutral OO language in the manner of C++, with explicit pointers and program-specified storage reclamation. Java uses OOP to capture the functionality of exception handling, multi-threading, enumeration types, and other facilities that are not necessarily related to object orientation. Ada supplies specific features for such functionality, independent of its OO model. Java is oriented towards manipulating dynamic data structures. Ada offers more opportunities for optimization and run-time efficiency, and greater flexibility in the choice of programming styles.

1 Introduction

Ada [1] and Java [2] both offer comprehensive support for Object-Oriented software development, but through rather different approaches and, perhaps confusingly, at times using the same terms or syntactic forms with different meanings. This paper contrasts the two languages' OO facilities from the perspectives of semantics, expressiveness/style, and efficiency. It is a major update to [3], taking into account the new facilities in both Ada 2005 and Java 1.5.

2 Object and Class

Ada and Java differ in several fundamental ways with respect to their support for Object-Oriented Programming (OOP):

- The role of the class construct
- Whether pointers are implicit or explicit
- Whether automatic storage reclamation ("garbage collection") is provided

F. Kordon and T. Vardanega (Eds.): Ada-Europe 2008, LNCS 5026, pp. 115–129, 2008.
© Springer-Verlag Berlin Heidelberg 2008

Java's class construct serves multiple purposes, as illustrated by the three occurrences of the class name in the following example:

```
class Fum{
 Fum f = new Fum();
 . . .
}
```

The class name denotes:

- a *module* for defining the members of the class (e.g. methods, fields),
- a *data type* for references to instances of that class or any of its subclasses, and
- a *constructor* for instances of that specific class

Java lacks an explicit pointer facility but instead is "reference-based": declaring a variable of class Fum reserves space only for a reference to an object. The reference, null by default, can designate an allocated instance from class Fum or from any of its subclasses. Garbage collection is provided.

Ada supplies separate features — the package, the tagged type, and the standard function facility — to capture the several purposes of a Java class name. A Java class thus generally corresponds to an Ada package whose specification immediately declares a tagged type. Since Ada is a traditional stack-based language where references (access values) need to be explicit, an Ada package declaring a tagged type T will generally declare an access-to-T'Class type. A function (possibly parameterized) delivering a value of type T corresponds to a general Java constructor. In simple situations a no-arg constructor may be modeled by default initializations for fields in the tagged type, and a constructor with arguments can sometimes be modeled by discriminants to the tagged type.

An Ada implementation is permitted but not required to supply garbage collection, and thus the application program generally needs to attend to storage reclamation through unchecked deallocation, storage pools, or controlled types.

Java uses traditional OOP method invocation syntax: an instance method foo from class Bar is invoked via ref.foo(parameters) where ref is a (non-null) reference to an object of class Bar or any of its subclasses; ref is passed as an implicit parameter named this. Ada 2005 allows the same syntax, but the target of the operation corresponds to an explicit formal parameter (rather than an implicit this parameter as in Java).

An Ada tagged type has data components only, and these components are always per-instance. Java allows a per-instance field to be declared final (meaning that it is a constant), whereas in Ada a record component other than a discriminant is always a variable rather than a constant.

Both languages allow setting a default value for a field/component.

A Java instance method takes an implicit parameter, this, which is an object reference. The corresponding Ada construct is a primitive subprogram taking an explicit parameter of the tagged type; a parameter of a tagged type is passed by reference. A Java static data member ("class variable") or static method ("class method") is modeled in Ada by a variable or subprogram declared in the same package as the tagged type.

The languages' different philosophies towards pointers lead to different trade-offs. In Java, the implementation of objects (including arrays) through implicit references, and the existence of automatic storage reclamation, offer dynamic flexibility and notational succinctness, and free the programmer from the error-prone task of explicitly deallocating storage.[1] However, these same properties prevent Java from being used as a systems programming language. There is no way in Java to define a type that directly models, say, a data structure comprising an integer, a sequence of characters, and some bit flags, with each field at a particular offset. Instead, one must define the data structure in another language and then resort to native methods to access the components.

In Ada the choice of indirection in data structure representation is always explicit in the program. If one declares a `String`, then the array's storage is reserved directly as part of the elaboration of the declaration. The benefits are flexibility of style (the programmer, not the language, decides when indirection will be used), and run-time efficiency both in data space and time. Ada's discriminant facility allows defining a parameterized type with declaration-time control over size (number of elements in a component that is an array) and shape (which variant is present). Java has no such mechanism. The drawbacks to Ada's approach are some notational overhead to declare the necessary access types, run-time implementation complexity to deal with issues such as functions returning values of "unconstrained" types, and the need for the programmer to take care of dynamic storage management.

Both Java and Ada support abstract classes and abstract methods for such classes. The Ada terminology for these concepts is *abstract type* and *abstract operation*. In both languages an abstract class with abstract methods is to be completed when extended by a non-abstract class. An abstract class in Java can be used to work around Java's omission of a facility for passing methods as parameters, i.e., what in other languages would be called a pointer to a function.

3 Encapsulation and Visibility

3.1 Access Control

Both Java and Ada have mechanisms that enforce *encapsulation*; i.e., that control the access to declarations so that only those parts of the program with a "need to know" may reference the declared entities. Java accomplishes this with an *access control modifier* that accompanies a class or any of its members.

- A class may be declared `public`, in which case its name is accessible anywhere its containing package is accessible. If a class is not specified as public, then it is accessible only from within the same package.
- A member is only accessible where its class is accessible, and an access control modifier may impose further restrictions.
  - A `public` member has the same accessibility as its containing class.

---

[1] Garbage collection does not prevent storage leaks; e.g. an infinite loop may add a new element to a list at each iteration.

- A **protected** member is accessible to code in the same package, and also to subclasses.
- A **private** member is accessible only to code in the same class.
- If no access control modifier is supplied, then the effect is known as "package" accessibility: the member is accessible only to code in the same package.

The location of a declaration in an Ada package (visible part, private part, body) models the accessibility of the corresponding method or static field in Java (public, protected, and private, respectively). There is no direct Ada analog to Java's "package" accessibility. Moreover, modeling a Java class that contains a private per-instance data member in Ada requires some circumlocution: a tagged private type with a component that is an access value to an incomplete type whose full declaration is in the package body.

Ada's subtype facility provides a convenient way to show a program's intent; e.g.:

```
subtype SSN is String;
```

Lacking such a mechanism, Java requires defining a new class:

```
class SSN{ String s; }
```

but that induces run-time overhead; creating an **SSN** involves allocating not just the **String** object but also the **SSN** that contains a reference to the **String**.

3.2 "Final" Entities

Java allows the programmer to specify an entity as **final**, implying that its properties are frozen at the point of declaration. If a per-instance method in a class is declared final, then each subclass inherits the method's implementation and is not allowed to override it. (The application of **final** to a static method makes no sense semantically, since static methods are not inherited, but is permitted.) If a class itself is declared final, then no subclasses of it can be declared. If a variable is declared final, then it is a constant after its initialization.

The application of **final** to a method or class enables certain optimizations; for example, the invocation of a final method can be compiled with static rather than dynamic binding, since the called method is the same for each class in the hierarchy.

Java's notion of "final" has several analogs in Ada's semantic model. A final static variable directly corresponds to an Ada constant. A "blank final" instance variable corresponds to an Ada discriminant, which is set to a constant value when an object is created. A final method (which ensures that the same code is used for all classes in the hierarchy) somewhat corresponds to an Ada subprogram taking a class-wide parameter.

3.3 Separation of Interface and Implementation

Perhaps surprisingly, given the otherwise careful attention paid to encapsulation, Java does not separate a class into a specification and a body. Rather, the method bodies occur physically within the class declaration, thus revealing to the user of the class more information than is needed, and imposing recompilation costs when, for example, a method implementation changes. If one wants to make available the source code for a set of classes that reveals only the methods' signatures (and not their implementation) than a tool is needed to extract this from the compilable units.

Ada enforces a strict separation between a unit's specification and its body; the "package specs" that comprise a system's interface are legitimate compilation units and do not contain algorithmic code. The latter forms the implementation and is found in the package bodies. The price for the specification/body separation is some additional complexity in language semantics. For example, Ada is susceptible to "access before elaboration" problems, a sometimes subtle runtime error in which a subprogram is invoked before its body has been elaborated. Java allows forward references to classes and methods and thus the concept of "access before elaboration" does not arise. However, Java's rules for class and object initialization involve a variety of syntactic and semantic subtleties (static initializers, initialization blocks, class loading) and, although deterministic, are the source of traps and pitfalls, especially for interdependent classes.

3.4   Parameter Protection

Ada provides parameter modes (`in`, `out`, `in out`) that control whether the actual parameter may be updated by the called subprogram. Thus the programmer knows by reading a subprogram's specification whether its parameters may be updated.

Ada's access parameter mechanism provides a somewhat analogous facility, with the Ada 2005 `access constant` parameter indicating that the designated object may not be assigned via the formal parameter.

Java has no such mechanism: a method's implementation has read/write access to the objects denoted by its reference-type parameters. Thus in Java there is no way to tell from a method's signature whether it updates either the object denoted by its `this` parameter or the objects denoted by any other reference-type formal parameters. Research is underway on annotations to mark a formal parameter as "readonly" (yielding the same effect as Ada 2005's `access constant` parameters), e.g. [4]) but these are not in the Java language, and indeed they raise some semantic issues (e.g., [5]).

Java's "call by value" semantics implies that a modification to a formal parameter of a primitive type has no effect on the actual parameter. In order to update, say, an `int`, the programmer must either declare a class with an `int` member or use an `int` array with one element. Both styles are clumsier and less efficient than Ada's approach with an `out`, `in out`, or `access` parameter.

3.5   Data Abstraction and Type Differentiation

da's private type facility supports *data abstraction*: the ability to define a data type while exposing only the interface and hiding the representation. A variable of a private type is represented directly, not through a reference, and its operations are bound statically. Data abstraction in Java is part of the OO model, resulting in run-time costs for indirection, heap management, and dynamic binding.

A somewhat related facility is the ability to partition data into different types based on their operations, so that mismatches are caught at compile time. Ada's derived type and numeric type features satisfy these goals. Java does not have an analogous mechanism for its primitive types.

4   Modularization

Java has two main mechanisms for modularization and namespace control: the package and the class. Ada does not have a direct analog to the Java package; the way in which compilation unit names are made available to the Ada compiler is implementation dependent. On the other hand, Java does not have a feature with the functionality of Ada's child units, a facility that allows a hierarchical namespace for compilation units. Inner classes in Java need to be physically nested within a "top level" class and are analogous to nested packages, not child packages, in Ada.

In Ada, related "classes" (tagged types) may be defined in the same module (package). Although a somewhat similar semantic effect may be achieved in Java by defining static inner classes in an enclosing class, this usage is a bit clumsy and in practice most "interesting" classes are defined at the top level.

Classes in Java may be interdependent; the implicit reference semantics avoid what would otherwise be a circularity problem. For example:

```
class Foo{ Bar b; }
class Bar{ Foo f; }
```

Modeling such classes was a problem in Ada 95, but the Ada 2005 limited with mechanism, coupled with a generalization of anonymous access types, provides the necessary functionality:

```
limited with Bar_Pkg;              limited with Foo_Pkg;
package Foo_Pkg is                 package Bar_Pkg is
   type Foo is tagged                 type Bar is tagged
     record                             record
       B : access Bar_Pkg.Bar;            F : access Foo_Pkg.Foo;
     end record ;                       end record;
end Foo_Pkg;                       end Bar_Pkg;
```

5   Inheritance

Java and Ada support class hierarchies based on single inheritance, and also provide a simple form of multiple inheritance through a mechanism known as an interface.[2] Inheritance in Java is realized through class extension, and in Ada through type extension coupled with child package visibility semantics.

5.1   Simple Inheritance

In Java, each non-private instance method defined in the superclass is implicitly inherited by the subclass, with the superclass's implementation. The subclass may override with its own implementation any of these that the superclass did not specify as final. The `super.member` notation is used within an instance method to reference fields or methods defined for the immediate superclass. Static methods are not inherited.

If a Java class does not explicitly extend another class, then it implicitly extends the ultimate ancestral class `Object`. The `Object` class allows the user to define "generic"[3] container classes, heterogeneous arrays, and similar constructs.

Ada has no immediate analog to Java's `Object` class, although the types `Controlled` and `Limited_Controlled` in `Ada.Finalization` serve this role to some extent. This absence is not critical, since Ada's generic facility allows defining container data structures, and an access value designating a class-wide type offers heterogeneity. On the other hand, Java's provision of a "root" class is convenient since a number of useful methods are defined there, such as `toString()`.

Ada allows a (primitive) procedure to be declared as `null`. This is especially useful for abstract tagged types and interface types, since it is often desirable to have a simple non-abstract descendant type with a default "no-op" behavior for some (perhaps all) of the abstract procedures. In Java, the program must explicitly define a so-called "adapter" class, with empty bodies for the methods, to get this effect.

Both Java and Ada allow a reference to be viewed as though it designates an object of a different type in the same class hierarchy. In Java this is known as a *cast*, in Ada it is a *view conversion* to a class-wide type. The semantics is roughly the same in both languages, with cast/conversion always allowed "towards the root", and also permitted "away from the root" but with a run-time check that the designated object is in the target class or one of its subclasses. Unless the source type is either a (direct or indirect) ancestor or descendant of the target type, the cast/conversion is illegal in both languages.

In Java, selecting a member from a cast expression provides static binding using the reference type of the cast when the member is a field, but dynamic binding using the type of the designated instance when the member is a method. Strictly speaking, Ada has the same semantics (for a view conversion to a class-wide type), but Ada does not allow the same component name to be used in both a parent record and an extension part, so the issue of static versus dynamic interpretation of field names does not arise.

---

[2] Ada's interface feature, introduced in Ada 2005, was heavily influenced by its Java counterpart.

[3] Java 1.5 has introduced a generic mechanism that provides additional functionality; it is outside the scope of this paper.

A common OOP style is "passing the buck": the implementation of a method for a subclass invokes the overridden method from the superclass. Java uses a special syntax, `super.method(...)`, for this effect, but it applies only to the immediate superclass. The Ada style is to invoke the desired subprogram on a view conversion of the parameter to the desired ancestor specific tagged type. This is generally the immediate ancestor but in general may be at any higher level.

OOP provides the opportunity to make several kinds of mistakes. *Unintended inheritance* occurs when an instance method that is intended to override a superclass method is entered incorrectly, for example by misspelling the method name. The resulting program is still legal, and the superclass's method is implicitly inherited (rather than overridden), which was not the programmer's intent. In the other direction, *unintended overriding* occurs when an overridable instance method is added to an existing superclass and it has the same signature as a method already present in some subclass. When the subclass is recompiled, the previously defined method now overrides the method that was added to the superclass. This is likely to be an error.

In Java, unintended inheritance can be prevented by prepending the `@Override` annotation (added in Java 1.5) to the method signature. There is no language feature to prevent unintended overriding.

Ada 2005 has introduced syntax to prevent both sorts of errors, since a subprogram may be specified as `overriding` or `not overriding`.

5.2   Multiple Inheritance and Interfaces

Multiple inheritance — the ability to define a class that inherits from more than one ancestor — is a controversial topic in OO language design. Although providing expressive power, it also complicates the language semantics and the compiler implementation. C++ provides direct linguistic support (see [6] and [7] for arguments pro and con), as do Eiffel and Common Lisp; on the other hand, Smalltalk and Simula provide only single inheritance.

Java takes an intermediate position. Recognizing the problems associated with implementation inheritance, Java allows a class to extend only one superclass. However, Java has a class-like construct known as an *interface* and allows a class to inherit from — or, in Java parlance, *implement* — one or more interfaces. Thus a user- defined class always extends exactly one superclass, either `Object` by default or else a class identified in an `extends` clause, but may implement an arbitrary number of interfaces.

Like a class, an interface is a reference type, and it is legal to declare a variable of an interface type. Like an abstract class, an interface does not allow creation of instances.

- Each method defined by an interface is implicitly abstract (that is, it lacks an implementation) and public
- An interface is not allowed to have any static methods
- Each variable in an interface is implicitly static and final (constant)

An interface thus has no implementation and no "state". When a class implements an interface, it must provide a "body" for each method declared in the interface. The `instanceof` operator may be used to test whether an object is of a class that implements a particular interface.

Ada 2005's *interface types* are similar to the Java mechanism, providing single inheritance of implementation and multiple inheritance of specifications. A tagged type can have a parent that it extends, and one or more interfaces that it implements. An interface is an abstract type with no components. A non-abstract type that implements an interface must provide bodies for all inherited operations other than null procedures.

Ada provides a taxonomy of interfaces that unifies polymorphism and concurrency; this unification is a major advance in programming language design. If a type is declared to be a synchronized interface, it can be implemented either by a task type or a protected type. Thus an algorithm that uses such an interface describes an abstraction that can be implemented either with concurrent entities that have independent threads of control, or with passive data structures provided with locking and exclusive access. Java's `Runnnable` interface is somewhat similar but not as expressive.

```
type I1 is interface;
function Retrieve (Obj : I1) return integer is abstract;
procedure Modify (Obj : in out I1) is null;
...
type I2 is interface;
procedure Merge (Obj1, Obj2 : in out I2) is abstract;
...
type Root is tagged record
   Value : Integer;
end Root;
type Thing is new Root and I1 and I2 with record
   Size : Long_Float;
end record;
```

The package that contains the declaration of `Thing` must include declarations for operations `Retrieve` and `Merge`, which are abstract in its ancestors. Procedure `Modify` is declared as a null procedure and does not need to be overridden.

In both Java and Ada it is possible to define interfaces that cannot be jointly implemented. In Java the problem arises because overloading is not allowed based on method result. Thus there is no class that can implement both of the following interfaces:

```
interface I1{ void foo(); }
interface I2{ int foo(); }
```

In Ada the problem arises when two profiles differ in a formal parameter's subtype:

```
type I1 is interface;
procedure P(I : I1; N : Natural) is abstract;

type I2 is interface;
procedure P(I : I2; N : Integer) is abstract;
```

The clash is preventable in Ada, since one can adopt the convention that subprograms for interface types take parameters that are declared with base types and not subtypes. There is no such straightforward solution in Java, and incompatible interfaces can thus interfere with reuse and system composition.

5.3 Covariance

Java 1.5 added a feature that is sometimes known in OOP parlance as "covariance": the result type in an overriding method may be a subclass of the type that would be used if the method were inherited instead of overridden. As an example:

```
class Doctor{ ... }
class Hospital{
    Doctor chief(){ ... } // The chief of a Hospital is a Doctor
}
class EyeDoctor extends Doctor{...}
class EyeHospital extends Hospital{
    @overriding
    EyeDoctor chief(){ ... }
    // The chief of an EyeHospital is an EyeDoctor
}
```

The declaration of `EyeHospital.chief()` would have been an illegal overloading in earlier versions of Java, but it is considered as an overriding method (emphasized by the annotation) in Java 1.5.

The Ada version of this example would be expressed a bit differently. Instead of declaring `Chief` for `Hospital` to return `Doctor` (which would be inherited by `EyeHospital` even if an explicit `Chief` were declared there to return an `EyeDoctor`), the `Chief` function for `Hospital` should be declared to return `Doctor'Class`. Then it could be overridden for `EyeHospital`, with result type still `Doctor'Class`, but with the returned value now an `EyeDoctor`. Thus a class-wide result type has the effect of covariance without the need for a special rule.

6   Summary of Overloading, Polymorphism and Dynamic Binding

Java and Ada both allow overloading, but Ada is more general in allowing overloading for operator symbols and also overloading of functions based on the result type.

Polymorphism, the ability of a variable to be in different classes of an inheritance hierarchy at different times, is implicit in Java. If p is declared as a reference to class C, then p can designate an instance of either C or any of its direct or indirect subclasses. In contrast, polymorphism is explicit in Ada, through a variable of a class-wide type, or access-to-classwide type. In Java a variable of type Object is completely polymorphic, capable of designating an object from any class. The closest Ada analog is a variable of an access type whose designated type is Ada.Finalization.Controlled'Class, which can designate an object of any type derived from the predefined type Controlled.

Instance method invocation in Java is in general bound dynamically: in a call p.foo() the version of foo() that is invoked is the one defined by the class of the object that p designates. Static binding applies, however, in several situations: an invocation super.method(...); an invocation of a final method; or an invocation of a private method (from within the class defining the method). A static method is also bound statically. Ada subprograms calls are in general bound statically: dynamic binding only occurs when the actual parameter is of a(n) (access-to) class-wide type T'Class and the called subprogram is a primitive operation for the tagged type T.

In Java there is an important (but perhaps subtle) difference in the semantics between an invocation of a method on super versus on any other reference. If p is a reference to an object of class C, then the invocation p.foo() is dynamically bound based on the type of the designated object, but super.foo() is statically resolved to foo() defined for C's superclass. Confusingly, this.foo() is bound dynamically, in contrast to super.foo(). The Ada view conversion approach has more consistent semantics.

In Ada, an object X of a class-wide type T1'Class can be "view converted" to a specific tagged type T2 that is either a descendant or ancestor of T1, with a run-time check that X is in T2'Class if T2 is a descendant of T1. If the view conversion T2(X) is passed as an actual parameter to a primitive operation of T2, the binding is static, not dynamic. Java lacks an equivalent facility for forcing static binding. Even if a reference x to a t1 object is cast to type t2, a method invocation ((t2)x).f() is dynamically bound to the method f() in t1, not the version in t2. The Ada analog to a Java cast is thus a view conversion to a class-wide type, not to a specific type.

In Ada it is possible to obtain dynamic binding through access values designating aliased class-wide variables rather than allocated objects; this avoids the overhead of heap management. Java has no such mechanism: all objects go on the heap.

7   User-Controlled Basic Behavior

A number of operations dictate the fundamental behavior for instances of a data type, including construction/initialization and finalization. Both Java and Ada allow the author of the type to specify these operations' availability and implementation, though with some stylistic and semantic differences.

7.1 Construction/Initialization

A Java class may include one or more constructors; a constructor is similar to a method but with special syntax and semantics; it is called during object creation/allocation.

A constructor has the same name as the class and lacks a return type. It may have a **throws** clause.[4] Java's overloading rules allow the declaration of multiple constructors; this is a common style. A constructor is invoked as an effect of an object allocation, after the object's instance variables have been set to their default values and after any explicit initializers have been executed.

An explicit constructor invocation is only permitted as the first statement of another constructor; the invocation will either specify **this** (for a constructor in the same class) or **super** (for a constructor in the superclass). If the first statement of a constructor is not an explicit invocation of another constructor, then an implicit call of the no-arg superclass constructor **super()** is inserted. (It is an error if no such constructor is accessible in the superclass.)

A subtle error in Java is to invoke an instance method for a class in a constructor for that class. Since a constructor is called before the explicit initializations of the instance fields have been performed, there is the risk of the constructor accessing a field and obtaining the language-defined default value (whatever corresponds to zero for that type) rather than the intended initialized value.

Ada has no immediate analog to Java constructors, but simulates their effect through functions returning a value of the given type, initialization procedures, and controlled types. A type derived from **Controlled** can be provided with an explicit **Initialize** procedure that is invoked whenever an object of the type is created. Controlled types can also be provided with an **Adjust** procedure, which is invoked whenever an object of the type is assigned to another. This corresponds to the actions of a C++ copy constructor. The closest analog to **Adjust** in Java is the control over cloning (through the **Cloneable** interface and the **clone()** method inherited from **Object**).

7.2 Finalization

The root class **java.lang.Object** supplies a protected method **finalize()** that can be overridden to do any resource cleanup required before the object is garbage collected. For example, if an object contains fields that reference open files, then these files should be closed when the object is reclaimed, versus waiting until program termination.

Finalization in Ada differs from Java both stylistically and semantically. Since Ada does not guarantee garbage collection, finalization is often used in Ada to obtain type-specific storage management such as reference counts. In Java there

---

[4] Although propagating an exception from a constructor may appear to risk leaving the new object in an inconsistent state, it would only cause problems in the rare situation where the constructor had first copied the **this** reference to a static field. Programming conventions (deferring such assignments until immediately before returning) would avoid such problems.

is no need for finalize to do storage reclamation. Semantically, **Finalize** is called in Ada not only when a controlled object is deallocated but also when it goes out of scope or is the target of an assignment. Moreover, since the Java language does not define when garbage collection occurs, a programmer cannot predict exactly when **finalize()** will be called, or the order in which finalizers are executed. In fact, the JVM may exit without garbage collecting all outstanding objects,

Table 1. *Comparison of OOP in Ada 2005 and Java*

	Ada 2005	**Java**
Class	• Class as module is package • Class as data template is (discriminated) tagged type	• Combines module and data template
Pointers	• Explicit (access values)	• Implicit
Storage reclamation	• Garbage collection, if provided by implementation • Controlled type or storage pool defined by class author • Unchecked deallocation by application programmer	• Implementation-provided garbage collection (no explicit free)
Instance method invocation	• subprogram(obj,...) • obj.subprogram(...)	• obj.method(...)
Inheritable entity	• Primitive subprogram for a tagged type	• Non-private, non-final instance method
Single inheritance	• A type that is derived from a tagged type	• A class that extends a superclass
Multiple inheritance	• A type that is derived from a tagged type and one or more interface types	• A class that extends a superclass and implements one or more interfaces
Polymorphism	• Explicit through object of (access to) class-wide type	• Implicit for any variable of a class or interface type
Method binding	• Static except for primitive operation invoked on parameter of (access to) class-wide type	• Dynamic except for methods that are static, final, private, or invoked on super
Fundamental operations	• Controlled types (Initialize, Finalize, Adjust)	• Constructors • finalize() • clone • equals()
Encapsulation	• Placement of entity declaration in a package (visible part, private part, body) • Child unit	• Access modifier (public, protected, private, none) for class member

implying that some finalizers might never be invoked. In brief, finalization in Java has rather ill-defined semantics; the programmer cannot know when, if at all, `finalize()` is invoked on a given object.

A Java object is not necessarily freed immediately after being finalized, since the `finalize()` method may have stored its `this` parameter in an outer variable, thus "resurrecting" it ([8], p. 114). Nonetheless the JVM invokes `finalize()` only once. In Ada, under some circumstances the `Finalize` procedure will be invoked automatically several times on the same object.[5] The programmer can attend to such a possibility by implementing `Finalize` to be "idempotent" (i.e. applying it multiple times has the same effect as applying it once), for example by storing a `Boolean` component in the controlled object that keeps track of whether finalization has already occurred.

In Java, an exception thrown by `finalize()` is lost (i.e., not propagated), despite the fact that the signature for `finalize` in class `Object` has a `throws` clause. In Ada it is a bounded error for a `Finalize` procedure to propagate an exception.

8   Conclusions

As can be seen in the comparison summary (Table 1), both Ada and Java are *bona fide* Object-Oriented languages. Java treats object orientation as its central mission; this brings a number of advantages (consistent integration of features, safe automatic storage reclamation, dynamic flexibility in data structures) but also some drawbacks (run-time overhead due to implicit heap usage and management, absence of several fundamental data structuring facilities, awkwardness in applying an OO style to a problem whose essence is process/function-related; implementation challenges in trying to deploy Java in domains requiring real-time predictability or safety-critical certification). Ada treats object orientation as one methodology, but not necessarily the only one, that might be appropriate for a software developer, and hence its OO support complements and supplements a more traditional set of stack-based "third-generation language" features. For example, in many situations simple Ada83-style data encapsulation (Ada private types) will be sufficient; the full generality of OOP is not needed.

Ada's advantages include run-time efficiency — a program only incurs heap management costs if it explicitly uses dynamic allocation — design method neutrality, and standardization. On the other hand, Ada induces a heavier notation and the need for applications to attend to storage management versus relying on a garbage collector.

Java 1.5 brought some relatively minor enhancements to its OOP support:[6] the ability for an overriding method to specify a result type that is a subclass of

---

[5] This will occur when `Finalize` is first invoked implicitly during assignment to an object of a non-limited controlled type, and the object subsequently undergoes finalization ([9], §7.6.1).

[6] Templates are a major new feature introduced in Java 1.5 and are based on OOP semantics, but from a linguistic point of view they offer orthogonal functionality.

the result type of the method that otherwise would have been inherited, and an annotation to indicate that a method is overriding. In contrast, the Ada 2005 OOP enhancements were significant, including `object.subprogram()` notation, interface types, syntax to make explicit a subprogram's intent as either overriding or not overriding, and features such as `limited with` clauses that make it easier to specify cyclic dependences across modules. With these sorts of improvements, Ada 2005 offers at least comparable OOP support to Java's and in some ways surpasses it.

Acknowledgements

The author is grateful to Ed Schonberg and Bob Duff (AdaCore), and to the anonymous referees, for their commments and suggestions.

References

1. ISO/IEC JTC1/SC 22/WG 9. Ada Reference Manual – ISO/IEC 8652:2007(E) with Technical Corrigendum 1 and Amendment 1 – Language and Standard Libraries (2007)
2. Gosling, J., Joy, B., Steele, G., Bracha, G.: The Java Language Specification, 3rd edn. Addison-Wesley, Reading (2005)
3. Benjamin, M., Brosgol, A.: Comparison of the Object-Oriented Features of Ada 95 and Java. In: Proc. TRI-Ada 1997. ACM, New York (1997)
4. Tschantz, M.S.: Javari: Adding Reference Immutability to Java. Master's thesis, Massachusetts Institute Of Technology (August 2006)
5. Boyland, J.: Why we should not add readonly to Java (yet). In: ECOOP 2005 Workshop FTfJP, vol. 5(5) (June 2006) (special issue)
6. Waldo, J.: The case for multiple inheritance in C++. In: Waldo, J. (ed.) The Evolution of C++, pp. 111–120. MIT Press, Cambridge (1993)
7. Cargill, T.A.: The case against multiple inheritance in C++. In: Waldo, J. (ed.) The Evolution of C++, pp. 101–110. MIT Press, Cambridge (1993)
8. Flanagan, D.: Java in a Nutshell, 5th edn. O'Reilly & Associates, Sebastopol (2005)
9. ISO/IEC JTC1/SC 22/WG 9. Annotated Ada Reference Manual – ISO/IEC 8652:2007(E) with Technical Corrigendum 1 and Amendment 1 – Language and Standard Libraries (2007)

A Framework for CFG-Based Static Program Analysis of Ada Programs

Raul Fechete, Georg Kienesberger, and Johann Blieberger

Institute for Computer-Aided Automation, TU Vienna
Treitlstr. 1-3, A-1040 Vienna, Austria
{fechete,kienes,blieb}@auto.tuwien.ac.at

Abstract. The control flow graph is the basis for many code optimisation and analysis techniques. We introduce a new framework for the construction of powerful CFG-based representations of arbitrary Ada programs. The generated data holds extensive information about the original Ada source, such as visibility, package structure and type definitions and provides means for complete interprocedural analysis. We use ASIS-for-GNAT as an interface to the Ada environment and extract the needed information in a single traversal of the provided syntax trees. In addition, further refinement of the resulting data structures is done.

1 Introduction

Many control and data flow analysis approaches [1,2,3,4,5,6] rely on the representation of a program in form of a *control flow graph* (CFG) [7].

We introduce a framework that generates CFG-based data structures holding comprehensive information about the original Ada source. The packages and CFGs of the input program are structured in trees according to their hierarchical organisation. We also use trees to represent complex expressions, allowing an in-depth analysis of the control flow. Types and variables are saved together with their complete definitions, thereby providing means to track them over several inheritance levels. Furthermore, we facilitate interprocedural analysis by referencing the target CFG in each subprogram call.

During the transformation, we extract the needed information from the *abstract syntax trees* (AST) [7] provided by ASIS-for-GNAT. Afterwards, in a post transformation phase, we further refine the resulting structures.

2 The Library

We designed *Ast2Cfg* as a library that uses ASIS [8] to get the information that is needed to build the CFG for a given Ada program. In fact we use the ASIS-for-GNAT implementation of the ASIS standard. Therefore, the so-called *tree files* for an Ada program, which are generated by GNAT [9], are used as input. Then ASIS provides us with the abstract syntax tree of the input program. During the traversal of this AST, which is done using *depth first search* (DFS)

F. Kordon and T. Vardanega (Eds.): Ada-Europe 2008, LNCS 5026, pp. 130–143, 2008.

```
with Ada.Text_IO; use Ada.Text_IO; with Ast2Cfg.Pkgs; use Ast2Cfg.Pkgs;
with Ast2Cfg.Control; with Ast2Cfg.Flow_World; with Ast2Cfg.Output;

procedure Run is
    World: Ast2Cfg.Flow_World.World_Object_Ptr;
    Pkgs: Pkg_Class_Ptr_List.Object;
    Pkg:  Pkg_Class_Ptr := null;
begin
    -- Initialisations
    Ast2Cfg.Output.Set_Level(Ast2Cfg.Output.Warning);
    Ast2Cfg.Control.Init;

    -- Fill the World with flow data
    World := Ast2Cfg.Control.Generate;

    -- Output the name of all top-level packages
    Pkgs := Ast2Cfg.Flow_World.Get_Pkgs(World.all);
    Pkg_Class_Ptr_List.Reset(Pkgs);
    while Pkg_Class_Ptr_List.Has_Next(Pkgs) loop
        Pkg_Class_Ptr_List.Get_Next(Pkgs, Pkg);
        Put_Line(Get_Name(Pkg.all));
    end loop;

    -- Finalisation
    Ast2Cfg.Control.Final;
end Run;
```

Fig. 1. A small application using Ast2Cfg

[10], we simultaneously build the corresponding CFG. Next, right after some refinement, the control flow information is made available to the library user in form of a single object, the *flow world*. Figure 1 shows a small application that uses Ast2Cfg to output the name of all top-level packages of the adt-files in the current directory.

We already developed a simple program, called *Cfg2Dot*, that uses the Ast2Cfg library to output the CFG for a program in dot graphics format [11]. Ast2Cfg, Cfg2Dot and additional documentation [12] are available from http://cfg.w3x.org.

2.1 The World Object

All information gathered during the transformation phase is saved in an object of type World_Object. It contains a list of package objects (Pkg_Object) that correspond to the top-level packages of the analysed Ada program.

Pkg_Object is derived from the abstract Flow_Object. The same applies to CFG_Object, that represents a control flow, and Node_Object, which is used by CFG_Object. Also, as described in detail below, each of these types has a series of subclasses such that a more fine-grained classification is possible. Where necessary, the derived types are also grouped into specifications and bodies. Figure 2 shows an overview of the class hierarchy where rectangles with dashed lines represent abstract types and those with solid lines concrete ones.

Since in Ada subprograms and packages may be declared within each other we have to keep track of such nesting relationships. Every flow object has a list of predecessors and successors. While node objects use those lists to build up a CFG, package and CFG objects use them to represent the nesting structure we

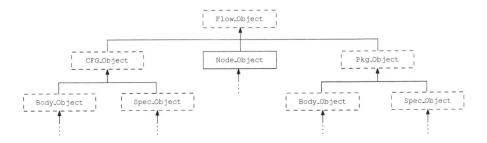

Fig. 2. An overview of the class hierarchy for the flow types

call *Pkg/CFG tree*. In other words, if B is declared within A, B is a successor of A and A a predecessor of B.

Another important tree structure is the *parameter tree* that we generate whenever an expression is encountered. A parameter tree is saved directly in the flow object that contains the expression and holds information on the used variables, functions, etc. and their nesting. As a result a parameter tree is a complete hierarchical representation of an expression, allowing the user to implement powerful static analysis algorithms.

Figure 3 shows the Cfg2Dot output for the single assignment statement `C(1) := Outer(A, Inner(X => B))`; where A and B are variables, C is an array and `Inner` and `Outer` are functions. The CFG consists of a single assignment node with two parameter trees, highlighted by dashed lines: one for the part to the left of the assignment operator and one for the right hand side. Every level in the parameter tree represents a nesting level in the underlying expression.

Flow Object. Every flow object has a unique id which may be tested for equality. In addition, flow objects have names. However, for node objects which are derived from flow objects, the name is empty in most cases. Furthermore, lists of variable declarations, generic formal parameters and renamings are available. Finally, we also store a list of with, use and use type clauses in every flow object.

CFG Types. CFG objects use node objects to represent the control flow information of different Ada entities like subprograms, blocks, initialisation sequences etc. Therefore in every CFG object we save a reference to the root node, the total number of nodes (without those in parameter trees) and, since many CFG objects represent subprograms, a list of parameters.

CFG_Object itself is declared abstract, hence all actual CFG objects have to be of one of the more specific, concrete subtypes. In the simplest case a subprogram has to be represented, which is done by either creating a Proc_Object for a procedure and, in case of a function, a Func_Object. For a *block*, which is located within some other CFG object, we create a separate Block_Object. Next we insert a *call node*, which is used to represent a subprogram call, at the position where the block used to be within the enclosing CFG. So, in fact,

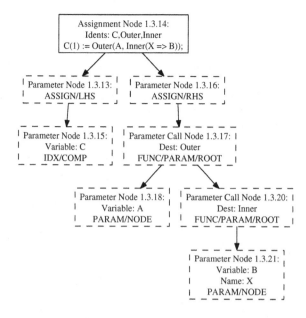

Fig. 3. A node with two parameter trees

a block is handled like a parameterless procedure, called when the block is declared. We transform an initialisation sequence of a package body into a so-called Init_Object and create an Except_Object for every exception handler.

In case we encounter a task body, a Task_Object is created where every accept block is represented separately by an Entry_Object. As it was the case with simple blocks, we link such an Entry_Object to its enclosing task by using a call node. Furthermore, we also map the protected entries of a protected object to entry objects. To represent the abortable part of a select – then abort statement we use an Abort_Object, which is, again, linked to the enclosing CFG using a call node.

Finally, there are three CFG objects which actually do not contain any control flow information. The main reason why we use them is that because of their position in the Pkg/CFG tree we are able to keep track where they are defined and can gain visibility information later on. So for a task type declaration we create a Task_Type_Object, while a simple task specification is represented by a Single_Task_Object. Finally, whenever we encounter a generic procedure or a generic function specification we create a Generic_Object.

Package Types. The Pkg_Object, like the CFG_Object, is abstract, which is why variables have to be of a more specific subtype. The main purpose of package objects is to help building the Pkg/CFG tree, and therefore the successor and predecessor lists are the most important components. Another component every package object except for the Prot_Object and the Def_Object has, is a list of the variables that are declared within.

For uniformity reasons we introduce an artificial default package of type Def_Object which contains CFGs that do not have an enclosing package such as library level procedures. A Prot_Object represents the body of a protected object or type, which may contain subprograms and entries. We map the specification that belongs to such a Prot_Object to a Prot_Type_Object in case of a protected type declaration and to a Single_ Prot_Object otherwise. The body of a generic package requires no special handling, however, we transform the corresponding specification into a Gen_Object.

Finally, for representing ordinary packages not mentioned above, we use a Simple_Spec_Object and, in case there is an accompanying body, a Simple_Body_Object.

Node Types. Any node that is not treated specifically as described below is of type Node_Object. If a statement has a label, then the label is saved as the name of the node representing this statement. Also, for every node we store a string that holds at least part of the code that this node is representing. Furthermore, all nodes have a *right hand side parameter tree*, and the Assign_Node_Object, which corresponds to an assignment statement, also has a *left hand side parameter tree* for the part to the left of the assignment operator. Finally, for every node we save the Asis.Element that is the source of this node. The Asis.Element can be seen as a link back into the ASIS AST. Consequently additional information can be acquired by analysing the AST starting at the element of an arbitrary node.

As already mentioned, we not only use a Call_Node_Object for the representation of a subprogram call, but also in several situations that are treated similarly. Clearly, the most important component of a call node is the reference to its destination CFG. We derived several subtypes from Call_Node_Object to convey additional information on the type of the call. So, for example we use an Accept_Node_Object to link an Entry_Object to its enclosing task body, while we represent a call of such an entry with an Entry_Call_Node_Object. Likewise an Abort_Node_Object links the abortable part of a select – then abort statement into its CFG. Finally, there is a subtype of Call_Node_Object that we exclusively use within parameter trees to represent a function call: the Param_Call_Node_Object.

Whenever we encounter a goto we use a Goto_Jump_Node_Object to point to the destination of the goto. Moreover we create an Exit_Jump_Node_Object for every exit statement within a loop. Note that the target of an exit jump node is empty in case it exits the innermost enclosing loop. For a return statement, we also create a special node, which is of type Return_Node_Object. A Loop_Node_Object marks the header of a loop, and the two concrete subtypes enable to distinguish between a while or for loop and a simple loop statement.

A parameter tree is built by nodes of type Param_Node_Object, Param_Alloc_Node_Object and the already mentioned parameter call nodes. We use the Param_Node_Object to save the name of the variable that was supplied as a parameter and the name of the parameter itself, in case it is known. The

Param_Alloc_Node_Object, however, represents a dynamic allocation using the new keyword.

Whenever we encounter an if or case statement, a special header node of type Branch_Node_Object is created so that its successors contain the branching conditions. After such a node with a branching condition the subgraph for the actual branch follows, until control flow is united again in an end node.

3   Transformation

We obtain the control flow data from the AST by using a two-phase mechanism. The first step, the *transformation*, includes extracting information from the tree and building the raw flow structure. The second one, the *post transformation*, further refines the output of the former.

The information retrieval is constructed on an inorder traversal skeleton provided by ASIS. The program walks the tree one node at a time, generating three types of events.

1. A *PreOp* event is triggered when the traversal reaches a node for the first time, before any other processing is done.
2. A *PostOp* event is triggered immediately after the traversal has left a node, as soon as all processing involving it has finished.
3. A *CHF* (child-has-finished) event provides us with a binary relation between a parent and a child node and is thereby context-sensitive. The previous two events, however, are context-insensitive, bearing no information of a node's relatives. CHF is triggered for each of a node's children, right after their processing has finished.

The event triggering traversal imposes a state-machine-like architecture on our transformation mechanism. We employ stacks to hold the current traversal state and three callback functions, one for each event named above. Since each method must be able to handle any of the ASIS node types, all three have a symmetrical structure.

One of the strengths of the ASIS abstract syntax trees is that they employ a relatively small set of node types, to describe any program, regardless of its complexity. To achieve this goal, ASIS combines the available types to ample configurations, creating specialised subtrees.

The Ada syntactical constructs can be divided into classes, with the members of each class sharing a common syntax subtree configuration. Usually, each ASIS type has its own case branch in the callback functions, but we take advantage of the tree similarities, by pulling the corresponding branches together.

As an example, let us consider the variable declarations, the component declarations of the aggregate types and the subprogram parameter specifications. A typical subtree for one of the declarations above holds the name of the new entity, its type and its initialisation expression. The only node that tells us what kind of tree this is, is the root. This information, however, is transparent to the handling mechanism of the tree. The complete information about the new entity

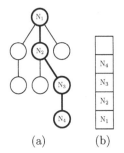
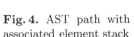

(a)   (b)

Fig. 4. AST path with associated element stack

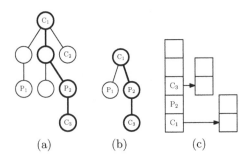

(a)   (b)   (c)

Fig. 5. AST path with associated flow tree, flow stack and node stacks

is gathered in an interim storage common to all the declarations of this class, and only the PostOp handling of the root node decides where the data should be transferred in the flow world.

The example above is also illustrative for the use of the interim storage, the *transformation data container* (TDC). Many ASIS types can, however, be added to the flow world immediately upon being reached. As an example, let us consider the handling of statements. Their flow world counterparts are the CFG nodes, and a statement PreOp triggers automatically the addition of a node to the current flow entity.

3.1   Element Stack

The *element stack* is the backbone of the AST traversal. It holds the path from the tree root to the current node. The stack grows with each PreOp event, as the search goes deeper, and diminishes with each PostOp event, as it returns.

Figure 4(a) shows an AST with the thicker edges and nodes indicating the current traversal state. The nodes in the active path are marked N_1 to N_4 with no regard to their syntactical value in the original program. Figure 4(b) displays the corresponding element stack state.

Keeping only a pointer to the current node is not enough, because for each node in the path we must be able to store additional information. We may need to access this information repeatedly, as the search keeps returning to this element. Such information is the count of already visited children, i.e. the number of CHF events, and the corresponding flow world structure for this node, e.g. a CFG node for a statement or a package pointer for the root of a package declaration subtree.

The element stack also provides us with an additional consistency check. The flow structure on top must also be the current one in the flow world.

3.2   Flow Stack

Ada allows both the nesting of subprograms in packages and vice versa. This fact leads to complex nesting hierarchies. We will represent these relationships in the flow world using a tree structure, that we call the *flow tree*. Its root is the outermost package or CFG. The children of a node in the flow tree represent the structures immediately nested in the construct the parent node stands for. The tree only describes the nesting of packages and CFGs. No information about other nesting relationships, like that of loops, is saved in the flow tree.

Due to similar considerations as in the case of the AST, we will also employ a stack (the *flow stack*) to keep the active path in the current flow tree.

Figure 5(a) depicts an AST with the thicker edges and nodes indicating the current traversal state. The nodes P_1 and P_2 represent packages, whereas C_1 to C_3 represent CFGs. We can clearly see, that the AST describes an Ada program built of a subprogram C_1. Immediately nested in this CFG, are the packages P_1 and P_2 and the CFG C_2. Nested in the package P_2 is the CFG C_3. The purpose of the empty nodes in the same figure, is to underline the fact, that even though a package or CFG has to be situated in the AST subtree rooted in the node of its enclosing structure, it does not, however, from a syntactical point of view, have to be an immediate child of it.

Figure 5(b) displays the current flow tree and the active path in it. Please note that the tree does not hold the CFG C_2, since the AST traversal has not reached it yet.

Figure 5(c) shows the current state of the flow stack. Each CFG on the stack also holds a reference to a node stack (see Sect. 3.3).

3.3   Node Stack

In the vast majority of the cases, an AST statement node undergoes a one-to-one transformation to a CFG node. Each time the traversal reaches a new statement, we add a new node at the end of the presently open CFG. As explained earlier, the current flow structure can be found on top of the flow stack.

We now need a mechanism to keep track of the last node that has been appended. In the standard scenario, the next node will be saved as successor of the former. In some cases, on the other hand, we would need information about several previous nodes, so keeping only one pointer proves to be insufficient. We opt again for a stack structure, but this time, with slightly different semantics.

The *node stack* usually holds only one element, maintaining the pointer to the last node that has been appended. This pointer is replaced each time a new node is added to the CFG. The stack grows only when explicit information about nodes handled in the past is necessary. This need arises in two cases:

1. When processing loops, we must not lose track of the loop head. The last node in the block must be linked back to it.
2. When processing if statements, we must not lose track of the if head. This node must be linked to all the decision branches.

Figure 6(a) depicts the standard scenario: an AST describing a subprogram P with two statements A and B. The nodes are added one after the other to the graph. In each of the two transformation steps, we see the graph and the associated node stack. The stack remains one level high in both cases.

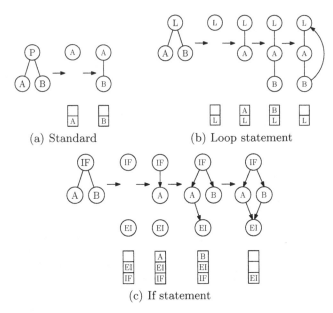

(a) Standard   (b) Loop statement

(c) If statement

Fig. 6. CFG construction examples with node stack

Figure 6(b) shows a loop transformation: the AST is composed of a loop L holding two statements A and B. This time, the node stack holds the loop head at all times. The inner nodes are being saved on the stack one level higher, so when the loop finishes, we have the possibility to link B, in this case, back to L.

Figure 6(c) illustrates an if transformation: the AST describes a program built of an if statement with two alternatives A and B. This time, our stack must hold two extra nodes: the if head and the endif node. The former must be linked to each of the alternatives, while each branch must have a link to the latter. We use the endif node to pull all the branches back together, and thereby improve the CFG readability without adding alien control flow semantics to it. At the end of each alternative, we perform the described linking operations, and restore the if-endif stack structure. When the processing finishes we leave only the endif node behind. Semantically, this is the last node in the CFG so far.

The standard scenario works only with the stack's top and is thereby oblivious of the lower levels. This allows us to perform the special if and loop operations completely transparent to the rest of the transformation.

Please note that all three ASTs depicted in Fig. 6 have a similar configuration. Only their head nodes (P, L and IF) identify their type.

3.4   Parameter Stack

The statement is the basic control flow unit in ASIS while the CFG node is its basic counterpart in the flow world. ASIS has, however, other control flow relevant structures that cannot be represented as nodes. Such are the function calls, which are categorised as expressions. For each non-trivial call, i.e. other

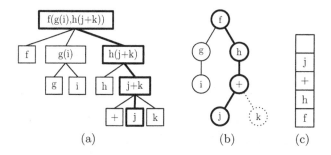

Fig. 7. AST path with associated parameter tree and stack

than an operation symbol like +, the execution leaves the original control flow temporarily and passes over to the function's body. This makes it imperative to save them in the CFG too.

A function call can also be nested inside another, as parameter of the former. These compositions can be structured into trees, with the primary called function in the root, and its parameters as children. The definition is recursive and the tree grows as the nesting hierarchy becomes deeper. Such parameter trees provide excellent means for static parameter aliasing, i.e. for determining the parameters used in function calls, regardless of the nesting depth.

When constructing parameter trees, we need to store the current path in them. Again, the best way to do so is to employ a stack, the *parameter stack*.

Figure 7 depicts a possible parameter tree construction scenario [12]. In Fig. 7(a) we can see an abstract syntax subtree describing a complex function call. The thick edges and nodes mark the current traversal state.

Figure 7(b) shows the corresponding parameter tree generated so far, with the thick edges standing for the current traversal state. The primary function f resides in the root. g and h are the functions used as parameters for f. The nesting, and therefore the tree, ends with the variables i, j and k. The edge and node for the variable k are dotted, displaying its future position. It has not been added so far, since the AST traversal has not reached it yet.

Figure 7(c) depicts the present state of the parameter stack. It is clearly visible that the current path in the tree is saved on the stack.

4   Post Transformation

4.1   Loop Refinement

After the transformation phase, for and while loops without exit or return statements are already represented correctly. However, simple loops and loops that contain exit or return statements need some refinement. For example consider the loop in Fig. 8(a). First, there should be no edge from the loop header to the loop end, since there is no condition in the header. Second, there should be an edge from the node containing the exit statement to the loop end. Figure 8(b) shows the refined, correct representation of this loop.

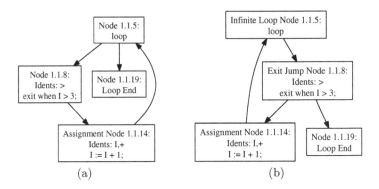

Fig. 8. Cfg2Dot output for a simple loop before (a) and after (b) loop refinement

Loop refinement is done after the main transformation phase, when the preliminary CFG has already been built. Consequently, we need to find the loops first. This has to be done since ASIS provides information only on the loop headers in a convenient way. Also, due to the considerable complexity of the traversal itself, it is easier to construct a raw version of the graph without extensive control flow semantics, and to gather this information in the post transformation phase. For that purpose, we employ Tarjan's algorithm for constructing the loop forest as it is presented by Ramalingam [13]. This algorithm needs the set of backedges of a CFG, which is why we first compute them using a simple DFS. This is possible since in a reducible CFG every retreating edge is a backedge [7].

The loop refinement is done in the `Collapse` procedure of Tarjan's algorithm. Every found loop results in a call of `Collapse` which takes the loop header and the body as parameters. After every node in the loop body is collapsed on its header, we collect the exit jump nodes for the current loop and those for outer loops in two different lists. The list with the exit jump nodes for outer loops is retained between different calls to `Collapse`.

Next, we determine the edge to the first statement after the loop which, at the current stage, is the only edge that points outside the loop. After that, we connect the exit jump nodes for the current loop and, in case the current loop has a label, also search the list with the exit jump nodes for outer loops. Note that Tarjan's algorithm always finds inner loops first, so that an exit jump node is always found before the corresponding loop. Finally, in case the current loop is a simple `loop` statement, we remove the edge from the loop header to the loop end. Return statements are handled in a similar way.

However, if the loop does not contain an `exit` statement, and therefore is an endless loop, there is the chance that some nodes, right after the loop, are not reachable any more by following only successor links. Apart from the problem of memory leakage, the fact that they still may be reached by traversing the CFG backwards, using only predecessor links, makes proper deallocation of those nodes necessary. So before the edge from loop header to loop end is removed, its target node is saved and handled later on (see Sect. 4.3).

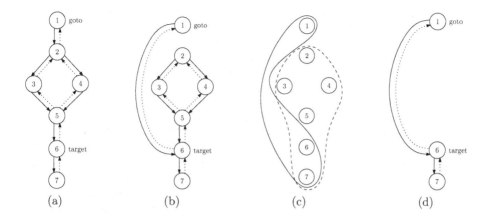

Fig. 9. Removing dangling nodes from the CFG

4.2   Connecting Gotos

During the transformation phase we only stored the target of a goto statement as a string but did not add an appropriate edge to the CFG. Instead, we connected the goto jump node to the node for the statement right after the goto. Now we have to remove that edge, and add one correctly representing the jump to the target of the goto.

Since the labels of a statement were also saved as strings, we basically build two lists during a DFS: a list of sources containing all found goto jump node objects and another one containing all nodes with at least one label, that is, all targets. Note that a goto statement itself may also be a target. Then we connect each node in the list of sources to the corresponding target and remove the existing, auxiliary edge.

However, as with endless loops, there may be unreachable statements following a goto. We will have to remove and correctly deallocate the nodes representing these statements later (see Sect. 4.3), which is why we store the target of the auxiliary edge.

4.3   Removing Dangling Nodes

As stated previously, we have to remove the subgraphs no longer reachable by only following their successor links. For example consider Fig. 9 where solid lines represent successor links and dotted lines correspond to predecessor links.

After we connect the goto node to its target as shown in Fig. 9(b) there now is a subgraph, rooted at Node 2, that is only reachable by following the predecessor link from Node 6 to Node 5.

We first perform a DFS on the CFG and add all reachable nodes to a set. In Fig. 9(c) this set is surrounded by a solid edge. Next, at each node that may be the root of an unreachable subgraph we start another DFS and create a second set containing all visited nodes. In our example in Fig. 9(c) this set is surrounded by a dashed edge. Finally we subtract the set with the nodes that are reachable through normal DFS from the set containing the nodes of unreachable subgraphs and remove the resulting nodes as shown in Fig. 9(d).

5   Performance

To measure the performance of Ast2Cfg, we recorded the execution time of Cfg2Dot, which introduces only minimal overhead. The test was performed with the Linux command *time* on a machine with a single Athlon XP 2800+ processor and a gigabyte of RAM. We generated the tree files for the contents of the include directories of a typical GNAT and ASIS-for-GNAT installation. The generation of the 588 tree files with a total of 426.4 MB lasted approximately 91 seconds. Then we used Cfg2Dot to generate 5472 separate CFGs in 213 seconds.

6   Conclusions and Future Work

We developed a framework for static program analysis, which provides a CFG-based structure of Ada programs. Since currently, neither GNAT nor ASIS, fully support the Ada 2005 standard, it was not possible for us to fully implement it either. However, our work already covers most of the language specification. Ast2Cfg is therefore still in an early stage, and will be developed further.

Apart from the simple Cfg2Dot utility, there are already two projects in the field of static control flow analysis that use Ast2Cfg.

The first one aims at the detection of *busy waiting*. Busy waiting is a form of synchronisation [14] that is considered bad practice since it results in a severe overhead and even may be responsible for system failure because of race conditions [15]. Busy waiting occurs whenever a loop is only exited in case the value of a variable is changed from outside the loop. That is, the loop exit condition is not influenced from within the loop. To be able to statically detect such occurrences the algorithm proposed by Blieberger et al. [15] is implemented and extended in order to yield more accurate results.

The second project's goal is to detect *access anomalies*. They are an issue concerning multitasking environments employing non-protected shared memory areas. They occur when several concurrent execution threads access (write-write, or read-write) the same memory area without coordination. [16]

An implementation of the analysis framework proposed by Blieberger et al. [17] aims at detecting such access anomalies by means of static analysis.

References

1. Allen, F.E.: Control flow analysis. In: Proceedings of a symposium on Compiler optimization, pp. 1–19 (1970)
2. Ryder, B.G., Paull, M.C.: Elimination algorithms for data flow analysis. ACM Comput. Surv. 18(3), 277–316 (1986)

3. Fahringer, T., Scholz, B.: A unified symbolic evaluation framework for parallelizing compilers. IEEE Trans. Parallel Distrib. Syst. 11(11), 1105–1125 (2000)
4. Blieberger, J.: Data-flow frameworks for worst-case execution time analysis. Real-Time Syst. 22(3), 183–227 (2002)
5. Allen, F.E., Cocke, J.: A program data flow analysis procedure. Commun. ACM 19(3), 137 (1976)
6. Sreedhar, V.C., Gao, G.R., Lee, Y.F.: A new framework for elimination-based data flow analysis using dj graphs. ACM TOPLAS 20(2), 388–435 (1998)
7. Aho, A.V., Sethi, R., Ullman, J.D.: Compilers. Addison-Wesley, Reading (1986)
8. International Organization for Standardization: ISO/IEC 15291:1999: Information technology — Programming languages — Ada Semantic Interface Specification (ASIS). ISO, Geneva, Switzerland (1999)
9. AdaCore: ASIS-for-GNAT User's Guide. Revision 41863 (January 2007)
10. Sedgewick, R.: Algorithms, 2nd edn. Addison-Wesley, Reading (1988)
11. Gansner, E.R., North, S.C.: An open graph visualization system and its applications to software engineering. Software — Practice and Experience 30(11), 1203–1233 (2000)
12. Fechete, R., Kienesberger, G.: Generating control flow graphs for Ada programs. Technical Report 183/1-139, Institute for Computer-Aided Automation, TU Vienna, Treitlstr. 1-3, A-1040 Vienna, Austria (September 2007)
13. Ramalingam, G.: Identifying loops in almost linear time. ACM Trans. Program. Lang. Syst. 21(2), 175–188 (1999)
14. Andrews, G.R.: Concurrent programming: principles and practice. Benjamin-Cummings Publishing Co. Inc., Redwood City (1991)
15. Blieberger, J., Burgstaller, B., Scholz, B.: Busy wait analysis. In: Reliable Software Technologies - Ada-Europe, pp. 142–152 (2003)
16. Schonberg, D.: On-the-fly detection of access anomalies. In: PLDI 1989: Proceedings of the ACM SIGPLAN 1989 Conference on Programming language design and implementation, pp. 285–297. ACM Press, New York (1989)
17. Burgstaller, B., Blieberger, J., Mittermayr, R.: Static Detection of Access Anomalies in Ada95. In: Pinho, L.M., González Harbour, M. (eds.) Ada-Europe 2006. LNCS, vol. 4006, pp. 40–55. Springer, Heidelberg (2006)

A Type-Safe Database Interface

Florian Villoing and Emmanuel Briot

AdaCore, 46 rue d'Amsterdam, 75009 Paris, France
villoing@adacore.com, briot@adacore.com

Abstract. This paper describes the design and implementation of a type-safe, vendor-neutral Application Programming Interface (API) to interact with a database system. It reviews the current practice in this area and summarizes the problems and limitations, and shows some solutions that were developed in response. The paper explains the benefits that Ada brings to the task of writing a high level SQL API.

1 Introduction

Many applications need to store persistent data. The amount of data can vary, of course, but tends to grow with the use of the application, and it therefore generally needs to be structured to facilitate its retrieval.

Database Management Systems (DBMS) vendors provide off-the-shelf solutions, with the relational model being by far the most popular. In a relational DBMS, servers are accessed through a Standard Query Language called SQL. The products in this area, either proprietary (such as Oracle and DB2) or open source (such as PostgreSQL [1] or MySQL [2]), are now very mature.

Ada itself does not specify a standard interface for accessing those servers. However, various libraries are available, sometimes provided by the DBMS vendors themselves (although in general they provide only a C API), and sometimes through open source software. Two such open source libraries are GNADE [3] and APQ [4]. The first part of this article describes a number of solutions currently available.

Ada is a strongly typed language, designed so that compilers can provide early warnings about potential errors in the code (uninitialized variables, unused parameters, etc.). However, when the program needs to access a database, this paper will show that the current solutions do not provide the necessary type-safety and early warnings.

As part of AdaCore's customer support infrastructure, we have developed a number of tools internally to integrate our support services (such as report tracking) with data about our customers. This integration includes managing customer and contact information, tracking email exchanges with customers, and making this information available to customers themselves through web interfaces. Since we needed to integrate a large amount of information, it was natural to use a DBMS (PostgreSQL in our case). The development was carried out in Ada. As we quickly encountered the limitations described in the first part of this article, we started developing an in-house system to overcome them. This

F. Kordon and T. Vardanega (Eds.): Ada-Europe 2008, LNCS 5026, pp. 144–157, 2008.

article describes the solution we ended up with and explains some of the design choices we made.

The resulting library has not yet been made widely available, although this is likely to happen in the future. This library has some PostgreSQL-specific parts, although, as we will show, it should be easy to adapt it to other systems. It is also a layer on top of GNADE, but that too could be changed if there was a need.

2   Review of Existing SQL Solutions

There are several ways to interact with a relational database. All end up sending a query (written in SQL) to the server, and reading the result.

A DBMS always comes with an applica-tion programming interface (API), generally written in C, that allows a program to in-teract with the underlying database. Such an API typically provides subprograms to send a SQL query to the database, retrieve the exit status of the query, and access the data returned by a SELECT query. The data itself is often returned as tuples of strings, which the application needs to convert to the proper types.

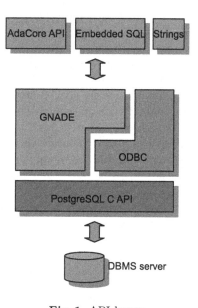

Using the API provided by the DBMS has one major drawback: it is tightly coupled with the underlying database. If the DBMS needs to be changed (or even when upgrad-ing to a newer version), the code must be adapted in all the places where interactions take place. This is partly mitigated by the fact that DBMS APIs usually provide inter-faces with a similar level of abstraction.

Since the API is generally low-level, a change in the database schema has implicit

Fig. 1. API layers

(and possibly hard-to-deduce) effects on the code. For instance, changing the name of a column in a table requires the programmer to search for all occur-rences of the column throughout the code, and rename them all.

The Open Database Connectivity (ODBC [5]) offers a way to solve the first issue, by abstracting the access to the database. The core ODBC library on the one hand provides an API that is common to all DBMS, and on the other hand is responsible for translating calls to the API into calls to the DBMS-specific API. This way the DBMS-specific details are hidden from the user, who can switch from one DBMS to another without modifying the application. ODBC, however, has a reputation for being much slower than the corresponding DBMS-specific API.

The ODBC approach solves the transition issue that arises in the vendor-specific approach. However, it remains relatively difficult to integrate in the code, getting values from local variables, and reading the result into some other variables. All communication is through strings and is therefore not type safe. Moreover, the same issue arises when the database schema is changed, and the code for the entire program needs to be reviewed in such cases.

There are several Ada bindings available that provide one or both of these two approaches (vendor-specific and ODBC). APQ was initially designed as a PostgreSQL-only API, and has subsequently been extended to other DBMS. It does not provide an ODBC binding, however. It also tries to provide a relatively high-level binding, using only Ada types and isolating the application from the underlying C types. GNADE covers more DBMS systems, both through a DBMS-specific API for each of these, and through an ODBC interface.

As mentioned above, regardless of the communication layer chosen, the SQL queries themselves are ultimately transferred to the server as strings. If one directly uses either the ODBC or the vendor-specific API, the code will still contain those queries as strings, with the limitations mentioned earlier.

Software developers have thus designed a standard way to write SQL queries, while providing a tighter integration with the rest of the source code. This is called "Embedded SQL". The query is written as part of the code itself, in a section marked by special keywords. A preprocessor is then used to transform the embedded SQL sequence into calls to the DBMS API (or possibly to ODBC, although this is rarely used in this context). The conditions used in the SQL query can directly contain variables from the code. The result is made available through variables (generally cursors, i.e. iterators over all matching tuples).

```
EXEC SQL DECLARE BEGIN
  empno : SQL_Standard.INTEGER;
EXEC SQL END-EXEC
EXEC SQL
  WHENEVER SQLERROR raise My_Exception;
EXEC SQL
  DECLARE cursor FOR
    SELECT empno INTO :empno FROM employees
    WHERE manager = :to_find;
```

Fig. 2. Embedded SQL example (from GNADE [6])

This embedded SQL somewhat improves code readability (fewer function calls), at the cost of using a preprocessor. The latter means that compiling the application involves an additional step, and, more importantly, the source files themselves are no longer valid Ada, which complicates using them in standard Integrated Development Environments (IDEs).

The embedded SQL solution also has several limitations: it does not ensure that the SQL query is syntactically correct (for example there may be mismatched parenthesis, or missing FROM statements in select queries), nor does it solve the maintenance problem when the database schema is changed. The next section of this article will describe a solution that addresses these two issues.

3   Integrity and Type-Safety in SQL Queries

For the development of the AdaCore information system, we selected the Post-greSQL DBMS. Thus the abstraction offered by ODBC was not needed, and we decided to develop a framework based on direct use of the PostgreSQL API through the binding provided by GNADE.

The problems we needed to solve through this framework were the following:

1. Integrity of the queries with regard to the database schema
   Whenever the database schema changes, we must have a way to know which part of the code becomes invalid. Relying on run-time testing is error prone.
2. Checking SQL syntax at compile time
   It should be impossible, or at least difficult, to write syntactically invalid SQL queries.
3. Easy interaction with Ada variables
   It should be straightforward to use local program variables in the query, in particular in the WHERE clause of SELECT statements.
4. Ensure type-safety
   To the extent possible, the interface should ensure that the type of an Ada variable matches the type stored in the database.

3.1   Database Schema and Query Consistency

As noted in the previous section, we want to verify the correctness of a SQL query as early as possible in the development process, i.e., at compile time.

A first step toward that goal is to generate some Ada code from the database content as part of the compilation process, and use this generated code when writing our queries. We generate an Ada package that declares string constants representing the various database elements such as table names and field names (see figure 3). These constants are used when writing SQL queries in the user code (see figure 4).

```
package Database is
    package Table1 is
        T : constant String := "table1";
        S_Field1 : constant String := "field1";
        S_Field2 : constant String := "field2";
        Field1 : constant String := T & "." & S_Field1;
        Field2 : constant String := T & "." & S_Field2;
    end Table1;
    ...
end Database;
```

Fig. 3. The generated package Database

```
declare
   Id    : constant Integer := 12;
   Query : constant String :=
              " SELECT " & Table1.Field1 & " FROM " & T
              & " WHERE " & Table1.Field2 & " = "
              & Integer'Image (Id);
begin
   ...
end
```

Fig. 4. User code using the generated package

This brings two improvements, solving the first issue mentioned earlier:

− Typing mistakes in the name of database entities are avoided
  Depending on the context, we need either a fully qualified name for the fields
  or just a simple name (in an **INSERT** query for instance). This is why our
  package contains two variants for each field.
− Whenever the database schema changes, the code no longer compiles
  If for instance we rename a column that is used in one of the SQL queries,
  say "field1" in the example above, we will get a compilation error because
  the constant **Field1** no longer exists.

The Database Package Generation. The
Database package generation is achieved
through the **package_builder** tool. This
tool works in two steps. Firstly, it accesses
the database in order to collect information about its structure. This is done using
GNADE and SQL queries, since in PostgreSQL, a database schema is stored in a
database itself. Then the **database.ads** file
is generated using the Templates Parser [7]
that comes with AWS and an Ada template,
database.tads. database.ads must be re-
generated every time the database schema
changes. This could in fact be done before
each compilation, but that would require a
running database environment to recompile

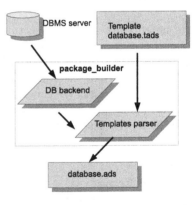

Fig. 5. database.ads generation

the application, which would be an unnecessary additional constraint.

The tool needs to access specific internal code of the DBMS to query the schema,
since SQL does not provide a standard way to retrieve that information. This is
DBMS specific, and needs to be rewritten when moving to another system. It is
quite limited in scope, though, which makes it relatively easy to port.

Figure 6 shows the template that can be used to generate the Database package in Figure 3. From the database schema, **package_builder** produces a set of

```
package Database is
  ...
  @@TABLE@@  @@--  For each table
    package @_CAPITALIZE:TABLE_NAME_@ is
       T :  constant String := "@_TABLE_NAME_@";

     @@TABLE@@  @@--  For each field
       S_@_CAPITALIZE:FIELD_NAME_@ : constant String := "@_TABLE_NAME_@";
     @@END_TABLE@@

     @@TABLE@@  @@--  For each field
       @_CAPITALIZE:FIELD_NAME_@ : constant String :=
          T & "." & S_@_CAPITALIZE:FIELD_NAME_@;
     @@END_TABLE@@

    end @_CAPITALIZE:TABLE_NAME_@;
  @@END_TABLE@@
end Database;
```

Fig. 6. The `Database` package template

internal vectors that are then processed through the template, to generate an actual Ada package.

In addition, a few Ada constants, extracted from the database, are also generated (see figure 7). These allow the use of Ada identifiers in the application and avoid the need to reference the internal identifiers used by the database system. This is a fast and effective way to implement the application. Ultimately, the code must remove the use of such constants, since changes to the database (when installing in another context for instance) might break the application.

```
Contract_Type_Subscription : constant Contract_Type_Id := 1;
Contract_Type_Service : constant Contract_Type_Id := 2;
```

Fig. 7. Generated constants

This solution has proved very flexible when we needed to enhance the generated packages, as we will see in the following sections. Generally the templates file is the only file that needs to be modified, which makes maintenance easier compared to enhancing `package_builder.adb` if it generated the `database.ads` files by printing strings directly.

3.2 Syntactically Correct SQL Queries

Although the above solution provides a partial solution, it is still possible to write an invalid query. For instance, we might omit a closing parenthesis, or forget the `FROM` part of our `SELECT` statement. To solve this, we have developed another package called SQL, which provides a set of functions that help write the SQL queries.

As figure 8 shows, we no longer write a string directly. Instead, the query is generated on the fly through calls to Ada subprograms like SQL_Select or SQL_Insert. This comes from the idea that an SQL query consists of several clauses that are not all of the same kind: immediately after a SELECT should come a list of fields, and a FROM clause expects a list of tables as its parameter. New types were therefore introduced to represent such constraints, replacing the string constants generated previously. Queries are thus written in terms of SQL_Table, SQL_Field, SQL_Criteria and SQL_Assignment. Constructors are provided to create new instances of those types, which are no longer compatible with the predefined type String.

The "=" operator is redefined, which helps create instances of SQL_Criteria to build the WHERE clause. It expects as usual two operands: one a SQL_Field and the other an Integer. Other overridings are provided for the predefined types. The & operator is overridden to build lists (of tables or fields).

The SQL package supports most of the SQL language structures, including all its operators (such as "in" and "like"), nested queries, function calls, insertion and deletion of rows, and so on.

```
declare
    Id    : constant Integer := 12;
    Query : constant SQL_Query := SQL_Select
      (Fields => Field1 & Field2,
       From   => T,
       Where  => Field2 = Id);
begin
    ...
end
```

Fig. 8. Syntactically correct SQL queries

This new version also automatically knows whether SQL expects a fully qualified name for fields, or a simple name, so we no longer need to generate both Field1 and S_Field1 as before. The templates used to generate database.ads have been enhanced so that instances of SQL_Table and SQL_Field are directly generated.

This solution solves issues 2 and 3 that we highlighted at the beginning of this section.

Compared to the use of strings, or to the use of embedded SQL, this solution is very flexible in the way that queries are built: the types we have redefined are not constrained, and can therefore be built on the fly, for instance as part of more complex Ada statements (figure 9).

This limits the amount of code duplication: very often the fields expected from a query are the same, and there are just one or two conditions that change. Most of the code is shared, except the condition that is built dynamically.

```
declare
   W : SQL_Criteria;  -- controlled, initialized to No_Criteria
   Q : SQL_Query;
begin
   if <has_id> then
      W := W and Field2 = Id;
   end if;
   Q := SQL_Select (Fields => Field1, Where => W);
end;
```

Fig. 9. Incremental build of SQL queries

It is worth noting that this SQL package is independent of the actual DBMS system (unless some non-standard SQL extensions are used, but they are clearly documented and the programmer has full knowledge of such things), and of the actual connection layer (ODBC or vendor-specific).

The SQL package provides a way to automatically complete the FROM and GROUP BY clauses of an SQL query. They are computed from the values provided for the other clauses. This eases the writing of SQL queries as well as their maintenance. For instance, it ensures on the one hand that only the necessary tables are listed in the FROM clause of a SELECT query even after some columns have been removed from the SELECT clause. On the other hand, if a column from another table is added to the SELECT clause, the corresponding table will be automatically added to the FROM clauses, thus reducing the probability of introducing discrepancies in the SQL queries.

3.3   Bringing Type-Safety to SQL Queries

The generated package Database is still not perfect. There is no way to ensure that we are not mixing a constant representing a table with a constant representing a column, or that a condition used in a WHERE clause is actually a Boolean expression.

It also does not prevent mixing variables of different types. For instance, in the above example there is no indication of whether Field2 is actually an integer (as its comparison with Id seems to imply), or a string, or some other type.

As a result, we decided to change the generated package so that the fields are no longer all of type SQL_Field, but instances of derived types instead, which we have called SQL_Field_Integer, SQL_Field_Text,...

By redefining the appropriate operators and functions, we ensure that the resulting SQL query is valid syntactically, and that type safety can be checked at compile time by the compiler itself.

As visible Figure 10, each column of a table is accessed through a primitive operation of the Table object. Using primitive functions rather than constants closely associates the field with the actual table. In SQL, a given query might reference the same table multiple times under different names (the "as" keyword in SQL). As a result, the Ada code would create two instances of Table, one for each name used in the query, and would call the primitive function of each of these two instances depending on the context. Syntactically, thanks to Ada 2005's dotted notation, the source code is the same regardless of whether constants or primitive operations are used. The other reason for using primitive operations, and therefore binding the field name and its table, is to have an unambiguous representation of the query in memory, which helps to implement the previously-mentioned auto-completion.

Using the SQL_Field_* types associates semantic information with a column, compared to the previous manipulation of the SQL_Field type. For example, an attempt to write a criterion for a WHERE clause in which Field1 of type SQL_Field_Integer is compared to a Boolean variable will be caught and rejected by the compiler. This provides a solution to the fourth issue mentioned at the beginning of this section.

```
package Database is
   package Table1 is
      type Table is  new SQL_Table with null record;
      function Field1 (Self : Table) return SQL_Field_Integer;
      function Field2 (Self : Table) return SQL_Field_Boolean;
   end Table1;
   Table1 : aliased constant T_Table1.Table;
   ...
end Database;
```

Fig. 10. The enhanced generated package Database

4   Safe Execution of SQL Queries

So far we stayed focused on how to write the actual SQL queries. But there are still a number of ways in which a database interface could help prevent errors. Our library provides some of these mechanisms. They are described below and are part of a package called SQL_Exec.

4.1   Network Failures and Database Connection

A DBMS system is implemented as a client-server interface. The server generally runs on a different machine, which introduces an additional possibility for failure in the execution of queries.

Our library automatically reconnects to the server should the connection be down. It then attempts to re-execute the current query, up to a certain number of times. All of this is transparent to the rest of the application.

4.2   Caching

In a given database, there are often some tables that act as enumerated types and do not change very often. An example in our information system technology is the list of possible priorities for a support ticket, or the various engineers to whom such a ticket can be assigned.

In addition, these tables are needed often, since they provide information that a user can directly manipulate: it is for example much easier to manipulate "enhancement request" than the corresponding internal id. Thus, each time information is presented to the user we need to perform a search of the ticket priority table, and every time the user enters information we need to convert it to the internal ids.

In order to improve performance, the SQL_exec package provides an optional caching system whereby the result of queries can be cached. Whenever the user executes a query that has been cached previously, no network communication is necessary, just a search in a local hash table, which is generally much faster.

The difficulty here is to ensure integrity when the database is changed. Our application automatically invalidates the cache every hour, which is good enough to ensure that the copy of the data is not too obsolete, and that a change in one of the enumeration tables becomes visible after at most one hour.

In addition, our web servers provide a special URL that forces an immediate reset of the cache.

When we implemented this cache, we saw a dramatic improvement in the speed of our web servers. The following figures come from a test that issued hundreds of queries against typical pages in our internal Customer Relationship Management (CRM) system. The PostgreSQL database is running on a remote host across the Atlantic. The measurements are derived from two cases:

1. The first test is for a page that lists details for a specific customer. In this test, none of the queries can be cached, because the information is too volatile. This test provides the worst-case scenario for the caching system, and ensures that activating the cache, even if there is no hit, does not impact performance.
2. The second test lists details for a specific ticket. Here, 43% of the queries can be cached (1190 out of 2706 upon 100 executions) because they are used to query information such as the possible assignees for a ticket, or its possible status. This information almost never changes, so is cached for efficiency. In addition to the database queries, this test also parses mailboxes, and therefore runs much more slowly.

	Without caching	With caching	Improvement
Test 1	1m9.943s	1m9.190s	−1.01%
Test 2	4m41.678s	2m50.359s	−65.3%

Fig. 11. Impact of the caching system

The results for the first case show that the caching system has no effect when not used (the minor difference is most likely related to a different load on the system, and was sometimes in favor of caching, sometimes against). The second case however shows the major speed improvement that can be expected.

4.3 SQL Transactions and Error Handling

There are various ways in which a query may fail:

- a `SELECT` query may fail because it is referencing invalid tables or columns (although queries written through our SQL package should not have such errors);
- the connection to the database may be invalid (although, as we mentioned earlier, our library automatically tries to reconnect);
- the query might be executed in the middle of a failed SQL transaction, which is invalid;
- an `INSERT` query may fail because some constraint is not satisfied;
- a `DELETE` query may fail because there is no matching line in the table, and so on.

In all of these cases, the way the DBMS reports the error may vary. This also depends on the connection layer (ODBC or vendor specific) that is used. Sometimes an exception will be raised, and sometimes an exit status is set.

The `SQL_Exec` package attempts to isolate the rest of the application from these features and to provide a consistent error-handling mechanism.

Often a specific customer action results in a sequence of SQL queries that must be executed either in their entirety or not at all; i.e. if one of them fails, then the whole sequence must be canceled, and no change should be visible to the rest of the database.

SQL supports this requirement through transactions. These are sequences of SQL queries that are executed in a "sandbox", until either the whole sequence is validated successfully (i.e. `COMMIT`'d), or canceled (i.e. `ROLLBACK`'d).

As an example, suppose that your application should insert an element in a table A and upon success insert it in table B. But if the insertion in B fails you do not want it to remain in A since that would be a database corruption.

In the case of PostgreSQL, it is also faster to execute queries in a transaction and commit them afterward, since less locking occurs.

The `SQL_Exec` package provides an enhanced support for transactions, and automatically starts a new transaction whenever a change of the database is about to take place (if there is no running transaction already). It then provides a subprogram so that the user can commit or rollback the whole transaction depending on the success of its queries.

We consider this to be an important step towards safe execution of an application that relies on a database in the sense that even if something unexpected happens while the application is running, the integrity of the database is automatically preserved. A user action that result in the insertion of data in the database will either be performed entirely or be rejected as a whole.

4.4 Multi-tasking Issues

In the context of an application such as an information system that includes web servers, one has to be careful about issues specific to multi-tasking. A web server is typically a multi-tasking application. There is a pool of threads running concurrently and each thread handles one request at a time.

Multi-tasking raises some subtle issues, and indeed a problem may arise in connection with transactions. The troublesome scenario occurs when a single connection to the database is shared by all threads in the application, and indeed this situation arose in the initial implementation of our tools.

For example, assume that a client request leads to the execution of the transaction described above. The transaction is started, the element is added to table A. In the mean time, another client request leads to the execution of a query whose execution fails. That marks the transaction as "in error". In this case, the transaction initiated by the first client will be rolled back. This is unfortunate and in more complex situations can be very troublesome.

This example demonstrates that each thread must use a distinct database connection.

4.5 Suggested Code Organization

This section describes an effective software architecture for code that stores data in a DBMS, based on our implementation experience.

One difficulty is that very often various parts of the code need to access similar, but not quite the same, data (say the list of support tickets assigned to one of the staff members, or the list of support tickets that are marked as urgent). If the code duplicates the queries, changing the database schema will force the rewrite of several parts of the code. Fortunately, with the approach described in this paper, the compiler will tell us which parts need updating. But it still remains a tedious job.

Another issue is that data structures tend to be organized in the same way as the database tables, although Ada provides much more advanced data structures.

Historically, our information system used flat text files to store the various pieces of information, and it was a large (although rewarding) effort to integrate all these into a single source of data in a DBMS. If some day we decide to move to some other technology (perhaps a remote web server queried through SOAP), we would like to reduce the porting effort and minimize the changes to the application.

One feature that our library has not been handling so far is how to read the result of queries from the DBMS. For that we rely on GNADE and its PostgreSQL-specific interface. Should we move to another DBMS, we will have to rewrite a part of our application. If the queries are found all over the code, that means examining and changing code throughout the application. Once again, the compiler would help and point out what needs to be changed, but it would still be a major effort.

Based on these considerations, we now try to write the SQL queries only in a limited number of shared packages, which the rest of the code uses. The rest of the code stays away from SQL itself. These packages provide the results of the queries through Ada 2005 containers.

For efficiency, the SQL strings returned by the query are converted to scalar types (Boolean, Integer, etc.) as much as possible. There remain cases where the result is actually a string. Since the queries are shared, it often happens that part of the result is not needed by the part of the application that requested it (say the "first name" column, when that part of the application is just trying to validate a login).

Once again for efficiency, the C strings (aka `char*`) are not converted immediately to `String_Access`, only on demand. That saves memory and system calls.

The last aspect of efficiency is that the Ada 2005 lists that represent a multiline result are not created immediately. Instead, we store the result of the query itself (GNADE has the type `Result` which we have made reference-counted for that purpose) and publish it as an `Unparsed_List` type. That way no memory allocation takes place until the data actually gets used. That makes it relatively cheap to share queries.

5   Conclusion

The framework and tools we have put in place integrate the application code tightly with the database schema. This brings safety: many errors are detected at compile time, whereas they would have been caught only at run time otherwise, either during the testing phase or, worse, only after the application has been put into production.

There are several aspects that could be enhanced. Parts of the library are specific to Postgres (most notably the generation of `database.ads` and retrieval of query results). Auto-completion of queries is very useful and helps in maintaining complex queries. It is however not as smart as we would sometimes wish it: for instance, it would be nice if it could automatically complete the WHERE clause to join tables. Since the library works by representing queries in memory, it could be enhanced to easily connect to several databases in parallel: for readonly queries, we could connect to one or more slaves of the DBMS to provide load balancing, while all write queries would be done on the common master (in the case of a CRM system, there are many more read-only queries).

With respect to performance, there is only a small additional overhead. This is negligible compared to the cost of transfering queries and their results over the network.

Internal discussions are in progress concerning the release of this library. Additional work is needed, in particular a few contributions to the GNADE package.

References

1. PostgreSQL 8.3.0 Documentation,
   http://www.postgresql.org/docs/8.3/static/index.html
2. MySQL 6.0 Reference Manual,
   http://dev.mysql.com/doc/refman/6.0/en/index.html
3. Erdmann, M.: GNADE user's guide,
   http://gnade.sourceforge.net/gnade/gnade.pdf
4. Gay, W.W.: APQ home page, http://home.cogeco.ca/~ve3wwg/software.html

5. ODBC–Open Database Connectivity Overview, `http://support.microsoft.com/kb/110093`
6. Erdmann, M.: Embedded SQL with GNADE, `http://gnade.sourceforge.net/#ESQL`
7. Templates Parser User's Guide, `https://libre.adacore.com/aws/templates_parser-gpl-2.3.0.pdf`
8. Erdmann, M.: GNAT Ada Database Development Environment. In: Blieberger, J., Strohmeier, A. (eds.) Ada-Europe 2002. LNCS, vol. 2361, pp. 334–343. Springer, Heidelberg (2002)
9. North, K.: Understanding multidatabase APIs and ODBC (1994), `http://www.dbmsmag.com/9403d13.html`
10. IBM, SQL Reference Volume 1, `ftp://ftp.software.ibm.com/ps/products/db2/info/vr9/pdf/letter/en_US/db2s1e90.pdf`
11. Dewar, R.B.K.: Quality control in a multi-platform multi-product software company (June 2001), `http://www.adacore.com/2001/03/02/quality-control-in-a-multi-platform-multi-product-software-company/`

StateML+: From Graphical State Machine Models to Thread-Safe Ada Code[*]

Diego Alonso, Cristina Vicente-Chicote, Juan A. Pastor,
and Bárbara Álvarez

Departamento de Tecnologías de la Información y las Comunicaciones
División de Sistemas y Ingeniería Electrónica (DSIE)
Universidad Politécnica de Cartagena, 30202 Cartagena, Spain
{diego.alonso,cristina.vicente,
juanangel.pastor,balvarez}@upct.es

Abstract. This paper presents the StateML+ tool aimed at designing state-machines and automatically generating thread-safe and multi-tasking modular Ada code from them, following a Model-Driven Engineering approach. The StateML+ meta-model is an extension of a previous version, and now it offers improved modeling capabilities, which include regions and macro-state definition. In this paper, a case study regarding the design of a robotic system will be used to demonstrate the benefits of the proposed approach.

Keywords: Model-Driven Engineering, Model-To-Text Transformation, Finite State Machines, Thread-Safe Code Generation, Eclipse platform.

1 Introduction

Model-Driven Engineering (MDE) technologies offer a promising approach to address the inability of third-generation languages to alleviate the complexity of platforms and express domain concepts effectively [1]. Objects are replaced by models, and model transformations appear as a powerful mechanism to automatically and incrementally develop software [2].

The work presented in this paper starts from the definition of the *ACRoSeT* [3] abstract architectural framework, aimed at developing abstract software components for tele-operated robots. This framework allows designers to define the software architecture of a robotic system in terms of abstract (platform independent) robotic components. *ACRoSET* components are designed taking into account both structural and behavioral aspects.

Although the adoption of *ACRoSET* for component-based robotic system design has demonstrated many advantages, the translation of its abstract components into concrete ones has not been automated yet and, thus, it remains an error-prone process. This is one of the current aims of our research group and this paper covers it partially.

To tackle the problem of automatically translating *ACRoSET* abstract components into concrete ones, we propose a MDE approach based on a previous experience,

---

[*] This research has been funded by the Spanish CICYT project MEDWSA (TIN2006-15175-C05-02) and the Regional Government of Murcia Seneca Program (02998-PI-05).

F. Kordon and T. Vardanega (Eds.): Ada-Europe 2008, LNCS 5026, pp. 158–170, 2008.
© Springer-Verlag Berlin Heidelberg 2008

already published in [4]. In that work, we presented a basic state-machine meta-model, called StateML, and a graphical modeling tool built on top of it, which allowed designers to depict and to validate very simple state-machine models. These models could then be automatically translated into Ada code using a model-to-text transformation, also implemented as part of that work.

State machines provide very powerful behavioral descriptions. This is why they are quite commonly used for modeling general-purpose processes and, in particular, why they have been extensively adopted by the robotics community. Even when using a Component-Based Software Development (CBSD) [5] approach for robotic application design, as the one proposed in *ACRoSET*, state-machines are a very appropriate and natural way for describing component behavior, since they allow designers to define how components react to different external and internal stimuli. In addition, state machines provide a very natural and precise notation for describing aspects such as concurrency.

However, in order to model ACRoSET abstract components, the state-machine models built using the previous StateML tool presented in [4] was not expressive enough, since it did not include mechanisms to model concurrency. Thus, instead of tackling the whole problem of translating ACRoSET abstract components into concrete ones, we decided to first complete the state-machine models and the translation of the component behavior part, leaving the structural aspects for a later stage.

In this vein, this paper presents the extended StateML⁺ meta-model, which includes all the concepts needed to model the behavior of *ACRoSET* abstract components, including those related to concurrency. Besides, the new tools implemented on top of this meta-model are also presented, i.e. a new graphical model editor and a new automatic model-to-code transformation, which generates a thread-safe Ada code implementation of the input state-machine model. Although developed in the context of *ACRoSeT*, StateML⁺ can be used as a stand-alone tool by any designer who wants to generate a multi-threaded Ada skeleton from a hierarchical state machine.

Before entering into details, the following section presents an outline of the research goals covered in this paper. Then, the rest of the paper is organized as follows. Firstly, section 2 presents the extended StateML⁺ meta-model, and the graphical modeling tool implemented to support the newly added elements. This section also presents a case study on robotics that will be used through the rest of the paper to illustrate the benefits of the proposed approach. Then, the automatic model-to-code transformation, from StateML⁺ models to thread-safe Ada code, is presented in section 3. Finally, section 4 presents the conclusions and some future research lines.

1.1 Goals of the Paper

In reactive systems, software commonly interacts simultaneously with multiple external elements (sensors, actuators, robots, conveyor belts, etc.). Actually, the real-world is inherently concurrent and this must be somehow captured in software applications. This obviously requires using platforms and programming languages which provide concurrency mechanisms.

As previously stated, the StateML meta-model did not offer any mechanism to model concurrency, although in [4] we proposed this extension as a future work. The main goal of this paper is to show how we have addressed this extension presenting the improved StateML⁺ meta-model, which now can deal with concurrency aspects. To achieve this goal, the following sub-goals have been addressed:

- Firstly, the state-machine meta-model was extended with new concepts in order to improve its modeling capabilities. Among others, it now includes orthogonal regions to represent independent and concurrently active states. The extension of the meta-model implied the addition of a comprehensive set of OCL (*Object Constraint Language*) [6] expressions in order to complete the syntax and the semantics of the meta-model, as it will be further explained in section 2.1.
- A new graphical modeling tool was also developed to allow designers to graphically define state-machine models and to validate them against the meta-model and the set of additional OCL constraints. This tool was validated building different robotic-related case studies, such as the one presented in section 2.2.
- A suitable design pattern [7] had to be selected in order to perform the model-to-code transformation. This implied reviewing some of the architectural patterns that could cope with the *run-to-completion* semantics associated to the state-machine artifacts. After a careful reviewing process, the *Reactor Pattern* [8] was finally selected, as it will be further justified in section 3.1.
- Finally, a new *MOFScript* [9] model-to-code transformation was implemented in order to generate thread-safe Ada code from any input state-machine model. This transformation, which implements the selected *Reactor Pattern,* is detailed in section 3.2.

After covering these goals, the paper will present some conclusions and future research lines.

2 StateML⁺: Improving FSM Modeling Capabilities

As stated in the introduction, this paper presents StateML⁺, which is an improved version of StateML, already presented in [4]. The state-machine meta-model included in StateML was designed as a quite simplified version of the UML 2.x [10] counterpart.

In StateML, designers could model state-machines consisting of states linked by transitions, which could be external or internal, depending on whether the state was actually exited or not. Designers could also include in their models one initial pseudo-state (to initialize the state-machine and to mark the first state to be executed) and one or more final states (to mark the state-machine execution end). The StateML meta-model was enriched with a complete set of OCL constraints in order to assert that models built from it were syntactically and semantically correct.

In spite of the good results obtained by the StateML tools, it was quite clear that its modeling capabilities were very limited, particularly to modeling real world system behavior. As already stated, one of the biggest limitations of StateML was the lack of macro-states and orthogonal regions, since (1) macro-states help avoiding state explosion in state-machines [11], and (2) orthogonal regions make it possible to model the concurrent aspects of a state.

The new StateML⁺, presented in this paper, tries to overcome the limitations of the previous version, extending the underlying state-machine meta-model with orthogonal regions (among other modeling elements), and, thus, providing extended modeling capabilities. Accordingly, the graphical modeling tool (see section 2.2), and the automatic model-to-Ada transformation (see section 3) have also been extended to support the new StateML⁺ extended meta-model.

2.1 The StateML⁺ Extended Meta-Model

The StateML⁺ extended meta-model is shown in Fig. 1. As justified before, when compared to the previous version (StateML meta-model [4]), the main difference is the inclusion of the Region concept, which now plays a central role. The elements included in the meta-model and the relationships existing between them are briefly described next.

- **Region.** As previously stated, this concept has been newly added to the meta-model. Each Region is contained in a State, but a special one, called *topRegion*, which is contained in the StateMachine itself. In this new version, Regions contain Vertexes and Transitions, which were directly stored in the StateMachine in the previous StateML version.
- **StateMachine.** As already explained, in this new version of the meta-model, the StateMachine contains a *topRegion* instead of directly containing the Vertexes and Transitions that constitute the state machine. Besides, it has a unexpectedTransitionPolicy property which can take values {IGNORE, NOTIFY_ERROR}. According to the value of this property, the StateMachine will react differently when it receives an event which does not trigger any of the outgoing transitions of the current state. Specifically, the StateMachine will ignore the unexpected event if the IGNORE value has been selected, and it will call an error handler otherwise (NOTIFY_ERROR value selected). This fact is considered as a "semantic variation point" in the UML 2.x specification and was outlined in [4] as a future improvement of StateML.
- **State.** In this extended version of the meta-model it is possible to create States containing Regions which may contain other States (and Transitions), up to any nesting level. Thus, this structure allows for creating macro-states. The State element has also been enriched with three boolean properties named hasOnEntry, hasDo, and hasOnExit, which allow designers to establish whether the implementation of the State will have any of these operations. These boolean properties are parsed during the model-to-Ada transformation step, as it will be widely explained in section 3.2.
- **Transition.** This element remains similar to the one included in the previous version. It keeps the kind property, which can take values {INTERNAL, EXTERNAL} as before, and includes two new boolean properties requiresGuard and hasFire, which control whether the designer wants a Transition to have a guard and a fire operation. These boolean properties, together with those added to the State element, are used during the model-to-Ada transformation step.

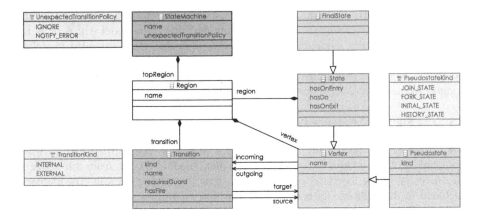

Fig. 1. The StateML⁺ extended meta-model

- **Pseudostate.** This element remains identical to the one included in StateML, i.e. it only includes a property kind of type PseudostateKind. However, as shown in Fig. 1, the PseudostateKind enumerated type has been enriched with new elements to cope with the new needs derived from the inclusion of Regions in the meta-model. Thus, the property kind can now take values {INITIAL_STATE, HISTORY_STATE, JOIN_STATE, FORK_STATE}. The syntax, and the semantics of these pseudo-states has been taken form the one defined in the UML 2.x specification [10], and it is summarized next.

  » **INITIAL_STATE / HISTORY_STATE.** Initial vertexes represent a default vertex that is the source for a single Transition to the default State of a Region. In the case of HISTORY_STATEs, they have the ability to "remember" the last active State the Region was in before exiting (the Region). Thus, when the Region is entered again, the HISTORY_STATE re-starts the last active State execution again. There can be at most one initial vertex (either INITIAL_STATEs or HISTORY_STATEs) in a Region. The outgoing Transition from the initial vertex can not have either a fire operation or a guard.

  » **JOIN_STATE.** JOIN_STATE Pseudostates allow to merge several Transitions emanating from source States belonging to orthogonal Regions, enabling their synchronization. The Transitions entering a JOIN_STATE Pseudostate cannot have either guards or fire operations.

  » **FORK_STATE.** FORK_STATE Pseudostates allow to split an incoming Transition into two or more Transitions terminating on orthogonal target States (i.e., States in different Regions of a macro-state). The Transitions outgoing from a FORK_STATE Pseudostate must not have guards or fire operations.

The StateML⁺ meta-model extension made arise many additional syntactic and semantic constraints, which could not be directly expressed in the meta-model, given the limitations of using a MOF [12] meta-class diagram. As a consequence, a comprehensive set of OCL [6] constraints had to be implemented to cope with the new modeling restrictions. For space reasons, only two of these constraints are included in this paper (see Table 1).

Next section presents the new graphical model editor built to support the new modeling capabilities of StateML⁺, together with a robotic system case study developed using this new tool.

Table 1. Two of the OCL constraints included to complete the formal syntax of StateML⁺

Target domain element: `Transition`

Description: *Pseudostates cannot have internal transitions*

OCL rule:

```
self.kind=TransitionKind::INTERNAL
    implies not(self.source.oclIsTypeOf(Pseudostate))
```

Target domain element: `Transition`

Description: *External Transitions from INITIAL, HISTORY, and FORK and to JOIN Pseudostates must have requiresGuard=false and hasFire =false*

OCL rule:

```
((self.kind=TransitionKind::EXTERNAL)        and
 ((self.source.oclIsTypeOf(Pseudostate))
or
    (self.target.oclIsTypeOf(Pseudostate))) and
 ((self.source.oclAsType(Pseudostate).kind=
        PseudostateKind::INITIAL_STATE )
or (self.source.oclAsType(Pseudostate).kind=
        PseudostateKind::HISTORY_STATE )
or (self.source.oclAsType(Pseudostate).kind=
        PseudostateKind::FORK_STATE )
or (self.target.oclAsType(Pseudostate).kind=
        PseudostateKind::JOIN_STATE )))
implies
    (self.requiresGuard=false and self.hasFire=false)
```

2.2 Building Graphical StateML⁺ Models: A Case Study on Robotics

A new graphical modeling tool has been developed to support the new modeling capabilities of StateML⁺ and also the new restrictions needed to complete the meta-model specification, as previously introduced in section 2.1.

As the previous version of the tool, the StateML⁺ graphical model editor was implemented using the Eclipse Graphical Modeling Framework (GMF). Thus, we followed a similar approach as the one described in [4] but, in this case, the new elements included in the StateML⁺meta-model and the new OCL constraints were taken into account.

As shown in Fig. 2, the new tool offers a richer palette, where the user can now select new elements such as `Region` or the new different kinds of pseudo-states.

Besides, users can validate their models both against the meta-model and against the newly added set of additional OCL constraints, thus assuring that their models are totally correct before proceeding to the model-to-code transformation step.

In order to test both the new modeling capabilities of the StateML$^+$ meta-model, the graphical modeling tool built on top of it, and the automatic model-to-Ada code transformation implemented afterwards, we needed a simple yet real-world case study. Given that, as stated in the introduction, our application domain is very related to robotics, we decided to use the state machine model proposed in [13] and depicted in Fig. 2.

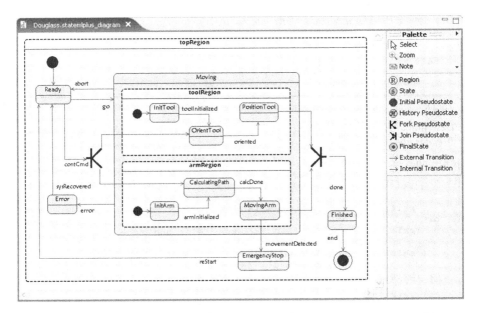

Fig. 2. State-machine model depicted using the StateML$^+$ graphical modeling tool. This state machine models the behavior of the robotic arm used as the case study in this paper.

The state-machine model shown in Fig. 2 models the behavior of a robotic arm which holds a tool (e.g. a gripper, a welder, etc.). As the movement of the arm and the movement of the tool are independent of each other, they have been modeled with two orthogonal regions (toolRegion and armRegion) to show this independence. Each of these regions contains the states in which the tool or the arm can be in, independently of the current state of the other region. The rest of the states (i.e. Ready, Error, EmergencyStop and Finished) are directly contained in the topRegion of the state-machine. In addition:

- An initial pseudo-state has been added to each region to mark its default initial state, i.e. where the region starts its execution. This restriction is checked by an OCL expression.

- A `fork` pseudo-state has been included in the `topRegion` to split the `contCmd` transition from the `Ready` state to two states included in the orthogonal regions defined in the `Moving` state.

- A `join` pseudo-state has also been added to the `topRegion` to synchronize the outgoing transition from the `Moving` state, i.e. from two of the internal states belonging to its internal regions.

This case study uses all the new elements added to StateML⁺, showing a simple yet rich enough case study. This case study has served also as the input to test our model-to-Ada code transformation that is explained in the following section.

3   From StateML⁺ Models to Thread-Safe Ada Code

The meta-model of a system plays a central and fundamental role in the MDE paradigm, since it is the basis that supports the rest of the MDE development process, namely: model creation and model transformations [14]. Therefore, changing the meta-model implies updating the graphical model editor and the model-to-Ada transformation that were previously developed for the StateML tool.

The model-to-Ada transformation, which is described in section 3.2, has suffered a deep modification and now generates Ada code that can cope not only with the new modeling capabilities of StateML⁺ but that is also ready to be included in any multi-tasking application. Besides, we have seized the fact that we should update the model transformation to include some of the characteristics that were outlined as "future work" in the previous StateML tool [4].

Section 3.1 briefly describes some of the architectural design pattern that could have been used to implement the concurrency aspects derived as a consequence of the improvement of the StateML tool, together with the main characteristic of the chosen implementation pattern: the *Reactor/Dispatcher* pattern.

3.1   Decoupling State Activities Execution from State-Machine Management: Using the Reactor Pattern

One of the main challenges of the model-to-code transformation of the state machine artifact resides in the *run-to-completion* semantics associated to the state machine. The run-to-completion semantics, as appears in the UML superstructure (see [10], chapter 13) specifies that:

"An event occurrence can only be taken from the pool and dispatched if the processing of the previous event occurrence is fully completed. Before commencing on a run-to-completion step, a state machine is in a stable state configuration, with all entry/exit/internal activities (but not necessarily state (do) activities) completed. The same conditions apply after the run-to-completion step is completed. Thus, an event occurrence will never be processed while the state machine is in some intermediate and inconsistent situation. The run-to-completion step is the passage between two state configurations of the state machine. The run-to-completion assumption simplifies the transition function of the state machine, since concurrency conflicts are avoided during the processing of event, allowing the state machine to safely complete its run-to-completion step".

This run-to-completion requirement was not a problem in the previous StateML tool, as it does not allow the creation of regions, and thus there is always one and only one active state. But, in StateML$^+$, the presence of regions breaks this rule, as there may be many active states inside any given macro-states. A possible alternative consists of the execution of every active state in its own thread. But using multi-threading in such an uncontrolled way has the following drawbacks:

- Threading may be inefficient and non-scalable.
- Threading may require the use of complex concurrency control schemes throughout the state machine code.
- Concurrency usually implies longer development times, as it has its own problems.

In our case, it was very advisable to come up with a scalable solution according to the number of states appearing in the model, and that could shorten implementation time from the former model-to-Ada transformation.

The *Reactor/Dispatcher* architectural pattern [8] provides a solution that accomplish this requirement. This pattern allows event-driven applications to de-multiplex and dispatch service requests that are delivered to an application from one or more clients. The handlers of these service requests are registered within a reactor thread that runs an infinite loop in which the registered handlers are run sequentially. The reactor thread provides a way to add and remove event handlers at run-time, so the application can adapt itself to changing requirements. The use of the Reactor pattern has allowed us to:

- Achieve "concurrency" for the states contained in orthogonal regions, eliminating the need of complex synchronization mechanisms and shortening in this way the implementation time of the transformations.
- Decouple the state machine management and the short duration activities involved in the run-to-completion semantics of the state-machine (transitions, entry and exit actions execution) from the long duration activities that may be associated to states.

However, the Reactor pattern is not suitable for long duration activities, as they are executed sequentially by the Reactor. Thus, the main liability has been the need of constraint the duration of the activities associated to states. Activities should be of short duration, though they are repeated every time the Reactor executes its cycle while the state machine remains in the given state. In this case, the reactor pattern can be seen as a cyclic executive scheduler. Long duration activities are more effectively handled using separate threads. This can be achieved via other patterns, such as Active Object or Half Sync/Half Async [8]. In general, the Reactor pattern is difficult to test and debug, but in our case simplicity helps avoiding these drawbacks.

3.2 Model-To-Ada Transformation: Implementing the *Reactor Pattern*

As said before, the Reactor pattern will be use to embed the run-to-completion semantics of the state-machine artifact in the resulting Ada code implementation of a StateML$^+$ model. In this case, the handlers executed by the reactor task are the Do_Activity associated to each state, while the events that trigger their execution are the transitions of the state-machine. When a transition occurs, the activity associated to the new state is registered in the reactor while the activity associated to the old state is removed from it. The same happens when entering or exiting a macro-state with orthogonal regions.

Fig. 3 shows the UML package diagram that describes the structure of the Ada code generated after the model-to-code transformation, which generates:

- A main procedure, called **Simulator**, which contains a command-line program that can command and control the generated state machine. This program is used only for different testing purposes. The state-machine is completely usable on itself without this procedure.

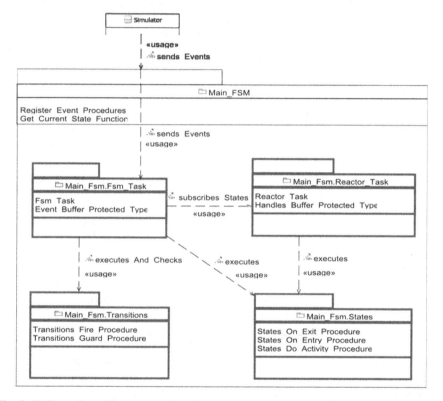

Fig. 3. UML package diagram showing the structure of the generated Ada code. Highlighted packages (those with a thicker border) are private childs of the outer package.

- A package, which name depends on the name of the state-machine model name (**Main_Fsm** in Fig. 3), implements all the structure and control logic of the state machine. This package contains: (1) the private child packages (depicted in Fig. 3 with a thicker border) that implement the different modules of the Reactor pattern as it will be explained in the following items, (2) the parameter-less procedures that signal the event occurrence that may trigger the fire of a transition of the state-machine, (3) a function to get the state machine current state and the corresponding types to correctly deal with it, and (4) the procedures that notify that an unexpected event has happened (these procedures are created when using the NOTIFY_ERROR value in the unexpectedTransitionPolicy property of the State-machine, see section 2.1).

- A private child package, named **Main_Fsm.Fsm_Task**, which contains a protected buffer to store event signaling and the task that controls the flow of states. The protected buffer accomplishes two main objectives: (1) it decouples event signaling from event processing, just as the Reactor pattern specifies, by using the *Command* design pattern [7], and (2) it makes the use of StateML$^+$ state-machines in multi-threaded applications possible. The task created in this package is in charge of controlling the state-machine and changing its state, depending on the received event. This task embodies the *run-to-completion* semantics that is associated to the state-machine execution, which includes event processing, entry/exit/fire activities execution and state change, but not do_activity execution.

- Another private child package, named **Main_Fsm.Reactor_Task,** that plays the role of the reactor that corresponds to its name. This package contains the list of currently active states (those whose Do_Activity has to be executed), together with the reactor task in charge of sequentially executing them. The list of activities to be executed is maintained and updated by the **Main_Fsm.Fsm_Task** when it processes an event that changes state. This design decision frees the **Fsm_Task** from executing the Do_Activity, so it can process the next event as soon as it completes the *run-to-completion* step.

- The private child package **Main_Fsm.Transitions** contains the specification and empty bodies of (1) the procedures that describe the activity that should be executed when a transition is fired (named Fire_XXX_Transition), and (2) the functions that check whether the transition should be executed or not, that is, the guard of the transition (Can_Fire_XXX_Transition). All of these subprograms are automatically generated if the corresponding attribute of the Transition is set (hasFire for generating the fire procedure and requiresGuard for the guard function). Of course, all these subprograms must be filled-in by the developer of the final application. Besides generating the specification of these subprograms, the transformation also generates the corresponding calls to these subprograms inside the procedures that control the state machine flow (implemented in the **Main_Fsm.Fsm_Task** package). This design decision eliminates the generation of unneeded code and reduces the number of subprogram calls, making the application smaller and more efficient.

- Another private child package, named **Main_Fsm.States**, contains the definition of all the states of the state-machine as well as the specification of the procedures that should be executed when entering (On_Entry procedure), exiting (On_Exit procedure) or when staying (Do_Activity procedure) in the state. As in the case of the Transition concept above, the specification, empty body and corresponding subprogram invocations are generated depending on the value of the hasOnEntry, hasOnExit and hasDo properties of the States.

The body of the reactor task contains a **select** statement to perform an Asynchronous Transfer Control (ATC) [15] back to the reactor. In the case in which the reactor is executing the Do_Activity of the state that is going to be exited as a consequence of the received event, this ATC will abort the corresponding procedure, as the execution of the state machine artifact demands.

Finally, to end this section about the model-to-Ada transformation of a StateML$^+$ model, it only remains to explain the implementation of the different values of the unexpectedTransitionPolicy attribute of the State-Machine concept. As was said in section 2, UML 2.x says that the behavior of the state machine after receiving an event that does not trigger the fire of any of the transitions of the current state is undefined (UML calls this a "semantic variation point"). The StateML$^+$ completes this lack definition by offering the designer two possible alternative behaviors when state machine receives such a transition: it may silently ignore the unexpected transition or it may call a registered procedure to notify other parts of the program the occurrence of this condition.

In the later case, two new procedures, named Subscribe_Handler and Erase_Handler, are added to the generated **Main_Fsm.Fsm_Task** package in order to allow interested units to subscribe to the occurrence of unexpected transitions. These handlers will be sequentially called by the state machine when it detects such an unexpected transition.

4   Conclusions and Future Research

State-machines have been used in software system design since the early 1970s, being part of many software applications and, for their characteristics they are particularly useful in the embedded system domain. As a consequence, many tools have been developed to describe and generate executable code for these artifacts. Among these tools, probably one of the most widely used is STATEMATE [11].

The OMG adopted state-machines to describe the behavior of the elements that appear in their UML standard. As a consequence, new UML-compliant tools appeared in the marketplace allowing designers to use this artifact in their designs. However, as the scope of these tools is wider than just generating code for state-machines, they commonly produce complex and cumbersome code, making it difficult to extract the state machine code. In this sense, the main advantage of the MDE approach is that developers can decide the abstraction level, the scope of their applications and the way models are transformed into code, having full control over the development process.

This paper has presented an extended version of the previously developed StateML tool, aimed at designing non-hierarchical state-machines and generating the corresponding Ada code implementation. According to the research objectives outlined in the introduction of the paper, the improved StateML$^+$ meta-model now allows designers to model the behavior of the ACRoSeT abstract components and to generate the corresponding Ada implementation. Therefore, the work presented in this paper represents a first and decided step in the road to implementing a full MDE process for generating robotic applications.

The extended StateML$^+$ meta-model and tools now include many improvements over the previous versions, being these the most important: (1) the addition of regions, which enable the creation of hierarchical and concurrent state-machines, (2) a better implementation of the *run-to-completion* semantics associated to the state-machine artifact, and (3) the generated Ada code is thread-safe and ready for working in a multi-tasking environment. We are still working on some additional improvements in the following directions:

- To allow designers to define different concurrency policies for each state. This would allow them to decide whether the `do_activity` of a state should be executed in the Reactor or in a new thread created for this purpose.
- To implement and test alternative design patterns, such as the *Proactor* or the *Active Object* [8] ones, which may help improving the overall system flexibility, as explained in section 3.1.
- To define additional model-to-text transformations to different target languages. Finding alternatives to Ada can be a tough work, as there are not many languages providing such a good multi-task support.

References

1. Schmidt, D.: Model-Driven Engineering. IEEE Computer 39, 25–31 (2006)
2. Bézivin, J.: On the Unification Power of Models. Software and Systems Modeling 4, 171–188 (2005)
3. Álvarez, B., Sánchez, P., Pastor, J.Á., Ortiz, F.J.: An architectural framework for modeling teleoperated service robots. Robotica 24, 411–418 (2006)
4. Alonso, D., Vicente-Chicote, C., Sánchez, P., Álvarez, B., Losilla, F.: Automatic Ada Code Generation Using a Model-Driven Engineering Approach. In: Abdennahder, N., Kordon, F. (eds.) Ada-Europe 2007. LNCS, vol. 4498, pp. 168–179. Springer, Heidelberg (2007)
5. Szyperski, C.: Component Software - Beyond Object-Oriented Programming. Addison-Wesley / ACM Press (2002)
6. OMG: Object Constraint Language (OCL) Specification v2.0. The Object Management Group (2006)
7. Gamma, E., Helm, R., Johnson, R., Vlissides, J.: Design Patterns: Elements of Reusable Object-Oriented Software. Addison-Wesley Professional, Reading (1995)
8. Schmidt, D., Stal, M., Rohnert, H., Buschmann, F.: Pattern-Oriented Software Architecture. In: Patterns for Concurrent and Networked Objects, vol. 2. Wiley, Chichester (2000)
9. The Eclipse MOFScript subproject., http://www.eclipse.org/gmt/mofscript/
10. OMG: Unified Modeling Language: Superstructure v 2.0. The Object Management Group (2005)
11. Harel, D., Naamad, A.: The STATEMATE semantics of statecharts. ACM Transactions on Software Engineering Methodology 5, 293–333 (1996)
12. OMG: Meta-Object Facility Specification v2.0. The Object Management Group (2004)
13. Douglass, B.P.: Real Time UML: Advances in the UML for Real-Time Systems. Addison-Wesley Professional, Reading (2004)
14. Sendall, S., Kozaczynski, W.: Model transformation: the heart and soul of model-driven software development. IEEE Software 20, 42–45 (2003)
15. Burns, A., Wellings, A.: Concurrent and Real-time Programming in Ada 2005. Cambridge University Press, Cambridge (2007)

Experience in the Integration of Heterogeneous Models in the Model-driven Engineering of High-Integrity Systems

Matteo Bordin, Thanassis Tsiodras, and Maxime Perrotin

University of Padua, Department of Pure and Applied Mathematics,
via Trieste 63, 35121 Padua, Italy
mbordin@math.unipd.it
Semantix Information Technologies, K. Tsaldari 62, 11476, Athens, Greece
ttsiodras@semantix.gr
European Space Agency, Keplerlaan 1, 2201 AZ Noordwijk, The Netherlands
maxime.perrotin@esa.int

Abstract. The development process of high-integrity systems has shifted from manual coding to designing with modeling tools that verify the correctness of the design well before production. The parallel application of several different modeling tools in the design of separate parts of the same system is now a common industrial practice. The advantage of using several, domain-specific tools is however balanced by an increasing complexity in the integration phase: it is indeed necessary to guarantee the correctness of the interaction of the several subapplications, which also includes the integration of the source code automatically generated by the different modeling tools. This constitutes a major concern for the introduction of several modeling tools in the industrial community, as well as for certification institutes. In this paper we present our practical experiences in the definition of a computer-aided sound development process to permit model-driven integration of heterogeneous models.

Keywords: Model-driven Integration, High-Integrity Systems, Automated Code Generation.

1 Introduction

The development of high-integrity systems stands to gain much from exploitation of different tools and languages in the implementation of a component based system. For example, in the domain of space-related applications (which is our main domain of interest), the system implementation is usually co-developed by several different providers, each one using a tool specifically suited for a particular subset of the application: Matlab [1] for the implementation of algorithms, SDL [2] for state machine logic, UML2 [3] for object-oriented architectures, AADL [4] or the emerging SysML [5] for system modeling, etc. The use of domain-specific tools offers two main advantages: (i) domain-specific semantics greatly simplifies the design and verification of a precise kind of applications; and (ii) the mentioned tools usually provide for automated source code generation through a

F. Kordon and T. Vardanega (Eds.): Ada-Europe 2008, LNCS 5026, pp. 171–184, 2008.

specifically tailored process (for example, the code generator which comes with SCADE has been qualified for DO-178B level A systems [6]).

The exploitation of several, domain-specific tools providing automated code generation to implement the functional specification surely decreases the verification and validation costs; but it also increases the criticality of the integration phase, as the switch from *software* modeling to *system* modeling - which is the design of the system architecture - may negatively affect the semantics of common data types and the non-functional properties of the system. Currently, the integration process is handled manually, making it very error-prone and a possible source of defects.

The idea we present in this paper is to exploit model-driven technologies to automate the integration phase, guaranteeing that the whole process can be applied in domains subject to strict certification standards. Model-Driven Engineering (MDE, [7]) is currently one of the main innovation vectors in software engineering. The whole idea at the heart of model-driven engineering is to promote the use of a formal, high-abstraction, representation of the system, a *model*, during each phase of the development cycle. In a model-driven development process, models are designed, analyzed, transformed, verified and executed. The notion of *model transformation* is particularly meaningful in MDE. Models are usually designed at a very high abstraction level, which may be agnostic on aspects such as target execution platform, deployment, and distribution middleware: a model transformation which takes as input the model *and* the platform specification may automatically generate the implementation of the system for a particular platform. Ideally, the developers do not need to cope with low-level representations of the system at all: the generation of source code is for example *just one* of the several possible transformations a model is subject to. In mainstream software engineering, model-driven engineering has *de facto* taken the name of the OMG initiative named Model-Driven Architecture (MDA, [8]); MDE is however not limited to the OMG world: SCADE or Matlab Simulink [9] are indeed excellent examples of MDE infrastructures because they permit to design, verify and deploy systems using a high-abstraction modeling semantics. Another key aspect of model-driven engineering is the concept of domain-specific metamodeling (DSM), which is the definition of design languages and tools to fully support MDE in a particular domain.

Model-driven principles and technologies have already been applied to the integration problem [10]: the OMG MOF facility is by itself an integration framework for heterogeneous metamodels. The most common domain for the application of model-driven integration is enterprise computing. One of the most typical application is the reverse engineering of legacy components (usually in the from of source code, CORBA interfaces, XML) to UML models, so as to permit the generation of a middleware layer to interface the components [11]. Another common application is the interoperaction between metadata defined with domain-specific metamodels which are all traced to a common metamodel, usually in the form of UML profiles [12].

Our first main contribution to the field of model-driven integration is the domain we target: high-integrity systems, in particular in the space domain. The most well-known (and probably unique) example of model integration in the high-integrity domain is the SCADE Simulink Gateway which permits to import Simulink models in SCADE, modify them and generate code using the SCADE code generation engine. As a first notable difference, we aim to integrate models designed with *radically* different tools *along* with their generated code. The models we plan to integrate are *functional* models because they represent the functional (sequential) specification of the system. The integration process must thus guarantee that the interaction between the models designed with different tools does not corrupt the properties proved during the modeling phase and that the interfacing of the generated code does not corrupt the semantics of the exchanged data: the solution of this last problem cannot be found in mainstream technologies like CORBA, SOAP or WEB-services, because of the peculiarities of the target domain (embedded systems with strict performance and predictability requirements). Finally, we also wish to verify system-level properties (in particular the timing behaviour) of the integrated system via model-based analysis: to achieve this goal, the integration process must be able to extract the information relevant to the analysis from the imported models.

1.1   The Overall Picture

The work presented in this paper is part of a toolchain infrastructure for the design, verification and implementation of high-integrity real-time systems. The main aim of our work is to define a new development process for high-integrity systems and develop a set of tools to support it. We have already developed a full Eclipse plug-in for the design of high-integrity, real-time systems. The plug-in is based on a domain-specific metamodel called RCM [13]. The RCM metamodel is conceptually traceable to a UML2 profile: it allows functional modeling by means of class and state machine diagrams and system modeling through component and deployment diagrams. The RCM metamodel guarantees that any designed system abides by the constraints enforced by the Ravenscar Computational Model [14] and can thus be statically analyzed for its timing behavior. The timing analysis is automatically performed on the model itself and encompasses logically and physically distributed systems [15]. The plug-in also comes with an automated code generation engine targeting Ada 2005 [16], which achieve 100% code generation for the concurrent and distributed architecture of the system [13].

2   System Models as an Integration Framework

The notion of *heterogeneity* entails that functional models are defined with different semantics: in MDE terms, we would say that the metamodel underlying each model is potentially different. This is in fact the case, as tools like SCADE, SDL and UML have their own semantics; the same fact applies also to manually written code, as a programming language - or more accurately, its grammar and semantics - is by itself a metamodel.

The place where the (different) semantics of (heterogeneous) functional models fit together is the *system model*, which is the model representing the overall system in terms of both functional and non-functional (like concurrency and deployment) features. We believe that a system model should be considered as a true integration framework — a pivotal representation of the system — because this is the place where software and system semantics merge: only in a system model is it possible to assure the correct interaction between integrated models and verify system-level properties which are affected by both the software and system modeling process. Our metamodel of choice for system modeling is the RCM metamodel, briefly introduced in section 1.1 and described in [13] and [17].

Merging heterogeneous functional models within a single system model may render particularly challenging to:

1. verify that the functional models do not interfere with the synchronization mechanism of the concurrent architecture;
2. assure that the concurrent architecture does not corrupt the properties of functional models by introducing race condition or deadlocks;
3. guarantee that the (possibly remote) interactions between heterogeneous functional models are semantically preserving, which basically means they do not corrupt the passed data;
4. keep the software and system view consistent with each other.

Coping with items 1 - 2 above is straightforward. If the concurrent semantics is prohibited in functional models, then the functional specification cannot affect the synchronization of the system; it is quite easy to identify the elements (or key words in a programming language) related to concurrency in the metamodel for functional modeling and prohibit their use. Tools for functional modeling usually permit to express some sort of aggregation properties for services accessing the same functional state: a SCADE block or a UML class are such examples. In order to avoid the corruption of the functional specification by the concurrent execution of the system, it is enough to constrain the concurrent semantics to permit at most one task at a time to access a functional model — in other words, to have a single executer behind the state machine underlying the functional model[1]. This constraint leaves two possible choices for stateful functional models: (i) a single dedicated task always executes the state machine; or (ii) each triggering procedure of the state machine presents a synchronization protocol assuring mutual access to the whole functional state. Stateless functional models (for example mathematical functions) do not require any particular attention in deciding their concurrent behavior. By choosing the concurrent semantics in a way the aforementioned constraints are guaranteed, no race condition may happen; deadlocks can also be prevented by enforcing the immediate priority ceiling protocol [18] and implementing remote communication with an asynchronous, message-based protocol.

---

[1] We do not consider non-intersecting, parallel state machines within the same class.

To guarantee semantic preservation of exchanged data (point 3) we use ASN.1 [19] for data modeling and an appropriate compiler to generate stubs to convert the raw representation of data between different languages/architecture: it is however less clear how we can integrate with the code generated by different modeling tools (SCADE, SDL, etc.). View-consistency (point 4) requires more attention and is strongly related with *cross-cutting* concerns. Cross-cutting concerns are aspects of the system affected by both the software and the system modeling process. A typical example of cross-cutting concerns is the definition of (execution/information/data) flows: they of course depend on the connection between component instances and on their deployment; but they also depend on the functional specification, which basically tells which services are invoked in response to the execution of a functional procedure. A sound determination of flows is a fundamental requirement for several kinds of model-based analysis, it being related to, for example, timing performance or security preservation. In the scope of our experimentation, we used the modelization of execution flows to perform model-based timing analysis [15].

3   Semantic Preservation in Practice

Three main dimensions require particular care if several modeling tools are exploited: (i) the semantics of common data types, and in particular their physical representations on different execution platforms; (ii) the integration of the code generated by the different modeling tools; and (iii) the extraction and evaluation of cross-cutting concerns.

3.1   Data Semantics Preservation

Abstract Syntax Notation One [19,20] (ASN.1) is a standard and flexible notation that allows detailed data structure representation, as well as portable and efficient encoding and decoding of data into bitstreams.

In the context of our work, ASN.1 was used as the center of a "star formation"; *all* the communication taking place between the subsystems (possibly modeled in different modeling tools) is done through ASN.1 messages. This enforces a common semantic "contract" between the communicating entities, in terms of what information is exchanged; ASN.1 therefore guarantees the semantic equivalence of the data types used in the different modeling tools.

To enforce this semantic equivalence contract, a semantic translation takes place immediately after the definition of the ASN.1 grammar that describes the exchanged data. The ASN.1 definitions of the messages form the basis; the desired target definitions are the semantically equivalent ones in the data definition languages offered by the modeling tools. A custom tool was built [21] that reads the ASN.1 definitions and translated them into the equivalent data definitions, to the extent supported by the target modeling tool languages (e.g. Lustre (for SCADE), SDL (for ObjectGeode), etc).

The translation process is guided from the overall system view; by parsing it and learning about the implementation platform of each subsystem, the translation tool is in a position to know the desired target language per message and accurately translate it preserving the semantic information.

As an example, from this ASN.1 data definition:

```
EXAMPLE  DEFINITIONS IMPLICIT TAGS ::= BEGIN PosData ::=
[APPLICATION 1] SEQUENCE {
    x INTEGER, y INTEGER,
    description OCTET STRING (SIZE(1..80))
} END
```

we get this translation in Lustre:

```
let type System_Types
    PosData = [x : int, y : int, description : char^ 80];
tel;
```

This translation is in fact the key to guarantee semantic consistency; e.g. the team developing a subsystem in SCADE will use the structure definitions as they are generated from the translation tool, knowing in advance that this process will neither introduce new content nor prune existing ones. If there is information in the ASN.1 definitions that is not translatable to the target modeling tool language, the translation tool will complain and warn the user about it - providing early feedback about the potential loss of information and preventing side effects from this loss. Notice also that by using the overall system view, the tool knows exactly what targets it needs to generate code for, thus being minimal and complete - optimal - in the generated definitions.

3.2   Integration of Generated Code

Creating semantically equivalent definitions is the first step - it guarantees that all subsystems will be functionally modeled with equivalent message definitions. This is not enough, however. Each modeling tool follows its own scheme in terms of how it generates code. To be precise, the code generated by the tools can be conceptually split in two categories:

– Code that implements the logic of the subsystem: state machines, algorithmic descriptions of work to be done in response to incoming signals, etc
– Code that describes the data structures of the exchanged messages

Since the data definitions have been produced by the translation tool, the data structures generated are certainly equipped with the same data. The details however - e.g. variable names, ordering, language-specific type definitions, etc - vary a great deal between different modeling tools. As a consequence, the actual generated code cannot interoperate as it is; error-prone manual labour is required to "glue" the pieces together. This is the source of multiple problems[2], and it is

---

[2] http://awads.net/wp/2005/12/05/ten-worst-software-bugs/

another reason for using ASN.1: by placing it at the center of a star formation amongst all modeling tools, the "glue-ing" can be done automatically:

– An ASN.1 compiler is used to create encoders and decoders for the messages exchanged between subsystems [22]
– Another custom tool is used [21], that creates mapping code ("glue" code); code that translates the data at runtime between the data structures of the ASN.1 compiler, and the data structures generated by the modeling tools.

As long as the mapping is a well defined one - that is, as long as the modeling tools follow specific rules in how they translate message data into data structures - this mapping work is feasible *at compile time*. This translation tool starts from the overall system view, just as the first one (Section 3.1) did: it learns about all the "paths" that messages have to go across, and thus, it knows what kind of glue code to generate at the source and the destination of each message exchange.

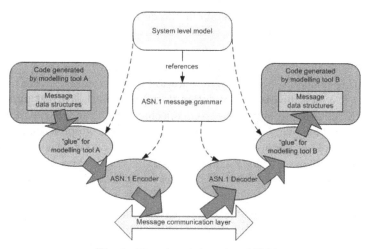

Fig. 1. Mapping data using ASN.1

This process is significantly easier to test and verify - compared to the manual translation process that would have to take place in its absence. Instead of painstakingly checking all the manually written code parts that marshal data back and forth between the data structures of the modeling tools' generated code, the only tests that need to be done are performed on the code generating primitives, that is; mapping of integers, mapping of floating point numbers, mapping of strings, etc. When each category has been tested and is known to be handled in the correct manner, *no further testing is necessary*, regardless of the complexity of the message structure itself. This significantly lessens the effort required to use complex messages in the exchanges taking place between different modeling tools.

Additionally, this glue layer offers a central point for tool-indifferent marshalling: common mapping API can be developed that pertain to specific type mapping and tool categories; as an example, SCADE/Lustre are just one of the technologies adhering to a synchronous modeling paradigm; common patterns for all such tools can be extracted into a message marshalling portability layer.

Here is an example declaration section from the glue code generated:

```
#include <stdlib.h> /* for size_t */ int
Convert_From_ASN1C_To_TCLink_In__TC_Parser__Id(
    void *pBuffer, size_t iBufferSize);
```

A number of marshalling functions are generated, one (or more) per message marshalling interface: they convey the message data as (pBuffer, iBufferSize) pairs into the appropriate data structures generated by the modeling tools; data are passed via (pBuffer, iBufferSize) pairs because it is a language-neutral representation of a series of octet - the ASN.1 message. Their implementation is completely automated, and their code generation process can cope with arbitrarily complex message definitions in a transparent way. The end user simply calls them, without ever worrying about the details of the mapping code.

3.3   Managing Cross-Cutting Concerns

Cross-cutting concerns (as the representation of functional provided/required services or the identification of execution flows) require the correct understanding of both the software and the system specification. A simple but illustrative example is the following. Given a state machine SM, suppose that the state entered by invoking method p() includes, among its actions, the invocation of method r() on object o (a class member). It is evident that there is a flow from p() to o.r(), but from the pure software specification it is not possible to determine which object resolves the invocation, because this information is contained in the deployment diagram where objects are linked; similarly the semantics of the invocation of o.r() is obscure in the functional model, as it may be synchronous or asynchronous, local or remote: this information is again contained in the system specification. On the other side, by looking at a pure system specification (it being written in RCM, SysML or AADL), it is not possible to determine the functional behavior behind the invocation of a service, as the action semantics is not completely visible from a system model. The current industrial practice would require the *manual* translation of cross-cutting concerns from a software to a system model (or viceversa): for example, flows may be manually identified in the system level, assuming the designer has a complete knowledge of the underlying functional specification. This process is inevitably error-prone: design errors may of course be caught during the verification phase, but this approach still requires additional manual intervention and thus increases the cost of validation. The presence of several possible modeling tools (each one with its own metamodel), makes it even harder for the designer to completely understand all possible formalisms for software design and extract the required information from the software models. Furthermore, to correctly identify cross-cutting concerns, the designer is actually required to define a semantic mapping between the metamodel used for system modeling and the metamodel(s) for software modeling. Industrial practitioners often seem to overlook the hidden complexity of that kind of mapping, which is definitely a potential source of inconsistency between system and software models.

In order to try to overcome the limits intrinsic to the manual nature of coping with cross-cutting concerns, we reasoned on the possibility of automating the interchange of semantic information between software and system models, and in particular to automatically import heterogeneous functional models in the system model. In section 2 we have acknowledged the pivotal role of the system model: our idea is to automatically determine the system representation of (part of) cross-cutting concerns by *importing* software models into the system model; in this manner, the design process would be guided by the automatically imported information, avoiding errors and inconsistencies between the system and software specification by construction. The import of a functional model is basically a model transformation which transforms a functional model conforming to the metamodel of the tool used to design it, to a model which conforms to the RCM metamodel: the first metamodel is said to be the *source* metamodel, while the second is the *target* metamodel. When importing a functional model, two distinct options are possible: we can import the *entire* semantics of the source model or we can extract *just* the information required to create a valid RCM model. In the first case, we should guarantee that the target metamodel (RCM) is expressive enough for every possible functional metamodel and develop a complex model transformation encompassing the *entire* semantics of the source metamodel: this solution may not even be possible to implement. In the case of importing a selected subset of the functional model, we are required to extract *only* the information that is needed for an RCM model: basically, the target metamodel specifies which kind of semantics must be present in the source metamodel to permit a meaningful import process. The required subset of semantics of the source metamodel is usually determined by the needs for system-level model-based analysis and code generation: in our case, to perform model-based timing analysis, we are interested in just provided/required services of each functional model and in their relation (basically, the execution flow: which required service is invoked during the execution of a provided one). In order to obtain the best cost/benefit ratio, we chose the second option.

The following step is the definition of the semantic mapping between the source metamodel and the RCM metamodel. From a purely conceptual point of view, a semantic mapping requires the comparison of the semantics of two different languages and the definition of a series of functions to move from the source to the target metamodel. Unfortunately, a mathematically sound methodology to specify *and* prove semantic mappings in MDE is yet to come: we thus still rely on the comparison of the language standards to define the model transformations. On a more pragmatic dimension, the model transformation requires to extract a set of information from a functional model, which may come in the form of a textual language (SDL, SCADE) or via an XML-based representation (UML2). If the source model is encoded using the latest (meta)modeling technologies, the model importer can exploit state-of-the-art tools to directly transform the source model into the target model. On the other side, importing a model specified via a textual language is more complex, because it requires a sort of "double-pass" transformation: first the model is parsed, then it must be transformed into an XML tree on which perform a model transformation.

The import process creates RCM entities representing the imported functional models within the functional view of an RCM model. Such entities are basically read-only, because they were designed, verified and deployed (transformed to code) with extern modeling tools. At the same time, the generated entities are marked with an appropriate tag to permit the RCM code generator to generate the code required to interface with the source generated by the original modeling tool. Once the software model is imported into an RCM model, the RCM representations of system-level provided/required services and possible execution flows are *automatically* determined out of the functional specification (see [17] for a complete explanation): it is thus impossible for system-level properties to be specified in a manner which is inconsistent with the imported software models. From this perspective, the RCM metamodel presents a clear advantage over other system modeling languages: it guarantees view consistency by strongly relating semantic element of each view. The RCM system model thus contains all the information required to perform model-based timing analysis: from this point on, the verification process proceeds as described in [15].

At the moment, we have developed prototype importers of UML2, Object-Geode (SDL) and SCADE (Lustre) models into an RCM model: the UML2 importer is not particular interesting because, since RCM mimics the UML2 semantics, its development is purely a technical (not conceptual) exercise; SDL and SCADE importers are indeed worth of additional explanation. The tools we used to parse and transform SDL and SCADE models are, respectively, OpenArchitectureWare xText and the Atlas Transformation Language (ATL).

Importing SCADE models. In order to preserve the properties of SCADE blocks (verified and proved with the appropriate modeling tool), we decided to prohibit the invocation of extern operations from within a SCADE block. For this reason, a SCADE block is always the leaf of an execution flow: in other words, it does not present required interfaces. The importing process of SCADE block is thus quite simple: it is simply mapped as a RCM class providing the service(s) offered by the block.

Importing SDL models. The import of SDL models is more complicated because they may have both provided and required interfaces - meaning that it is necessary to extract not only provided and required services, but also the execution flow. After the parsing, the transformation process is divided into three main steps:

1. Each SDL process is mapped onto an RCM class in the functional model: the accepted input signal are mapped as public methods of the class.

2. The output signals or calls executed by the SDL process compose the required interface of the RCM class: they are grouped by their target element, which may be another SDL state machine, a SCADE block or an UML class.
3. For every output signal or call sent in response to an input signal, an execution flow between the method corresponding to the input signal and the required interface corresponding to the output signal or call is generated in the RCM class.

All information imported from the SDL model are automatically represented in the system view, thanks to the view consistency enforced by the RCM metamodel. To some extent, the SDL importer is still primitive because it does not take into account conditional execution: *all* possible execution flows are considered *at the same time*, even those which are mutually exclusive. For the purpose of timing analysis, this limit induces a clear pessimism, because the worst case execution path is composed by the union of *all* paths. To limit the pessimism, in the first prototype of our tool we permit to manually select which flows must be considered for the analysis: we are aware that a manual intervention may potentially corrupt the model consistency, but we consider this solution as a temporary defect induced by technical reasons, rather than by conceptual difficulties.

4   Results and Discussion

To evaluate our approach and the tools we developed, we designed a simple example using the RCM metamodel and related tools. The prototype is a simplification of the software architecture of a subset of the embedded software of a satellite, in particular the positioning and guidance and navigation system: it is composed by communicating applications designed in SCADE (algorithmical computations), SDL (state machines modeling) and RCM (system modeling). The prototype has been demonstrated during the final review of the ASSERT project (cf. the Acknowledgements section). The designed system is an approximation of a real-life architecture, but it demonstrates most of the components categories usually present in this family of applications; our purpose of evaluating our approach in model-driven integration of heterogenous models is adequately illustrated by this simplified prototype. Our evaluation is based on a set of metrics quite common in model-driven development, namely semantic preservation in model transformations, ease of model-based analysis, model-to-code traceability and the quality and size of generated code.

The prototype importer tools developed to generate RCM functional models from SCADE and SDL models enabled us to accurately determine the system-level representation of provided and required services; at the same time, possible execution paths are identified during the importing process, permitting a safer identification of the flows of interest for model-based (timing) analysis: with the described approach, the identification of cross-cutting concerns cannot be a possible cause of semantic inconsistency anymore. The presence of an XML-based and well-defined metamodel for all involved modeling tools is a highly desired requirement to simplify any importing process by using more productive modeling technologies: modeling technologies using XML and OCL (or equivalent) -based technologies render the development of the model importer/analysis tools easier and more cost effective. The effort we spent in developing an SDL importer (starting from a textual specification) is a practical indication of the truth behind this statement: state-of-the-art modeling technologies permit much easier model query and manipulation, thanks to the exploitation of domain-specific tools; as an exemplary quantitative evaluation, *just* the implementation (and *not* the conception of the semantic mapping) of a UML2 importer from an EMF-based implementation took us less than half of the time than the development of the corresponding tool for SDL. Our belief is strengthened by the general industrial trend toward some sort of XML-based metamodeling technology, even for languages originally born as a pure textual specification such as SCADE or AADL (cf. the TOPCASED project).

Our automated code generation process proved to be useful and efficient when applied to the described test case: the code generated from SCADE and Object-GEODE (an SDL tool) could be *automatically* integrated with the code generated from the system view (designed in RCM) to implement the concurrent and deployment architecture of the system. From a quantitative point of view, the amount of generated code is comparable in sheer size to the source generated to handle the concurrent and distribution infrastructure, but probably not more than what we would have written in a manual development process: such an evaluation is a good empirical estimation of the productive advantages of the developed tools. We are currently working to integrate the overall transformation chain (including the code generator for RCM models and the tools described in sections 3.1 and 3.2) within a single Eclipse plug-in: in this manner, we plan to decrease the effort required by the end user to generate code integrating heterogenous models within a single system model.

From a purely technological point of view, the results we achieved are quite important, since they represent one of the first (if not *the* first) successful attempt to apply model-driven integration in the space application domain: our test case — while simple — is a valid proof of concepts and exploits tools widely used in the industrial community. Some concerns however still remain.

First, some optimization concerns: while ASN1 modeling is surely an effective way to guarantee the preservation of the semantics of data types across different languages/architectures, when the interacting subsystems are designed in the same modeling tool and they "live" in the same process space, they can communicate more optimally (speed-wise) by directly accessing each other's data structures. This would avoid the overhead of needless data conversions. On the code generation side, the choice of *always* passing through ASN1 (un)marshalling has two main drawbacks: (i) it induces a penalty on the execution time: the penalty is not evident in the model and cannot be evaluated on the functional specification (it is introduced by the code generator), making it difficult to perform accurate model-based timing analysis; and (ii) it makes model-to-code traceability difficult, as the invocation of any required service is actually mapped as an invocation to a sort of middleware composed by the ASN1 (un)marshallers, instead of a proper method invocation like in the originating model. To partially overcome the cited problems, we may consider to extend our tools to apply ASN1 (un)marshalling only when strictly required and add traceability information to the generated code.

5   Conclusion

In this paper we have described an experimental approach to model-driven integration for the development of high-integrity systems exploiting multiple modeling tools. By identifying in the system model the place where heterogeneous models should be integrated, we developed a set of tools allowing a highly automated integration process encompassing model importing and automated generation of glue code. The main difference of our approach when compared to mainstream solutions is its focus on integrating radically different models *and* their generated code, with particular attention for the consistency of cross-cutting concerns and the verification of system-level properties in the *integrated* system model: the integration process indeed also includes the extraction of information relevant to model-based analysis from the imported models. During our investigation, two main results rose. First of all, multiple-view consistency emerged as a highly desirable property for system modeling languages aiming to support model-based analysis in the high-integrity domain: contrary to the RCM metamodel, current state-of-the-art modeling languages do not enforces any form of view consistency, forcing the designer to manually guarantee it. In addition, selective[3] model import via automated model transformations showed to be a worthy solution for analysis-oriented model-driven integration.

The industrial need for the developed technologies is strongly related to the heterogeneity of modeling tools/platforms/architectures for the domain of interest: the more the variety, the more useful our tools are. In *current-generation* systems the weight of the side-effects introduced by the chosen technological solutions is not small, in particular for what regards model-based analysis, model-to-code traceability and performance; *next-generation* applications are however expected to drastically increase their complexity, along with the amount of exploited modeling formalisms and programming languages: the recent rise of AADL, SysML and RTSJ are a clear example of this trend. We thus expect the integration issue to gain more and more importance in the development of future systems; the industrial community must then strive to find effective and cost-wise solutions to solve it: the approach we presented in this paper is a good starting point in that direction and surely a valid reference milestone for future improvements.

Acknowledgments. The research work from which this paper has originated was carried out in the ASSERT project (IST-FP6-2004 004033) partially funded by the European Commission as part of the 6th Framework Programme. The authors gratefully acknowledge Yuri Yushtein (European Space Agency) for his valuable suggestions.

---

[3] Only part of the imported models is mapped onto the target metamodel.

References

1. Matlab: http://www.mathworks.com/
2. SDL: Specification and Description Language, http://www.sdl-forum.org/
3. OMG: UML2 Metamodel Superstructure (2005)
4. AADL: Architecture Analysis and Design Language, http://www.aadl.info
5. SysML: Systems Modeling Language, http://www.omgsysml.org/
6. RTCA: Radio Technical Commission for Aeronautics, rtca.org
7. Schmidt, D.C.: Guest Editor's Introduction: Model-Driven Engineering. Computer 39(2), 25–31 (2006)
8. The Object Management Group: (Model Driven Architecture), www.omg.org
9. Mathworks: (Simulink), http://www.mathworks.com/products/simulink/
10. Denno, P., Steves, M.P., Libes, D., Barkmeyer, E.J.: Model-driven integration using existing models. IEEE Software 20(5), 59–63 (2003)
11. E2E: Model Driven Integration: Transparent Virtualization of Distributed Applications (E2E technical white paper), http://www.e2ebridge.com/live/files/E2E-WP-MDI-070112en.pdf
12. Noogle, B.J., Lang, M.: Model Driven Information Architecture. TDAN.com (2002), http://www.tdan.com/view-articles/4989
13. Bordin, M., Vardanega, T.: Correctness by Construction for High-Integrity Real-Time Systems: a Metamodel-driven Approach. In: Reliable Software Technologies - Ada-Europe (2007)
14. Burns, A., Dobbing, B., Vardanega, T.: Guide for the Use of the Ada Ravenscar Profile in High Integrity Systems. Technical Report YCS-2003-348, University of York (2003)
15. Panunzio, M., Vardanega, T.: A Metamodel-Driven Process Featuring Advanced Model-Based Timing Analysis. In: Abdennahder, N., Kordon, F. (eds.) Ada-Europe 2007. LNCS, vol. 4498, pp. 128–141. Springer, Heidelberg (2007)
16. Bordin, M., Vardanega, T.: Automated Model-Based Generation of Ravenscar-Compliant Source Code. In: Proc. of the 17th Euromicro Conference on Real-Time Systems (2005)
17. Bordin, M., Vardanega, T.: A Domain-specific Metamodel for Reusable, Object-Oriented, High-Integrity Components. In: OOPSLA DSM 2007. ACM, New York (2007)
18. Goodenough, J.B., Sha, L.: The priority ceiling protocol: a method for minimizing the blocking of high priority Ada tasks. In: IRTAW 1988: Proc. of the second international workshop on Real-time Ada issues, pp. 20–31 (1988)
19. ITU-T: (Rec. X.680-X.683, ISO/IEC: Abstract Syntax Notation One (ASN.1))
20. Dubuisson, O.: ASN.1 - Communication between heterogeneous systems (2000)
21. Semantix Information Technologies: The ASSERT project ASN.1 toolchain (2002), http://www.semantix.gr/assert/
22. asn1c: The Open Source ASN.1 compiler (2002-2007), http://lionet.info/asn1c/

A Systematic Approach to Automatically Generate Multiple Semantically Equivalent Program Versions*

Sri Hari Krishna Narayanan and Mahmut Kandemir

Computer Science and Engineering Department
The Pennsylvania State University, University Park, PA 16802, USA
{snarayan,kandemir}@cse.psu.edu

Abstract. Classic methods to overcome software faults include design diversity that involves creating multiple versions of an application. However, design diverse techniques typically require a staggering investment of time and manpower. There is also no guarantee that the multiple versions are correct or equivalent. This paper presents a novel approach that addresses the above problems, by automatically producing multiple, semantically equivalent copies for a given array/loop-based application. The copies, when used within the framework of common design diverse techniques, provide a high degree of software fault tolerance at practically no additional cost. In this paper, we also apply our automated version generation approach to detect the occurrence of soft errors during the execution of an application.

1 Introduction

Design diversity is a technique used for achieving a certain degree of fault tolerance in software engineering [1,2,3,4,5]. Since exact copies of a given program cannot always improve fault tolerance, creating multiple, different copies is essential [6]. However, this is not a trivial task as independently designing different versions of the same application software can take a lot of time and resources, most of which is spent verifying that these versions are indeed semantically equivalent and they exhibit certain diversity which helps us catch design errors as much as possible (e.g., by minimizing the causes for identical errors). The problem becomes more severe if a large number of versions are required.

Automatically generating different versions of a given program can be useful in two aspects, provided that the versions generated are sufficiently diverse for catching the types of errors targeted. First, design time and cost can be dramatically reduced as a result of automation. Second, since the versions are generated automatically, we can be sure that they are semantically equivalent save for the errors of interest. However,

* This work is supported in part by NSF grants # 0720645 , # 0702519 and support from the Gigascale Systems Research Focus Center, one of the five research centers funded under SRCs Focus Center Research Program. The authors would like to thank the anonymous reviewers for their helpful remarks. The authors would like to thank Seung Woo Son and Shiva Prasad Kasiviswanathan for their suggestions. Finally, the authors would like to thank, our shepherd, Dr. Erhard Plödereder who helped finalize the paper.

F. Kordon and T. Vardanega (Eds.): Ada-Europe 2008, LNCS 5026, pp. 185–198, 2008.

as mentioned earlier, these versions should be sufficiently different from each other, depending on the types of errors targeted.

Numerical applications which make extensive use of arrays and nested loops are good candidates for automatic version generation as they are amenable to be analyzed and restructured by optimizing compilers. Current compilers restructure such applications to optimize data locality and improving loop-level parallelism as well as for other reasons [7,8,9,10]. The main stumbling block to full fledged re-ordering of computations are data dependences in the program code.

The main contribution of this paper is a tool that generates different versions of a numerical application automatically *a priori*. The tool generates these versions by restructuring the given application code in a systematic fashion using the concept of *data tiles*. A data tile is a portion of an array which may be manipulated by the application. Hence, an array can be thought of as a series of data tiles. Given such a series of data tiles, of a particular size and shape, we can generate a new version of the code by restructuring the code in such a fashion that the accesses to each tile are completed before moving to the next tile. As a result, computations are performed on a per tile basis. Therefore, a different tile shape or a different order of tiles (to the extent allowed by data) gives an entirely different version of the application, thereby contributing to diversity. In this paper, we also present a method for selecting the tile shapes as well as method to systematically reorder them based on the number of versions required.

We apply our tool to the emergent architectural challenge of soft errors. Soft errors are a form of transient errors that occur when charged neutrons strike logic devices which hold charges to indicate the bit that they represent [11,12,13,14]. A neutron strike can change the charge held on the device either by charging or discharging it. This change in charge can lead to a bit flip in memory or logic components of the system which can affect the end results generated by the application. We show how the tool can be used to detect errors that remain undetected by a state of the art architectural recovery approach.

The remainder of this paper is organized as follows. Section 2 presents the theory behind the proposed approach. Section 3 presents implementation details of our tool as well as results obtained using a scientific benchmark. Section 4 concludes the paper by summarizing our major contributions and giving a brief outline of the planned future work.

2   Detailed Analysis

This section explains the details of the approach proposed to automatically create the multiple versions of a given array/loop based application. Our goal is to obtain different (but semantically equivalent) versions of a given code fragment by restructuring the fragment based on a data tile shape. The input to our approach is a code fragment that consists of the series of loop nests and the data array(s) that is accessed in the fragment. The loop nests in the fragment contain expressions, called array references, that access locations within the array. Figure 1(a) shows an example code fragment and the array being accessed in the loop nests.

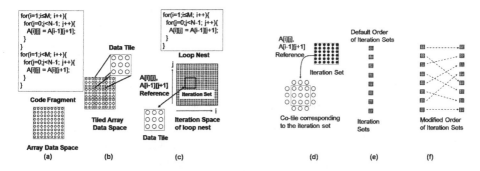

Fig. 1. (a) A code fragment. (b) Data tiles formed from a seed tile. (c) Iteration set that accesses the data in a data tile. (d) Co-tile identification. (e) Default order of iteration sets. (f) New order of iteration sets, as a result of restructuring.

Our approach first creates a *seed tile* which is a uniquely shaped subsection of the array (selection of a seed tile is detailed in Section 2.7). Using this seed tile as a template, we logically divide the array into multiple sections called *data tiles* as shown in Figure 1(b). In the following paragraphs we discuss what is performed on a particular data tile.

In the next stage shown in 1(c), we identify for each loop nest the array references that accesses locations within the data tile. Then, for each loop nest, we use these references to determine the set of iterations that access this particular data tile. The iterations from a loop nest that are associated with a particular data tile are called the *iteration set* of that data tile with respect to that loop nest.

Now, let us consider the case for a particular iteration set associated with a data tile. It is possible that these iterations access array locations outside the data tile as well. These external locations are called the *extra tile*, and the original data tile and the extra tile are collectively referred to as the *co-tile*. Figure 1(d) shows the co-tile corresponding to an iteration set.

Our idea is to first identify, for each combination of data tile and loop nest, the associated iteration set. Once we have the iteration set corresponding to a data tile and loop nest, we can execute all the computations that should take place on that pair. The original code can therefore be thought of as the default order of iteration sets shown in Figure 1(e). Next, in order to create new codes, we systematically re-order the iteration sets to create multiple different sequences as shown in Figure 1(f). Each unique order of iteration sets leads to a unique version of the code. Such a re-ordering is legal provided that data dependences do not exist between iteration sets. Data dependences, impose an ordering constraint on the iteration sets and prevent full fledged re-ordering. If dependences do exist between the iteration sets, we explore other data tile shapes to arrive at a dependence free group of iteration sets.

The rest of this section details our approach. After presenting basic definitions in Section 2.1, Section 2.2 presents our method of forming data tiles. Section 2.3 shows how iteration sets and co-tiles are calculated. Our algorithm to detect dependences (legality requirements) are presented in Section 2.4. Section 2.5 shows how the iteration sets are systematically re-ordered. Section 2.6 presents the overall algorithm used to create multiple versions of code. Section 2.7 discusses how data tiles of different shapes and sizes are created, and Section 2.8 explains how we deal with code that accesses multiple arrays.

2.1 Basic Definitions

This subsection presents important definitions that we use to formalize our approach.

- Program : A program source code fragment is represented as $\mathcal{P} = \{\mathcal{N}, \mathcal{A}\}$, where $\mathcal{N}$ is a list of loop nests and $\mathcal{A}$ is the set of arrays declared in $\mathcal{P}$ that are accessed in $\mathcal{N}$. Figure 2 shows the benchmark source code fragment employed.
- Array : An array $\mathcal{A}_a$ is described by its dimensions, δ, and the extent (size) in each dimension, γ, $\mathcal{A}_a = \{\delta, \gamma\}$. For example, the array DW defined in the code fragment in Figure 2 can be expressed as $DW = \{3, \{10, 10, 4\}\}$ in our framework.
- Loop Nest : A loop nest $\mathcal{N}_i$, is represented as $\{\alpha, \mathcal{A}_{\mathcal{N}}, \mathcal{I}, \mathcal{L}, \mathcal{U}, \mathcal{S}, \psi\}$, where α is the number of loops in the nest and $\mathcal{L}, \mathcal{U}$, and $\mathcal{S}$ are vectors that give, respectively, the values of the lower limit, upper limit, and the step of the loop index variables which are given in $\mathcal{I}$. It is assumed that at compile time all the values of these vectors are known. The body of the loop nest is represented by ψ. The arrays accessed within $\mathcal{N}_i$ are represented as $\mathcal{A}_{\mathcal{N}_i}$ where $\mathcal{A}_{\mathcal{N}_i} \subseteq \mathcal{A}$, i.e., each loop nest typically accesses a subset of the arrays declared in the program code. For example, the second loop nest in Figure 2 can be represented as

$$N_1 = \left\{ 3, DW, \begin{bmatrix} N \\ J \\ I \end{bmatrix}, \begin{bmatrix} 1 \\ 2 \\ 2 \end{bmatrix}, \begin{bmatrix} 4 \\ 10 \\ 10 \end{bmatrix}, \begin{bmatrix} 1 \\ 1 \\ 1 \end{bmatrix}, \psi \right\}.$$

- Loop Body : A loop body is made of a series of statements which use the references to the arrays $\mathcal{A}$ declared in $\mathcal{P}$. Consequently, loop body ψ can be expressed as a set of references.
- Iteration : For a loop nest, $\mathcal{N}_n$, an iteration is a particular combination of legal values that its index variables in $\mathcal{I}$ can assume. It is expressed as $\mathcal{I}_\sigma$, and it represents an execution of the loop body.
- Iteration Space : The iteration space of a loop nest $\mathcal{N}_i$ is the set of all iterations in the loop nest.
- Data Space : The data space of a data structure (e.g., an array) are all the individual memory locations that form the data structure in question.
- Reference : It is an element of ψ expressed as $(\psi_p^{r/w} = \{\mathcal{N}_n, \mathcal{A}_A, L, o\})$. It is an affine relation from the iteration space of a loop nest $\mathcal{N}_n = \{\alpha, \mathcal{A}_n, \mathcal{I}, \mathcal{L}, \mathcal{U}, \mathcal{S}, \psi\}$ to the data space of an array $(\mathcal{A}_a = \{\delta, \gamma\})$. From compiler theory [7], it is known that this relation can be described by $Li + o$ where i is a vector that captures the loop indices of $\mathcal{N}$, L is a matrix of size $\delta * \alpha$, and o is an offset displacement vector. As an example, the reference $A[i + j - 1][j + 2]$ is represented by

$$\psi_p^{r/w} = \begin{bmatrix} 1 & 1 \\ 0 & 1 \end{bmatrix} * \begin{bmatrix} i \\ j \end{bmatrix} + \begin{bmatrix} -1 \\ 2 \end{bmatrix}.$$

A reference within the body of a loop nest helps us calculate the locations of an array that the loop nest accesses. Further, a reference can be a read reference, which

```
int DW[10][10][4];

for (N=1;N<=4;N++) {
  for (J=2;J<=10;J++)
   DW[1][J][N] = 0;
}

for (N=1;N<=4;N++) {
  for (J=2;J<=10;J++)
   for (I=2;I<=10;I++)
    DW[I][J][N] = DW[I][J][N]
                   -R*(DW[I][J][N]
                   -DW[I-1][J][N]);
}

for (N=1;N<=4;N++) {
  for (J=2;J<=10;J++)
   DW[10][J][N] = T1*DW[10][J][N];
}

for (N=1;N<=4;N++) {
  for(II=3; II<= 9; II++)
   for (J=2;J<=10;J++)
    DW[II][J][N] = DW[II][J][N]
                    -R*(DW[II][J][N]
                    -DW[II+1][J][N]);
}
```

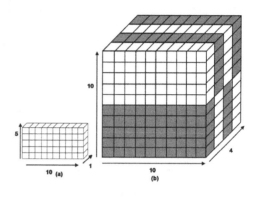

Fig. 2. A code fragment with four loop nests and an array

Fig. 3. (a) Seed tile for the array DW in the code fragment of Figure 2. (b) The array DW divided into multiple tiles using the seed tile

means that an array location is read from, or a write reference, which means that an array location is written to. This is identified by attaching a r/w superscript to the reference. Hence, $\psi_p^r(\mathcal{N}_n)$ represents the set of all array locations read by the reference in loop nest $\mathcal{N}_n$.

2.2 Data Tile Formation

In this paper, we use the concept of data space tiling to logically divide the data space of an array into multiple sections. This subsection provides the theoretical basis and the algorithm used to perform tiling.

- Data Tile : A data tile $D_{\mathcal{A}_a,\mathcal{L},\mathcal{U}}$ is a regular subpart (region) of the array $\mathcal{A}_a$. The size of the data tile in each dimension is given by the difference between $\mathcal{L}$ and $\mathcal{U}$ plus 1. It is assumed that the size of a data tile is not zero in any dimension. Based on the definition of a data tile, data space of $D_{\mathcal{A}_a,\mathcal{L},\mathcal{U}}$ can be formally expressed as follows:

$$D_{\mathcal{A}_a,\mathcal{L},\mathcal{U}} = \{\{d_1, d_2..d_\delta\} \mid \mathcal{L}_1 \leq d_1 \leq \mathcal{U}_1$$
$$\&\& \quad \mathcal{L}_2 \leq d_2 \leq \mathcal{U}_2 ... \&\& \quad \mathcal{L}_\delta \leq d_\delta \leq \mathcal{U}_\delta\}$$

- Seed Data Tile : A data tile, $D_{\mathcal{A}_a,\mathcal{L},\mathcal{U}}$, is described as a seed data tile if $\mathcal{L} = \mathbf{0}$. This tile is used (as a template) to partition the array $\mathcal{A}_a$ into further tiles. As an example, Figure 3(a) shows a seed tile for the array DW that is defined in Figure 2, and Figure 3(b) illustrates how DW is partitioned into multiple tiles using this seed tile. This partitioning is outlined in Algorithm 1. Multiple seed tiles can simply formed by

Algorithm 1. $DataTile(D_{\mathcal{A}_a}, \mathcal{L}, \mathcal{U})$

```
 1: Tile_list := ∅
 2: for iδ = 1 to γδ by U[δ] do
 3:     L'[δ] := iδ
 4:     U'[δ] := min(iδ + U[δ] − 1, γδ)
 5:     for iδ−1 = 1 to γδ−1 by U[δ − 1] do
 6:         L'[δ − 1] := iδ−1
 7:         U'[δ − 1] := min(iδ−1 + U[δ − 1] − 1,
 8:                                                    γδ−1)
 9:         .
10:         .
11:         for i1 = 1 to γ1 by U[1] do
12:             L'[1] := i1
13:             U'[1] := min(i1 + U[1] − 1, γ1)
14:             Tile := DA_a,L',U'
15:             Tile_list := Tile_list ⋃ Tile
16:         end for
17:     end for
18: end for
19: Return Tile_list
```

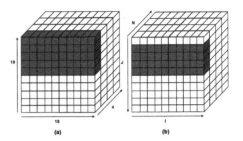

Fig. 4. The iteration set corresponding a data tile in the array DW (accessed by the code fragment in Figure 2) and the second loop nest in the code fragment

changing the values of the entries of $\mathcal{U}$. By supplying different seed tiles as input to Algorithm 1, we are able to split an array into differently shaped tiles.

2.3   Iteration Set and Co-tile Formation

An iteration set is associated with a loop nest $\mathcal{N}_n$, and a data tile $D_{\mathcal{A}_a}, \mathcal{L}, \mathcal{U}$. It is the subset of the iteration space of $\mathcal{N}_n$, in which the elements (iterations) have the property that $\psi_p^{r/w}(\mathcal{I}_\sigma) \in D_{\mathcal{A}_a}, \mathcal{L}, \mathcal{U}$. That is, it is the set of all iterations in a particular loop nest that accesses the locations in a given data tile. We can calculate the iteration set $I(D_{\mathcal{A}_a}, \mathcal{L}, \mathcal{U}, \mathcal{N}_n)$ of data tile $D_{\mathcal{A}_a}, \mathcal{L}, \mathcal{U}$ and loop nest $\mathcal{N}_n$ as

$$I(D_{\mathcal{A}_a}, \mathcal{L}, \mathcal{U}, \mathcal{N}_n) = \bigcup_{\psi_p^{r/w} \in \psi} \bigcup_{\mathcal{I}_\sigma \in \mathcal{N}_n} \{\ \mathcal{I}_\sigma\ |\ \{\psi_p^{r/w}(\mathcal{I}_\sigma) \cap D_{\mathcal{A}_a}, \mathcal{L}, \mathcal{U}\} \neq \emptyset\ \}. \tag{1}$$

Figure 4 shows the iteration set corresponding to the data tile of the array DW and the second loop nest in the code given in Figure 2. It is possible that the iteration set $I(D_{\mathcal{A}_a}, \mathcal{L}, \mathcal{U}, \mathcal{N}_n)$ accesses locations in the array $\mathcal{A}_a$ that lie outside the data tile, $D_{\mathcal{A}_a}, \mathcal{L}, \mathcal{U}$. In other words, $(\bigcup_{\psi_p} \psi_p(I(D_{\mathcal{A}_a}, \mathcal{L}, \mathcal{U}, \mathcal{N}_n))) - D_{\mathcal{A}_a}, \mathcal{L}, \mathcal{U} \neq \emptyset$ may be true.

Recall that our overall goal is to capture all the computations that need to be performed by a loop nest on a data tile. As a consequence, we need to express the extra locations that are accessed by the iteration set. As mentioned earlier, the extra locations and the original data tile together are called the co-tile of the iteration set and is given by:

$$C_{D_{\mathcal{A}_a}, \mathcal{L}, \mathcal{U}, \mathcal{N}_i} = \bigcup_{\forall \psi_p \in \mathcal{N}_n} \psi_p(I(D_{\mathcal{A}_a}, \mathcal{L}, \mathcal{U}, \mathcal{N}_n)) \tag{2}$$

Using the formulation for iteration set in Equation (1), the formulation for a co-tile given in Equation (2) and the list of all data tiles generated by Algorithm 1, we can

---

Algorithm 2. $Dependence Detector(Tile\_list)$

1: Dep_Array := 0
2: **for all** $D_m \in$ $Tile\_list$ **do**
3:   **for all** $\mathcal{N}_i \in \mathcal{N}$ **do**
4:     calculate $I_{D_m, \mathcal{N}_i}$
5:   **end for**
6: **end for**
7: **for all** $D_m \in$ $Tile\_list$ **do**
8:   **for all** $\mathcal{N}_i \in \mathcal{N}$ **do**
9:     **for all** $D_n \in$ $Tile\_list$ **do**
10:       **for all** $\mathcal{N}_j \in \mathcal{N}$ **do**
11:         **if** $\{(\bigcup_{\psi_p^w} \psi_p^w (I_{D_m, \mathcal{N}_i})) \cap (\bigcup_{\psi_{p'}^r} \psi_{p'}^r (I_{D_n, \mathcal{N}_j}))\} \neq \emptyset \|$
            $\{(\bigcup_{\psi_p^r} \psi_p^r (I_{D_m, \mathcal{N}_i})) \cap (\bigcup_{\psi_{p'}^w} \psi_{p'}^w (I_{D_n, \mathcal{N}_j}))\} \neq \emptyset \|$
            $\{(\bigcup_{\psi_p^w} \psi_p^w (I_{D_m, \mathcal{N}_i})) \cap (\bigcup_{\psi_{p'}^w} \psi_{p'}^w (I_{D_n, \mathcal{N}_j}))\} \neq \emptyset$ **then**
12:           Dep_Array$_{m,i,n,j}$:= 1
13:         **end if**
14:       **end for**
15:     **end for**
16:   **end for**
17: **end for**
18: Return Dep_Array

---

now generate a list of all iteration set/co-tile pairs. The default list of pairs describes the default program behavior (i.e., without any restructuring). It is this behavior that we want to change while maintaining the same semantics as the original code.

2.4 Data Dependences Across Iteration Sets

All iterations in the given program fragment are executed in a default order called the program order. This program order can be extended to the pairs of iteration sets and co-tiles. In order to change the code, the execution of iteration sets must be re-ordered. A fundamental restriction on whether we can re-order the iteration sets are ordering relations among them, which are also known as *data dependences*.

The execution order of any two iterations can be arbitrary with respect to each other as long as these two iterations do not have any data dependence between them. A data dependence exists between two iterations within a loop nest if one iteration reads a value of a variable computed by another iteration or if both iterations compute the value of the same variable [7].

Consequently, in order to re-order any two iteration sets, there should not be any data dependence there between them. Furthermore, if we want to arbitrarily re-order all the iteration sets, there should not be any data dependence between any two iteration sets. Otherwise, it is possible that the wrong data is read by one iteration set or written by another iteration set. The rest of this sub-section presents our algorithm to detect data dependences between iteration set and co-tile pairs. This analysis is different from conventional data dependence analysis as we perform it at an iteration set and co-tile granularity.

Formally, two iterations $\mathcal{I}_\sigma$ and $\mathcal{I}'_\sigma$ within a nest $\mathcal{N}_n$ have a data dependence between them if and only if

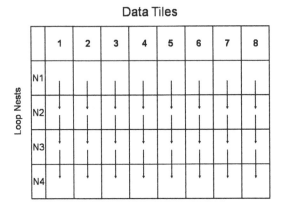

Fig. 5. Arrows indicate the data dependence between iteration sets formed by loop nests in Figure 2 and data tiles formed using the seed tile in Figure 3(a)

$$\psi_p^r(\mathcal{I}_\sigma) = \psi_{p'}^w(\mathcal{I}_\sigma') || \psi_p^w(\mathcal{I}_\sigma) = \psi_{p'}^r(\mathcal{I}_\sigma') || \psi_p^w(\mathcal{I}_\sigma) = \psi_{p'}^w(\mathcal{I}_\sigma') \qquad (3)$$

is true, where $\psi_p^{r/w}$ and $\psi_{p'}^{r/w}$ are two references that appear in $\mathcal{N}_n$.

This formulation can be extended to iteration sets and the co-tiles that are accessed in them. In the context of our paper, a dependence is said to exist between two iteration sets if and only if,

$$\{(\bigcup_{\psi_p^w} \psi_p^w(I(D_{\mathcal{A}_a}, \mathcal{L}, \mathcal{U}, \mathcal{N}_n))) \cap (\bigcup_{\psi_{p'}^r} \psi_{p'}^r(I(D_{\mathcal{A}_a}, \mathcal{L}', \mathcal{U}', \mathcal{N}_{n'})))\} \neq \emptyset ||$$

$$\{(\bigcup_{\psi_p^r} \psi_p^r(I(D_{\mathcal{A}_a}, \mathcal{L}, \mathcal{U}, \mathcal{N}_n))) \cap (\bigcup_{\psi_{p'}^w} \psi_{p'}^w(I(D_{\mathcal{A}_a}, \mathcal{L}', \mathcal{U}', \mathcal{N}_{n'})))\} \neq \emptyset ||$$

$$\{(\bigcup_{\psi_p^w} \psi_p^w(I(D_{\mathcal{A}_a}, \mathcal{L}, \mathcal{U}, \mathcal{N}_n))) \cap (\bigcup_{\psi_{p'}^w} \psi_{p'}^w(I(D_{\mathcal{A}_a}, \mathcal{L}', \mathcal{U}', \mathcal{N}_{n'})))\} \neq \emptyset$$

$$(4)$$

is true.

Based on Equation (4), Algorithm 2 detects the data dependences between the iteration sets formed from a list of data tiles. As we are not interested in re-ordering the iterations within an iteration set, dependence detection is performed at the level of loop nest granularity. The algorithm sets $Dep\_Array[m, i, n, j]$ to 1 if a dependence exists between the iteration set $I_{D_m, \mathcal{N}_i}$ and the iteration set $I_{D_n, \mathcal{N}_j}$, where D_m and D_n are data tiles created by Algorithm 1. For two iteration sets associated with the same loop nest, the dependence flows from the iteration set that contains the earlier iterations to the other iteration set. Let us now discuss what the matrix Dep_Array represents. The dependence relations between iteration sets can be described by a graph in which the nodes are the individual iteration sets. A directed edge from the node that represents iteration set $I_{D_m, \mathcal{N}_i}$ to the node that represents $I_{D_n, \mathcal{N}_j}$ means that $I_{D_n, \mathcal{N}_j}$ is dependent on $I_{D_m, \mathcal{N}_i}$. Consequently a node that represents an iteration set that is independent of all other iteration sets has a fan-in value of zero in this graph. Given these observations, we can conclude that the matrix Dep_Array is simply the representation of this

Position	Code Version
	1 2 3 4 5 6 7 8
1	1 2 3 4 5 6 7 8
2	2 3 4 5 6 7 8 1
3	3 4 5 6 7 8 1 2
4	4 5 6 7 8 1 2 3
5	5 6 7 8 1 2 3 4
6	6 7 8 1 2 3 4 5
7	7 8 1 2 3 4 5 6
8	8 1 2 3 4 5 6 7

Fig. 6. The different orders of iteration sets in the different versions of the code

Algorithm 3. $VersionGenerator(P_o, V)$

1: Generate Seed Tile
2: Create Iteration Sets and Partitions
3: Verify dependences
4: **while** Dependences exist **do**
5:    **if** Generate New Seed Tile() == failure **then**
6:       Return Error
7:    **end if**
8:    Create Iteration Sets and Partitions
9:    Verify dependences
10: **end while**
11: Create V Versions

graph in an adjacency matrix form. The dependence relations between iteration sets is represented pictorially in Figure 5.

At this point, we have generated a list of iteration sets which when executed individually perform all the computations that should be performed on a particular data tile by the associated loop nest. However, it is possible that two iteration sets, $I_{D_n, \mathcal{N}_j}$ and $I_{D_{n'}, \mathcal{N}_j}$, which are associated with the same nest and have a dependence between them, might intersect. That is, some iterations may belong to both $I_{D_n, \mathcal{N}_j}$ and $I_{D_{n'}, \mathcal{N}_j}$. In order to produce code that is semantically identical to the original code, the intersecting iterations need to be associated with only one of the iteration sets. Assuming that the iteration set $I_{D_{n'}, \mathcal{N}_j}$ is dependent on $I_{D_n, \mathcal{N}_j}$, the intersecting iterations are executed by $I_{D_{n'}, \mathcal{N}_j}$. That is, $I_{D_{n'}, \mathcal{N}_j}$ is set to $I_{D_{n'}, \mathcal{N}_j} - (I_{D_n, \mathcal{N}_j} \cap I_{D_{n'}, \mathcal{N}_j})$.

2.5 Re-ordering Iteration Sets

The key requirement for full re-ordering of iteration sets is that there should be no data dependence at all between iteration sets. However, this behavior is not exhibited by most real applications. Therefore, we relax this requirement and allow reordering when the only dependences are between iteration sets corresponding to the same data tile. That is, directed edges of the form, $I_{D_n, \mathcal{N}_i}$ to $I_{D_n, \mathcal{N}_j}$ which represents data dependences between iteration sets associated with the same data tile are allowed. Once this condition has been satisfied, we first group all the iteration sets associated with each tile. Then, we partition the groups of iteration sets into V groups, where V is the number of versions of code that are required and number each partition from 1 to V. We use this numbering to create a circular sequence over all the iteration set partitions. That is, to create the ith version of the code the order of iteration set partitions is : $i, i + 1 \ldots V - 1, V, 1, 2 \ldots i - 2, i - 1$. Figure 6 presents the orders of partitions when V is 8.

2.6 Generating Multiple Versions

This section describes Algorithm 3 to create the multiple versions of an input program. The input to the algorithm is the original program P_o and number of versions, V, of the code that are desired. In order to create a semantically equivalent version of P_o, a new seed element (that has not been used previously) is formed. Then, using this seed element, the data space of P_o is broken up into further data tiles.

Using these data tiles and the loop nests in P_o, the dependence graph between the iteration sets that correspond to these data tiles is created. If there are no dependences between iteration sets corresponding to different data tiles, then the different versions of the code are created using orders as explained in Section 2.5. If however, dependences do exist, a new seed tile is used. If no satisfactory seed tile can be found, an error is reported. In order to generate the actual code, we rely on the Omega Library [15] which is a polyhedral tool in which iteration spaces can be described using Presburger arithmetic [16]. Given the description and order of the iteration tiles, the *codegen* utility of the Omega Library is used to generate the actual loop nests. Once the loops have been generated, they are combined so that the generated code is as compact as possible. However, the combining is done such that the order between the iteration sets remains the same. In fact, the combining method simply generates loops that iterate over the partitions of iteration sets. A portion of the semantically equivalent version of the code corresponding to one data tile is shown in Figure 7.

2.7   Data Tile Selection

So far we have ignored the problem of generating the actual seed tiles which divide the array data space into its component tiles.

The potential space to explore in order to select appropriate seed tiles is vast. We first trim this space by considering only those tiles whose boundaries are parallel to the axes of the array that is being tiled. The rationale be-

```
int DW[10][10][4];

for (J=2;J<=5;J++)
  DW[1][J][1] = 0;

for (J=2;J<=5;J++)
  for (I=2;I<=10;I++)
    DW[I][J][1] = DW[I][J][1]  -R*(DW[I][J][1]
                                 -DW[I-1][J][1]);

for (J=2;J<=5;J++)
  DW[10][J][1] = T1*DW[10][J][1];

for(II=3; II<= 9; II++)
  for (J=2;J<=5;J++)
    DW[II][J][1] = DW[II][J][1]  -R*(DW[II][J][1]
                                   -DW[II+1][J][1]);
```

Fig. 7. The code generated for one data tile of the code given in Figure 2

hind this is that the output codes generated using such tiles tend to be simpler that those generated using arbitrary tiles. That is, if the array is δ-dimensional, the seed is shaped regularly, and the references from the loop nest to the array are through *affine* expressions; then iteration sets that access the data tiles are regular in shape.

Further, as we require V different versions, we assume that the size of the seed tile should imply that there are V data tiles. This also implies that the iteration sets in an iteration set partition are all associated with the same data tile.

Let us consider a δ-dimensional array, $A[n_1, n_2, ..n_\delta]$ for which V unique seed tiles are required. As A is δ-dimensional, any seed tile of A, $S[s_1, s_2, ..s_\delta]$, is also δ-dimensional. Therefore, the problem of finding the values of $s_1, s_2, ..s_\delta$ which defines the shape of the seed tile translates into the problem of selecting an appropriate value of s_i from the factors of n_i such that $\sum_i s_i = V$. As n_i is bounded by the array size large, the number of combinations from which $S[s_1, s_2, ..s_\delta]$ is selected is not very large.

2.8   Handling Multiple Arrays

Our formulation so far has assumed that the references in the loop nests (of the code for which we meant to generate multiple versions) access a single array. In order to extend our approach to multiple arrays, we first need to extend the concept of an iteration set. An iteration set is now associated with a loop nest as well as data tiles belonging to different arrays. As a result, the iteration set is expressed as $I_{\{D\},\mathcal{N}_j}$, where $\{D\}$ is the set of data tiles (from different arrays) which are accessed in that iteration set. If the loop nest associated with the iteration set does not contain references that access an array $\{D\}$ will not contain a data tile from that array. Consequently, dependences between two iteration sets can potentially occur if they both access a common location in any array used by the program.

Another consideration with multiple arrays is how the seed tile for each array is created. One approach is to simply have the same seed tile for each array. Another approach is to create different seed tiles for different arrays, where the shape of a seed tile associated with one array is independent of the seed tile chosen for another array. In yet another approach, a seed tile is created for a chosen array $\mathcal{A}_s$ with a fixed number of elements. The ratio of the elements in a seed tile for an array $\mathcal{A}_{s'}$ is fixed relative to the number of elements in a seed tile used for $\mathcal{A}_s$, and based on the number of elements in this seed tile, the shape of the tiles is determined. Consequently, by changing the number of elements in the seed tile used for $\mathcal{A}_s$ the seed tile used for $\mathcal{A}_{s'}$ is changed. As each approach potentially gives us different versions of code, the approach we choose depends on the number of versions that need to be created. The default approach used is the one in which each tile in each array is of the same shape.

3   Implementation and Experiments

While our automated approach can be useful in any scenario where multiple versions of the same code are needed, we focus on one particular scenario in this work. This section first describes the targeted scenario where our proposed approach is applied. It then illustrates the architecture of the tool that is created based on the approach. Finally, it describes the experiments conducted using the tool in the targeted scenario. As mentioned earlier, soft errors are a growing threat to the correct execution of an application [11,12,13]. A soft error is defined as an unwanted change in the state of a bit in a computer's component such as the memory system. It can result from particle strikes on logic devices which cause the bit represented by the device to flip. Increased scaling of technology has exacerbated this problem [14]. As result, the problem of soft errors has received considerable attention with many proposed hardware as well as software solutions. In chip multiprocessor (CMP) architectures, redundant-threading (RT) is one of the ways to overcome soft errors [17]. In an RT framework the same code is simultaneously executed across all the processors and periodically the results are compared to check if the computed results across the different threads agree. If they agree, it is assumed that no error has occurred as only a single soft error is expected in any single thread and in any time frame. Another way is to run the code multiple times one after another and to check whether the results from each run agree with each other. Obviously, running each version simultaneously, if the resources are available, is the

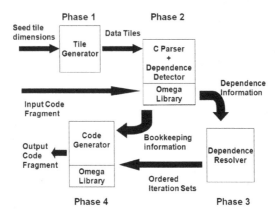

Fig. 8. Details of the flow within the tool. Phase 1 involves the creation of data tiles (Section 2.2) using a unique seed tile (Section 2.7). Phase 2 involves the parsing of the input code fragment, formation of iteration sets (Section 2.3), and detection of data dependences between them (Section 2.4). Phase 3 re-orders iteration sets (Section 2.5). Finally, phase 4 generates the output code fragment using the Omega Library (Section 2.6).

preferred option as it results in a faster finish time for the thread. The disadvantage is that in a CMP that is based on the shared memory concept, threads that operate simultaneously in the RT framework would read the same data from memory in close temporal proximity. Therefore, if a datum in memory is corrupted by a soft error, running the same code multiple times in parallel could result in the corrupted value being read by all threads. Such a read could result in the wrong result being computed and this error would remain undetected in current techniques. Although error correcting codes (ECC) have been proposed to overcome errors in the caches, ECC is not a viable solution in all computing systems due to the high costs it involves, especially form the power consumption angle [18,19]. Furthermore, ECC would not catch multiple errors, which would be detected by our method.

We propose to use our automatic versioning algorithm to create multiple versions of the thread. These versions, when run in parallel, will access data in different temporal orders. Thus, the proposed approach will achieve temporal diversity without increasing the overall execution time. As a result, a particular datum which is corrupted at some time during the execution of the threads, could be accessed before corruption by one thread and after corruption by another. Therefore, it is possible that the changed value of the datum will be observable in the results of the different threads. Obviously, if the datum does not affect the end result, the proposed approach would perform exactly like the RT case and declare that no soft error has occurred. However, if that datum affects the end results, our approach is more likely to detect it. A tool was implemented based on the data tile based code restructuring approach (see Figure 8). This tools uses the Omega Library to evaluate the relations described in Section 2 and to generate the loops corresponding to the final relations using the Library's *codegen* utility on each relation one by one [20]. The tool was used to automatically create eight versions of the *tsf* benchmark shown in Figure 2 using the seed tile shown in Figure 3(a). Each version used a different order of iteration tiles shown in Figure 6. Therefore, each iteration set

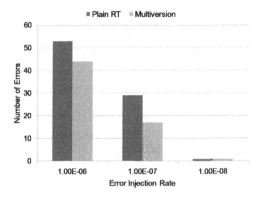

Fig. 9. The graph shows the number of errors in the array DW for different error injection rates using the default RT scheme and the proposed approach

will execute at a particular time slot in at least one version. In an error free scenario, the different versions should generate the *same* results. However, in case of a soft error, two versions may differ in the results generated for a particular iteration set. In that case, the version that scheduled the iteration set earlier than the other is assumed to be the correct one. That is, the error is assumed to have occurred between the executions of the earlier set and set executed later.

We ran the original benchmark in conjunction with a fault injection module [21] to simulate execution under the soft error scenario. This setup was used to record the *stage* at which each error was injected and where in the memory space it occurred. Then, each automatically generated version of the code was run under the error injection mode using the previously recorded error occurrence and the results were compared with each other. A simple arbiter is used to reason about the results that are generated. If the results of any data tile in the automatically generated versions were different, the arbiter chose the results of the version in which the iteration tile corresponding to the data tile is executed earlier. In order to simulate RT, the errors recorded earlier are injected for each version, one at a time. At each stage, any error that is not injected into the memory is assumed to be caught, but any changes to the memory itself are allowed to propagate. Figure 9 shows the number of remaining errors in the proposed approach as compared to the standard RT approach (which uses the same version in each processor) for different injection rates. It can be seen that the proposed approach reduces the number of errors that affect the end result.

4   Concluding Remarks

This paper presents a tool that uses code restructuring techniques to automatically generate multiple semantically equivalent versions of a given numerical application that is organized as a series of loops that access data in arrays. We created different versions of the code that differ in the order in which they access the data and used these different versions of the code to detect the occurrence of soft errors during the execution of the code. We believe that, this tool provides an inexpensive and automated method to enable fault tolerance to critical applications. Our planned future work includes developing more techniques to generate seed tiles easily and developing techniques to generate more compact code. We also plan to use our tool in other scenarios that benefit from multiple versions.

References

1. Avizienis, A.: On the implementation of nversion programming for software fault tolerance during execution. Proceedings of the IEEE 66(10), 1109–1125 (1978)
2. Elmendorf, W.: Fault-tolerant programming. In: FTCS-2, pp. 79–83 (1972)
3. Randell, B.: System structure for software fault tolerance. IEEE Trans. on Software Engineering SE-1(2), 220–232 (1975)
4. Horning, J.J., et al.: A program structure for error detection and recovery. In: Operating Systems, Proceedings of an Int. Symposium, pp. 171–187. Springer, Heidelberg (1974)
5. Pullum, L.: A new adjudicator for fault tolerant software applications correctly resulting in multiple solutions. In: Digital Avionics Systems Conference, pp. 147–152 (1993)
6. Pullum, L.L.: Software Fault Tolerance Techniques and Implementation. Artech House (2001)
7. Wolfe, M.: High Performance Compilers for Parallel Computing. Addison-Wesley, Reading (1996)
8. Wolfe, M.J.: Optimizing Supercompilers for Supercomputers. MIT Press, Cambridge (1990)
9. Kodukula, I., et al.: Data-centric multi-level blocking. In: PLDI, pp. 346–357 (1997)
10. Kadayif, I., Kandemir, M.: Data space-oriented tiling for enhancing locality. Trans. on Embedded Computing Sys. 4(2), 388–414 (2005)
11. Michalak, S., Harris, K., Hengartner, N., Takala, B., Wender, S.: Predicting the number of fatal soft errors in los alamos national laboratory's asc q supercomputer. IEEE Transactions on Device and Materials Reliability 5(3), 329–335 (2005)
12. Wang, N., Quek, J., Rafacz, T.: patel, S.: Characterizing the effects of transient faults on a high-performance processor pipeline. In: DSN 2004: Proceedings of the 2004 International Conference on Dependable Systems and Networks, p. 61 (2004)
13. Patel, J.: Characterization of soft errors caused by single event upsets in cmos processes. IEEE Trans. Dependable Secur. Comput. 1(2), 128–143 (2004)
14. Degalahal, V., Ramanarayanan, R., Vijaykrishnan, N., Xie, Y., Irwin, M.J.: The effect of threshold voltages on the soft error rate. In: International Symposium on Quality Electronic Design, pp. 503–508 (2004)
15. Kelly, W., et al.: The omega calculator and library v1.1.0. Technical report, Dept. of CS, Univ. of Maryland (1996)
16. Kreisel, G., Krivine, J.L.: Elements of mathematical logic. North-Holland Pub. Co., Amsterdam (1967)
17. Reinhardt, S., Mukherjee, S.: Transient fault detection via simultaneous multithreading. SIGARCH Comput. Archit. News 28(2), 25–36 (2000)
18. Chen, C., Hsiao, M.: Error-correcting codes for semiconductor memory applications: a state of the art review. Reliable Computer Systems - Design and Evaluation, 771–786 (1992)
19. Pradhan, D.K. (ed.): Fault-tolerant computer system design (1996)
20. Kelly, W., et al.: Code generation for multiple mappings. Technical report, Dept. of CS, Univ. of Maryland (1994)
21. Gurumurthi, S., Parashar, A., Sivasubramaniam, A.: Sos: Using speculation for memory error detection. In: Workshop on High Performance Computing Reliability Issues (2005)

Increasing Confidence in Concurrent Software through Architectural Analysis

Robert G. Pettit IV

The Aerospace Corporation, 15049 Conference Center Drive,
Chantilly, Virginia, USA 20151
rob.pettit@aero.org

Abstract. Mission critical real-time and embedded software systems often use significant degree of concurrency within their architecture designs. Experience has shown that common problems surrounding the design of these systems include underspecified performance requirements; underspecified state-dependent behavior; and inadequately capturing concurrent interactions. Dynamic architectural models capturing the overall behavioral properties of the software system are often constructed using ad hoc techniques with little consideration given to the resulting performance or implications of concurrent behavior until the project reaches implementation. To address this issue and thus increase the confidence that a concurrent software architecture design will behave as desired, we have developed an approach to augment UML-based software designs with colored Petri nets, thus increasing the analytical capabilities at design time. An illustration of this approach using a rover control case study is included in this paper.

1 Introduction

Mission critical real-time and embedded software systems often use significant degree of concurrency within their architecture designs. Experience[1,2] has shown that common problems surrounding the design of these systems include underspecified performance requirements; underspecified state-dependent behavior (e.g. a lack of state machines); and inadequately capturing concurrent interactions. Dynamic architectural models capturing the overall behavioral properties of the software system are often constructed using ad hoc techniques with little consideration given to the resulting performance or implications of concurrent behavior until the project reaches implementation. Efforts to analyze the behavior of these architectures typically occur through opportunistic rather than systematic approaches and are inherently cumbersome, unreliable, and unrepeatable.

One means of increasing confidence that concurrent software architectures result in the desired behavioral aspects is to provide greater emphasis on architectural analysis during the design stage. The approach taken in this paper is to integrate formalisms (specifically colored Petri nets) within the software architecture design and to thus increase the analytical capabilities that can be applied to the design.

For the software architecture design, we start with a set of concurrently executing objects and the messages that are passed between them. This is expressed in the

F. Kordon and T. Vardanega (Eds.): Ada-Europe 2008, LNCS 5026, pp. 199–210, 2008.

Unified Modeling Language (UML) [3] using interaction diagrams. The UML is used for this design as its adoption is quite prevalent among software engineers and it provides a means of capturing concurrently executing objects (i.e *active objects*) in a manner intuitive to the software architect.

The approach used in the paper [4] then augments the native object-oriented design by seamlessly integrating an underlying colored Petri net (CPN) representation and then using the CPN model to analyze the concurrent behavior of the architecture. Results from the analysis can be applied back to the original UML design in order to increase the confidence that the final implementation of the design will be satisfactory in terms of the concurrent behavior.

The remainder of this paper includes a brief background on related works and an overview of colored Petri nets; a description of how UML-based software architecture models are augmented with CPN behavioral templates; and an illustration of applying the modeling and analysis techniques using a case study of an autonomous rover.

2   Overview of Colored Petri Nets for Modeling Concurrency

The basic notation for Petri nets is a bipartite graph consisting of places and transitions that alternate on a path and are connected by directional arcs. In general, places are represented by circles, whereas transitions are represented by bars or boxes. Tokens are used to mark places, and under certain conditions, actions associated with transitions are allowed to occur, thus causing a change in the placement of tokens.

When a transition occurs, that transition is said to be *fired*. A transition can only be fired if each of the input places to the transition contains at least one token. The transition is then said to be *enabled*. The firing of a transition results in the removal of a token from each input place and the addition of a token to each output place.

When a transition is enabled, we know that it will be fired. However, in the basic Petri net model, there is no timing constraint that can be used to determine *when* the transition will be fired. There are variations of the basic model that allow timing constraints to be introduced (e.g. timed Petri nets). These variations will be briefly mentioned as they apply to creating the templates used in this paper.

A colored Petri net is a special case of Petri net in which the tokens have identifying attributes; in this case the color of the token [20]. At first, colored Petri nets seem less intuitive than the basic Petri net. However, by allowing the tokens to have an associated attribute, colored Petri nets scale to large problems much better than the basic Petri net.

Petri net models can be mixed to provide a hybrid Petri net model that supports multiple characteristics. These hybrid models prove useful in modeling real-time systems by allowing the combinations of such attributes as timing constraints and colored tokens.

The Petri net system used in this research follows Jensen's [20] colored Petri nets, which support hierarchical construction and the inclusion of timing information. The basic notation for these Petri nets is illustrated in Figure 1. As seen in this figure, ovals represent places and boxes represent transitions. Each place must be labeled with a particular color set indicating the color (or type) of tokens that may reside on that place. Transitions may perform behavior as simple as moving a token from one place to another. More often, though, they may contain additional information such as guard conditions that place explicit conditions on the firing of the transition; code regions that may perform complex transformations on the tokens; or time regions that may be used to increment the time stamp on tokens. Additionally, transitions form the basis for hierarchical construction in the CPN model. "Substitution transitions" may be created that are decomposed into lower level CPN segments. This feature allows an engineer to view the CPN model at different levels of abstraction, depending on the desired focus for modeling and analysis.

Fig. 1. CPN Notation

2.1 Related Works

There are many existing works dealing with the use of Petri nets for describing software behavior. As they relate to this paper, the existing works can be broadly categorized into the modeling of software code and the modeling of software designs. Our approach differs from the former by choosing to focus on analyzing the software design rather than to delay performance analysis to the software code. Specifically, this research focuses on the modeling and analysis of concurrent object-oriented software designs.

In terms of object-oriented design, the related Petri net research can be broadly categorized into three areas. New development methodologies [5-8] involve the creation of development processes where the software engineer applies Petri net modeling as the primary tool for capturing concurrent behavior among objects. Object-oriented extensions to Petri nets [9-11] involve extending existing Petri net formalisms to support object-oriented constructs.

The integration of Petri nets with existing object-oriented methodologies [12-19] involves identifying ways to augment mainstream design practices and notations with an underlying Petri net formalism. It is within this last category that our work falls. Our approach does not seek to replace UML models with Petri nets. Nor do we seek to extend the definition of CPNs beyond the current standard. Rather, one of the goals of this research falls into the last category above as one of our primary goals is to provide a method that requires no additional tools or language constructs beyond those currently available for the UML and CPN definitions. Within this category of related research, the main features that distinguish our approach from other related works include our focus on the concurrent software architecture design and the use of consistent, reusable CPN templates to model the behavior of concurrent objects and their interactions (rather than a direct, but not reusable CPN translation).

3 Modeling UML Architectures with Colored Petri Nets

The approach used in this paper for developing executable models for concurrent software designs is to model object behavior in the form of behavioral design patterns (BDP), which are then mapped to Colored Petri Net (CPN) templates [4]. Each BDP represents the behavior of an individual object together with associated communication constructs between that object and other objects with which it collaborates. The BDP for a given object is identified by its UML stereotype. In this approach we utilize the stereotypes from the COMET software design method [21] as shown in Figure 2. An example of a behavioral design pattern for an asynchronous device input concurrent object is given in Figure 3a.

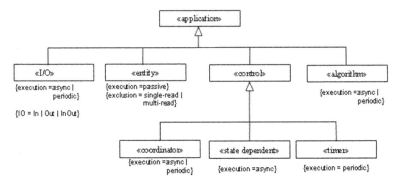

Fig. 2. Stereotype Hierarchy of Behavioral Roles

For each BDP, a self-contained CPN template is designed, which by means of its places, transitions, and tokens, models a given concurrent behavioral pattern. Figure 3b depicts the CPN template for an asynchronous device input concurrent object. Each template is generic in the sense that it provides a basic behavioral pattern and component connections for the concurrent object but does not contain any application-specific information. Furthermore, concurrent component templates are designed such that they can be interconnected via connector templates.

The software architecture is organized using the concept of components and connectors, in which concurrent objects are designed as components that can be connected through passive message communication objects and entity objects. Using this approach, a concurrent software architecture is described in terms of interconnected concurrent behavioral design patterns (i.e. components), which are then mapped to a CPN model by connecting the corresponding CPN templates. The CPN templates are elaborated to include application specific behavior necessary to conduct our analyses. This additional information is captured in the UML model via tagged values and includes:

- Execution Type: passive, asynchronous, or periodic
- IO: input and/or output
- Communication Type: synchronous or asynchronous
- Activation Time: periodic activation rate

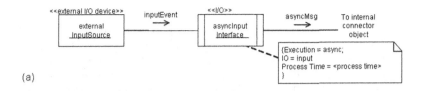

(a)

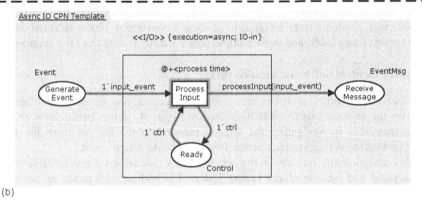

(b)

Fig. 3. Asynchronous Input Concurrent Object: (a) Behavioral Design Pattern; (b) CPN Template

- Processing Time: estimated execution time for one cycle
- Operation Type: read or write
- Statechart: for each «state dependent» object.

To illustrate pairing these architectural parameters with BDPs, refer once again to Fig. . In Fig. (a) we have an active object, "asyncInputInterface" that implements the I/O behavioral pattern as indicated by its stereotype. Furthermore, tagged types are used to capture specific architectural properties of the object, namely that it executes asynchronously; handles only input; and has a yet-to-be specified processing time of <process time>. The resulting CPN representation in Fig. (b) reflects these parameters with the selection of an asynchronous, input-only CPN template and by setting the time inscription on the Process Input transition to @+<process time>.

This <process time> parameter is an estimate for the time required by the object to complete one activation cycle. Initially, this is simply an analyst's best estimate. However, as additional platform specific information is known, this parameter can be updated to increase the fidelity of the model [22].

Once the CPN model is fully elaborated, it is analyzed in a CPN tool (e.g. by simulation or state space analysis) and the results used to reason about the original UML software architecture.

4   Case Study: Rover Control

To illustrate this CPN modeling and analysis approach, this section introduces a case study based on the Lego® Robotics Invention System™ (RIS), commonly known as

Mindstorms™[23]. The case study was employed in the context of a graduate software project laboratory course at George Mason University [24]. This project consisted of designing and constructing software on the RIS to implement an autonomous rover employing an infrared light sensor and two motors. The goal of the rover was to search an area for colored discs, while staying within the course boundary and avoiding obstacles. In this project, the light sensor was used as the sole input sensor, responsible for detecting boundary markings, obstacle markings, and discs according to different color schemes. Students were required to develop a concurrent, object-oriented design for the system using UML and to then implement the design using the Java language.

4.1 Rover Control Software Architecture

While there were some variations across student designs, one plausible architecture model for the autonomous rover is illustrated in Figure 4. In this particular scenario, we are interested in navigating the course; responding to changes from the light sensor; and taking the appropriate action based on the detection event.

In this design, there are three active, concurrently executing objects (*detect*, *rover*, and *nav*) and one passive object (*map*). External I/O objects (depicted as actors in Figure 4) are also shown for receiving light sensor input and for modeling output to the two motors. Each of the objects is stereotyped according to the hierarchy previously shown in Figure 1, thus indicating the behavioral design pattern (BDP) implemented by each object. Further details about the behavioral properties are augmented with architectural parameters as follows:

The *detect*, *rover*, and *nav* objects all operate asynchronously and have an Execution Type tagged value of "async". As the input interface for the light sensor, the *detect* object has an IO tagged value of "input". All messages between the active

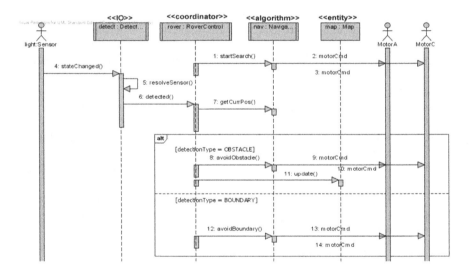

Fig. 4. Sequence Diagram for Rover control

objects have a Communication Type tagged value of "synchronous", indicating synchronous, buffered communication. This particular design decision was made to decrease the risk of missing a boundary or obstacle detection event. Other design choices for this system would be to employ FIFO or priority queuing. The effects of these design decisions could also be analyzed using the techniques presented in this paper, but are not shown due to space limitations. Finally, the *update()* operation on the *map* object has an Operation Type tagged value of "writer".

4.2 CPN Architecture Representation

Using the above design information, we can now begin to construct a Colored Petri Net (CPN) representation of the software architecture. Using a top-down approach we start with a context level model, capturing the system as a black box (transition) and external sensors and actuators represented as places. This model, allowing us to focus on the highest level of abstraction with observed inputs and outputs is shown in Figure 5.

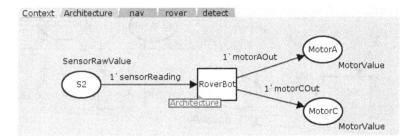

Fig. 5. RoverBot Context Level CPN Model

Moving forward, the second step is to decompose the RoverBot system-level transition into a layer of abstraction representing the concurrent object architecture. This architecture level model is shown in Figure 6. At this level, each of the active objects from Fig. is represented as its own transition (box) in the CPN model. Each of these will be further decomposed to implement the specific CPN template matching the objects behavioral design pattern. We have also included the single «entity» object containing map data and it is represented by a place for the map data to be stored along with a transition and two places representing the behavior for calling the *update()* operation. Finally, as all message communication between active objects in the RoverBot system is synchronous, there is a CPN place modeling a buffer for the synchronous communication between *detect* and *rover* and between *rover* and *nav*. Notice that our external input and output places have also been carried down to this level as well.

Once an architecture-level model is established, each of the transitions representing an active object is then decomposed by applying the CPN template associated with the behavioral design pattern of that object. For the asynchronous, input-only «IO» object, *detect*, this CPN object-level model is shown in Figure 7. Here, the CPN template has been inserted and instantiated specifically for the *detect* object by setting the object ID to "1" as seen by the number appended to place and transition names. The specific control token, C1 has also been added as has the function for processing detections, *detection (sensorReading)*. To maintain consistency, the main transition of this template, Pin1, has also been connected to the sensor input place and to the roverBuf message buffer place. Additionally, an initial estimate for the processing time (21 ms) was applied to the <process time> paramter.

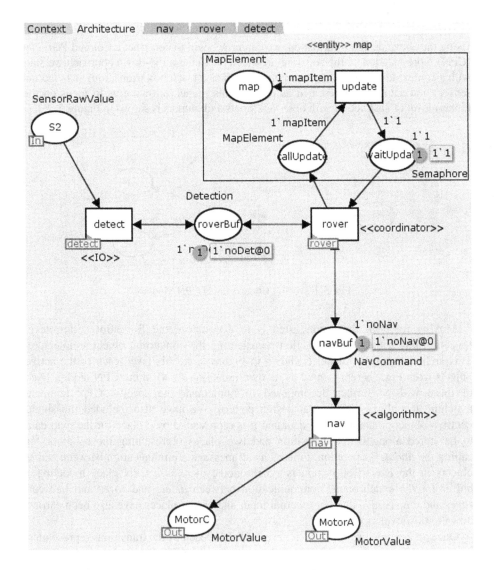

Fig. 6. RoverBot CPN Architecture

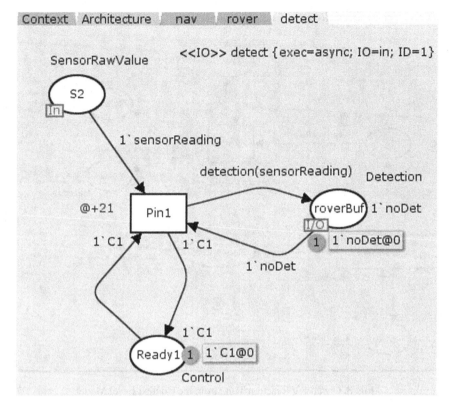

Fig. 7. Detect Object CPN Template with Time

4.3 Analysis of Rover Software Architecture

Recall from the sequence diagram of Fig. that the primary purpose of the autonomous rover system is to navigate an area, mapping objects discovered by the light sensor and taking evasive action when the light sensor detects obstacles or course boundaries. To begin analyzing this behavior with the corresponding CPN model, we use a test driver to provide simulated input events at random intervals. One of the first things we want to discover is how quickly the architecture responds to the detection of an obstacle or boundary. This can be analyzed from the context-level model by taking the difference in time stamps from the time an obstacle or boundary event arrives on the light sensor place to the time that a command is issued to the motors. For example, in Figure 8, the first obstacle was detected at time 6459 (all time is in milliseconds in this model). From the timestamps on the Motor places, we can see that from the time an input arrives to the time the system responded, there was an elapsed time of 31ms. The degree to which the CPN model represented the ultimate implementation of this design was validated using student implementations for the project [24].

The analytical CPN information could then be used, along with the speed of the rover, to determine if the reaction time is sufficient using this software architecture and this particular platform. Other forms of analysis could include altering the architecture

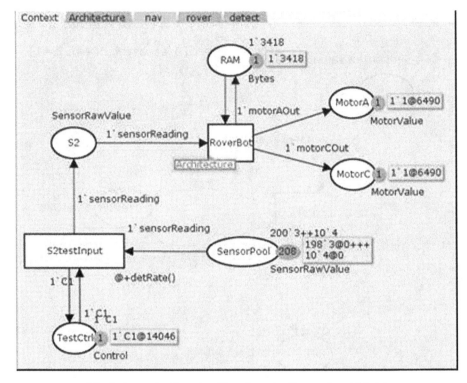

Fig. 8. Observing Reaction Time from the Context Level Model

to explore "what if" scenarios. Such examples could include changing the assumptions about hardware device performance or changing message communication mechanisms from synchronous to asynchronous. Additionally, one could perform some level of state space analysis on the CPN model to investigate conditions that may arise in a deadlocked state. One could also drill down through the CPN model to observe interactions at the architecture level or within an individual object. Additional resources can also be added to model such aspects as memory consumption as was done with the RAM place in Figure 8. Further details on resource modeling is discussed in [22].

5 Conclusions and Future Research

The ultimate goal of this research effort is to provide an automated means of translating a UML concurrent software architecture design into an underlying CPN representation that can then be used to conduct behavioral analysis and applying the results to the original UML model. To date, we have developed a method for systematically translating a UML software architecture design (represented as an interaction diagram of concurrent objects) into a CPN representation. This method employs reusable, consistent CPN segments that model the behavior of a set of objects according to their stereotyped behavioral roles. Once the CPN representation has been created, the properties of Petri nets (along with the corresponding tool support) allow for analysis to be performed on a number of aspects related to the behavior of the concurrently executing objects. By constructing a CPN representation that maintains the structure of the concurrent object architecture, the results from the CPN analysis can easily be applied to the original UML model. By conducting analyses on the concurrent architecture early in the project lifecycle, we can increase the confidence that the final implementation will meet the desired behavior. Furthermore, we are more likely to find and correct problems at a time when it is significantly less costly (in terms of both time and money) to fix them.

The current state of this research provides a systematic method for translating a concurrent software design captured in UML to an underlying CPN model. We have also given examples of how to apply various CPN analysis techniques and have expanded the modeling capabilities to handle the inclusion of platform specific characteristics. Future research in this area will need to investigate approaches to facilitate the automated translation from a UML model into a CPN model. Furthermore, most of the analysis conducted with this research effort has focused on the use of simulations for functional and performance. Additional research need to be conducted to explore the use of state space analysis and to determine how scalable such state space analysis would be for larger systems. Such state analysis properties of CPNs are quite powerful and could be used to analyze such features as the absence of deadlock conditions as well as system-wide state changes.

In conclusion, this paper has provided a brief description of a systematic and repeatable method for translating concurrent UML software architectures into an underlying CPN model. This CPN model may then be analyzed for functionality and performance and thus provide insight to the software engineer regarding the concurrent behavior of the design. By adjusting the software design based on the results from the CPN analysis, an engineer may increase confidence in the software architecture design, identifying and avoiding concurrent behavioral problems earlier in the lifecycle.

References

1. Pettit, R.G., Street, J.A.: Lessons Learned Applying UML in the Design of Mission Critical Software, In: Proc. UML 2004, Lisbon, Portugal (October 2004)
2. Pettit, R.G.: Lessons Learned Applying UML in Embedded Software Systems Design. In: Proc. WSTFEUS 2004, Vienna, Austria (May 2004)
3. OMG, The Unified Modeling Language®, Version 2.1.2, The Object Mangagement Group (November 2007)
4. Pettit, R.G., Gomaa, H.: Modeling Behavioral Design Patterns of Concurrent Objects. In: Proc. 28th International Conference on Software Engineering (ICSE), Shanghai, China (May 2006)
5. Baldassari, M., Bruno, G., Castella, A.: PROTOB: an Object-Oriented CASE Tool for Modeling and Prototyping Distributed Systems. Software-Practice & Experience 21, 823–844 (1991)
6. Mikolajczak, B., Sefranek, C.A.: Integrating Object Oriented Design with Concurrency Using Petri Nets. In: IEEE International Conference on Systems, Man and Cybernetics, Piscataway, NJ, USA (2001)
7. Aihua, R.: An Integrated Development Environment for Concurrent Software Developing Based on Object Oriented Petri Nets. In: Fourth International Conference/Exhibition on High Performance Computing in the Asia-Pacific Region, Los Alamitos, CA, USA (2000)

8. He, X., Ding, Y.: Object Orientation in Hierarchical Predicate Transition Nets. In: Concurrent Object-Oriented Programming and Petri Nets. Advances in Petri Nets, pp. 196–215. Springer, Berlin (2001)

9. Biberstein, O., Buchs, D., Guelfi, N.: Object-Oriented Nets with Algebraic Specifications: The CO-OPN/2 Formalism. In: Agha, G.A., De Cindio, F., Rozenberg, G. (eds.) APN 2001. LNCS, vol. 2001, pp. 73–130. Springer, Heidelberg (2001)

10. Camurri, A., Franchi, P., Vitale, M.: Extending High-Level Petri Nets for Object-Oriented Design. In: IEEE International Conference on Systems, Man and Cybernetics, New York, NY, USA (1992)

11. Hong, J.E., Bae, D.H.: Software Modeling and Analysis Using a Hierarchical Object-Oriented Petri Net. Information Sciences 130, 133–164 (2000)

12. Azzopardi, D., Holding, D.J.: Petri Nets and OMT for Modeling and Analysis of DEDS. Control Engineering Practices 5 (1997)

13. Lakos, C.A.: Object Oriented Modelling with Object Petri Nets. In: Agha, G.A., De Cindio, F., Rozenberg, G. (eds.) APN 2001. LNCS, vol. 2001, pp. 1–37. Springer, Heidelberg (2001)

14. Maier, C., Moldt, D.: Object Coloured Petri Nets- A Formal Technique for Object Oriented Modelling. In: Concurrent Object-Oriented Programming and Petri Nets. Advances in Petri Nets, pp. 406–427. Springer, Berlin (2001)

15. Saldhana, J.A., Shatz, S.M., Zhaoxia, H.: Formalization of Object Behavior and Interactions from UML Models. International Journal of Software Engineering & Knowledge Engineering 11, 643–673 (2001)

16. Baresi, L., Pezze, M.: On Formalizing UML with High-Level Petri Nets. In: Agha, G.A., De Cindio, F., Rozenberg, G. (eds.) APN 2001. LNCS, vol. 2001, pp. 276–304. Springer, Heidelberg (2001)

17. Hansen, K.M.: Towards a Coloured Petri Net Profile for the Unified Modeling Centre for Object Technology, Aarhus, Denmark, Technical Report COT/2-52-V0.1 (DRAFT) (2001)

18. Jørgensen, J.B.: Coloured Petri Nets in UML-Based Software Development - Designing Middleware for Pervasive Healthcare. In: CPN 2002, Aarhus, Denmark (2002)

19. Bordbar, B., Giacomini, L., Holding, D.J.: UML and Petri Nets for Design and Analysis of Distributed Systems. In: International Conference on Control Applications, Anchorage, Alaska, USA (2000)

20. Jensen, K.: Coloured Petri Nets: Basic Concepts, Analysis Methods, and Practical Use, vol. I-III. Springer, Berlin (1997)

21. Gomaa, H.: Designing Concurrent, Distributed, and Real-Time Applications with UML. Addison-Wesley, Reading (2000)

22. Pettit, R.G., Gomaa, H.: Analyzing Behavior of Concurrent Software Designs for Embedded Systems. In: Proc. ISORC 2007, Santorini, Greece (2007)

23. Lego, "Lego Mindstorms", http://mindstorms.lego.com

24. Pettit, R.: SWE 626: Software Project Lab for Real-Time and Embedded Systems. George Mason University (2006)

Fast Scheduling of Distributable Real-Time Threads with Assured End-to-End Timeliness

Sherif F. Fahmy[1], Binoy Ravindran[1], and E.D. Jensen[2]

[1] ECE Dept., Virginia Tech, Blacksburg, VA 24061, USA
[2] The MITRE Corporation, Bedford, MA 01730, USA

Abstract. We consider networked, embedded real-time systems that operate under run-time uncertainties on activity execution times and arrivals, node failures, and message losses. We consider the distributable threads abstraction for programming and scheduling such systems, and present a thread scheduling algorithm called QBUA. We show that QBUA satisfies (end-to-end) thread time constraints in the presence of crash failures and message losses, has efficient message and time complexities, and lower overhead and superior timeliness properties than past thread scheduling algorithms. Our experimental studies validate our theoretical results, and illustrate the algorithm's effectiveness.

1 Introduction

Some emerging, networked embedded real-time systems (e.g., US DoD's Network Centric Warfare systems [1]) are subject to resource overloads (due to context-dependent activity execution times), arbitrary activity arrivals, and arbitrary node failures and message losses. Reasoning about *end-to-end* timeliness is a difficult and unsolved problem in such systems. A distinguishing feature of such systems is their relatively long activity execution time scales (e.g., milliseconds to minutes), which permits more time-costlier real-time resource management.

Maintaining end-to-end properties (e.g., timeliness, connectivity) of a control or information flow requires a model of the flow's locus in space and time that can be reasoned about. Such a model facilitates reasoning about the contention for resources that occur along the flow's locus and resolving those contentions to optimize system-wide end-to-end timeliness. The *distributable thread* programming abstraction which first appeared in the Alpha OS [2], and later the Real-Time CORBA 1.2 standard directly provides such a model as their first-class programming and scheduling abstraction. A distributable thread is a single thread of execution with a globally unique identity that transparently extends and retracts through local and remote objects. We focus on distributable threads as our end-to-end programming/scheduling abstraction, and hereafter, refer to them as *threads*, except as necessary for clarity.

Contributions. In this paper, we consider the problem of scheduling threads in the presence of the previously mentioned uncertainties, focusing particularly on (arbitrary) node failures and message losses. Past efforts on thread scheduling

F. Kordon and T. Vardanega (Eds.): Ada-Europe 2008, LNCS 5026, pp. 211–225, 2008.

(e.g., see [3] and references therein) can be broadly categorized into two classes: *independent node scheduling* and *collaborative scheduling*. In the independent scheduling approach, threads are scheduled at nodes using propagated thread scheduling parameters and without any interaction with other nodes. Thread faults are managed by *integrity protocols* that run concurrent to thread execution. Integrity protocols employ failure detectors (or FDs), and use them to detect thread failures. In the collaborative scheduling approach, nodes explicitly cooperate to construct system-wide thread schedules, detecting node failures using FDs while doing so. In this work, we compare QBUA to three previous thread scheduling algorithms, HUA, CUA, and ACUA (see [3] and references therein).

HUA is an independent scheduling algorithm, which sometimes may make locally optimal decisions that may not be globally optimal. This is overcome by CUA and ACUA, which are collaborative scheduling algorithms that use uniform consensus [4] for unanimously deciding on system-wide thread schedules in the presence of node failures. In [3], it is shown that ACUA has superior timeliness properties (e.g., lower number of missed deadlines) than HUA and CUA. In addition, HUA and CUA consider synchronous computational models (i.e., those with deterministically bounded time variables). In contrast, ACUA considers the partially synchronous model in [5], where message delay and message loss are probabilistically described. Though this increases ACUA's coverage[1], the algorithm has high overhead, thereby only allowing threads that can tolerant this large overhead to reap the algorithm's superior timeliness.

In this paper, we present a collaborative scheduling algorithm called the *Quorum-Based Utility Accrual scheduling* (or QBUA) that precisely overcomes ACUA's overhead disadvantage. The algorithm considers the partially synchronous model in [5], and uses a Quorum set of nodes for majority agreement on constructing system-wide thread schedules. We show that QBUA satisfies thread time constraints in the presence of node crash failures and message losses, has efficient message and time complexities that compare favorably with other algorithms in its class, and lower overhead and superior timeliness than past algorithms including CUA and HUA. We also show that the algorithm's lower overhead enables it to allow more threads to benefit from its superior timeliness, than that allowed by past algorithms.

2   Models and Objective

Distributable Thread Abstraction. Distributable threads, our computing abstraction, execute in local and remote objects by location-independent invocations and returns. The portion of a thread executing an object operation is called a *thread segment*. Thus, a thread can be viewed as being composed of a concatenation of thread segments. A thread can also be viewed as being composed of a

---

[1] As defined in [6], coverage is the decreasing likelihood for the algorithm's timing assurances to be violated, when the underlying synchrony assumptions are violated at run-time (e.g., due to overloads or other exigencies). This likelihood reduces when coverage increases.

sequence of *sections*, where a section is a maximal length sequence of contiguous thread segments on a node. A section's first segment results from an invocation from another node, and its last segment performs a remote invocation. We assume that execution time estimates of sections of a thread are known when the thread arrives into the system and are described using TUFs (see our timeliness model). The sequence of remote invocations and returns made by a thread can typically be estimated by analyzing the thread code. The total number of sections of a thread is thus assumed to be known a-priori. The application is thus comprised of a set of threads, denoted $\mathbf{T} = \{T_1, T_2, \ldots\}$ and the set of sections of a thread T_i is denoted as $[S_1^i, S_2^i, \ldots, S_k^i]$. See [7] for more details.

Timeliness Model. We specify the time constraint of each thread using a Time/ Utility Function (TUF) [8]. A TUF allows us to decouple the urgency of a thread from its importance. This decoupling is a key property allowed by TUFs since the urgency of a thread may be orthogonal to its importance. A thread T_i's TUF is denoted as $U_i(t)$. A classical deadline is unit-valued—i.e., $U_i(t) = \{0, 1\}$, since importance is not considered. Downward step TUFs generalize classical deadlines where $U_i(t) = \{0, \{m\}\}$. We focus on downward step TUFs, and denote the maximum, constant utility of a TUF $U_i(t)$, simply as U_i. Each TUF has an initial time I_i, which is the earliest time for which the TUF is defined, and a termination time X_i, which, for a downward step TUF, is its discontinuity point. $U_i(t) > 0, \forall t \in [I_i, X_i]$ and $U_i(t) = 0, \forall t \notin [I_i, X_i], \forall i$.

System Model. Our system consists of a set of client nodes $\coprod = \{1, 2, \cdots, N\}$ and a set of server nodes $\Pi = \{1, 2, \cdots, n\}$ (*server* and *client* are logical designations given to nodes to describe the algorithm's behavior). Bi-directional logical communication channels are assumed to exist between every client-server and client-client pair. We also assume that the basic communication channels may loose messages with probability p, and communication delay is described by some probability distribution. On top of this basic communication channel, we consider a reliable communication protocol that delivers a message to its destination in probabilistically bounded time provided that the sender and receiver both remain correct, using the standard technique of sequence numbers and retransmissions. We assume that each node is equipped with two processors: a processor that executes thread sections on the node and a scheduling co-processor as in [2]. We also assume that nodes in our system have access to GPS clocks that provides each node with a UTC time-source with high precision (e.g., [9]) and are equipped with appropriately tuned QoS FDs [5]. Further details about our system model are provided in [7].

Exceptions and Abort Model. Each section of a thread has an associated exception handler. We consider a termination model for thread failures including time-constraint violations and node failures. In the case of time constraint-violation or node failure, these exception handlers are triggered to restore the system to a safe state. The exception handlers we consider have time constraints expressed as relative deadlines. See [7] for more details.

Failure Model. The nodes are subject to crash failures. When a process crashes, it loses it state memory — i.e., there is no persistent storage. If a crashed client node recovers at a later time, we consider it a new node since it has already lost all of its former execution context. A client node is *correct* if it does not crash; it is *faulty* if it is not correct. In the case of a server crash, it may either recover or be replaced by a new server assuming the same server name (using DNS or DHT — e.g, [10] — technology). We model both cases as server recovery. Since crashes are associated with memory loss, recovered servers start from their initial state. A server is *correct* if it never fails; it is *faulty* if it is not correct. QBUA tolerates up to $N - 1$ client failures and up to $f^s_{max} \leq n/3$ server failures. The actual number of server failures is denoted as $f^s \leq f^s_{max}$ and the actual number of client failures is denoted as $f \leq f_{max}$ where $f_{max} \leq N - 1$.

Scheduling Objectives. Our primary objective is to design a thread scheduling algorithm to maximize the total utility accrued by all threads as much as possible. The algorithm must also provide assurances on the satisfaction of thread termination times in the presence of (up to f_{max}) crash failures. Moreover, the algorithm must exhibit the best-effort property (see Section 1 of [7] for details).

3   Algorithm Rationale

QBUA is a collaborative scheduling algorithm, which allows it to construct schedules that result in higher system-wide accrued utility by preventing locally optimal decisions from compromising system-wide optimality. It also allows QBUA to respond to node failures by eliminating threads that are affected by the failures, thus allowing the algorithm to gracefully degrade timeliness in the presence of failures. There are two types of scheduling events that are handled by QBUA, viz: a) local scheduling events and b) distributed scheduling events.

Local scheduling events are handled locally on a node without consulting other nodes. Examples of local scheduling events are section completion, section handler expiry events etc. For a full list of local scheduling events please see Algorithm 7 in [7]. Distributed scheduling events need the participation of all nodes in the system to handle them. In this work, only two distributed scheduling events exit, viz: a) the arrival of a new thread into the system and b) the failure of a node. A node that detects a distributed scheduling event sends a START message to all other nodes requesting their scheduling information so that it can compute a <u>S</u>ystem <u>W</u>ide <u>E</u>xecutable <u>T</u>hread <u>S</u>et (or SWETS). Nodes that receive this message, send their scheduling information to the requesting node and wait for schedule updates (which are sent to them when the requesting node computes a new system-wide schedule). This may lead to contention if several different nodes detect the same distributed scheduling event concurrently.

For example, when a node fails, many nodes may detect the failure concurrently. It is superfluous for all these nodes to start an instance of QBUA. In addition, events that occur in quick succession may trigger several instances of QBUA when only one instance can handle all of those events. To prevent this, we use a quorum system to arbitrate among the nodes wishing to run QBUA. In order to perform this arbitration, the quorum system examines the time-stamp of incoming events. If an instance of QBUA was granted permission to run *later* than an incoming event, there is no need to run another instance of QBUA since information about the incoming event will be available to the version of QBUA already running (i.e., the event will be handled by that instance of QBUA).

4   Algorithm Description

As mentioned above, whenever a distributed scheduling event occurs, a node attempts to acquire permission from the quorum system to run a version of QBUA. After the quorum system has arbitrated among the nodes contending to execute QBUA, the node that acquires the "lock" executes Algorithm 1. In Algorithm 1, the node first broadcasts a start of algorithm message (line 1) and then waits $2T$ time units[2] for all nodes in the system to respond by sending their local scheduling information (line 2). After collecting this information, the node computes SWETS (line 3) using Algorithm 4. After computing SWETS, the node contacts affected nodes (i.e. nodes that will have sections added or removed from their schedule as a result of the scheduling event).

Algorithm 1. Compute SWETS

1: Broadcast start of algorithm message, START;
2: Wait $2T$ collecting replies from other nodes;
3: Construct SWETS using information collected;
4: Multicast change of schedule to affected nodes;
5: return;

Algorithm 2 shows the details of the algorithm that client nodes run when attempting to acquire a "lock" on running a version of QBUA. The algorithm is loosely based on Chen's solution for FTME [11]. Upon the arrival of a distributed scheduling event, a node tries to acquire a "lock" on running QBUA (the try_1 part of the algorithm that starts on line 3).

The first thing that the node does (lines 4-5) is check if it is currently running an instance of QBUA that is in its information collection phase (line 2 in Algorithm 1). If so, the new event that has occurred can simply be added to the information being collected by this version of QBUA. However, if no current instance of QBUA is being hosted by the node, or if the instance of QBUA being hosted has passed its information collection phase, then the event may have to spawn a new instance of QBUA (this starts at line 6 in the algorithm).

The first thing that Algorithm 2 does in this case is send a time-stamped request to the set of server nodes, Π, in the system (lines 8-10). The time-stamp is used to inform the quorum nodes of the time at which the event was detected by the current node. Beginning at line 3, Algorithm 2 collects replies from the servers. Once a sufficient number of replies have arrived (line 14), Algorithm 2 checks whether its request has been accepted by a sufficient ($\lceil \frac{2n}{3} \rceil$ see Section 5) number of server nodes. If so, the node computes SWETS (lines 15-16).

---

[2] T is communication delay derived from the random variable describing the communication delay in the system.

On the other hand, if an insufficient number of server nodes support the request, two possibilities exist. The first possibility is that another node has been granted permission to run an instance of QBUA to handle this event. In this case, the current node does not need to perform any additional action and so releases the "lock" it has acquired on some servers (lines 17-21).

The second possibility is that the result of the contention to run QBUA at the servers was inconclusive due to differences in communication delay.   For

---

Algorithm 2. QBUA on client node i

1: *timestamp*; // time stamp variable initially set to nil
2: **upon thread arrival or detection of a node failure:**
3:    try_1:
4:       **if** *a current version of QBUA is waiting for information from other nodes* **then**
5:          Include information about event when computing SWETS;
6:       **else**
7:          *timestamp* ← GetTimeStamp;
8:          **for** *all* $r_j \in \Pi$ **do**
9:             resp[j] ← (nil, nil);
10:            **send** (REQUEST, *timestamp*) to r_j;
11:         **repeat**
12:            **wait until**   [received (RESPONSE, *owner*, t) from some r_j];
13:            **if** $(c_1 \neq owner$ *or timestamp* $= t)$ **then**   resp[j] ← $(owner, t)$;
14:            **if** *among resp[], at least m of them are not* (nil, nil) **then**
15:               **if** *at least m elements in resp[] are* (c_1, t) **then**
16:                  **return** Compute SWETS;
17:               **else if** *at least m elements in resp[] agree about a certain node* **then**
18:                  **for** *all* $r_k \in \Pi$ *such that resp[k]* $\neq (nil, nil)$ **do**
19:                     **if** *resp[k].owner* $= c_1$ **then**
20:                        **send** (RELEASE,*timestamp*) to r_k;
21:                  Skip rest of algorithm; //Event is already being handled
22:               **else**
23:                  **for** *all* $r_k \in \Pi$ *such that resp[k]* $\neq (nil, nil)$ **do**
24:                     **if** *resp[k].owner* $= c_1$ **then**
25:                        **send** (YIELD,*timestamp*) to r_k;
26:                     **else**
27:                        **send** (INQUIRE,*timestamp*) to r_k;
28:                     resp[k] ← (nil, nil);
29:         **until** *forever* ;
30:      $exit_1$:
31:         *oldtimestamp* ← *timestamp*;
32:         *timestamp* ← GetTimeStamp;
33:         **for** *all* $r_k \in \Pi$ **do**
34:            **send** (RELEASE, *oldtimestamp*) to r_j;
35:            **return**;
36: **upon receive** (CHECK, t) from r_j
37:    **if** *for all instances of QBUA running on this node, timestamp* $\neq t$ **then**
38:       **send** (RELEASE, t) to r_j;
39: **upon receive** (START) from some client node
40:    Update RE_j^i for all sections;
41:    **send** σ_j and RE_j^i's to requesting node;

---

example, assume that we have 5 servers and three clients wishing to run QBUA and all three clients send their request to the servers at the same time, also assume different communication delay between each server and client. Due to these communication differences, the messages of the clients may arrive in such a pattern so that two servers support client 1, another 2 servers support client 2 and the last server supports client 3. This means that no client's request is supported by a sufficient — i.e., $\frac{2n}{3}$ — number of server nodes. In this case, the client node sends a YIELD message to servers that support it and an INQUIRE message to nodes that do not support it (line 22-28) and waits for more responses from the server nodes to resolve this conflict. Lines 30-35 release the "lock" on servers after the client node has computed SWETS, lines 36-38 are used to handle the periodic cleanup messages sent by the servers and lines 39-41 respond to the START of algorithm message (line 1, Algorithm 1).

Algorithm 3. QBUA on server node i

1:   $c_{owner}[]$; Array of nodes holding lock to run QBUA
2:   $t_{owner}[]$; $t_{owner}[i]$ contains time-stamp of event that triggered QBUA for node in $c_{owner}[i]$
3:   $t_{grant}[]$; $t_{grant}[i]$ contains time at which node in $c_{owner}[i]$ was granted lock to run QBUA
4:   $R_{wait}[]$; $R_{wait}[i]$ is waiting queue for instance of QBUA being run by $c_{owner}[i]$;
5:   **upon receive** $(tag,\ t)$
6:     $CurrentTime \leftarrow$ GetTimeStamp;
7:     **if** $(c_1,\ t')$ *appears in* $(c_{owner}[],t_{owner}[])$ *or* $R_{wait}[]$ **then**
8:       **if** $t < t'$ **then** Skip rest of algo; //This is an old message

9:     **if** $tag = REQUEST$ **then**
10:       **if** $\exists\ t_{grant} \in t_{grant}[]$ *such that* $t \leq t_{grant}$ **then**
11:         send (RESPONSE, c, t_{grant}) to c_1; //where $c \leftarrow c_{owner}[i]$, such that $t_{grant}[i] = t_{grant}$;
12:         Enqueue (c_1, t) in $R_{wait}[i]$, such that $t_{grant}[i] = t_{grant}$;
13:         Skip rest of algorithm;

14:       **else**
15:         AddElement($c_{owner}[], c_1$);
16:         AddElement($t_{owner}[], t$);
17:         AddElement($t_{grant}[], CurrentTime$);
18:         send (RESPONSE, c_1, t) to c_1;

19:     **else if** $tag = RELEASE$ **then**
20:       Delete entry corresponding to c_1, t from $c_{owner}[]$, $t_{owner}[]$, $t_{grant}[]$, and $R_{wait}[]$;

21:     **else if** $tag = YIELD$ **then**
22:       **if** $(c_1,\ t) \in (c_{owner}[],\ t_{owner}[])$ **then**
23:         For i, such that $(c_1,\ t) = (c_{owner}[i],\ t_{owner}[i])$
24:         Enqueue $(c_1,\ t)$ in $R_{wait}[i]$;
25:         $(c_{wait}, t_{wait}) \leftarrow$ top of $R_{wait}[i]$;
26:         $c_{owner}[i] \leftarrow c_{wait}$; $t_{owner}[i] \leftarrow t_{wait}$;
27:         $t_{grant}[i] \leftarrow CurrentTime$;
28:         send (RESPONSE, c_{wait}, t_{wait}) to c_{wait};

29:       **if** $c_1 \notin c_{owner}[]$ **then**
30:         $(c, t_p) \leftarrow (c_{owner}[i], t_{owner}[i])$, for min i such that $t \leq t_{grant}[i]$;
31:         send (RESPONSE, c, t_p) to c_1;

32:     **else if** $tag = INQUIRE$ **then**
33:       $(c, t_p) \leftarrow (c_{owner}[i], t_{owner}[i])$, for min i such that $t \leq t_{grant}[i]$;
34:       send (RESPONSE, c, t_p) to c_1;

35: **upon suspect that** $c_{owner}[i]$ has failed:
36:     HandleFailure($c_{owner}[i], c_{owner}[], t_{owner}[], t_{grant}[], R_{wait}[]$);
37: **periodically**:
38:     $\forall\ c_{owner} \in c_{owner}[]$:
39:       send (CHECK, t_{owner}) to c_{owner}; //NB. t_{owner} is the entry in $t_{owner}[]$ that corresponds to c_{owner}.

Algorithm 3 is run by the servers, the function of this algorithm is to arbitrate among the nodes contending to run QBUA so as to minimize the number of concurrent executions of the algorithm. Since there may be more than one instance of QBUA running at any given time, the server nodes keep track of these instances using three arrays. The first array, $c_{owner}[]$, keeps track of which nodes are running instances of QBUA, the second, $t_{owner}[]$, stores the time at which a node in $c_{owner}[]$ sends a request to the servers (i.e., the time at which that node detects a certain scheduling event), and $t_{grant}[]$ keeps track of the time at which server nodes grant permission to client nodes to execute QBUA. In addition, a waiting queue for each running instance of QBUA is kept in $R_{wait}[]$.

When a server receives a message from a client node, it first checks to see if this is a stale message (which may happen due to out of order delivery). A message from a client node, c_1, that has a time-stamp older than the last message received from c_1 has been delivered out of order and is ignored (line 7-8). Starting at line 9, the algorithm begins to examine the message it has received. If it is a REQUEST message, the server checks if the time-stamp of the event triggering the message is *less* than the time at which a client node was *granted* permission to run an instance of QBUA. If such an instance exists, a new instance of QBUA is not needed since the event will be handled by that previous instance of QBUA. Algorithm 3, inserts the incoming request into a waiting queue associated with that instance of QBUA and sends a message to the client (lines 10-13).

However, if no current instance of QBUA can handle the event, a client's request to start an instance of QBUA is granted (lines 14-18). If a client node sends a YIELD message, the server revokes the grant it issued to that client and selects another client from the waiting queue for that event (lines 21-31). This part of the algorithm can only be triggered if the result of the first round of contention to run QBUA is inconclusive (as discussed when describing Algorithm 2). Recall that this inconclusive contention is caused by different communication delays that allow different requests to arrive at different severs in different orders. However, all client requests for a particular instance of QBUA are queued in $R_{wait}[]$, therefore, when a client sends a YIELD message, servers are able to choose the highest priority request (which we define as the request with the earliest time-stamp and use node id as a tie breaker). Thus, we guarantee that this contention will be resolved in the second round of the algorithm. Lines 32-34 show servers' response to INQUIRE messages and lines 35-39 show the clean up procedures to remove stale messages. See [7] for how we handle failures (line 36).

Algorithm 4 is used by a client node to compute SWETS once it has received information from all other nodes in the system (line 2 in Algorithm 1). It performs two basic functions, first, it computes a system wide order on threads by computing their global Potential Utility Density (PUD). It then attempts to insert the remaining sections of each thread, in non-increasing order of global PUD, into the scheduling queues of all nodes in the system. After the insertion of each thread, the schedule is checked for feasibility. If it is not feasible, then the thread is removed from SWETS (after scheduling the appropriate exception handler if necessary).

First we need to define the global PUD of a thread. Assume that a thread, T_i, has k sections denoted $\{S_1^i, S_2^i, \cdots, S_k^i\}$. We define the global remaining execution time, GE_i, of the thread to be the sum of the remaining execution times of each of the thread's sections. Let $\{RE_1^i, RE_2^i, \cdots, RE_k^i\}$ be the set of remaining execution times of T_i's sections, then $GE_i = \sum_{j=1}^{k} RE_j^i$. Assuming that we are using step-down TUFs, and T_i's TUF is $U_i(t)$, then its global PUD can be computed as $T_i.PUD = U_i(t_{curr} + GE_i)/GE_i$, where U is the utility of the thread and t_{curr} is the current time. Using global PUD, we can establish a system wide order on the threads in non-increasing order of "return on investment". This allows us to consider the threads for scheduling in an order that is designed to maximize accrued utility [12].

We now turn our attention to the method used to check schedule feasibility. For a schedule to be feasible, all the sections it contains should complete their execution before their assigned termination time. Since we are considering threads with end-to-end termination times, the termination time of each section needs to be derived from its thread's end-to-end termination time. This derivation should ensure that if all the section termination times are met, then the end-to-end termination time of the thread will also be met.

For the last section in a thread, we derive its termination time as simply the termination time of the entire thread. The termination time of the other sections is the latest start time of the section's successor minus the communication delay. Thus the section termination times of a thread T_i, with k sections, is:

$$
S_j^i.tt = \begin{cases} T_i.tt & j = k \\ S_{j+1}^i.tt - S_{j+1}^i.ex - T & 1 \leq j \leq k-1 \end{cases}
$$

where $S_j^i.tt$ denotes section S_j^i's termination time, $T_i.tt$ denotes T_i's termination time, and $S_j^i.ex$ denotes the estimated execution time of section S_j^i. The communication delay, which we denote by T above, is a random variable Δ. Therefore, the value of T can only be determined probabilistically. This implies that if each section meets the termination times computed above, the whole thread will meet its termination time with a certain, high, probability (see Lemma 6 in [7]).

In addition, each section's handler has a **relative** termination time, $S_j^h.X$. However, a handler's **absolute** termination time is relative to the time it is released, more specifically, the **absolute** termination time of a handler is equal to the sum of the **relative** termination time of the handler and the failure time t_f (which cannot be known a priori). In order to overcome this problem, we delay the execution of the handler as much as possible, thus leaving room for more important threads. We compute the handler termination times as follows:

$$
S_j^h.tt = \begin{cases} S_k^i.tt + S_j^h.X + T_D + t_a & j = k \\ S_{j+1}^h.tt + S_j^h.X + T & 1 \leq j \leq k-1 \end{cases}
$$

where $S_j^h.tt$ denotes section handler S_j^h's termination time, $S_j^h.X$ denotes the relative termination time of section handler S_j^h, $S_k^i.tt$ is the termination time of thread i's last section, t_a is a correction factor corresponding to the execution time of the scheduling algorithm, and T_D is the time needed to detect a failure by our QoS FD [5]. From this termination time decomposition, we compute latest start times for each handler: $S_j^h.st = S_j^h.tt - S_j^h.ex$ for $1 \leq j \leq k$, where $S_j^h.ex$ denotes the estimated execution time of section handler S_j^h. In Algorithm 4, each node, j, sends the node running QBUA its current local schedule σ_j^p. Using these schedules, the node can determine the set of threads, Γ, that are currently in the system. Both these variables are inputs to the scheduling algorithm (lines 1 and 2 in Algorithm 4). In lines 3-6, the algorithm computes the global PUD of each thread in Γ.

Before we schedule the threads, we need to ensure that the exception handlers of any thread that has already been accepted into the system can execute to completion before its termination time. We do this by inserting the handlers of sections that were part of each node's previous schedule into that node's current schedule (lines 7-9). Since these handlers were part of σ_j^p, and QBUA always maintains the feasibility of a schedule as an algorithm invariant, we are sure that these handlers will execute to completion before their termination times.

In line 10, we sort the threads in the system in non-increasing order of PUD and consider them for scheduling in that order (lines 11-21). In lines 13-14 we mark as failed any thread that has a section hosted on a node that does not participate in the algorithm. If the thread can contribute non-zero utility to the system and the thread has not been rejected from the system, then we insert its sections into the scheduling queue of the node responsible for them (line 17).

Algorithm 4. ConstructSchedule

1: **input:** Γ; //Set of threads in the system
2: **input:** σ_j^p, $H_j \leftarrow$ nil; //σ_j^p: Previous schedule of node j, H_j: set of handlers scheduled
3: **for** *each* $T_i \in \Gamma$ **do**
4:      **if** *for some section* S_j^i *belonging to* T_i, $t_{curr} + S_j^i.ex > S_j^i.tt$ **then**
5:         $T_i.PUD \leftarrow 0$;
6:      **else** $T_i.PUD \leftarrow \frac{U_i(t_{curr}+GE_i)}{GE_i}$;

7: **for** *each task* $el \in \sigma_j^p$ **do**
8:      **if** *el is an exception handler for section* S_j^i **then** Insert(el, H_j, $el.tt$);

9: $\sigma_j \leftarrow H_j$;
10: $\sigma_{temp} \leftarrow$ sortByPUD(Γ);
11: **for** *each* $T_i \in \sigma_{temp}$ **do**
12:      $T_i.stop \leftarrow false$;
13:      **if** *did not receive* σ_j *from node hosting one of* T_i *'s sections* S_j^i **then**
14:         $T_i.stop \leftarrow true$;

15:      **for** *each remaining section,* S_j^i, *belonging to* T_i **do**
16:         **if** $T_i.PUD > 0$ *and* $T_i.stop \neq true$ **then**
17:            Insert(S_j^i, σ_j, $S_j^i.tt$);
18:            **if** $S_j^h \notin \sigma_j^p$ **then** Insert(S_j^h, σ_j, $S_j^h.tt$);
19:            **if** *isFeasible*(σ_j)=*false* **then**
20:               $T_i.stop \leftarrow true$;
21:               Remove(S_k^i, σ_k, $S_k^i.tt$) for $1 \leq k \leq j$;
22:               **if** $S_j^i \notin \sigma_j^p$ **then** Remove(S_j^h, σ_j, $S_j^h.tt$);

23: **for** *each* $j \in N$ **do**
24:      **if** $\sigma_j \neq \sigma_j^p$ **then** Mark node j as being affected by current scheduling event;

After inserting the section into its corresponding ready queue (at a position reflecting its termination time), we check to see whether this section's handler had been included in the previous schedule of the node. If so, we do not insert the handler into the schedule since this has been already taken care of by lines 7-8. Otherwise, the handler is inserted into its corresponding ready queue (line 18). Once the section, and its handler, have been inserted into the ready queue, we check the feasibility of the schedule (line 19). If the schedule is infeasible, we remove the thread's sections from the schedule (line 21). However, we first check to see whether the section's handler was part of a previous schedule before we remove it (line 22). We perform this check before removing the handler because if the handler was part of a previous schedule, then its section has failed and we should keep its exception handler for clean up purposes. Finally, if the schedule of any node has changed, these nodes are marked to have been affected by the current instance of QBUA (lines 23-24). It is to these nodes that the current node needs to multicast the changes that have occurred (line 4, Algorithm 1). In order to test the feasibility of a schedule, we need to check if all the sections in the schedule can complete before their derived termination times. The full algorithm is depicted in Algorithm 6 in [7]. QBUA's dispatcher is shown in Algorithm 7 in [7]. Only two scheduling events result in collaborative scheduling, viz: the arrival of a thread into the system, and the failure of a node, all other scheduling events are handled locally. Since we are talking about a partially synchronous system, the FD we use to detect node failures can make mistakes. Thus, QBUA may be started due to an erroneous detection of failure. The this can be reduced by designing a QoS FD [5] with appropriate QoS parameters.

5 Algorithm Properties

We establish several properties of QBUA. Due to space limitations, some of the properties and all of the proofs are omitted here, and can be found in [7]. Below, T is the communication delay, and Γ is the set of threads in the system.

Lemma 1. *A node determines whether or not it needs to run an instance of QBUA at most $4T$ time units after it detects a distributed scheduling event, with high, computable probability, P_{lock}.*

Lemma 2. *Once a node is granted permission to run an instance of QBUA, it takes $O(T + N + |\Gamma| \log(|\Gamma|))$ time units to compute a new schedule, with high, computable, probability, P_{SWETS}.*

Theorem 3. *A distributed scheduling event is handled at most $O(T + N + |\Gamma| \log(|\Gamma|) + T_D)$ time units after it occurs, with high, computable, probability, P_{hand}.*

Lemma 4. *The worst case message complexity of the algorithm is $O(n + N)$.*

Theorem 5. *If all nodes are underloaded, no nodes fail (i.e. $f = 0$) and each thread can be delayed $O(T + N + |\Gamma| \log(|\Gamma|))$ time units once and still be schedulable, QBUA meets all the thread termination times yielding optimal total utility with high, computable, probability, P_{alg}.*

Theorem 6. *If $N - f$ nodes do not crash, are underloaded, and all incoming threads can be delayed $O(T + N + |\Gamma| \log(|\Gamma|))$ and still be schedulable, then QBUA meets the execution time of all threads in its eligible execution thread set, Γ, with high computable probability, P_{alg}.*

Lemma 7. *QBUA has a quorum threshold, m, (see Algorithm 2) of $\lceil \frac{2n}{3} \rceil$ and can tolerate $f^s = \frac{n}{3}$ faulty servers.*

Theorem 8. *QBUA has a better best-effort property than HUA and CUA and a similar best-effort property to ACUA.*

Theorem 9. *QBUA has lower overhead than ACUA and its overhead scales better with the number of node failures.*

Theorem 10. *QBUA limits thrashing by reducing the number of instances of QBUA spawned by concurrent distributed scheduling event.*

6   Experimental Results

We performed a series of simulation experiments on ns-2 to compare the performance of QBUA to ACUA, CUA and HUA in terms of Accrued Utility Ratio (AUR) and Termination-time Meet Ratio (TMR). We define AUR as the ratio of the accrued utility (the sum of U_i for all completed threads) to the utility available (the sum of U_i for all available jobs) and TMR as the ratio of the number of threads that meet their termination time to the total number of threads in the system. We considered threads with three segments. Each thread starts at its origin node with its first segment. The second segment is a result of a remote invocation to some node in the system, and the third segment occurs when the thread returns to its origin node to complete its execution. The periods of these threads are fixed, and we vary their execution times to obtain a range of utilization ranging from 0 to 200%. For fair comparison, all algorithms were simulated using a synchronous system model, where communication delay varied according to an exponential distribution with mean and standard deviation 0.02 seconds but could not exceed an upper bound of 0.5 seconds. Our system consisted of fifty client nodes and five servers. In our experiments, the utilization of the system is considered the *maximum* utilization experienced by any node.

QBUA is a collaborative scheduling algorithm, as such, its strength lies in its ability to give priority to threads that will result in the most system-wide accrued utility even if the sections of those threads do not maximize local utility on the nodes they are hosted. The thread set that highlights this property contains threads that would be given low priority if local scheduling is performed but should be assigned high priority due to the system-wide utility they accrue. Therefore, we chose a thread set that contains high utility threads that have one section with above average execution time (resulting in low PUD for that section) and other sections with below average execution times (resulting in high PUD for those sections). Such thread sets test the ability of the algorithm to take advantage of collaboration to avoid making locally optimal decisions that would compromise global optimality. We also conducted experiments under a broad range of thread sets. Those results are omitted here due to space constraints; they can be found in [7] and they all exhibit the same trend.

As Figures 1 and 2 show, the performance of QBUA during underloads, in the absence of failure, is similar to that of other algorithms. However, during overloads, QBUA begins to outperform other algorithms due to its better best effort property. During overloads, QBUA accrues, on average, 17% more utility that CUA, 14% more utility than HUA and 8% more utility than ACUA. The maximum difference between the performance of QBUA and other algorithms in our experiment was the 22% difference between ABUA's and CUA's AUR at the 1.88 system load point. Throughout our experiment, the performance of ACUA was the closest to QBUA with the difference in performance between these two algorithms getting more pronounced as system load increases (the largest difference in performance is 11.7% and occurs at about 2.0 system load). The reason for this is that QBUA has a similar best-effort property to ACUA (see Theorem 8). In addition, the difference between these two algorithms becomes more pronounced as system load increases because the scheduling overhead becomes more apparent at high system loads, allowing QBUA, with its lower overhead, to scale better with system load. Also, QBUA does not accrue 100% utility during all cases of underload; as the load approaches 1.0 some deadlines are missed because the overhead of QBUA becomes more significant at this point. This is also true for other collaborative scheduling algorithms such as CUA and ACUA, and, to a lesser extent, for non-collaborative scheduling algorithms such as HUA.

Figures 3 and 4 show the effect of failures on QBUA. In these experiments we programmatically fail $f_{max} = 0.2N$ nodes — i.e., we fail 20% of the client nodes. From Figure 3, we see that failures do not degrade the performance of QBUA compared to other scheduling algorithms — i.e., the relationship between the utility accrued by QBUA to the utility accrued by other scheduling algorithms remains relatively the same in the presence of failures. However, QBUA accrues, on average, 18.5% more utility than CUA, 13.6% more utility than HUA and 9.9% more utility than ACUA. Both ACUA and CUA suffer a further loss in performance relative to QBUA in the presence of failures because their time

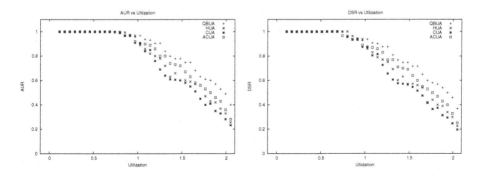

Fig. 1. AUR vs. Utilization (no failures)   **Fig. 2.** TMR vs. Utilization (no failures)

complexity is a function of the number of node failures, therefore they have higher overheads in the presence of failures. In Figure 4 we compare the behavior of QBUA in the presence of failure to its behavior in the absence of failure.

As can be seen, QBUA's performance suffers a degradation in the presence of failures. This degradation is most pronounced during underloads, and becomes less pronounced as the system load is increased. This occurs because, during underloads all threads are feasible and therefore the failure of a node deprives the system of the utility of all the threads that have a section hosted on that node. However, during overloads, not all sections hosted by a node are feasible, thus the failure of that node only deprives the system of the utility of the feasible threads that have a section hosted by that node. Thus the loss of utility during overloads is less than during underloads.

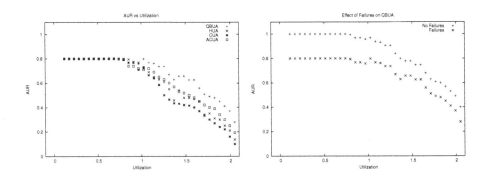

Fig. 3. AUR vs. Utilization (failures)   **Fig. 4.** Effect of failures on QBUA

7   Conclusions

We presented a collaborative scheduling algorithm for distributed real-time systems, QBUA. We showed that QBUA has better best-effort properties and message and time complexities than previous distributed scheduling algorithms. We validated our theoretical results using ns-2 simulations. The experiments show that QBUA outperforms other algorithms most during overloads in the presence of failure, due to its better best-effort property and its failure invariant overhead.

References

1. Cares, J.R.: Distributed Networked Operations: The Foundations of Network Centric Warfare. iUniverse, Inc. (2006)
2. Clark, R., Jensen, E., Reynolds, F.: An architectural overview of the alpha real-time distributed kernel. In: 1993 Winter USENIX Conf., pp. 127–146 (1993)
3. Fahmy, S.F., Ravindran, B., Jensen, E.D.: Scheduling distributable real-time threads in the presence of crash failures and message losses. In: ACM SAC, Track on Real-Time Systems (to appear, 2008),
   http://www.real-time.ece.vt.edu/sac08.pdf

4. Aguilera, M.K., Lann, G.L., Toueg, S.: On the impact of fast failure detectors on real-time fault-tolerant systems. In: Malkhi, D. (ed.) DISC 2002. LNCS, vol. 2508, pp. 354–370. Springer, Heidelberg (2002)

5. Chen, W., Toueg, S., Aguilera, M.K.: On the quality of service of failure detectors. IEEE Transactions on Computers 51(1), 13–32 (2002)

6. Hermant, J.F., Lann, G.L.: Fast asynchronous uniform consensus in real-time distributed systems. IEEE Transactions on Computers 51(8), 931–944 (2002)

7. Fahmy, S.F., Ravindran, B., Jensen, E.D.: Fast scheduling of distributable real-time threads with assured end-to-end timeliness. Technical report, Virginia Tech, ECE Dept. (2007), http://www.real-time.ece.vt.edu/RST_TR.pdf

8. Jensen, E., Locke, C., Tokuda, H.: A time driven scheduling model for real-time operating systems. IEEE RTSS, 112–122 (1985)

9. Sterzbach, B.: GPS-based clock synchronization in a mobile, distributed real-time system. Real-Time Syst. 12(1), 63–75 (1997)

10. Druschel, P., Rowstron, A.: PAST: A large-scale, persistent peer-to-peer storage utility. In: HOTOS 2001, pp. 75–80 (2001)

11. Chen, W., Lin, S., Lian, Q., Zhang, Z.: Sigma: A fault-tolerant mutual exclusion algorithm in dynamic distributed systems subject to process crashes and memory losses. In: PRDC 2005, pp. 7–14. IEEE Computer Society, Washington, DC (2005)

12. Clark, R.K.: Scheduling Dependent Real-Time Activities. PhD thesis, CMU CMU-CS-90-155 (1990)

RCanalyser: A Flexible Framework for the Detection of Data Races in Parallel Programs

Aoun Raza and Gunther Vogel

University of Stuttgart
Institute of Software Technology, Universitaetsstrasse 38
70569 Stuttgart, Germany
{raza,vogel}@informatik.uni-stuttgart.de

Abstract. Creating multiple threads for performance gain is not only common for complex computations on supercomputers but also for ordinary application programs. Multi-threaded/parallel programs have many advantages but also introduce new types of errors that do not occur in purely sequential programs. Race conditions are one important class of these special problems because the effects of race conditions occur nondeterministically and range from incorrect results to unexpected program behaviour. This paper presents RCanalyser, a tool for the detection of race conditions, which is based on a $Must\_Locks$ analysis using a flexible interface for the integration of different points-to analyses. As the problem of detecting race conditions is NP-hard in the general case, the tool is restricted to the detection of so-called data races [1]. The tool is able to analyse C/C++programs that use thread APIs for the implementation and synchronization of concurrent units. We applied the tool to a set of real programs, which use the POSIX thread API, and present results and statistics.

1 Introduction

In parallel programs, different threads are created and often communicate with each other. Different communication methods are available for these interactions, e.g., message passing or shared memory. Furthermore, threads may need to claim other system resources that are shared among them. As multiple threads try to access shared resources, their actions must be protected through some synchronisation mechanism to avoid interleaving. Absence of such a mechanism during these accesses can lead to inconsistent states of shared resources, which can result in abnormal or unpredictable program behavior. An important class of inter-process or inter-thread anomalies is race conditions. A race condition occurs when different threads simultaneously perform read and write access on shared data without prior synchronization. Such erroneous situations tend to be very difficult to detect or to recreate by test runs; they arise in real-life execution as an inexplicable, sudden, and not re-creatable, sometimes disastrous malfunction of the system. Debugging of parallel programs requires tools and mechanisms that can discover such situations and assist programmers in locating the culprit source code. Moreover, for parallel programs using shared resources, mechanisms are required to determine when a race condition can manifest and, to provide further assistance in locating it. Due to their critical effects on the deterministic behaviour of software, guidelines on thread programming have been devised to avoid data races [2]. However, this

F. Kordon and T. Vardanega (Eds.): Ada-Europe 2008, LNCS 5026, pp. 226–239, 2008.

can restrict a programmer's benefits achievable through full use of the concurrency features of a programming language.

Many research communities have investigated this issue and have proposed different dynamic and static techniques to detect race conditions [3,4,5,6,7,8,9,10]. The available race detection techniques exhibit different limitations depending on the nature of analyses underneath, i.e., dynamic or static analyses. Some of them raise the degree of false positives while others impose overhead in terms of time and space complexity [11].

This paper presents the tool RCanalyser, which performs flow- and context-sensitive analyses of the program to find a *Probable_Lock* for each shared variable. Further, it provides the flexibility to combine different points-to analysis mechanisms while present tools do not incorporate points-to analysis or cover only simple aspects. Our mechanism performs detection of data races based on locks and shared variable analysis. Shared variable discovery has a major effect on the accuracy of data race detection. Therefore, unlike others [4,12], in our approach we first discover shared variables and then investigate if they are consistently protected. For the safe detection of accesses to shared variables and the execution of synchronization operations, knowledge about the potential targets of pointers is essential. RCanalyser is a part of the Bauhaus [13] tool suite and uses its interface for different points-to analysis techniques implemented in the infrastructure which helps us to increase the precision for those programs which heavily use pointers. This paper is structured as follows; section 2 discusses the related work in this area. In section 3 we explain our definitions and terminology for the scope of this paper. The design and implementation of RCanalyser is described in section 4. Section 5 presents the evaluation of RCanalyser. Finally, section 6 concludes the paper and discusses future trends.

2   Related Work

Since the detection of race conditions in parallel programs is notoriously difficult, a large community has focused on this issue. In fact, it is quite difficult to detect such problems by manually testing the programs. Additionally, most of the existing concurrent software systems are written in C. Therefore, the need of an efficient mechanism for detecting parallel program anomalies is always present. As a consequence of difficulties involved in the race detection process, tools and mechanisms which provide automatic detection are extremely valuable. Hence, there has been a substantial amount of past work in building tools for analysis and detection of data races [3,4,5,6,7,8,9,10]. These tools are either based on the verification of access event ordering or they verify a locking discipline for mutual exclusion [7]. This means, if there is no unordered access to a shared variable such that at least one access is a write, the program is free from race conflicts. Similarly, if the accesses to shared variables in a program obey a locking discipline then the program is race free. In the traditional manner, the research can be categorised as on-the-fly, ahead-of-time, and post-mortem techniques. These techniques exhibit different strengths for race detection in programs. The ahead-of-time approaches encompass those detection techniques that apply static analysis and compile-time heuristics while on-the-fly approaches are dynamic in nature.

In well-known techniques and tools *RacerX, Locksmith* and *Chord* are based on static analysis, whereas *Eraser* uses dynamic analysis. RacerX [4] performs a flow-sensitive inter-procedural analysis to extract lock-set information and uses it for race and dead-lock detection. It detects multi-threaded parts of the program and shared accesses that can be dangerous. However, RacerX assumes that code segments which are protected through locks perform parallel accesses to shared variables which may not be true if they are contained in threads which do not run in parallel. Eraser [5] employs a binary code instrumentation approach for runtime race detection, which is further extended for Java by [7] [6]. Chord [14] detects race conditions in Java programs by employing a combination of static analyses (reachability, aliasing, escape and lockset analyses) for successive reduction of memory access pairs. Locksmith [12] assumes the common approach that shared memory locations are consistently protected by a lock (*consistent correlation*). It uses a constraint-based analysis that context-sensitively infers the consistent correlation, and uses its outcome to check the proper guarding of locations by locks. However, these tools have restrictions in terms of time and space complexity. Some of them use very naive points-to information. Therefore, the need for a scalable solution is always present considering the pervasive presence of complex multi-threaded applications.

3   Terminology

Here we present the terminologies and definitions, which are used throughout this paper.

3.1   Threads

In sequential programs there is only one thread, which controls the execution of the program in a defined order. However, a sequential execution on a multi-processor system is unable to utilize the multiple processors in an efficient manner. Further, sequential programs cannot support the response time characteristics required in complex systems. These problems are alleviated by parallel programs by creating multiple threads of control. Unlike processes, threads share the same memory area and resources. Communication among threads is achieved through shared program memory. In this paper the term thread is used to refer to a POSIX thread, which is defined by the tuple

$$t = (id, attributes, start\_routine, data)$$

Each thread has a unique id, attributes (e.g., scope, state, stacksize, etc. or can be NULL if default attributes are meant to be used), a procedure to start with and some data that can be either a shared resource or specific to it.

Threads Execute in Parallel: Threads which are active at the same time may run in parallel. On a single processor system threads execute concurrently (logical parallelism), whereas on a multi-processor system they can truly run in parallel. Unless the execution of threads depends on each other and is synchronised through some mechanism, this paper considers them to be running in parallel. Further, the execution of a thread is parallel to other threads if its execution is not deterministic with respect to those threads. If T represents the set of threads of a program and $SynchOrder$ is a relation of synchronization between threads t_i and t_j then the parallel relation is defined as follows:

$$t_i \| t_j \Leftrightarrow \neg SynchOrder(t_i, t_j)$$

The parallel relation $\|$ is symmetric, therefore if $t_i \| t_j$ then also $t_j \| t_i$. As threads are created dynamically we need a static representation for threads such that each static thread corresponds to a set of dynamic threads. In RCanalyser we chose invocation sites of thread-create functions for the representation of threads, as a call to a thread-create API might be performed in a loop with the same start routine and create multiple threads at runtime. There is no further distinction between the created threads and we consider the static thread having multiple instances. If the invocation is guaranteed to be performed only once in each execution of the program, the static thread is considered to be a single thread.

The parallel relation is reflexive *iff* multiple instances of a (static) thread are present in the program and might run in parallel.

3.2 Race Condition (RC)

A race condition can be formalised through different definitions, however for the scope of this paper the following equation defines a race for a memory location $m \in M$ as a symmetric binary relation $RC(m) \subseteq S(m) \times S(m)$. Where S is the set of all statements in a program source and $S(m)$ contains all those statements s which access a shared memory location m such that $S(m) \subseteq S$.

$$S(m) = \{s \mid m \in DEF(s) \cup USE(s)\}$$

As in standard data-flow analysis, the sets $DEF(s)$ and $USE(s)$ contain memory elements which are modified or read by the statement $s \in S(m)$. The set of shared memory locations M is defined in section 3.3. Race conditions relating to $m \in M$ are defined as

$$RC(m) = \{(s_i, s_j) \mid s_i \| s_j \wedge m \in DEF(s_i) \cap (DEF(s_j) \cup USE(s_j))\}$$

$s_i \| s_j$ represents the parallel relation between ststaments s_i, s_j and is defined in section 3.6.

3.3 Shared Accesses

Shared variables or memory locations (used interchangeably in this paper) are generally variables in parallel programs, which are accessed from more than one thread. Therefore shared memory locations are potential targets of data races. A shared memory location can include stack, global and heap variables. We do not consider volatile and atomic variables. Depending upon the requirements of the analysis compound objects and elements/components of these objects are distinguished. Additionally, a local variable whose reference is passed to other threads through a pointer also belongs to the category of shared memory locations. However, reference variables require special consideration because their accessibility to more than one thread does not necessarily result in the same memory location during dereference. RCanalyser can perform two different analyses for shared memory location for compound types and their elements: it can either consider an access to a compound object's element as an access to the whole compound object or consider all elements as individual variables in a program. Differentiation between elements of the compound object will decrease the number of false positives. Furthermore, local static variables are also treated as global variables because they remain preserved even after a call to the enclosing procedure has finished. With this, the set of shared memory locations M is defined as:

$$M = \{m \mid \exists s_i, s_j \in S : \exists t_i, t_j \in T :$$
$$(s_i \in statements(t_i) \land s_j \in statements(t_j) \land$$
$$(t_i \neq t_j \lor (t_i = t_j \land t_i \in mult\_inst))) \land m \in Nonlocals \land$$
$$m \in (DEF(s_i) \cup USE(s_i)) \land m \in (DEF(s_j) \cup USE(s_j))\}$$

In the above definition, T represents all threads of the program, $statements(t)$ contains all statements reachable by a thread t and $multi\_inst$ indicates if multiple active instances of a thread might exist at runtime. $Nonlocals$ are global variables accessible in all functions and procedures of a program but are not local to them. Further, they also include those references which escape their definition scope.

```
int *arrptr;

int *copy (int *p, int size)
    {
        int *tmp;
        tmp = malloc(size * sizeof(int));
        for(int i=0; i<size; i++) tmp[i] = p[i];
        return tmp;
    }

int main() {
    int a[5];
    ...
    arrptr = copy(&a, 5);
    ...
}
```

For example in the above code snippet `arrptr`, the allocated heap object and the array a are nonlocal objects.

Existing techniques [4,5] perform shared variable detection based on the underlying assumption that accesses to shared variables almost always follow a lock acquisition. By focusing on the lock variable relation, however, consideration of only such variables as shared can lead to false negatives of data races, because shared variables may be accessed without lock acquisition if a programmer assumes its access is safe without acquiring a lock e.g., in interactive user input. Therefore, we discover shared variables according to the above definitions and then detect if they need to be protected or not. For details see section 4.3

3.4 Critical Section (CS)

A critical section is a part of the program that accesses shared resources and needs to be executed atomically by threads, i.e., no other thread may enter a critical section if a thread is currently executing it. Critical sections are necessary to avoid inconsistent states of shared variables during successive operations. Critical sections implement mutual exclusion mechanisms, which prevent other threads to access the shared data simultaneously. Critical sections can be implemented using synchronization instructions such as semaphores, locks or synchronized objects. During execution a thread acquires a lock and enters the critical section. Meanwhile, other threads who want to acquire the lock before entering the critical region have to wait until the lock is released. On release waiting threads attempt to obtain the lock and execute their critical code. RCanalyser considers a section of the program protected by a lock as a critical section to be extended to the point where it finds a release statement for the lock. A critical section of a thread t can be defined as a single-entry single-exit sequence of statements between lock acquire and release statements in a thread t:

$$CS(l, t) = \{s_n \mid \exists \pi = (s_1, \ldots, s_n) :$$
$$\forall s_i \in \pi : s_i \in statements(t) \wedge$$
$$s_1 \text{ locks } l \wedge \nexists s_x \in \pi : \text{unlocks } l\}$$

This definition of a critical section does not differentiate between global locks and locks which are kept as fields of dynamic data-structure. If RCanalyser does not find any shared variables we argue that it is unnecessary to implement critical sections for mutual exclusion because threads do not contain accesses to shared variables and resources.

3.5 Locks and Thread Synchronisation

Critical sections are protected by locks or other synchronisation mechanisms. However, in the scope of this paper we consider locks as a mutual exclusion mechanism used for the protection of the critical sections. The term lock is synonymously used for mutex. Before entering into a critical section a thread must obtain the associated lock and on exit it must release the lock to allow other threads to execute their critical section. If the critical section contains more than one shared variable then all these variables are protected using the lock associated with this critical section. This condition must hold for all accesses to shared variables in critical sections in other threads, otherwise inconsistent lock protection to shared variables could lead to race conditions during accesses among different threads. A thread can contain nested critical sections accessing variables shared between different threads and protected through multiple locks. The only constraint is that threads must hold a common lock before performing accesses to shared variables, locks protecting critical sections may hold locks for the contained shared variables. All locks definitely held at a statement s in a thread t without considering path conditions can be defined as the set of $Must\_Locks$

$$Must\_Locks(s,t) = \{l \mid l \in Locks \wedge$$
$$\forall \pi = (t.entry, \ldots, s) : l \text{ is held at } s\}$$

In the above definition $Must\_Locks$ contains all locks held by a thread before executing a statement s. We define a function $LockCount(m, l)$ to compute the number of statements which hold the lock l and access the shared variable m.

$$Lock\_Count(m, l) = |\{s \in S(m) \mid l \in Must\_Locks(s, t)\}|$$

The $Lock\_Count(m, l)$ serves two purposes, first we use it to compute a single lock i.e., $Probable\_Lock(m)$ which must be obtained before an access to the shared variable m in a safe program. The computed lock has the highest acquisition number for shared variable m. Second, if two locks have the same acquisition number for a shared variable then both locks become plausible and are considered in $Probable\_Lock(m)$. However, during race detection accesses to the shared variable are considered unprotected due to inconsistent locking and both locks are reported to the user to decide the appropriate lock.

$$Probable\_Lock(m) = \{l \in Locks \mid$$
$$\forall l' \in Locks : l \neq l' \wedge Lock\_Count(m, l) \geq Lock\_Count(m, l')\}$$

3.6 Statements Exceuting in Parallel

The statements of two threads which run in parallel potentially participate in a race condition if they are not synchronised. However, if two threads run in parallel not all of their statements necessarily run in parallel. Statements accessing a shared resource can only happen in parallel if they are not synchronised through common locks, however, this does not represent their execution order i.e., a statement will happen before the other.

$$s_i \| s_j \Leftrightarrow \exists t_i, t_j \in T : s_i \in statements(t_i) \wedge s_j \in statements(t_j) \wedge$$
$$t_i \| t_j \wedge \not\exists l \in Locks : s_i \in CS(l, t_i) \wedge s_j \in CS(l, t_j)$$

Simultaneously reachable statements participate in a data race, therefore, statements in critical sections of two different threads with the same lock cannot execute concurrently. Additionally, statements cannot execute in parallel or perform parallel accesses, if there is a prior access to the must lock associated with shared variables.

4   Design and Implementation

The static recognition of race conditions in parallel programs is not a simple problem. Therefore many tools and mechanisms analyse the synchronisation structure of input programs and perform unsafe approximations to detect the absence of necessary synchronisation [4]. RCanalyser assumes that a shared variable is consistently protected by a single lock. Hence, if different locks protect a shared variable then the lock with a higher acquisition count will be considered. RCanalyser has been designed and implemented in six different stages as illustrated in figure 1. In the following sections we discuss them in detail.

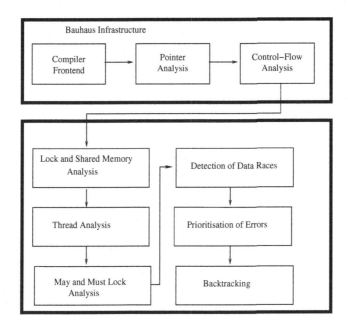

Fig. 1. The components of RCanalyser

4.1 Bauhaus Infrastructure

RCanalyser has been implemented on top of the Bauhaus infrastructure [13]. Bauhaus provides a base for implementing different high and low-level static program analyses. For our implementation we have used different Bauhaus features, e.g., an annotated abstract syntax graph (IML) for the full source program generated through language frontend and a local control-flow analysis to obtain intra-procedural control-flow graphs for all subprograms. The generic pointer analysis interface of Bauhaus provides us with different classical points-to analyses, e.g, Steensgaard [15], Das [16], and Andersen [17], which approximate the effects of pointers and determine the targets of indirect or dispatching calls.

4.2 Escape Analysis

If a majority of locks and shared variables are accessed via pointer dereferences in an analysed program, then the precision of the analysis depends directly on the quality of the pointer analysis. By inaccuracies of the points-to analysis, the degree of false positives will be high, since apparent accesses to shared variables will be noted through the analysis, which will not occur during execution of the program. Therefore, to mitigate the imprecise effect of points-to analyses, RCanalyser provides the flexibility to use different points-to analyses to achieve different levels of precision. Further, RCanalyser performs a thread specific escape analysis to improve the quality of error reports. RCanalyser checks if a local variable's reference is ever assigned to a pointer during execution and marks such locals as escaped references. If a reference never escapes its scope a race condition on such variable is considered spurious and ignored, because a flow- and context-insensitive points-to analysis result for a pointer can nevertheless contain this variable's reference.

4.3 Lock and Shared Variable Analyses

Shared variable analysis detects all variables which are accessed (read, write) in at least two threads. Therefore, all accesses to global and reference variables are computed on a per-thread basis. If a global variable is read or written in a statement by a thread it is immediately marked as a shared access. An access to a reference variable is registered as an access to all global or local variables to which it possibly refers. However, if a local variable's address is never assigned to a reference variable it cannot contribute in a data race and accesses to it are simply ignored. Shared variable analysis determines read and write accesses on a variable and stores this information for each thread in the program. Later this information is used to determine conflicts between threads.

The lock analysis is one of the most important parts of RCanalyser. RCanalyser performs a flow- and context-sensitive lock analysis as defined in [4]. The task of this analysis is to compute $Must\_Locks$ for each statement. It is important to note that it is not determined which lock in the program is always set for a statement, but all the acquired locks are computed. This benefits the analysis by providing the information if a lock is obtained on all paths in the program. However, due to flow- and context-sensitivity its runtime complexity can increase exponentially. The analysis is performed in a depth first search order. To determine all possible locks RCanalyser computes which locks are acquired before a procedure call and visits the control-flow-graph of the procedure to determine which locks are acquired and released during the procedure call. This result is propagated back to the call site and $Must\_Locks$ information is updated along the analysed path. If a procedure call contains more than one possibility to exit, then information propagated to the call site can contain different locks or locksets of $Must\_Locks$. Further analysis then has to compute $Must\_Locks$ within the context of each lock or lockset. The resulting $Must\_Locks$ of this procedure is saved in a cache to avoid a re-computation, in case the procedure is called again with the same locks. In the same manner $Must\_Locks$ information for statements is computed and saved in the cache.

4.4 Thread Analysis

Thread analysis computes which threads in the program can run in parallel. RCanalyser considers threads in parallel with other threads if their start and end is in the range of the other thread's execution span. To determine the execution span of threads, a global logical clock is defined in such a way that it is incremented each time a thread starts or gets joined by other threads independent from its runtime execution behavior. Execution span is calculated flow sensitively in topological ordering from the value of the global clock at a thread's creation call to its corresponding join call. Therefore, the termination of a thread in relation to other threads is defined by the clock count value when its join call is found. After execution spans are computed for all threads, a run in parallel relation between threads is computed for each thread. All threads which are alive during the execution span of a specific thread are considered to potentially run in parallel. Due to the symmetric nature of the run in parallel relation, the computation complexity is reducible.

4.5   Variable Lock Relation

The next step in RCanalyser is to determine $Must\_Locks$ for each shared variable as defined in section 3.5. For each shared variable we count the number of statements which access the shared variable and hold a specific lock l. The lock with the highest number of statements is considered as must lock for the shared variable. If the number of statements and lock acquisition count is equal then shared variables are consistently protected. If a statement appears in two critical sections protected through different locks which include accesses to a shared variable such that one critical section is nested in a thread and the other is not then there will be no data race on this variable if a common lock is held by both threads. This common lock will be considered as a must lock for this variable.

4.6   Detection of Data Races

Having computed the information about threads, shared variables and must locks, a potential data race can be determined by using the equation defined in section 3.2. If RCanalyser does not find a required lock for a shared variable v which is held at all parallel statements accessing v, we consider accesses to this variable as data races. However, read accesses are not considered as a data race, at least one single write access on a shared variable is necessary for a data race. It is possible that a thread makes a procedure call after obtaining a lock and another thread without acquiring a lock calls it and itself holds the lock for a shared variable, such a case will not fall in the category of race condition. Because a common lock is always held before the access is performed. Furthermore, accesses on a shared variable with different locks held in different threads will also indicate a race condition.

4.7   Prioritization and Backtraces

RCanalyser computes a prioritisation between detected data races depending upon the type of the shared variables and the threads' run in parallel information. The criterion followed for prioritisation based on severity and probability are

Prioritization: Severe Errors

- If a global variable is involved in a data race it has a high priority.
- The priority of a data race in a thread where must lock for a variable is not acquired is high as compared to the thread which acquires a lock for a shared variable but run in parallel with this thread.

Prioritization: Probable Errors

- If the involved variable is accessed in a loop the priority is high.
- For reference variables with many possible destinations the priority is low.
- If the accessed object is of a compound type, i.e., a structure or an array, the priority is low because the exact location index of the accessed element may be imprecisely calculated.
- When two threads who cannot possibly run in parallel access a shared variable without acquiring a common lock the priority of data race is also low.

The error reports can be viewed using RCanalyser interactive shell in the order of their priority. Backtraces report the path along which a data race can occur. If the path contains conditional statements the trace report represents which branch is considered.

5 Experimental Results and Evaluation

RCanalyser delivers results to our expectations, i.e., all locks are computed, and shared variables are recognised. It computes the parallel threads and must locks for each variable and partially excludes the variable initializations from data races, and successfully prioritizes the errors, depending upon their nature. Nevertheless, due to the conservative nature of analyses implemented by RCanalyser it can also report false positives. It can report a data race on a compound object accessed through a pointer even if different elements are involved during accesses. However, this can be mitigated by enabling the field sensitive points-to analysis for program variables. Similarly, it is undecideable to distinguish between different elements of an array object. An access to an array element is considered as an access to the complete array. RCanalyser performs a context- and flow-sensitive lock analysis. Therefore, the tool handles function calls precisely and it does not consider infeasible paths due to invocations of functions. Nevertheless, infeasible paths might be considered in local contexts because the tool does not evaluate conditions and always considers all paths after a branch.

Currently RCanalyser can be configured to detect races in POSIX/Apache Runtime Environment based multi-threaded C programs. The experimental results of our test suite downloaded from *sourceforge.net* are listed below. We have used *Das* analysis to compute points-to information for these programs. The result clearly shows the effective discovery of shared variables and number of threads in each program (columns *Sh Vars* and *Threads*). The results also illustrate that RCanalyser is scalable and can be applied to benchmarks with up to 6.1 kloc (same as Locksmith [12] tool.)

The column *Warnings* shows the number of locations where a race condition might manifest. The reported numbers are higher as compared to others [12], because, after locating the first unprotected access to a shared variable we record all following locations

Benchmark	KLOC	Threads	Sh Vars	Warnings	Unguarded	Real Races
aget-0.4	1.6	4	13	49	47	11
smtprc-2.0.3	6.1	3	10	200	180	7
ctrace-1.2	1.8	3	14	53	50	6
tplay-0.6.1	3.9	3	5	47	46	2

Fig. 2. Test Results

as well. The figures in column *Unguarded* describe program statements performing access to a shared variable without lock acquisition. These figures do not contain the locations where a lock has been held before access to a shared variable. It might be possible that these warnings are only about some shared variables which are targets of a data race. *Real races* presents the number of data races found after a careful inspection of unguarded program locations.

5.1 Discussion of Results

Due to the conservative nature of the static analyses in RCanalyser, it will safely find all potential race conditions in a program. But it may also report false positives which come from over-approximations done in the base analyses and RCanalyser itself.

In Figure 2 we can see that the differences of the number of *Warnings* and the number of *Real races* are still high. A detailed inspection lets us conclude that many of the reported false positives are manifestations of the features not yet present in our implementation.

A great deal of inaccuracy has its cause in an inadequate handling of (conceptual) reference parameters in our base analyses. The context- and flow-insensitive pointer analyses which are currently used in Bauhaus merge the targets of a reference parameter for multiple invocations of a subprogram. Therefore RCanalyser currently does not distinguish between different invocation contexts. The usage of a context-sensitive pointer analysis would bring a great benefit and is planned as a future work.

Another reason for false positives was the lack of path conditions in RCanalyser. The analysis currently considers all branches in the control flow of a program as equally feasible. A first step towards an improvement is the integration of a copy propagation analysis which lets us detect if a condition is always true or false. This helps us to remove dead code which can not contribute to a race condition. We expect another improvement from the implementation of a same-value analysis which determines if the values of different conditions are definitely the same. With that we are able to exclude infeasible paths as a reason for race conditions. A same-value analysis for thread variables will also mitigate the decision process of which thread gets joined or canceled at a given point, because thread identifier are integers and may get another value during program execution.

6 Conclusion and Future Work

Obtaining information about which threads run in parallel has significant applications in the detection of anomalies such as race conditions and deadlocks. Further, C-programs make intensive use of pointers, which make it difficult to find data races in parallel threads. Algorithms which can compute this information effectively and precisely are of great value. Previous approaches analyse programs without significant consideration of points-to information. We developed RCanalyser, a tool for the conservative detection of data races in multi-thread/parallel programs using $Must\_Locks$ analysis with flexibility to incorporate different points-to analysis mechanisms. The framework can handle multi-threaded programs of practical nature. The results have shown that due to the conservativeness of our technique and unavailability of a flow- and context-sensitive points-to analysis, it can produce false positives. However, RCanalyser can handle all types of pointer used in C programs. In the future, we plan to improve our mechanisms to correctly identify the accessed components of compound data types and thread escape analysis to optimize the precision and reduce the number of false positives. Additionally, we would like to implement a data-flow analysis for parallel programs in our framework to detect updates which may change thread identifiers. A further goal is to make RCanalyser more scalable to handle larger program code up 50-100K and incorporate the most used synchronization techniques e.g., condition variables, signal wait etc.

Acknowledgement

We would like to thank our colleagues at ISTE/PS department at university of Stuttgart and reviewers for their insightful comments on this paper.

References

1. Netzer, R.H.B., Miller, B.P.: What are race conditions?: Some issues and formalizations. ACM Letters on Programming Languages and Systems 1, 74–88 (1992)
2. Sun Microsystems, Inc.: Multithreaded Programming Guide (2002), http://docs.sun.com/app/docs/doc/806-6867/
3. Sterling, N.: WARLOCK - A Static Data Race Analysis Tool. In: USENIX Winter Technical Conference, pp. 97–106 (1993)
4. Engler, D., Ashcraft, K.: RacerX: Effective, Static Detection of Race Conditions and Deadlocks. In: Proceedings of the 19th ACM Symposium on Operating Systems Principles, pp. 237–252. ACM Press, New York (2003)
5. Savage, S., Burrows, M., Nelson, G., Sobalvarro, P., Anderson, T.: Eraser: A Dynamic Data Race Detector for Multi-Threaded Programs. In: Proceedings of the 16th ACM Symposium on Operating Systems Principles, pp. 27–37. ACM Press, New York (1997)
6. Choi, J.D., Lee, K., Loginov, A., O'Callahan, R., Sarkar, V., Sridharan, M.: Efficient and Precise Datarace Detection for Multithreaded Object-Oriented Programs. In: Proceedings of the ACM SIGPLAN Conference on Programming Language Design and Implementation, pp. 258–269. ACM Press, New York (2002)
7. von Praun, C., Gross, T.R.: Object Race Detection. In: Proceedings of the 16th ACM SIGPLAN Conference on Object Oriented Programming, Systems, Languages, and Applications, pp. 70–82. ACM Press, New York (2001)
8. Naumovich, G., Avrunin, G.S.: A Conservative Data Flow Algorithm for Detecting All Pairs of Statements that May Happen in Parallel. In: Proceedings of the 6th ACM SIGSOFT International Symposium on Foundations of Software Engineering, pp. 24–34 (1998)

9. Masticola, S.P., Ryder, B.G.: Non-concurrency Analysis. In: Proceedings of the fourth ACM SIGPLAN Symposium on Principles and Practice of Parallel Programming, pp. 129–138 (1993)
10. Burgstaller, B., Blieberger, J., Mittermayr, R.: Static Detection of Access Anomalies in Ada95. In: Pinho, L.M., González Harbour, M. (eds.) Ada-Europe 2006. LNCS, vol. 4006, pp. 40–55. Springer, Heidelberg (2006)
11. Raza, A.: A Review of Race Detection Mechanisms. In: Grigoriev, D., Harrison, J., Hirsch, E.A. (eds.) CSR 2006. LNCS, vol. 3967, pp. 534–543. Springer, Heidelberg (2006)
12. Pratikakis, P., Foster, J.S., Hicks, M.: LOCKSMITH: Context-Sensitive Correlation Analysis for Race Detection. In: Proceedings of the ACM SIGPLAN Conference on Programming Language Design and Implementation, pp. 320–331. ACM Press, New York (2006)
13. Raza, A., Vogel, G., Ploedereder, E.: Bauhaus – A Tool Suite for Program Analysis and Reverse Engineering. In: Pinho, L.M., González Harbour, M. (eds.) Ada-Europe 2006. LNCS, vol. 4006, pp. 71–82. Springer, Heidelberg (2006)
14. Naik, M., Aiken, A., Whaley, J.: Effective static race detection for java. In: Proceedings of the ACM SIGPLAN Conference on Programming Language Design and Implementation, pp. 308–319. ACM Press, New York (2006)
15. Steensgaard, B.: Points-to Analysis in Almost Linear Time. In: Proceedings of the 23rd ACM SIGPLAN-SIGACT Symposium on Principles of Programming Languages, pp. 32–41. ACM Press, New York (1996)
16. Das, M.: Unification-based Pointer Analysis with Directional Assignments. In: Proceedings of the ACM SIGPLAN Conference on Programming Language Design and Implementation, pp. 35–46 (2000)
17. Andersen, L.O.: Program Analysis and Specialization for the C Programming Language. PhD thesis, DIKU, University of Copenhagen (1994)

Can We Increase the Usability of Real Time Scheduling Theory?
The Cheddar Project

Frank Singhoff[1], Alain Plantec[1], and Pierre Dissaux[2]

[1] LISyC/University of Brest, 20, av Le Gorgeu, 29238 Brest Cedex 3, France
[2] Ellidiss Technologies, 24 quai de la douane, 29200 Brest, France
{singhoff,plantec}@univ-brest.fr, pierre.dissaux@ellidiss.com

Abstract. The Cheddar project deals with real time scheduling theory. Many industrial projects do not perform performance analysis with real time scheduling theory even if the demand for the use of this theory is large. The Cheddar project investigates why real time scheduling theory is not used and how its usability can be increased. The Cheddar project was launched at the University of Brest in 2002. This article presents a summary of its contributions and ongoing works.

1 Introduction

Real time scheduling theory provides algebraic methods and algorithms in order to predict the temporal behavior of real time systems. The foundations of real time scheduling theory were proposed in 1970 [1] and it leads to extensive researchs. Since 1990, it makes it possible the analysis of systems composed of periodic tasks sharing resources and running on a single processor [2]. Numerous operating systems provide features allowing the implementation of such applications. Some standards and compilers also provide tools to enforce that an application meets real time scheduling theory assumptions. The Ravenscar profile defined in the Ada 2005 standard allows this assumption checking [3].

Real time scheduling theory was successfully used in many projects [4]. Nevertheless, many practical cases also do not perform analysis with such a method even if our experience shows that the demand for the use of this analysis method is large.

Several reasons can explain why real time scheduling analysis is not applied as much as it could be. Of course, there exists some architectures on which real time scheduling analysis is difficult. For example, few analytical methods were proposed for the analysis of distributed systems [5]. Sometimes, there is no analytical method for architectures made of complex schedulers or task models. In these cases, a real time scheduling toolset should at least provide means to model the system and to run simulations.

Furthermore, we believe that this theory is not so easy to understand and to be applied for many engineers. Many analytical methods and algorithms were proposed during the last 30 years. Each analytical method allows to compute

F. Kordon and T. Vardanega (Eds.): Ada-Europe 2008, LNCS 5026, pp. 240–253, 2008.

different performance criteria. Each criterion requires that a set of assumptions must be meet by the investigated system. Then, it may be difficult for a designer to choose the relevant analytical method. Unfortunately, there is currently few supports by design languages and CASE tools which can help him to automatically apply real time scheduling theory.

This article presents three possible ways investigated by the Cheddar project in order to increase the usability of real time scheduling theory. Section 2 presents a set of tools which aims at helping the designer to automatically apply real time scheduling theory on an architecture model. Section 3 depicts how the use of an architecture design language can help the designer to apply real time scheduling theory. Section 4 presents a domain specific language and a set of tools that the designer can use when no analytical method can be applied in order to investigate performances of a specific architecture. Finally, section 5 is devoted to a conclusion and presents Cheddar project ongoing works.

2   Increasing the Usability of Real Time Scheduling Theory: Easing Analysis with Flexible Tools

Real time scheduling theory provides scheduling algorithms and algebraic methods usually called feasibility tests which help the system designer to analyze the timing behaviour of his architecture. With the Liu and Layland real time task model [1], each task periodically performs a treatment. This "periodic" task is defined by three parameters: its deadline (D_i), its period (P_i) and its capacity (C_i). P_i is a fixed delay between two release times of the task i. Each time the task i is released, it has to do a job whose execution time is bounded by C_i units of time. This job has to be ended before D_i units of time after the task wake up time. From this task model, some feasibility tests can provide a proof that an architecture will meet its periodic task performance requirements. Scheduling algorithms allow the designer to compute scheduling simulations of the architecture to analyze. Usually, simulations can not lead to a proof. However with deterministic schedulers and periodic tasks, scheduling simulation may lead to a schedulability proof if the designer is able to compute the scheduling during the base period [6]. Different kinds of feasibility tests exist such as tests based on processor utilization factor or tests based on worst case task response time. The worst case response time feasibility test consists in comparing the worst case response time of each task with their deadline. Joseph, Pandia, Audsley et al. [7] have proposed a way to compute the worst case response time of a task with pre-emptive fixed priority scheduler by:

$$r_i = C_i + \sum_{\forall j \in hp(i)} \left\lceil \frac{r_i}{P_j} \right\rceil C_j \qquad (1)$$

Where r_i is the worst case response time of the task i and $hp(i)$ is the set of tasks which have a higher priority level than i. This feasibility test must be extended to take into account task waiting time on shared resources, jitter on task release time or task precedency relationships. To apply a feasibility test, the designer must check that his design and his executive fulfill all the feasibility test assumptions. As an example, with the feasibility test of the equation (1), D_i must be less or equal than P_i and all tasks must have the same first release time. Then, for a designer who has not a deep knowledge of real time scheduling theory, verifying an architecture with feasibility tests becomes a difficult task because, for each part of the architecture to verify, he must (see figure 1):

1. Choose the performance criterion he would like to check.
2. Find the right model for each entity of his architecture. For example, should he model a function of his architecture as a set of periodic tasks or as a set of sporadic tasks ? The designer must select the right abstraction level which decreases the model complexity but which takes into account properties required for analysis.
3. Select a feasibility test which is able to compute the criterion chosen in (1) and which is compliant with the models chosen in (2). For such a purpose, he must check that his model is compliant with the feasibility test assumptions.

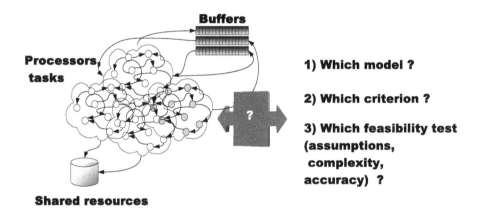

Fig. 1. From the modelling to the analysis

But of course, in many cases, this work can be quite simple since the studied architecture is simple too. A real time scheduling analysis toolset should actually provide several using levels. Several real time scheduling tools exist such as MAST [8], Rapid-RMA [9] or Cheddar. Cheddar is a toolset composed of an editor and of a framework. The designer can specify his architecture model with the Cheddar editor. However, it is expected that designers perform modelling with dedicated CASE tools. The Cheddar framework consists in a set of Ada packages which includes most current feasibility tests and most of the classical real time scheduling algorithms. This framework also offers a domain specific language together with an interpreter and a compiler, for the design and the analysis of schedulers which are not already implemented into the framework.

Cheddar offers different using levels depending on the architecture to analyze, on the CASE tool Cheddar is supposed to work with or on the knowledge of the designer. Typical use cases are:

- Just load an architecture model into the Cheddar editor and simply push a button to perform its analysis. In this case, Cheddar chooses the feasibility test, checks if the feasibility test assumptions are met and displays the result. It is assumed that the designer makes use of a design pattern handled by Cheddar. For example, the designer can model his architecture with the Ravenscar design pattern. Ravenscar is a part of the Ada 2005 standard [3]. It is a set of Ada program restrictions usually enforced at compilation time, which guaranties that the software architecture is real time scheduling theory compliant. Ravenscar is an Ada subset from which one can write applications composed of a set of tasks and shared data. Ravenscar assumes that tasks are scheduled with a fixed priority scheduler and that shared data are accessed with ICPP. This first way to use Cheddar is also the best suited for students who have to understand real time scheduling foundations.
- A second way is to let the designer choose which performance criteria to compute. The designer must handle the Cheddar editor menus to customized which criteria the Cheddar framework has to compute. In this case, feasibility test assumptions are always automatically checked by Cheddar.
- Third, if the scheduling algorithms or the feasibility tests implemented into Cheddar can not be applied, then the designer must extend the Cheddar framework. Two ways exist for such a purpose. The framework can be extended by the Cheddar domain specific language with the process explained in section 4. Otherwise, the designer manually implements the performance analysis tools. In this case, he must well understand the Cheddar framework design.

There exists many other ways to use a toolset such as Cheddar. As an example, Cheddar can be embedded into CASE tools such as Stood [10] or Ocarina [11] in order to increase its usability. In this case, the designer does not use the Cheddar editor anymore and the Cheddar framework is directly called by embedding CASE tools. Cheddar exports analysis results as an XML data stream which can be displayed back by the CASE tools. The next section presents how an architecture language can be used to achieve CASE tool and analysis tool interoperability.

3   Increasing the Usability of Real Time Scheduling Theory: From the Engineering Process to the Performance Analysis

A possible way to help the designer to apply real time scheduling theory, is to embed such a knowledge into the engineering process with the help of design languages and design patterns.

Panunzio and Vardanega have proposed a metamodel which permits the execution of timing analysis [12]. An UML profile called MARTE which allows such a timing analysis is also currently investigated by Frédéric et al. [13]. The SAE Architecture Analysis and Design Language (AADL) is a textual and a graphical language support for model-based engineering of embedded real time systems. AADL has been approved and published as SAE Standard AS-5506 [14]. AADL is used to design and analyze software and hardware architecture of embedded real-time systems. In the context of the Cheddar project, AADL was chosen to investigate how real time scheduling theory can be automatically applied. As Cheddar provides the most known real time scheduling feasibility tests and scheduling algorithms, it was primarily used in order to check that the first AADL standard can be actually analyzed with real time scheduling theory tools. Then, we have investigated how memory footprint analysis can be conducted with AADL [15] and finally, some design patterns expressed in AADL were proposed in order to ease interoperability between AADL tools [10].

3.1 Investigating AADL Suitability for Real Time Scheduling Theory

An AADL model is a set of hardware and software components such as data, threads, processes (the software side of a specification), processors, devices and busses (the hardware side of a specification). A data component may represent a data structure in the program source. An AADL data component can be implemented by an Ada tagged record. A thread is a sequential flow of control that executes a program. An AADL thread can be implemented by an Ada task. AADL threads can be released according to several policies: a thread may be periodic, sporadic or aperiodic. An AADL process models an address space. An AADL operational system instantiates a set of process components encompassing thread and data components that are bound to an execution platform composed of processor, memory and bus components. Properties can be defined for most of AADL components. A property is defined by a name, a value and a type. Information provided by component properties can be related to the component behavior, its state, the way it will be implemented in Ada or anything else that makes it possible to perform analysis.

Figure 2 shows an AADL specification. This specification contains a shared resource (called $R1$) accessed by two threads (threads $TH1$ and $TH2$). The threads and the shared resource are defined into one address space (process $proc0$). The process $proc0$ is bound to a processor called $cpu0$.

The first release of the AADL standard provides component properties required in order to apply the simplest real time scheduling analysis methods. Nevertheless, some properties were missing to apply several usual real time scheduling theory analysis methods. AADL provides a way to extend the AADL standard property sets. We have proposed a set of property extensions [16] to model:

- Usual properties of real time schedulers (eg. quantum, preemptivity, POSIX 1003.1b policies).

```
data shared_resource_type
end shared_resource_type;
data implementation shared_resource_type.Impl
    properties
        Concurrency_Control_Protocol => PRIORITY_CEILING_PROTOCOL;
end shared_resource_type.Impl;
thread task_type
    features
        can_access : requires data access shared_resource_type;
end task_type;
thread implementation task_type.Impl
    properties
        Dispatch_Protocol => Periodic;
        Period => 50;
        Compute_Execution_time => 3 ms .. 3 ms;
        Cheddar_Properties::POSIX_Scheduling_Policy => SCHED_FIFO;
        Cheddar_Properties::Fixed_Priority => 5;
        Cheddar_Properties::Dispatch_Jitter => 10;
end task_type.Impl;
processor a_cpu
end a_cpu;
processor implementation a_cpu.Impl
    properties
        Scheduling_Protocol => RATE_MONOTONIC;
        Cheddar_Properties::Scheduler_Quantum => 1;
        Cheddar_Properties::Preemptive_Scheduler => true;
end a_cpu.Impl;
process a_proc
end a_proc;
process implementation a_proc.Impl
    subcomponents
        TH1 : thread task_type.Impl;
        TH2 : thread task_type.Impl;
        R1 : data shared_resource_type.Impl;
    connections
        data access R1 - > TH1.can_access;
        data access R1 - > TH2.can_access;
end a_proc.Impl;
system a_system
end a_system;
system implementation a_system.Impl
    subcomponents
        cpu0 : processor a_cpu.Impl;
        proc0 : process a_proc.Impl;
    properties
        Actual_Processor_Binding => reference cpu0 applies to proc0;
end a_system.Impl;
```

Fig. 2. Example of an AADL model

- Usual thread properties such as fixed priority, jitter, offset, shared resource blocking time, ...
- Properties to define when shared resources are accessed by threads.
- And finally, the current AADL standard leading to some ambiguities, some properties to express thread precedency relationships which can not be computed from standard AADL connections.

Some of the lacks presented above will be fixed in the next AADL standard with the Behavioral Annex [17] and with some of the Cheddar properties which will be included in the standard AADL property set.

3.2   Memory Footprint Analysis with AADL

One of the most interesting part of an architecture design language as AADL, is that it allows performance analysis on multiple resources. This is especially mandatory with distributed real time systems which may be composed of several processors, memory units and communication devices. The figure 3 shows a distributed system composed of two processors exchanging messages througth a TCP/IP socket. With such a system, performance analysis on processors and memory units can not be performed independently:

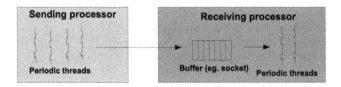

Fig. 3. Part of a distributed system

- In one hand, if the periodic receiving/sending threads have a high priority level, and then a short worst case response time, the required memory in the socket to store messages may be low.
- In the other hand, when sending/receiving threads have a long worst case response time, the memory requirement into the socket may be high if no message have to be lost.

By defining all the parts of a system, AADL allows such an analysis. As an example, in [18], Legrand et al. have proposed a set of feasibility tests based on queueing system. These feasibility tests were adapted to AADL in [15]. It was shown how to perform memory footprint analysis with AADL models containing event data ports. Event data ports represent connection points for transfer of messages that may be queued. For example, if both producers and consumers are periodic AADL thread exchanging messages through an event data port, L, the worst case number of messages in the event data port is equal to $L = 2.n$ if threads are harmonic, or $L = 2.n + 1$ otherwise. Where n is the number of producers. As any feasibility test, this memory footprint feasibility test has to meet several assumptions (eg. Kirchhoff's law).

3.3   About Interoperability between AADL Tools

Coupling of modelling and analysis tools requires that both ends strictly comply with the same semantic definition of the exchanged model. This is particularly important for real-time systems and software architectures. Such a guaranty can be brought by a standard use of the AADL all along the tool-chain. In the sequel, we show how AADL can be used as a pivot language between Cheddar and a modelling tool called Stood.

Stood is a software design tool that provides an extended support for AADL in addition to its compliancy with the HOOD methodology. Stood makes it possible to manage a complete software project by building libraries of reusable components, reversing legacy code and specifying the real time application as well as its execution platform. Most of the modelling activities can be performed graphically and the corresponding AADL code is automatically generated by the tool.

To ease interoperability between Stood and Cheddar, in [10], we have proposed a set of AADL design patterns which models usual real time synchronization/threads-communication paradigms (eg. ARINC 653 [19]):

1. **Synchronous data-flows design pattern:** This first design pattern is the simplest one. The data sharing is achieved by a clock synchronization of the threads as Meta-H [14] proposed it. In this synchronization schema, thread dispatch is not affected by the inter-thread communications that are expressed by pure data-flows. Each thread reads its input data ports at dispatch time and writes its output data ports at complete time. This design pattern does not require the use of a shared data component. In this simple case, the execution platform consists in one processor running a scheduler such as Rate Monotonic [1].

2. **Ravenscar design pattern:** Main drawback of the previous pattern is its lack of flexibility at run time. Each thread will always execute, read and write data at pre-defined times, even if useless. In order to introduce more flexibility, asynchronous inter-thread communications can be proposed. An example of such a run-time environment is given by the Ravenscar profile. In Ravenscar, threads access shared data components asynchronously according to priority inheritance protocols.

3. **Blackboard design pattern:** Ravenscar allows a thread to allocate/release several shared resources (eg. AADL data). Real time scheduling theory usually models such a shared resource as a semaphore, to represent, for example, a critical section. In classical operating systems, there exists many synchronization design patterns such as critical section, barrier, readers-writers, private semaphore, and various producers-consumers. The blackboard design pattern implements a readers-writers synchronization protocol. At a given time, only one writer can get the access to the blackboard in order to update the stored data, as opposed to the readers which are allowed to read the data simultaneously. The usual implementation of this protocol implies that readers and writers do not perform the same semaphore access, that requires extra analysis.

4. **Queued buffer design pattern:** In the blackboard design pattern, at any time, only the last written message is made available to the threads. Some real time executives provide communication features which allow to store all written messages in a memory unit. AADL also propose such a feature with event data ports or shared data components.

For each pattern, an applicative test case was described under the form of an AADL model which has been formatted in purpose to highlight some of the possible performance analysis that Cheddar is able to automatically compute (thread worst case response time, bound on shared resource blocking time, memory footprint analysis, ...) [10].

4   Increasing the Usability of Real Time Scheduling Theory: When No Feasibility Test Exists

Many practical cases can not be analyzed by real time scheduling theory feasibility tests. Complex industrial real time architectures frequently make use of specific task models or schedulers. In this case, no feasibility tests exists and building new feasibility tests is a difficult and expensive work. Furthermore, industrial real time systems may be composed of a large number of entities (eg. tasks, processors, memory units ...). These large scale systems can not be efficiently analyzed with model-checking. The only way people can expect to verify performances of such real time systems is to perform analysis with extensive simulations.

Languages and models were proposed for such a purpose. CPN tools [20] provides simulation features based on Petri Net for example. Unfortunately, the use of these general purpose simulation tools usually implies that the designer must model real time scheduling low level abstractions such as task preemption. A second way is to develop ad-hoc simulation programs, but this solution implies a very low reusability of the simulation programs. The Cheddar framework proposes a third way by the use of a domain specific language and a set of tools (compiler, interpreter, code generator ...). This domain specific language allows the designer to build models of his schedulers and tasks.

We also propose an engineering process from which the designer can test his models and automatically generate a simulation program. This model driven engineering process is implemented with Platypus [21].

4.1   A Language for the Modelling of Real Time Schedulers

Real time schedulers are composed of two different aspects:

1. Arithmetic and logical statements which allow to select a task amoung a set of ready tasks or to compute task priorities.
2. Temporal constraints and synchronizations between entities (eg. tasks and schedulers). These synchronizations describe how entities must work all together in order to share processors.

The Cheddar language is then defined by two parts : 1) a subset of Ada for the modelling of arithmetic and logical statements of the schedulers and 2) a timed automaton language for the synchronizations modelling scheduler and task relationships. A detailed description of this language is given into the Cheddar users's guide [22].

An Ada subset language. This part of the Cheddar language allows to express the arithmetic and logical statements on simulation data. Simulation data are associated to the entities composing the architecture to analyze (eg. task release time, scheduler quantum, shared resource protocol, ...). This language allows the designer to express sort rules as Earliest Deadline for example. A Cheddar program is organized in sub-programs called sections. These sub-programs are typed:

- Some sub-programs are devoted to data simulation declaration and initialization. They are called *start_section*.
- Some sub-programs allow to select a task amoung a set of ready tasks according to simulation data (eg. priority). These sub-programs are called *election_section*.
- Finally, some sub-programs contain statements which have to be ran at each unit of time before the task selection. They are called *priority_section*.

The language defines usual operators and statements. Schedulers can be modelled with loops, conditional tests or assignements. This domain specific language also provides statements and operators that are specific to real time scheduling theory. For example, the *uniform/exponential* statements customize the way random values are generated during simulations. The *lcm* operator computes last common multiplier of simulation data. The *max_to_index* operator looks for the ready task which has the highest priority level.

The language is typed and provides usual types as integer, boolean or string. Some types related to real time scheduling theory are also defined.

A timed automaton language. The second part of a Cheddar scheduler model is a network of timed automata. A scheduler model can contain timed automata similar to those proposed by UPPAAL [23,24]. UPPAAL is a toolbox for the modelling and the verification of real time systems.

A network of timed automata models timing and synchronization between schedulers and tasks. The Ada subset described above is enough to model schedulers which have fixed synchronization relationships between tasks and schedulers. By the past, we have shown that this language makes it possible the modelling of simple schedulers like Earliest Deadline First, Rate Monotonic ou Maximum Urgency First. However, some real time schedulers require the modelling of complex synchronizations. This is the case of hierarchical schedulers. An architecture based on hierarchical scheduling is an architecture in which several entities work all together for the processor sharing. Hierarchical scheduling has been initially proposed in the context of time sharing systems. In time sharing systems, hierarchical schedulers were proposed in order to define user-level scheduling policies (eg. fair process scheduling [25]). Today, hierarchical scheduling also exists in several real time system standards such as ARINC 653, POSIX 1003 or Ada 2005 [26,3,19].

Every automaton may fire a transition separately or synchronize with another automaton. Transitions may be guarded with time constraints. Delays can express time consumption at transition firing. Finally, at transition firing, automata may run Ada subset sections in order to compute task priorities or to choose the next task to run.

For further readings, a model of an ARINC 653 hierarchical scheduling modelled with the Cheddar language is given in [27].

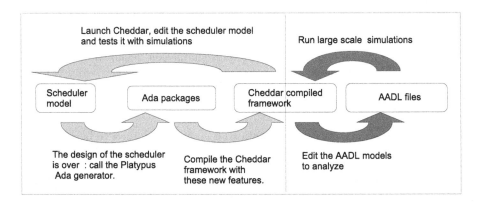

Fig. 4. A process to perform simulations from Cheddar scheduler models

4.2   Engineering Process of a Cheddar Scheduler Model: From the Model to the Scheduling Simulation

Figure 4 depicts the process that a designer runs to perform scheduling simulations with specific scheduler or task models:

1. With the Cheddar toolset the designer models a new scheduler. This model can be directly interpreted using the Cheddar framework. This feature eases the design step and allows the designer to perform small scheduling simulations.
2. When his scheduler has been tested, the designer can generate Ada packages implementing his scheduler into the Cheddar framework. The Ada package generator is implemented within Platypus. Platypus [21] is a meta-environment suitable for model driven engineering activities.
3. The generated Ada packages can be integrated into the Cheddar framework. The Cheddar framework is then compiled in order to enrich it with this new scheduler.
4. The designer can actually run large scale simulations with this new Cheddar framework embedding his scheduler. The designer makes use of his scheduler through this enriched Cheddar framework in the same way he will make use of standard schedulers manually implemented into Cheddar (eg. Rate Monotonic).

5   Conclusion and Ongoing Works

This article presents three possible ways investigated by the Cheddar project in order to increase the usability of real time scheduling theory. We have presented a set of tools which help the designer to apply real time scheduling theory. This toolset allows several levels of use and is able to perform analysis of models written with design languages such as AADL. We also have presented a domain specific language to investigate performances of architectures on which real time scheduling theory does not propose analytical method.

At the time we are writing this article, it is difficult to state if Cheddar has actually helped people to apply real time scheduling theory on practical cases. The toolset has been used to build many real time scheduling courses. It has been experimented in different research and development projects related to avionic or robotic applications, with different design languages. Besides these first encouraging results, the Cheddar project have raised several interesting open research questions.

First, Ellidiss technologies will distribute Cheddar with its modelling tool Stood. We expect to spread the use of real time scheduling theory on practitioners. For such a purpose, we have started to investigate how to apply Cheddar to modelling design patterns that practitioners usually handle with Stood [10]. For this project, we have chosen AADL as a pivot language between Stood and Cheddar.

Second, the Cheddar language we have defined to model schedulers was experienced in several projects. We know that this language is well suited for this purpose. The language is based on an Ada subset, which allows static analysis (eg. SPARK [28]) and on a timed automaton language which allows dynamic analysis (eg. model-checking with UUPPAL). We plan to investigate how Cheddar scheduler model analysis can help designers to compare their models.

Finally, the complexity of real time systems has been growing quickly for these 15 last years. In the past, the only resource requiring deep and accurate analysis was the processor. But now, many real time systems are distributed over several processors and several resources have to be managed all together: processors, communication networks and memory units. In the next months, we plan to focus on memory footprint analysis with queueing system models.

Acknowledgments

Cheddar is an open-source toolset and many people have helped the Cheddar team. The Cheddar team would like to thank all contributors (see http://beru.univ-brest.fr/~singhoff/cheddar/). Cheddar AADL analysis features rely on Ocarina [11]. We also would like to thank the Ocarina's Team (B. Zalila, J. Hugues, L. Pautet and F. Kordon).

References

1. Liu, C.L., Layland, J.W.: Scheduling Algorithms for Multiprogramming in a Hard Real-Time Environnment. Journal of the Association for Computing Machinery 20(1), 46–61 (1973)
2. Sha, L., Rajkumar, R., Lehoczky, J.: Priority Inheritance Protocols: An Approach to real-time Synchronization. IEEE Transactions on computers 39(9), 1175–1185 (1990)
3. Taft, S.T., Duff, R.A., Brukardt, R.L., Ploedereder, E., Leroy, P.: Ada 2005 Reference Manual. Language and Standard Libraries. International Standard ISO/IEC 8652/1995(E) with Technical Corrigendum 1 and Amendment 1. LNCS, vol. 4348(XXII). Springer, Heidelberg (2006)
4. SEI: The Rate Monotonic Analysis. Technical report, In the Software Technology Roadmap (2003), http://www.sei.cmu.edu/str/descriptions/rma_body.html
5. Tindell, K.W., Clark, J.: Holistic schedulability analysis for distributed hard real-time systems. Microprocessing and Microprogramming 40(2-3), 117–134 (1994)
6. Leung, J., Merril, M.: A note on preemptive scheduling of periodic real time tasks. Information processing Letters 3(11), 115–118 (1980)
7. George, L., Rivierre, N., Spuri, M.: Preemptive and Non-Preemptive Real-time Uni-processor Scheduling, INRIA Technical report number 2966 (1996)
8. Harbour, M.G., García, J.G., Gutiérrez, J.P., Moyano, J.D.: MAST: Modeling and Analysis Suite for Real Time Applications. In: Proc. of the 13th Euromicro Conference on Real-Time Systems, Delft, The Netherlands, pp. 125–134 (2001)
9. Tri-Pacific: Rapid-RMA : The Art of Modeling Real-Time Systems (2003), http://www.tripac.com/html/prod-fact-rrm.html
10. Dissaux, P., Singhoff, F.: Stood and Cheddar: AADL as a Pivot Language for Analysing Performances of Real Time Architectures. In: Proceedings of the European Real Time System conference, Toulouse, France (2008)
11. Hugues, J., Zalila, B., Pautet, L.: Rapid Prototyping of Distributed Real-Time Embedded Systems Using the AADL and Ocarina. In: 18th IEEE/IFIP International Workshop on Rapid System Prototyping (RSP 2007), Porto Allegre, Brazil (2007)
12. Panunzio, M., Vardanega, T.: A Metamodel-Driven Process Featuring Advanced Model-Based Timing Analysis. In: Abdennahder, N., Kordon, F. (eds.) Ada-Europe 2007. LNCS, vol. 4498, pp. 128–141. Springer, Heidelberg (2007)
13. Frédéric, T., Gérard, S., Delatour, J.: Towards an UML 2.0 profile for real-time execution platform modeling. In: Proceedings of the 18th Euromicro Conference on Real-Time Systems (ECRTS 2006) Work in progress session (2006)
14. Inc., S.: Architecture Analysis and Design Language (AADL) AS 5506. Technical report, The Engineering Society For Advancing Mobility Land Sea Air and Space, Aerospace Information Report, Version 1.0 (2004)
15. Singhoff, F., Legrand, J., Nana, L., Marcé, L.: Scheduling and Memory requirements analysis with AADL. In: ACM SIGAda Ada Letters, vol. 25(4), pp. 1–10. ACM Press, New York (2005)
16. Singhoff, F.: The Cheddar AADL property set (Release 2.x, LISyC Technical report, number singhoff-03-2007) (2007), http://beru.univ-brest.fr/~singhoff/cheddar
17. Inc., S.: AADL Annex Behavior (draft V1.6), AS 5506. Technical report, The Engineering Society For Advancing Mobility Land Sea Air and Space, Aerospace Information Report (2007)

18. Legrand, J., Singhoff, F., Nana, L., Marcé, L.: Performance Analysis of Buffers Shared by Independent Periodic Tasks, LISyC Technical report, number legrand-02-2004 (2004), http://beru.univ-brest.fr/~singhoff/cheddar
19. Arinc: Avionics Application Software Standard Interface. The Arinc Committee (1997)
20. Wells, L.: Performance Analysis using CPN Tools. In: Proceedings of the First International Conference on Performance Evaluation Methodologies and Tools 2006. ValueTools 2006. ACM Press, New York (2006)
21. Platypus Technical Summary and download (2007), http://cassoulet.univ-brest.fr/mme/
22. Singhoff, F.: Cheddar Release 2.x User's Guide, LISyC Technical report, number singhoff-01-2007 (2007), http://beru.univ-brest.fr/~singhoff/cheddar
23. Alur, R., Dill, D.L.: Automata for modeling real time systems. In: Paterson, M. (ed.) ICALP 1990. LNCS, vol. 443, pp. 322–335. Springer, Heidelberg (1990)
24. Behrmann, G., David, A., Larsen, K.G.: A Tutorial on UPPAAL, Technical Report Updated the 17th November 2004, Department of Computer Science, Aalbord University, Denmark (2004)
25. Kay, J., Lauder, P.: A Fair Share Scheduler. Communications of the ACM 31, 44–45 (1988)
26. Gallmeister, B.O.: POSIX 4: Programming for the Real World. O'Reilly and Associates, Sebastopol (1995)
27. Singhoff, F., Plantec, A.: AADL Modeling and Analysis of a hierarchical schedulers. In: ACM SIGAda Ada Letters, vol. 27(3), pp. 41–50. ACM Press, New York (2007)
28. Barnes, J.: High integrity software: The Spark approach to safety and security. Addison-Wesley Publishing Company, Reading (2003)

An Ada 2005 Technology for Distributed and Real-Time Component-Based Applications

Patricia López Martínez, José M. Drake, Pablo Pacheco, and Julio L. Medina

Departamento de Electrónica y Computadores, Universidad de Cantabria,
39005-Santander, SPAIN
{lopezpa,drakej,pachecop,medinajl}@unican.es

Abstract: The concept of interface in Ada 2005 significantly facilitates its usage as the basis for a software components technology. This technology, taking benefit of the resources that Ada offers for real-time systems development, would be suitable for component-based real-time applications that run on embedded platforms with limited resources. This paper proposes a model based technology for the implementation of distributed real-time component-based applications with Ada 2005. The proposed technology uses the specification of components and the framework defined in the LwCCM standard, modifying it with some key features that make the temporal behaviour of the applications executed on it, predictable, and analysable with schedulability analysis tools. Among these features, the dependency on CORBA is replaced by specialized communication components called connectors, the threads required by the components are created and managed by the environment, and interception mechanisms are placed to control their scheduling parameters in a per-transaction basis. This effort aims to lead to a new IDL to Ada mapping, a prospective standard of the OMG.

Keywords: Ada 2005, Component-based technology, embedded systems, real-time, OMG standards

1 Introduction[1]

While in the general-purpose software applications domain the component-based software engineering (CBSE) approach is progressing as a promising technology to improve productivity and to deal with the increasing complexity of applications, in the embedded and real-time systems domain, instead, its usage has evolved significantly slower. The main reason for this delay is that the most known CBSE technologies like EJB, .NET, or CCM, are inherently heavy and complex, they introduce not easily predictable overheads and do not scale well enough to fit the significant restrictions on the availability of resources usually suffered by embedded systems.

Trying to find an appropriate solution to this problem, european research projects like COMPARE[1] and FRESCOR [2], tackle from different points of view, the development

---

[1] This work has been funded by the European Union's FP6 under contracts FP6/2005/IST/5-034026 (FRESCOR project) and IST-004527 (ARTIST2 One) and by the Spanish Government under grant TIC2005-08665-C03 (THREAD project) and the ITEA SPICES project. This work reflects only the author's views; the EU is not liable for any use that may be made of the information contained herein.

F. Kordon and T. Vardanega (Eds.): Ada-Europe 2008, LNCS 5026, pp. 254–267, 2008.

of a real-time component-based technology compatible with the embedded systems constraints. Their approach is based on the usage of the Container/Component model pattern defined in the LwCCM specification developed by OMG [3], but avoiding the usage of CORBA as communication middleware, which is too heavy for this kind of applications. With this pattern, the interaction of the component with the run-time environment is completely carried out through the container, whose code is generated by automatic tools with the purpose of isolating the component developer from the details concerning the code of the execution environment.

The recent modification of the Ada language specification [4], so called Ada 2005, provides an enhanced option for the implementation of fully Ada native component-based technologies, which is really suitable for embedded platforms. Ada's native support for concurrency, scheduling policies, synchronization mechanisms, and remote invocations has always been a strength for implementing real-time and distributed systems. New to Ada 2005 is the concept of interface, which provides support for multiple inheritance. This is a key aspect in a component-based technology because it allows the components to inherit characteristics from both the technology with which they are developed as well as the application domain to which they belong. Besides, interfaces are used to encapsulate the services offered by the components (Facets in LwCCM) and also as the mechanism to make reference to the required services (Receptacles in LwCCM).

This paper proposes a component-based technology based on Ada. It implements the LwCCM framework, with the container/component model, and both the code of the environment and the code of the components are written in Ada 2005. The technology incorporates mechanisms to the running environment, and extends the specification of the components, in such a way that the timing behaviour of the final application is totally controlled by the automatically generated execution environment. In this way, real-time models of the application can be elaborated and analysed in order to verify its schedulability when the application is run in closed platforms, or to define the resource usage contracts required to operate in open environments like FRESCOR[2][5]. The description and deployment of applications and components in the technology follow the "Deployment and Configuration of Component-Based Distributed Applications" standard of the OMG [6] (D&C). The paper is focused in the description of the framework that is the base of the technology, particularly on the resources used to guarantee the required predictability.

Various proposals dealing with the adaptation of CBSE to real-time systems have appeared in the last years, though none of them have fully satisfied the industry requirements [7]. In the absence of a standard, some companies have developed their own solutions, adapted to their corresponding domains. Examples of that kind of technologies are Koala [8], developed by Philips, or Rubus [9], developed by Arcticus Systems and used by Volvo. These technologies have been successfully applied in the companies that created them, though none of them have stimulated an inter-enterprise software components market. However, they have served as the basis of other academic approaches. The Robocop component model [10] is based on Koala and adds some features to support analysis of real-time properties; Bondarev et al. [11] have developed an integrated environment for the design and performance analysis of Robocop models. Similarly, Rubus has been used as the starting point of the SaveCCT technology [12]; the component concept in SAVE is applied at a very low granularity. Under appropriate assumptions for concurrency, simple RMA analysis can be applied and the resulting timing properties introduced as quality attributes of the assemblies. SaveCCT focuses on control systems for the automotive domain. In a similar way, COMDES-II [13] encapsulates control tasks following a hierarchical composition scheme, applied in an ad-hoc C based RT-kernel. The technology presented in this paper follows the idea proposed by PECT (Prediction-Enabled Component Technology) [14]. Sets of constraints in the components allow one to predict the behaviour of an assembly of components. In our case, this approach is applied to obtain the complete real-time model of the application. Though the Ada language is significantly used in the design and implementation of embedded real-time systems, we have not found references of its usage in support of component-based environments. This is probably due to the lack of support for multiple inheritance in the previous versions of the language.

The rest of this paper is organized as follows. Section 2 describes the two main processes involved in a components technology, emphasizing the main contributions of the proposal. Section 3 describes in detail the reference model of the framework, and the aspects included for developing analysable applications. Section 4 details the architecture and classes to which a component is mapped in the technology. Finally, Section 5 and 6 shows some practical experiences, conclusions and future work.

2   Real-Time Component-Based Development

A component technology defines two different development processes, shown in Figure 1. The components development process comprises the specification, implementation, and packaging of components as reusable and independently distributable entities. The development of component-based applications includes specification, configuration, deployment and launching of applications built as assemblies of available components. Both processes are independent and they are carried out by different agents in different stages, however, they require to be coordinated because the final products of the first process are

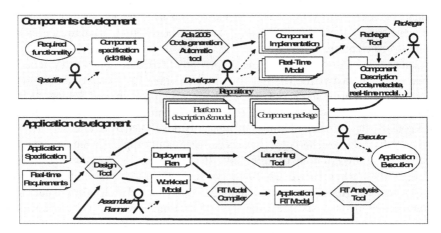

Fig. 1. Main processes in a component technology

the inputs for the second. So, in order to guarantee their coherence, a component technology must define a set of rules about the kind of products and information that are generated in each phase of the process, and the formats in which they are supplied. A key aspect in a component technology is the opacity of the components; during the process of application development, components must be used without any knowledge of the internal details of their implementation or code. To achieve this opacity, models and information concerning functional and non-functional aspects of the component must be added to its implementation in the package that describes the component.

A component development process starts when the "specifier", who is an expert in a particular application domain, creates the specification of a component with concrete functionality in the domain. The "developer" implements this specification and creates models that describe the installation requirements of the component. This work is supported by automatic tools, which generate the skeletons for the code of the component based on the selected technology. Therefore, the developer task is reduced to design and implement the specific business code of the component without having to be aware of internal details about the technology. Finally, the "packager" gathers all the information required to make use of the component, and creates and publishes the distributable element that constitutes the component. Relevant aspects of the proposed technology related to components development are:

- The methodology for functional specification of components and the framework proposed by the LwCCM specification have been adopted as the basis for the technology. Hence, a container/component model is used in the component implementations, but CORBA is replaced by simpler static communication mechanisms with predictable behaviour, and suitable for the execution platform. Remote communication between components is achieved by using connectors. They are special components whose code is completely generated by the tools and which encapsulate all the support for interactions among components.
- Since component implementations are generated in Ada2005, it has been necessary to define the set of Ada packages to which the components and the elements of the LwCCM framework are mapped. An automatic code generation tool has been developed. This tool takes the specification of a component as input and generates all the code elements that provide support for the component inside the framework.
- The technology follows the D&C specification for the description of the package that holds the distributable component.

In order to apply the technology to hard real-time component-based applications, both standard specifications, D&C and LwCCM, have been extended with new elements that are used to describe the temporal behaviour of components and the requirements they impose on the resources in order to meet timing requirements:

- D&C specification has been extended in order to associate a temporal behaviour model to the specifications and implementations of components. This real-time model is used to describe the temporal responses of the component and the configuration parameters that it requires. This paper does not detail the modelling approach used. For a complete explanation of the approach see [15]. The basic idea is that the real-time model of a component is a parameterized model, independent of the

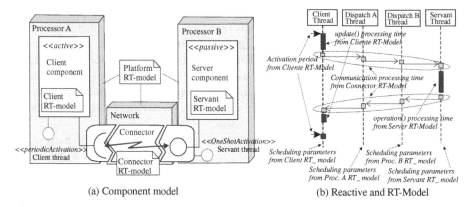

(a) Component model

(b) Reactive and RT-Model

Fig. 2. RT Modeling of component-based applications

application in which the component is used, which describes the component temporal behaviour through references to the models of the platform in which the component is executed and to the models of other components that it uses in order to implement its functionality. Once all these elements are known in the context of an application deployed in a concrete platform, as it is shown in Figure 2a, the real time model of the complete application can be generated by composition of the individual real-time models of the software and hardware components that form it. This model describes the set of real-time transactions [16] executed in the application, as the one in Figure 2b, and can be used to obtain the response time of services, analyse the schedulability or evaluate the scheduling parameters required to satisfy the timing requirements imposed to the application. In our case, the real-time models of the components are formulated according to the MAST model [16], so that the set of tools offered by the MAST environment can be used to analyse the system.

- The LwCCM functional specification of a component has been refined with the purpose of controlling threading characteristics of the components. These characteristics include the number and assignment of threads and scheduling parameters. A component can not create threads inside its business code. Instead of that, for each thread that a component requires, it declares a port in its specification. This port implements one of the predefined interfaces OneShotActivation or PeriodicActivation (see Section 3).
- Interception mechanisms are used to control the scheduling parameters with which each invocation received by a component is executed. The specification of a component declares the configuration parameters required to assign concrete values of these scheduling parameters to a component instance.

The application development process consists in assembling component instances, choosing them from those which have been previously developed, and stored in the repository of the design environment. This process is carried out by three different agents in three consecutive phases. The "assembler" builds the application choosing the required component instances and connecting them according to their instantiation requirements.

This work is led by the functional specification of the application, the real-time requirements of the application, and the description of the available components. The result of this first stage is a description of the application as a composite component, which is useful by itself. The "planner" (usually the same agent as the assembler) takes this description and designs a deployment model for the application. This model includes assigments of component instances to nodes and the communication mechanisms between them. The result of this stage is the deployment plan, which completely describes the application and the way in which it is planned to be executed. Finally, the "executor" deploys, installs, and executes the application, taking the deployment plan and the information about the execution platform as inputs. This labour is usually assisted by automatic tools. Relevant aspects of the proposed technology regarding application development are:

- As well as describing components, the D&C specification is the basis for the process of designing and deploying an application. D&C defines the structure of the deployment plan that leads this process. It describes the component instances that form the application, their connections, the configuration parameters assigned to each instance and the assignment of instances to nodes.
- A deployment tool processes the information provided by the deployment plan. It selects the code of the components suitable for the target platform and generates the code required to support the execution of the components in each node. Specifically, it automatically generates the connectors, which provide the communication mechanisms between remote component instances, as well as the code for the main procedures executed on each node.

The specific aspects included in the application development process to support hard real-time applications are:

- Once the planner has developed the deployment plan, the local or remote nature of each connection between component ports is defined. Then, an automatic tool generates the code of the connectors based on the selected communication service and its corresponding configuration parameters, which were assigned to the connection in the deployment plan. The communication service used must hold a predictable behaviour, hence, the tool generates also the real-time models that describe the temporal behaviour of those connectors.
- Once the connectors have been developed together with their real-time models, and based on the deployment plan, a tool elaborates the real-time model of the application by composition of the real-time models of the components that form it (connectors included) and the models of the platform resources. This model is used either to analyse the schedulability of the application under a certain workload, or to calculate the resource usage contracts necessary to guarantee its operation in an open contractual environment [5]. In the latter case, these contracts will be negotiated, prior to the application execution, by the launching tool.
- The execution environment includes a special internal service as well as interception mechanisms that are used to manage in an automated way the scheduling parameters of the threads involved in the application execution. The configuration parameters of this service, whose values may be obtained by schedulability analysis, are specified in the deployment plan and assigned to the service at launching time.

3   Reference Model of the Technology

The proposed technology is based on the reusability (with no modification) of the business code of the components, and the complete generation by automatic tools of the code that adapts the component to the execution environment. This code is generated according to the reference model shown in Figure 3. It takes the LwCCM framework as a starting point, and adds to it the features required to control the real-time behaviour of the application execution. Each of the elements that take part in the execution environment are explained below.

Component: A component is a reusable software module that offers a well-defined business functionality. This functionality is specified through the set of services that the component offers to other components, grouped in ports called *facets*, and the set of services it requires from other components, grouped in ports called *receptacles*.

With the purpose of having complete control of the threading and scheduling characteristics of an application, and in the look for being able to analyse it, components in our technology are passive. The operations they offer through their facets are made up of passive code that can call protected objects. But this does not mean that there can not be active components in the framework, concurrency is provided by means of *activation ports*. When a component requires a thread for implementing its functionality, it declares a port that implements one of the two special interfaces defined in the framework: OneShotActivation or PeriodicActivation. These ports are recognized by the environment, which creates and activates the corresponding threads for their execution once the component is instantiated, connected and configured. The interface OneShotActivation declares a run() procedure, which will be executed once by the created thread, while the interface PeriodicActivation declares an update() procedure, which will be invoked periodically. A component can declare several activation ports, each of them representing an independent unit of concurrency managed by the component, and which are independent of the business invocations.

Activation ports are declared in the component specification (in the IDL file), and all the elements required for their execution are created by the code generation tool. Their configuration parameters, which include the scheduling parameters of the threads as well as the activation period (in case of PeriodicActivation ports) are assigned for each component instance in the deployment plan.

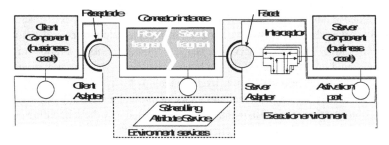

Fig. 3. Reference model of the technology

Adapter: An adapter is the part of the component's code which provides the run-time support for the business code. All the platform related aspects are included in the adapter. Its code is automatically generated according to the component/container model. With this programming approach the component developer does not need to know any detail about the underlying technology, he is only in charge of business code development.

Connector: A connector is the mechanism through which a component communicates with another component connected to it through a port. In our technology, a connector has the same structure as a component, but its business code is also generated by the deployment tool, based on:

- The interface of the connected ports. The connectors are generated from a set of templates which are adapted so that they implement the operations of the required interface.
- The location of the components (local vs remote), and the type of invocation (synchronous or asynchronous). Combinations among these different characteristics lead to different types of connectors. For local and synchronous invocations, the connector is not necessary, the client component invokes the operation directly on the server. For local and asynchronous invocations the connector requires an additional thread to execute the operation (obtained through activation ports). If the invocation is distributed, the connector is divided in two fragments: the *proxy fragment*, which is instantiated in the client node, and the *servant fragment*, which is instantiated in the server node. The communication between the two fragments is achieved by means of the communication service selected for the connection. In this case, the connector can also implement synchronous or asynchronous invocations, including the required mechanisms in the proxy fragment.
- The communication service or middleware used for the connection and its corresponding configuration parameters, which are assigned for each connection between ports in the deployment plan.

Interceptors: The concept of interception is taken from QoSforCCM [17]. It brings a way to support the management of non-functional features of the application. An interceptor allows to incorporate calls to the environment services inside the sequence of an invocation by executing certain actions before and after the operation is executed on the component. The support for interceptors is introduced in the adapter, so it is hidden to the component developer. Their introduction is optional for each operation, and it is specified in the deployment plan.

In our technology, interceptors are used to control the scheduling parameters with which each received invocation is executed. Based on the configuration parameters assigned to it in the deployment plan, each interceptor knows the scheduling parameter which corresponds to the current invocation, and uses the SchedulingParameterService to modify it in the invoking thread. With this strategy, different schemes for scheduling parameters assignment can be implemented. Besides common assignment policies, like Client Propagated or Server Declared [18], our technology allows to apply an assignment based on the transactional model of the application. With this policy, a service can be executed with different scheduling parameters inside the same end-to-end flow depending on the particular step inside the flow in which the invocation takes place. This scheme enables better schedulability results [19]. The values of these parameters are obtained from the analysis using holistic priority assignment tools like the ones included in MAST, which is used as analysis environment in our technology.

SchedulingParameterService: It is an internal environment service which is invoked by the interceptors to change the scheduling parameters of the invoking thread. The kind of scheduling parameters that will be effectively used depends strongly on the execution platform, it may be a single priority, deadline, or the contract to use in the case of a FRES-COR flexible scheduling platform.

4   Architecture of a Component Implementation

There are two complementary aspects that a component implementation must address:

- The component has to implement the functionality that it offers through its facets, making use of its own business logic and the services of other components.
- The implementation must include the necessary resources to instantiate, connect and execute the component in the corresponding platform. This aspect is addressed by implementing the appropriate interfaces which allow to manage the component in an standard way. In our case, those defined by LwCCM.

Each aspect requires knowledge about different domains. For the first aspect, an expert on the application domain corresponding to the component functionality is required. For the second, however, what it is required is an expert on the corresponding component technology. The proposed architecture for a component implementation tries to find an structural pattern to achieve independency of the Ada packages that implement each aspect. Besides, the packages that implement the technology related aspects are to be automatically generated according to the component specification. With this approach, the component developer only has to design and implement the business code of the component.

The proposed architecture is based on the reference one proposed by LwCCM, but adapted for:

- Making use of the abstraction, security and predictability characteristics of Ada.
- Including the capacity for controlling threading characteristics of the components.
- Facilitating the automatic generation of code taking the IDL3 specification of the component as input and generating the set of classes that represent a component in the technology.
- Providing a well-defined frame in which the component developer designs and writes the business code.

In the proposed technology, the architecture of a component is significantly simplified as a consequence of the usage of connectors. When two connected components are installed in different nodes, the client component interacts only with the proxy fragment of the connector, while the server component interacts only with the servant fragment of the connector. Therefore, all the interactions between components are local, since it is the connector who hides the communications mechanisms used for the interaction.

For each component, four Ada packages are generated. Three of them are completely generated by the tool, while the last package leaves the "blank" spaces in which the

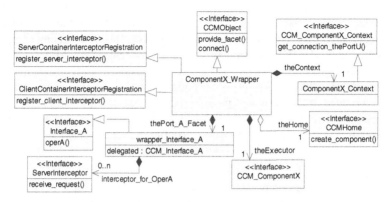

Fig. 4. Example of Component Wrapper Structure for ComponentX

component developer must include the business code of the component. The first module represents the adapter (or container) of the component. It includes the set of resources that adapt the business code of the component to the platform, following the interaction rules imposed by the technology. It defines three classes:

- The wrapper class of the component, called {ComponentName}_Wrapper, which represents the most external class of the component. It offers the equivalent interface of the component, which LwCCM establishes as the only interface that can be used by clients or by the deployment tool to access to the component. With this purpose, the class implements the CCMObject interface, which, among others, offers operations to access to the component facets, or to connect the corresponding server components to the receptacles. Besides, the capacity to incorporate interceptors is achieved by implementing the Client/ServerContainerInterceptorRegistration interfaces, a modified version of the interfaces with the same name defined in QoSCCM [17]. As it is shown in Figure 4, this class is a container which aggregates or references all the elements that form the component:
  - The component context, through which components access to their receptacles.
  - The home, which represents the factory used to create the component instance.
  - The executor of the component, which represents its real business code implementation. Its structure is explained below.
  - An instance of a facet wrapper class that is aggregated for each facet of the component. They capture the invocations received in the component and transfer them to the corresponding facet implementations, which are defined in the executor. The facet wrappers are the place in which the interceptors for managing non-functional features are included.
- The class that represents the context implementation, called {ComponentName}_ Context. It includes all the information and resources required by the component to access to the components which are connected to its receptacles.
- The {ComponentName}_Home_Wrapper, which implements the equivalent interface of the home of the component. It includes the class procedures (static) that are used as factories for component instantiation.

The rest of generated Ada packages contain the classes that represent the implementation of the business code of the component (the executor). The LwCCM standard fixes a set of rules that define the programming model to follow in order to develop a component implementation. Taking the IDL3 specification of a component, LwCCM defines a set of abstract classes and interfaces which have to be implemented, either automatically or by the user, to develop the functionality of the component. This set of root classes and interfaces are grouped in the generated package {ComponentName}_Exec. The {ComponentName}_Exec_Impl package includes the concrete classes for the component implementation which inherit from the classes defined in the previous package. The class that represents the component implementation, {ComponentName}_Exec_Impl, which is shown in Figure 5, has the following attributes:

- A reference to the component context. It is set by the environment through the set_session_context() operation, and it is used to access to the receptacles.
- An aggregated object of the {ComponentName}_Impl class, whose skeleton is generated by the tool and has to be completed by the developer.
- Each activation port defined in the specification of the component, represents a thread that is required by the component to implement its functionality. For implementing those threads two kinds of Ada task types have been defined. The OneShotActivationTask executes once the corresponding run() procedure of the port, while the PeriodicActivationTask executes periodically the update() procedure of the corresponding port. Both types of task receive as a discriminant during its instantiation, a reference to the data structure that qualify their execution, including scheduling parameters, period, state of the component and the procedure to execute. For each activation port defined in the component, a thread of the corresponding type is declared. They will be activated and terminated by the environment by means of standard procedures that LwCCM includes in the CCMObject interface to control the lifecycle of the component.

The {ComponentName}_Impl class, represented in Figure 5, is defined in a new package, in order to hide the environment internals to the code developer. It represents the reference frame in which the developer introduces the business code. Relevant elements of this class are:

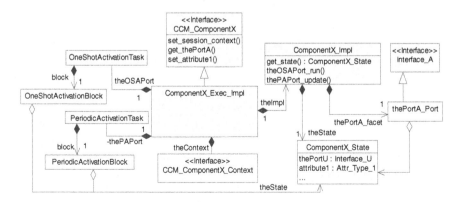

Fig. 5. Example of Component Implementation Structure for ComponentX

- For each facet offered by the component, a facet implementation object is aggregated. However, in the case of simple components, the class itself can implement the interfaces supported by the facets.
- All the implementation elements (facet implementations, activation tasks, etc.) operate according to the state of the component, which is unique for each instance. Based on that, the state has been implemented as an independent aggregated class, which can be accessed by the rest of the elements, avoiding cyclic dependencies.
- For each activation port defined in the component specification, the corresponding {PortName}_run() or {PortName}_update procedures are declared.

Most of the code of this class is generated automatically, the component developer only has to write the body of the activation port procedures (run or update), and the body of the operations offered by each of the facets implementations. The developer, who knows the temporal behaviour of the code, must also elaborate the real-time model of the component. In the case of a connector, the structure generated is exactly the same, but the "business" code, which in that case consists in the code required to implement remote invocations, is also automatically generated by the deployment tool.

The current available Ada mapping for IDL [20] is based in Ada95, so for the development of the code generation tool, it has been necessary to define new mappings for some IDL types in order to get benefit of the new concepts introduced in Ada 2005. The main change concerns to the usage of interfaces. The old mapping for the IDL "interface" type led to a complex Ada structure while now can be directly mapped to an Ada interface. Besides, some data structures defined in IDL, as for example the "sequence" type, can be implemented now with the new Ada 2005 containers.

5   Practical Experience

At the time of the first attempts made to validate the proposed technology, there was no real-time operating system with support for Ada 2005 applications, so the tests were run on a Linux platform, using the GNAT (GAP) 2007 compiler. The construction of the connectors for the communication between remote components, was made using the native Ada Distributed System Annex (DSA), Annex E of the Ada specification. The implementation of DSA used was GLADE [21]. Distributed test applications were developed and executed successfully. The platforms used in this evaluation were sufficient for the conceptual validation of the technology, since from the point of view of the software architecture the final code is equivalent, but of course, it is not appropriate for the validation of the timing properties of real-time applications.

The recently released new version of MaRTE_OS [22] provides now support for the execution of Ada 2005 applications, and allows to test the technology over a hard real-time environment. Still there is a lack for a real-time communication middleware. An enhanced version of GLADE that enables messages priority assignment exists for MaRTE_OS & GNAT [23], but it has not been ported to the new versions. To overcome this limitation, we have developed simpler connectors using a link layer real-time protocol. Our first tests on a real-time platform have been done with connectors that use directly the RT-EP [24] protocol for the communication between remote components.

The same application tested in the linux platform was used in MaRTE_OS, and as expectable, the code of the components did not require any modification, the only necessary change was the development of the new connectors suitable for the new communication service (RT-EP) used.

6   Conclusions and Future Work

This paper proposes a model based technology for the development of real-time component-based applications. The usage of the Ada language for its implementation, makes it particularly suitable for applications that run in embedded nodes with limited resources and strict timing requirements. The technology is based on the D&C and LwCCM standard specifications, which have been extended in order to support the development of applications with a predictable and analysable behaviour.

The key features of this technology have been specified and tested successfully. Nevertheless some challenges arise for this community to face. The most rewarding of them is the availability of an Ada native communication middleware, here used in the development of connectors, which must hold predictable behaviour, and allow a priority assigment for the messages based on the transactional (or so called end-to-end flow) model. Our aim is to develop the connectors using the Ada Distributed System Annex so that applications rely only on the Ada run-time infrastructure with no additional middleware, which is highly desirable to target small embedded systems.

As future work, some more tests have to be applied in order to quantify the concrete overheads introduced by the technology. A planned enhancement for the technology is the construction of a graphical environment to integrate all the stages of development of an application: design, code generation, analysis, and finally, execution. Another effort that has been started in the OMG and arise from this work is the elaboration of an updated version of the mapping from IDL to Ada 2005 [25].

References

[1]   IST project COMPARE: Component-based approach for real-time and embedded systems, http://www.ist-compare.org
[2]   IST project FRESCOR: Framework for Real-time Embedded Systems based on Contracts, http://www.frescor.org
[3]   OMG: Lightweight Corba Component Model, ptc/03-11-03 (November 2003)
[4]   Tucker Taft, S., Duff, R.A., Brukardt, R.L., Plödereder, E., Leroy, P.: Ada 2005 Reference Manual. LNCS, vol. 4348, pp. 43–48. Springer, Heidelberg (2006)
[5]   Aldea, M., et al.: FSF: A Real-Time Scheduling Architecture Framework. In: Proc. of 12th RTAS Conference, April 2006, San Jose, USA (2006)
[6]   OMG: Deployment and Configuration of Component-Based Distributed Applications Specification, version 4.0, Formal/06-04-02 (April 2006)
[7]   Möller, A., Åkerholm, M., Fredriksson, J., Nolin, M.: Evaluation of Component Technologies with Respect to Industrial Requirements. In: Proc. of 30th Euromicro Conference on Software Engineering and Advanced Applications (August 2004)
[8]   Ommering, R., Linden, F., Kramer, J.: The koala component model for consumer electronics software. IEEE Computer, IEEE, 78–85 (2000)

[9]   Lundbäck, K.-L., Lundbäck, J., Lindberg, M.: Component based development of dependable real-time applications Arcticus Systems, http://www.arcticus-systems.com

[10] Bondarev, E., de With, P., Chaudron, M.: Predicting Real-Time Properties of Component-Based Applications. In: Proc. of 10th RTCSA Conference, Goteborg (August 2004)

[11] Bondarev, E., et al.: CARAT: a toolkit for design and performance analysis of component-based embedded systems. In: Proc. of DATE 2007 Conference (April 2007)

[12] Åkerholm, M., et al.: The SAVE approach to component-based development of vehicular systems. Journal of Systems and Software 80(5) (May 2007)

[13] Ke, X., Sierszecki, K., Angelov, C.: COMDES-II: A Component-Based Framework for Generative Development of Distributed Real-Time Control Systems. In: Proc. of 13th RTCSA Conference (August 2007)

[14] Wallnau, K.C.: Volume III: A Technology for Predictable Assembly from Certifiable Components, Technical report, Software Engineering Institute, Carnegie Mellon University, April 2003, Pittsburgh, USA (2003)

[15] López, P., Drake, J.M., Medina, J.L.: Real-Time Modelling of Distributed Component-Based Applications. In: Proc. of 32h Euromicro Conference on Software Engineering and Advanced Applications, August 2006, Croatia (2006)

[16] González Harbour, M., Gutiérrez, J.J., Palencia, J.C., Drake, J.M.: MAST: Modeling and Analysis Suite for Real-Time Applications. In: Proc. of the Euromicro Conference on Real-Time Systems (June 2001)

[17] OMG: Quality of Service for CORBA Components, ptc/06-04-05 (April 2006)

[18] OMG: Real-Time CORBA Specification, v1.2 formal/05-01-04. Enero (2005)

[19] Gutiérrez García, J.J., González Harbour, M.: Prioritizing Remote Procedure Calls in Ada Distributed Systems. In: Proc. of the 9th Intl. Real-Time Ada Workshop, ACM Ada Letters, XIX, 2, pp. 67–72 (June 1999)

[20] OMG: Ada Language Mapping Specification - Version 1.2 (October 2001)

[21] Pautet, L., Tardieu, S.: GLADE: a Framework for Building Large Object-Oriented Real-Time Distributed Systems. In: Proc. of the 3rd IEEE Intl. Symposium on Object- Oriented Real-Time Distributed Computing, March 2000, Newport Beach, USA (2000)

[22] Aldea, M., González, M.: MaRTE OS: An Ada Kernel for Real-Time Embedded Applications. In: Strohmeier, A., Craeynest, D. (eds.) Ada-Europe 2001. LNCS, vol. 2043. Springer, Heidelberg (2001)

[23] López-Campos, J., Gutiérrez, J.-J., González-Harbour, M.: The Chance for Ada to Support Distribution and Real-Time in Embedded Systems. In: Llamosí, A., Strohmeier, A. (eds.) Ada-Europe 2004. LNCS, vol. 3063, pp. 91–105. Springer, Heidelberg (2004)

[24] Martínez, J.M., González, M.: RT-EP: A Fixed-Priority Real Time Communication Protocol over Standard Ethernet. In: Vardanega, T., Wellings, A.J. (eds.) Ada-Europe 2005. LNCS, vol. 3555, pp. 180–195. Springer, Heidelberg (2005)

[25] Medina, J.: Status report of the Ada2005 expected impact on the IDL to Ada Mapping. OMG documents mars/07-09-12 and mars/07-06-13 (2007), http://www.omg.org

Real-Time Distribution Middleware from the Ada Perspective*

Héctor Pérez, J. Javier Gutiérrez, Daniel Sangorrín, and Michael González Harbour

Computers and Real-Time Group
Universidad de Cantabria, 39005 - Santander, SPAIN
{perezh,gutierjj,daniel.sangorrin,mgh}@unican.es
http://www.ctr.unican.es/

Abstract. Standards for distribution middleware sometimes impose restrictions and often allow the implementations to decide on aspects that are fundamental to the correct and efficient behaviour of the applications using them, especially when these applications have real-time requirements. This work presents a study of two standard approaches for distribution middleware that can be used from Ada applications: RT-CORBA, and the Distributed Systems Annex (DSA) of Ada. The study focuses on the problems associated with the real-time behaviour of some implementations of these approaches, and on possible solutions that can be derived from our experience with Ada implementations. Moreover, the paper considers the problem of integration of the distribution middleware with a new generation of scheduling mechanisms based on contracts.

Keywords: distribution middleware, real-time, communications, RT-CORBA, Ada DSA, performance.

1 Introduction

The concept of a distributed application is not new; it has existed since two computers were first connected. However, the programming techniques of these systems have evolved greatly and they have become especially relevant in the last decade. Traditionally, message-passing mechanisms were used for communication among the parts of a distributed application where the communications among the application parts were done explicitly by the programmer. Since then, new object distribution techniques have evolved, for instance using Remote Procedure Calls (RPCs) that allow operations to be transparently used regardless of whether the functionality is offered in the local processor or in a remote one.

The object distribution paradigm is probably the most relevant in current industrial applications, and an important example is the CORBA standard [12] which provides a

---

* This work has been funded in part by the Spanish *Ministry of Science and Technology* under grant number TIC2005-08665-C03-02 (THREAD), and by the IST Programme of the European Commission under project FP6/2005/IST/5-034026 (FRESCOR). This work reflects only the author's views; the EU is not liable for any use that may be made of the information contained herein.

F. Kordon and T. Vardanega (Eds.): Ada-Europe 2008, LNCS 5026, pp. 268–281, 2008.
© Springer-Verlag Berlin Heidelberg 2008

language for the specification of interfaces (IDL, Interface Definition Language) that enables the use of different programming languages in the development of an application. There exist other distribution techniques of higher level coming from CORBA such as CCM (CORBA Component Model), or DDS (Data Distribution Service), but their degree of acceptance in industry is still lower compared to CORBA.

In addition to distribution standards, there are programming languages that allow the development of distributed applications. This is the case of Java (a *de facto* standard) with its specification for distributed systems, Java RMI (Java Remote Method Invocation) [17], based on the distribution of objects. Also, the Ada standard allows distribution through its DSA (Distributed Systems Annex, Annex E) [19], which supports both distribution of objects and RPCs.

This work will focus on analysing the real-time characteristics for distribution within the CORBA and Ada standards. It does not consider Java RMI because the real-time aspects of Java have not been fully addressed yet. RT-CORBA [13] offers the CORBA specification for real-time systems, and although Ada's DSA is not specifically designed for real-time systems, there are works that demonstrate that it is possible to write real-time implementations within the standard [14,7,8]. One goal of this paper is to make a comparative study of the scheduling models offered by these standards for implementing distributed real-time applications, an analysis of some of their implementations from the viewpoint of management of calls to remote resources, and an experimental evaluation on a real-time platform of the response times that can be obtained in remote calls in order to get an idea of the overheads introduced. Another objective of this work is to establish the basis for incorporating the experience acquired in systems programmed in Ada into the world of RT-CORBA.

The evolving complexity of real-time systems has lead to the need for using more sophisticated scheduling techniques, capable of simultaneously satisfying multiple types of requirements such as hard real-time guarantees and quality of service requirements, in the same system. To better handle the complexity of these systems, instead of asking the application to interact directly with the scheduling policies, scheduling services of a higher level of abstraction are being designed, usually based on the concept of resource reservations [2]. The FRESCOR European Union project [3] in which we are participating is aimed at investigating these aspects by creating a contract-based scheduling framework. In [8], some initial ideas were given about the integration of middleware and advanced scheduling services, and in this paper we extend those ideas to address the problem of handling distributed transactions.

The document is organized as follows. Section 2 is dedicated to the presentation of the basic characteristics of the distribution middleware based on RT-CORBA and Ada's DSA, and their implementations. Section 3 analyses in detail the aspects of scheduling, distribution mechanisms, and management of the remote calls proposed in the two standards and their implementations. The evaluation and discussion of the overheads in remote operations for these implementations is dealt with in Section 4. Section 5 proposes the integration of the distribution middleware with the framework for flexible scheduling. Finally, Section 6 draws the conclusions and considers future work.

2 Real-Time Distribution Middleware

This section will describe the scheduling models of RT-CORBA and of the DSA for the execution of remote calls and will discuss how the distributed transaction model can be supported. Furthermore, the different implementations to be analysed, all of which are open source code, will be briefly introduced.

A distributed transaction is defined as a part of an application consisting of multiple threads executing code in multiple processing nodes, and exchanging messages with information and events through one or more communication networks. In a transaction, events arriving at the system trigger the execution of activities, which can be either task jobs in the processors or messages in the networks. These activities, in turn, may generate additional events that trigger other activities, and this gives way to a chain of events and activities, possibly with end-to-end timing requirements [8]. This model is traditionally used for analysing the response time in real-time distributed applications. We will discuss how this model can be supported by the middleware.

2.1 RT-CORBA Model

The main characteristics of the architecture proposed by RT-CORBA in its specification [12] with respect to scheduling are the following:

- Use of threads as scheduling entities, for which an RT-CORBA priority can be applied and for which there are functions for conversion to the native priorities of the system on which they run.
- Use of two models for the specification of the priority of remote calls (following the Client-Server model): *Client_Propagated* (the invocation is executed in the remote node at the priority of the client, which is transmitted with the request message), and *Server_Declared* (all the requests to a particular object are executed at a priority preset in the server). In addition, it is possible for the user to define priority transformations that modify the priority associated with the server. This is done with two functions called *inbound* (which transforms the priority before running the server's code) and *outbound* (which transforms the priority with which the server makes calls to other remote services).
- Definition of *Threadpools* as mechanisms for managing remote requests. The threads in the pool may be preallocated, or can be created dynamically. There may be several groups of threadpools, each group using a specific priority band.
- Definition of *Priority-Banded Connections*. This mechanism is proposed for reducing priority inversions when a transport protocol without priorities is used.

The specification of RT-CORBA incorporates a chapter dedicated to dynamic scheduling, which basically introduces two concepts:

- The possibility of introducing other scheduling policies in addition to the fixed priority policy, such as, EDF (Earliest Deadline First), LLF (Least Laxity First), and MAU (Maximize Accrued Utility). The scheduling parameters are defined as a container that can contain more than one simple value, and can be changed by the application dynamically.

- The *Distributable Thread* that allows end-to-end scheduling and the identification of *Scheduling Segments* each one of which can be run on a processor. This concept is similar to the distributed transaction presented in [8].

RT-CORBA does not consider explicitly the possibility of passing scheduling parameters to the communications networks.

2.2 Ada DSA Model

Ada DSA does not have any mechanism for transmission of priorities and so its implementation is left up to the criterion of the implementation. The specification requires support for executing concurrent remote calls and for waiting until the return of the remote call. The communication among active partitions is carried out in a standard way using the Partition Communication Subsystem (PCS).

The concurrency and the real-time mechanisms are supported by the language itself with tasks, protected types and the services specified in Annex D. In [4], a mechanism for handling the transmission of priorities in the DSA is proposed. This mechanism is in principle more powerful than that of RT-CORBA, as it allows total freedom in the assignment of priorities both in the processors and in the networks used.

Ada included in its latest revision the scheduling policies EDF and Round Robin as part of its Real-Rime Systems Annex (Annex D). Nevertheless, it does not contemplate the existence of distributed transactions. Like RT-CORBA, Ada DSA does not consider the possibility of passing scheduling parameters to the communications networks.

2.3 Implementations Under Study

This work analyses and assesses the following implementations of RT-CORBA and the DSA:

- TAO [18] is an open source implementation of RT-CORBA that has been evolving for several years. The applications are programmed in C++ and the version we have used (1.5) runs on Linux and TCP/IP. It is offered as an implementation of the complete specification.
- PolyORB [15,20] is presented as a "schizophrenic" middleware that can support distribution with different personalities such as CORBA, RT-CORBA, or DSA. It is distributed with the GNAT compiler [1] and in principle it is envisaged for applications programmed in Ada. The version used (2007) supports CORBA and some basic notions of RT-CORBA (priorities and their propagation), and allows distribution through the DSA although it does not allow specifying scheduling parameters. The execution platform is Linux and TCP/IP.
- GLADE [14] is the original implementation of the DSA offered by GNAT [1] to support the development of distributed applications with real-time requirements. The scheduling is done through fixed priorities and implements two policies for distribution of priorities in the style of

RT-CORBA (Client Propagated and Server Declared). The 2007 version is used, and once again the execution platform is Linux and TCP/IP.

- RT-GLADE is a modification of GLADE that optimizes its real-time behaviour. There are two versions: in the first one [7], free assignment of priorities in remote calls is allowed (both in the processors and in the communication networks). The second version [8] proposes a way of incorporating distributed transactions into the DSA and giving support to different scheduling policies in a distributed system. The execution platform is MaRTE OS [9] and the network protocol is RT-EP [10]. This communication protocol is based on token passing in a logical ring over standard Ethernet, and it supports three different scheduling policies: fixed priorities, sporadic servers, and resource reservations through contracts [2,3].

3 Analysis of Distribution Middleware Implementations

The objective of this section is to analyse the scheduling aspects of the mechanisms for management of remote calls used by the implementations of RT-CORBA or DSA to support their respective specifications. It also discusses the properties of the solutions adopted and proposes some improvements that could be made both in the standards and in their implementations.

3.1 Implementations of RT-CORBA and DSA

From the viewpoint of management of remote calls, TAO defines several elements that can be configured [16]:

- Number of ORBs. The ORB is the management unit of the calls to a service. There may be several or only one, given that each ORB can accept requests from different parts of the application.
- The strategy of the concurrency server. Two models are defined: *Reactive*, in which a thread is executed to provide service to multiple connections; and *thread-per-connection*, in which the ORB creates a thread to serve each new connection.
- The threadpools. Two types of thread groups are defined with two different behaviours. In the *ORB-per-Thread* model each thread has an associated ORB that accepts and processes the services requested. In the *Leader/Followers* model the user can create several threads and each ORB will select them in turns so they await and process new requests arriving from the network.

For the management of remote calls, PolyORB defines the following configurable elements [15]:

- ORB tasking policies. Four policies are defined:
    - *No_Tasking:* the ORB does not create threads and uses the environment task to process the jobs

o   *Thread_Pool:* a set of threads is created at start-up time; this set can grow up to an absolute maximum, and unused threads are removed from it if its size exceeds a configurable intermediate value.

o   *Thread_per_Session:* a thread is created for each session that is opened

o   *Thread_per_Request:* a thread is created for each request that arrives and is destroyed when the job is done

- Configuration of the tasking runtimes. It is possible to choose among a Ravenscar-compliant, no tasking, or full tasking runtime system.

- ORB control policies. Four policies are defined that affect the internal behaviour of the middleware:

  o   *No Tasking:* a loop monitors I/O operations and processes the jobs

  o   *Workers:* all the threads are equal and they monitor the I/O operations alternatively

  o   *Half Sync/Half Async:* one thread monitors the I/O operations and adds the requests to a queue, and the other threads process them

  o   *Leader/Followers:* Several threads take turns to monitor I/O sources and then process the requests once arrived. However, if RT-CORBA is in use, the selected thread will add the request to an intermediate queue where another thread will process it at the proper priority.

The implementation of the DSA carried out in GLADE [14] defines a group of threads to process the requests with similar parameters to those of PolyORB in terms of the number of threads (minimum number of threads created at start-up time, stable value and absolute maximum), and uses another two intermediate threads for the requests; one awaits the arrival of requests from the network, and the other one processes these requests and selects one of the threads of the group to finally process the job.

The modifications made to GLADE to obtain the first version of RT-GLADE [7] eliminated one of the intermediate threads, so that there was a thread waiting for requests arriving from the net, which in turn activated one of the threads of the group to carry out the job. In the second version of RT-GLADE [8], an API was provided to allow an explicit configuration of the threads that execute the jobs, and they are designed to wait directly on the net. This is done through the definition of communication *endpoints* which handle the association with the remote thread and support the scheduling parameters for the network. These parameters, that can be complex, are associated with the appropriate entity when a distributed transaction is installed and do not need to be transmitted each time the remote service is called.

TAO, PolyORB, and GLADE all use the priority assignment policies defined in RT-CORBA. In contrast, in the first version of RT-GLADE [7] free assignment of priorities is allowed for the remote services and for the request and reply messages. This approach enables the use of optimization techniques in the assignment of priorities in distributed systems.

In the second version of RT-GLADE [8], the definition of the connection endpoints allows the programming of distributed transactions, which are identified just by specifying a small number at the beginning of the transaction. Moreover, the transaction is executed with the scheduling parameters associated to its threads and messages. This concept is similar to the distributable thread of RT-CORBA, except that this specification never takes the network scheduling into account. TAO implements this part of the dynamic scheduling of RT-CORBA, in which dynamic changing of the scheduling parameters of a scheduling segment is permitted [5].

In this work, we have made a prototype porting of PolyORB to the MaRTE OS [9] real-time operating system and we have adapted it to the RT-EP real-time network protocol [10]. The personality of CORBA (PolyORB-CORBA) allows the use of the control policies of the ORB defined in PolyORB. The DSA personality of PolyORB does not currently allow choosing among different control policies. For this personality (PolyORB-DSA), a basic version of the scheduling defined in [8] has been implemented over our real-time platform to obtain results comparable to those of RT-GLADE.

3.2 Discussion

Based on the analysis above, this subsection discusses some objectives that the real-time distribution middleware must pursue, and proposes solutions or extensions that the standards and/or the implementations should incorporate.

- Allow a schedulability analysis of the complete application. Although the middleware is executed in the processor, in many cases the timing behaviour of the networks has a strong influence on the overall response times, and therefore the networks should be scheduled with appropriate techniques [6]. The middleware should have the ability to specify the scheduling parameters of the networks through suitable models. RT-GLADE could be used as a reference [8].

- Transactions or distributable threads. In agreement with the previous point, the transactions or distributable threads should incorporate all the information about scheduling in the processors and networks, either in the model proposed by RT-CORBA or in the one proposed in RT-GLADE [8].

- Control of remote calls. The task models implemented in TAO and PolyORB can be used as a reference, adding an extra case in which there is one dedicated thread per kind of request, directly waiting on the net (as in the second version of RT-GLADE). The latter case can be useful in flexible scheduling environments when threads execute under contracts and the cost of negotiating or changing contracts is very high. In the case when there are intermediate threads for managing remote calls (GLADE, RT-GLADE or PolyORB) it is important to control their scheduling parameters. This is also the case of groups of threads in which threads can execute with different parameters each time.

- Allow the free assignment of scheduling parameters. This is the approach used in RT-GLADE. In RT-CORBA there is a specification for static real-time systems, and an extension for dynamic real-time systems (see Section 3 in [13]). The specification for static systems imposes restrictions on the assignment of priorities, but these restrictions are removed in the specification for dynamic systems, which allows implementations to define scheduling policies.

4 Evaluating Distribution Middleware Implementations

The objective of this section is to provide an idea about the predictability and the overhead introduced by the analysed implementations in a distributed application, but not to make a straight comparison among them, as they are of different nature.

In this work, we have made a prototype porting of PolyORB to the MaRTE OS [9] real-time operating system and we have adapted it to the RT-EP real-time network protocol [10]. The personality of CORBA (PolyORB-CORBA) allows the use of the control policies of the ORB defined in PolyORB. The DSA personality of PolyORB does not currently allow the definition of any particular control policy. For this personality (PolyORB-DSA), a basic version of the scheduling defined in [8] has been implemented over our real-time platform. Furthermore, GLADE 2007 has been modified to support the mechanisms included in the second version of RT-GLADE.

In flexible scheduling environments threads are executed under contracts and the cost of negotiating or changing them could be very high for the system. To minimize context switches and therefore fit those requirements, RT-GLADE uses dedicated threads that wait for the event arrivals and then process the received events. The *Leader/Followers* pattern uses a similar concept, with threads that perform both communication and processing roles, thus minimizing context switches. This pattern is the one that is most similar to the RT-GLADE approach, and consequently it will be used in this evaluation both for TAO and PolyORB.

A hardware platform consisting of two 800-MHz AMD Duron processors and a dedicated 100-Mbps Ethernet has been used. The following two software platforms have also been used:

- Linux kernel 2.6.10 with TCP/IP to evaluate the implementations of TAO (version 5.5), PolyORB (version 2.3) with CORBA personality and GLADE (version 2007).
- MaRTE OS 1.7 with RT-EP [10] to evaluate PolyORB-CORBA (version 2.3), PolyORB-DSA (version 2.3) and RT-GLADE (adapted from GLADE 2007).

The tests will measure the execution time of a remote operation that adds two integers and returns the result. The measurement is carried out from the time when the call is made until the response is returned. This operation will be carried out in two modes: alone, and with four other clients carrying out the same operation, but at a lower priority. The objective is not to obtain exhaustive measurements of the platform, but to get a rough idea of the performance (predictability and overheads) that can be achieved with the middleware. In all the tests the operation to be evaluated is executed 10,000 times, and the average, maximum, and minimum times are evaluated, together with the standard deviation and the relative frequency of time values that are within a deviation from the maximum of 10% of the difference between the maximum and average values.

Tables 1 and 2 show the results of the measurements taken with the Linux platforms, using the middleware configurations that introduce the least overhead. For the case of a single client in TAO the reactive concurrency model with a single thread in the group has been used. In PolyORB the model with full tasking without internal threads has been used for the experiment with one client. For the five-client case both in TAO and in

PolyORB a configuration of a group of 5 threads with a *Leader/Followers* model has been used. In GLADE, a static group of threads equal to the number of clients is defined. The priority specification model for TAO, PolyORB and GLADE was client propagated. In order to make the middleware overhead measurements more comparable, the temporal cost of using the net is also evaluated. Thus, Table 1 includes the average, maximum and minimum times for the case when a message is sent and a response is received; the program on the server side answers immediately upon reception.

Table 1. Measurements in Linux for oneclient (times in μs)

	Avg. Time	Max. Time	Min. Time	Std. Deviation	10% from Max. (%)
TAO	998	1380	914	75	0.06
PolyORB-CORBA	1424	4302	1189	373	0.01
GLADE	415	3081	340	261	0.02
Stand-alone network	129	678	118	40	0.12

Table 2. Measurements in Linux forthe highest priority client, five clients (times in μs)

	Avg. Time	Max. Time	Min. Time	Std. Deviation	10% from Max. (%)
TAO	1371	6376	889	356	0.02
PolyORB-CORBA	5399	11554	1593	1050	0.02
GLADE	1700	5953	595	496	0.12

In the results obtained for one client in Linux, it can be observed that GLADE achieves better average and minimum response times than TAO and PolyORB, which can be explained because it has a lighter code. The maximum times obtained for PolyORB and GLADE in the case of one client are much higher than the average times compared to TAO. The average numbers for one and five clients show large differences in PolyORB and GLADE, while in TAO they are relatively similar. We can conclude that this configuration of TAO makes a better management of the priorities and the queues on this platform.

Tables 3 and 4 show the results of the measurements carried out over the three implementations on the MaRTE OS/RT-EP platform. The configuration of PolyORB-CORBA is the same as for Linux. The PolyORB-DSA configuration creates a task explicitly to attend the remote requests. The group of threads for RT-GLADE is configured to be equal to the number of clients. As for RT-EP, the parameter corresponding to the delay between arbitration tokens is set to a value of 150 μs. This value limits the overhead in the processor due to the network. A simple transmission in the network is also evaluated for the same reason as in the case of Linux (see Table 3).

From the results obtained in the evaluation on the real-time platform, it can be observed that, firstly, the network protocol has a greater latency and it makes the times of a simple round-trip transmission higher than in Linux; the trade-off is that this is a predictable network with less dispersion among the values of the measurements.

Furthermore, the minimum and average times of RT-GLADE for one client are also greater than those of GLADE over Linux, although the maximum time remains within a bound indicating a much lower dispersion. An important part of the response times obtained for RT-GLADE is due to the network, but is also due to the operating system and the dynamic memory manager used [11] (to make the timing predictable). If we observe the times of RT-GLADE for five clients, we can see that only the minimum time is worse than in GLADE, although with less difference; in contrast the average time and specially the maximum are now clearly better. The increase in the maximum times of RT-GLADE with respect to the case of one client is reasonable and can be justified by the blocking times that can be suffered both in the processor and in the network.

Table 3. Measurements inMaRTE OS for oneclient (times in μs)

	Avg. Time	Max. Time	Min. Time	Std. Deviation	10% from Max. (%)
PolyORB-CORBA	2997	3012	2770	6	0.01
PolyORB-DSA	4117	4487	3835	300	42.50
RT-GLADE	1080	1151	955	23	0.03
Stand-alone network	959	964	707	3	0.01

Table 4. Measurements in MaRTE OS forthe highest priority client, five clients (times in μs)

	Avg. Time	Max. Time	Min. Time	Std. Deviation	10% from Max. (%)
PolyORB-CORBA	3527	6566	2748	727	0.11
PolyORB-DSA	4516	5299	3531	320	0.02
RT-GLADE	1000	1462	896	27	0.06

In the measurement of the times of PolyORB-CORBA over MaRTE OS we have found a great disparity of the measurements for five clients depending on the priorities used in them. This can be explained because of the architecture used to implement the *Leader/Followers* model. This is a part which could be improved by using an implementation model similar to TAO. In any case, the measurements reflected in Table 4 for PolyORB-CORBA with five clients have been obtained in a best-case scenario in which the low-priority clients are not preempted by any of the threads in the thread pool. Referring to PolyORB-DSA, the response times obtained are comparable to those of PolyORB-CORBA, but with higher predictability.

As a consequence of the response times of PolyORB over MaRTE OS, it is again shown, by comparing the results with those of RT-GLADE, that the pure implementation of the DSA can be much lighter than that of RT-CORBA. Comparing the tests of PolyORB-CORBA for one and for five clients it can be seen that there is an important difference between the minimum and maximum times for five clients, which is due to the priority inversion introduced by the intermediate tasks.

5 Integration of the Distribution Middleware with a Contract-Based Scheduling Framework

The FRESCOR (Framework for Real-time Embedded Systems based on COntRacts) EU project [3] has the objective of providing engineers with a scheduling framework that represents a high-level abstraction that lets them concentrate on the specification of the application requirements, while the system transparently uses advanced real-time scheduling techniques to meet those requirements. In order to keep the framework independent of specific scheduling schemes, FRESCOR introduces an interface between the applications and the scheduler, called the service contract. Application requirements related to a given resource are mapped to a contract, which can be verified at design time by providing off-line guarantees, or can be negotiated at runtime, when it may or may not be admitted. As a result of the negotiation a virtual resource is created, representing a certain resource reservation. The resources managed by the framework are the processors, networks, memory, shared resources, disk bandwidth, and energy; additional resources could be added in the future.

Careful use of virtual resources allows different parts of the system (whether they are processes, applications, components, or schedulers) to use budgeting schemes. Not only can virtual resources be used to help enforce temporal independence, but a process can interact with a virtual resource to query its resource usage and hence support the kinds of algorithms where execution paths depend on the available resources.

When distribution middleware is implemented on operating systems and network protocols with priority-based scheduling, it is easy to transmit the priority at which a remote service must be executed inside the messages sent through the network. However, this solution does not work if more complex scheduling policies, such as the FRESCOR framework, are used. Sending the contract parameters of the RPC handler and the reply message through the network is inefficient because these parameters are large in size. Dynamically changing the scheduling parameters of the RPC handler is also inefficient because dynamically changing a contract requires an expensive renegotiation process.

The solution proposed in [8] consisted in explicitly creating the network and processor schedulable entities required to establish the communication and execute the remote calls. The contracts of these entities are negotiated and created before they are used. They are then referenced with a short identifier that can be easily encoded in the messages transmitted. For identifying these schedulable entities the transactional model is used and the identifier, called an Event_Id, represents the event that triggers the activity executed by the schedulable entity.

In the current FRESCOR framework, support for the transactional model is being built. A tool called the Distributed Transaction Manager (DTM) is a distributed application responsible for the negotiation of transactions in the local and remote processing nodes in a FRESCOR system that implements the contract-scheduling framework. Managing distributed transactions cannot be done on an individual processing node because it requires dynamic knowledge of the contracts negotiated in the other nodes, leading to a distributed consensus problem. The objective of the Distributed Transaction Manager is to allow the remote management of contracts in distributed systems, including capabilities for remote negotiation and renegotiation, and management of the coherence of the results of these negotiation processes. In this way, FRESCOR provides support for distributed global activities or transactions consisting of multiple actions executed in processing nodes and synchronized through messages sent across communication networks.

The implementation of the DTM contains an agent in every node, which listens to messages either from the local node or from remote nodes, performs the requested actions, and sends back the replies. In every node there is also a DTM data structure with the information used by the corresponding agent. Part of this information is shared with the DTM services invoked locally from the application threads. This architecture could benefit from the presence of a distribution middleware, by making the agents offer operations that could be invoked remotely, thus simplifying the current need for a special communications protocol between the agents.

The current version of the transaction manager limits its capabilities just to the management of remote contracts. In the future, the DTM should also provide a full support for the transactional model, integrated with the distribution middleware. For this purpose the following services would need to be added to it:

- Specification of the full transaction with identification of its activities, remote services and events, and contracts for the different resources (processors and networks).
- Automatic deployment of the transaction in the middleware. This would require:
  - choosing unused Event_Ids for the transaction events
  - choosing unused ports in the involved nodes, for the communications
  - creating send endpoints for the client-side of the communications, using the desired contracts and networks
  - creating receive endpoints for the reception of the reply in the client-side of the communications, using the desired networks, ports, and event ids.
  - creating the necessary RPC handlers with their corresponding contracts
  - creating the receive endpoints of the server-side of the communications using the desired contracts and networks
  - creating the send endpoints of the server-side of the communication using the desired contracts and networks.

All this deployment would be done by the DTM from the information of the transaction, which could be written using a suitable deployment and configuration language. After this initialization, the transaction would start executing, its RPCs would be invoked and the middleware would automatically direct them through the appropriate endpoints and RPC handlers almost transparently. We would just specify the appropriate event ids.

With the described approach we would achieve a complete integration of the distribution middleware and the transactional model in a system managed through a resource reservation scheduler.

6 Conclusions and Future Work

The work presented here reports an analysis and evaluation of some implementations of distribution middleware from the viewpoint of their suitability for the implementation of real-time systems. Specifically, the following aspects have been highlighted: the way remote calls are managed, the mechanisms for establishing the scheduling parameters, and the importance of giving support to the transactions or distributable threads.

The time measurements have been carried out over Linux as the native operating system of the middleware analysed, and over a real-time platform based on the MaRTE operating system and the RT-EP real-time network protocol, to which PolyORB has been ported in this work. In the measurements obtained, it can be observed that the implementations of Ada's DSA are lighter than the implementations of RT-CORBA. This suggests that Ada is a good option for programming distributed systems, and that it could find its niche in medium-sized embedded distributed real-time systems. The measurements on the real-time platform also show that the predictability has a cost in terms of overhead in the network and in memory management.

Furthermore, new mechanisms for contract-based resource management in a distributed real-time system have been identified, and the necessity to integrate the distribution middleware with them has been described, together with some ideas on future work needed to support this integration.

Our work will continue with experimentation on the PolyORB real-time platform that we already have, given our experience in Ada and in GLADE. The objective will be to progress with the improvement of specific real-time aspects over this platform both for the DSA and for RT-CORBA, and to integrate the distributed transaction model along with their managers and the new contract-based scheduling mechanisms for processors and networks using the ideas described in this paper. The ultimate goal would be to make proposals for inclusion in the corresponding standards and implementations.

References

1. Ada-Core Technologies, The GNAT Pro Company, http://www.adacore.com/
2. Aldea, M., Bernat, G., Broster, I., Burns, A., Dobrin, R., Drake, J.M., Fohler, G., Gai, P., González Harbour, M., Guidi, G., Gutiérrez, J.J., Lennvall, T., Lipari, G., Martínez, J.M., Medina, J.L., Palencia, J.C., Trimarchi, M.: FSF: A Real-Time Scheduling Architecture Framework. In: Proc. of the 12th IEEE Real-Time and Embedded Technology and Applications Symposium, RTAS 2006, San Jose, CA, USA (2006)
3. FRESCOR project web page: http://frescor.org
4. Gutiérrez, J.J., González Harbour, M.: Prioritizing Remote Procedure Calls in Ada Distributed Systems. In: Proc. of the 9th International Real-Time Ada Workshop, ACM Ada Letters, June 1999, XIX, 2, pp. 67–72 (1999)
5. Krishnamurthy, Y., Pyarali, I., Gill, C., Mgeta, L., Zhang, Y., Torri, S., Schmidt, D.C.: The Design and Implementation of Real-Time CORBA 2.0: Dynamic Scheduling in TAO. In: Proc. of the 10th IEEE Real-Time and Embedded Technology and Applications Symposium (RTAS 2004), Toronto, Canada (May 2004)
6. Liu, J.: Real-Time Systems. Prentice-Hall, Englewood Cliffs (2000)

7. López Campos, J., Gutiérrez, J.J., González Harbour, M.: The Chance for Ada to Support Distribution and Real Time in Embedded Systems. In: Llamosí, A., Strohmeier, A. (eds.) Ada-Europe 2004. LNCS, vol. 3063. Springer, Heidelberg (2004)
8. López Campos, J., Gutiérrez, J.J., González Harbour, M.: Interchangeable Scheduling Policies in Real-Time Middleware for Distribution. In: Pinho, L.M., González Harbour, M. (eds.) Ada-Europe 2006. LNCS, vol. 4006. Springer, Heidelberg (2006)
9. MaRTE OS web page, http://marte.unican.es/
10. Martínez, J.M., González Harbour, M.: RT-EP: A Fixed-Priority Real Time Communication Protocol over Standard Ethernet. In: Vardanega, T., Wellings, A.J. (eds.) Ada-Europe 2005. LNCS, vol. 3555. Springer, Heidelberg (2005)
11. Masmano, M., Ripoll, I., Crespo, A., Real, J.: TLSF: A New Dynamic Memory Allocator for Real-Time Systems. In: Proc of the 16th Euromicro Conference on Real-Time Systems, Catania, Italy (June 2004)
12. Object Management Group. CORBA Core Specification. OMG Document, v3.0 formal/02-06-01 (July 2003)
13. Object Management Group. Realtime CORBA Specification. OMG Document, v1.2 formal/05-01-04 (January 2005)
14. Pautet, L., Tardieu, S.: GLADE: a Framework for Building Large Object-Oriented Real-Time Distributed Systems. In: Proc. of the 3rd IEEE Intl. Symposium on Object-Oriented Real-Time Distributed Computing (ISORC 2000), Newport Beach, USA (March 2000)
15. PolyORB web page, http://polyorb.objectweb.org/
16. Pyarali, I., Spivak, M., Schmidt, D.C., Cytron, R.: Optimizing Thread-Pool Strategies for Real-Time CORBA. In: Proc. of the ACM SIGPLAN Workshop on Optimization of Middleware and Distributed Systems (OM 2001), Snowbird, Utah (June 2001)
17. Sun Developer Network, http://java.sun.com
18. TAO web page, http://www.cs.wustl.edu/~schmidt/TAO.html
19. Tucker Taft, S., Duff, R.A., Brukardt, R.L., Plödereder, E., Leroy, P. (eds.): Ada 2005 Reference Manual. LNCS, vol. 4348. Springer, Heidelberg (2006)
20. Vergnaud, T., Hugues, J., Pautet, L., Kordon, F.: PolyORB: a Schizophrenic Middleware to Build Versatile Reliable Distributed Applications. In: Llamosí, A., Strohmeier, A. (eds.) Ada-Europe 2004. LNCS, vol. 3063. Springer, Heidelberg (2004)

Author Index

Lecture Notes in Computer Science

Sublibrary 2: Programming and Software Engineering

For information about Vols. 1– 4355
please contact your bookseller or Springer